Shojo Beat

ANONYMOUS NOISE

Ryoko Fukuyama

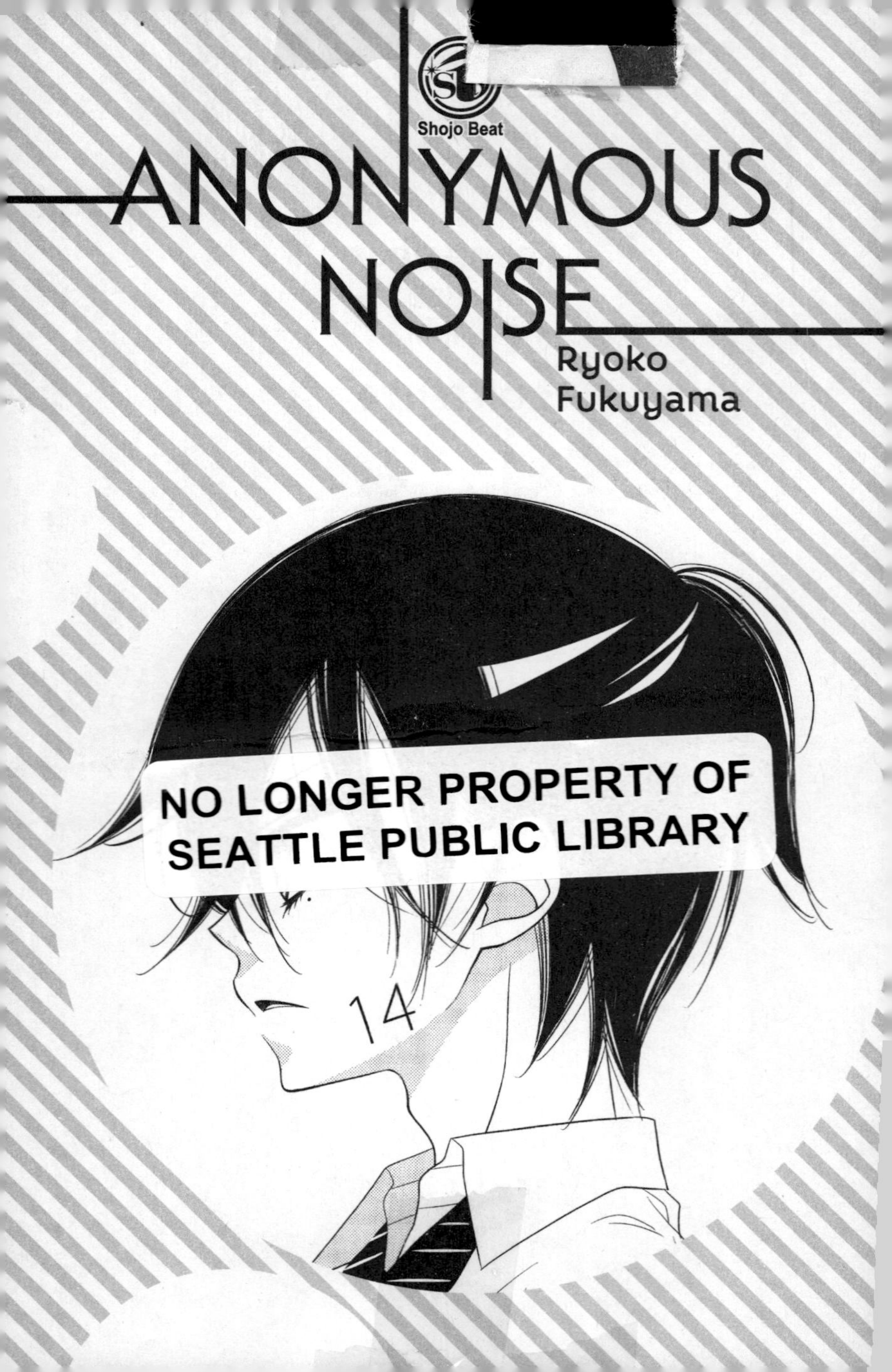

14

Anonymous Noise
Volume 14

CONTENTS

Song 76...............3

Song 77...............34

Song 78...............67

Song 79...............99

Song 80...............129

Song 81...............159

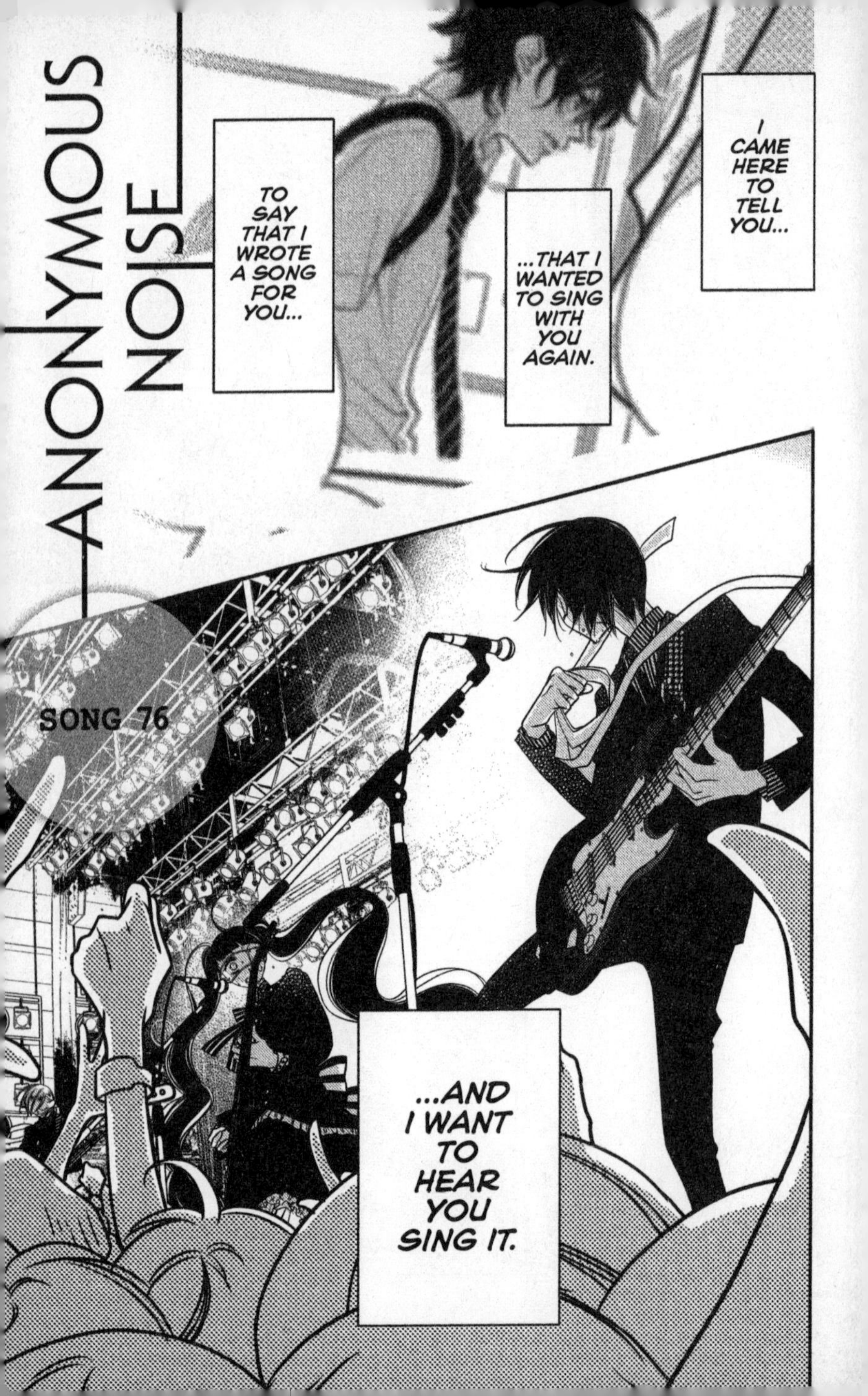
ANONYMOUS NOISE
SONG 76
I CAME HERE TO TELL YOU...
...THAT I WANTED TO SING WITH YOU AGAIN.
TO SAY THAT I WROTE A SONG FOR YOU...
...AND I WANT TO HEAR YOU SING IT.

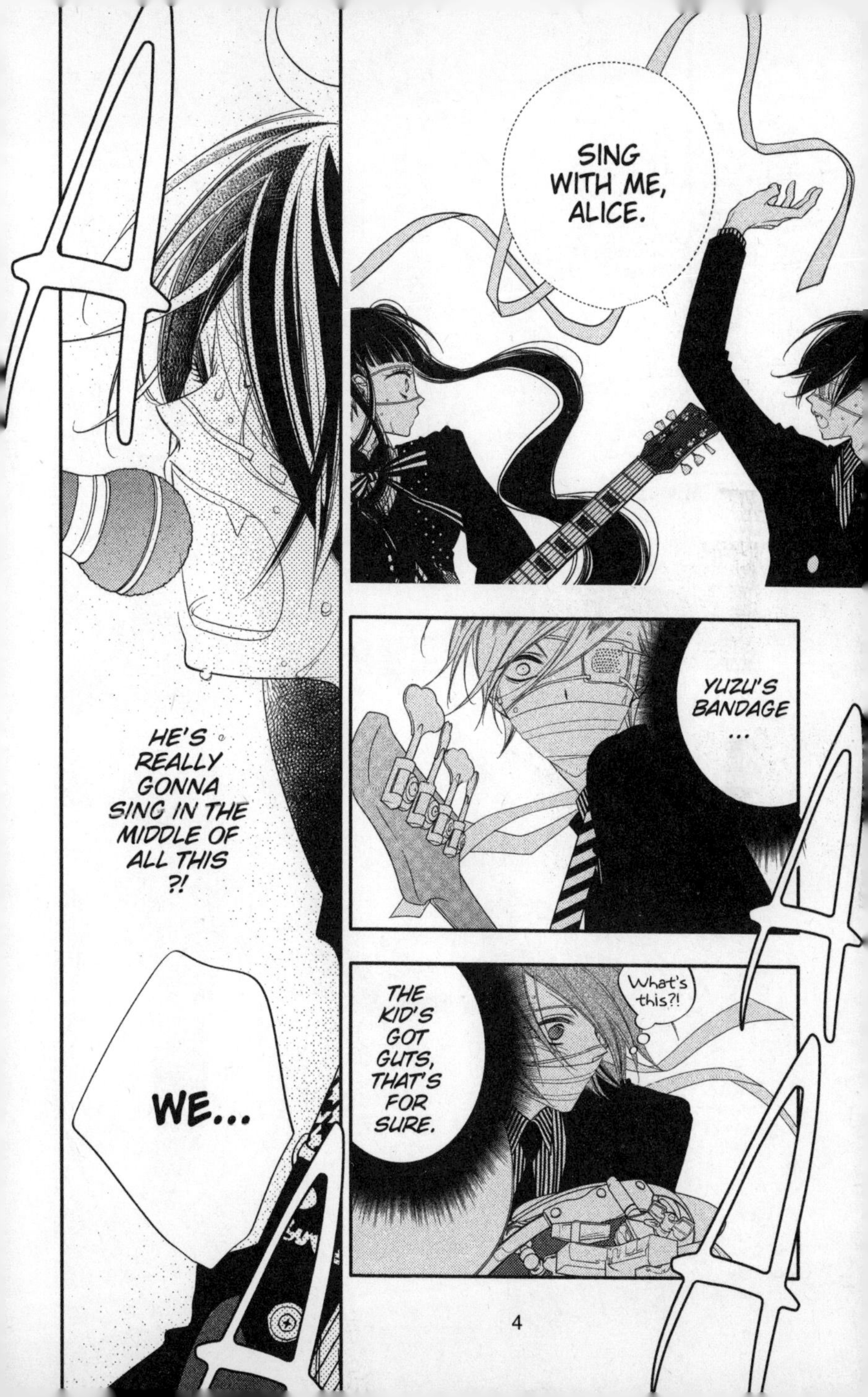
SING WITH ME, ALICE.
YUZU'S BANDAGE ...
What's this?!
THE KID'S GOT GUTS, THAT'S FOR SURE.
HE'S REALLY GONNA SING IN THE MIDDLE OF ALL THIS ?!
WE...

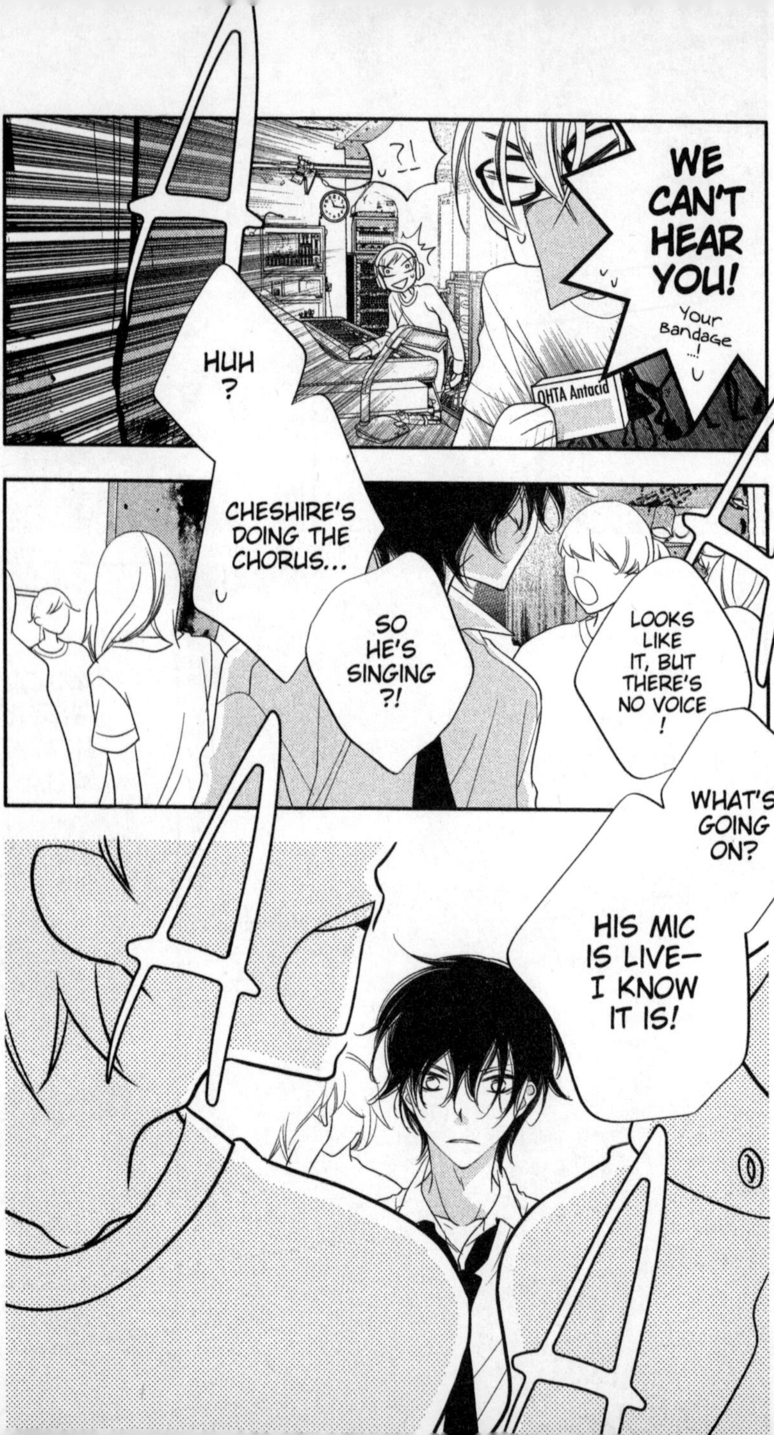
WE CAN'T HEAR YOU!
Your Bandage ...!
?!
OHTA Antacid
HUH?
CHESHIRE'S DOING THE CHORUS...
SO HE'S SINGING?!
LOOKS LIKE IT, BUT THERE'S NO VOICE!
WHAT'S GOING ON?
HIS MIC IS LIVE— I KNOW IT IS!

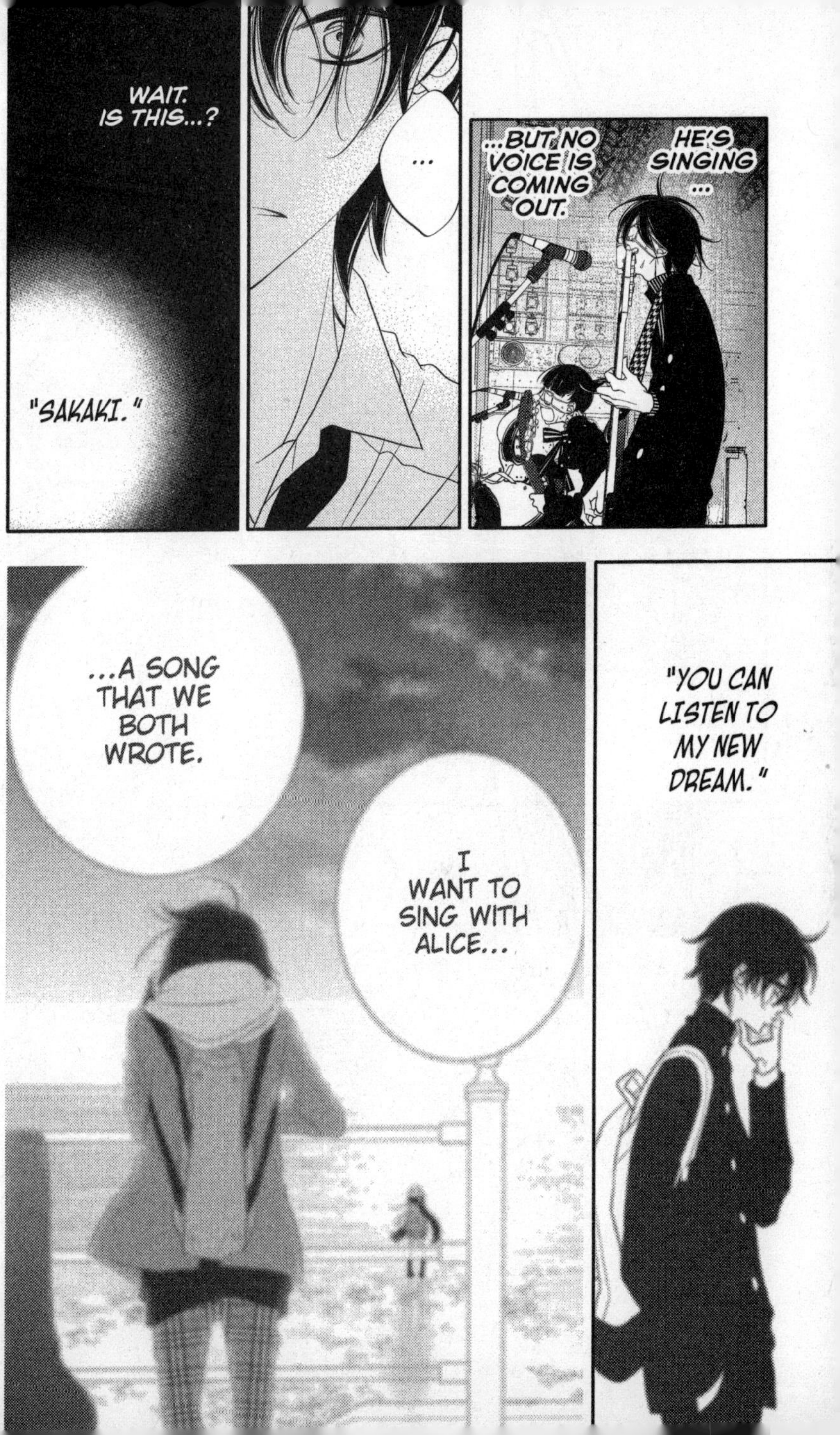
HE'S SINGING ...
...BUT NO VOICE IS COMING OUT.
...
WAIT. IS THIS...?
"SAKAKI."
"YOU CAN LISTEN TO MY NEW DREAM."
I WANT TO SING WITH ALICE...
...A SONG THAT WE BOTH WROTE.

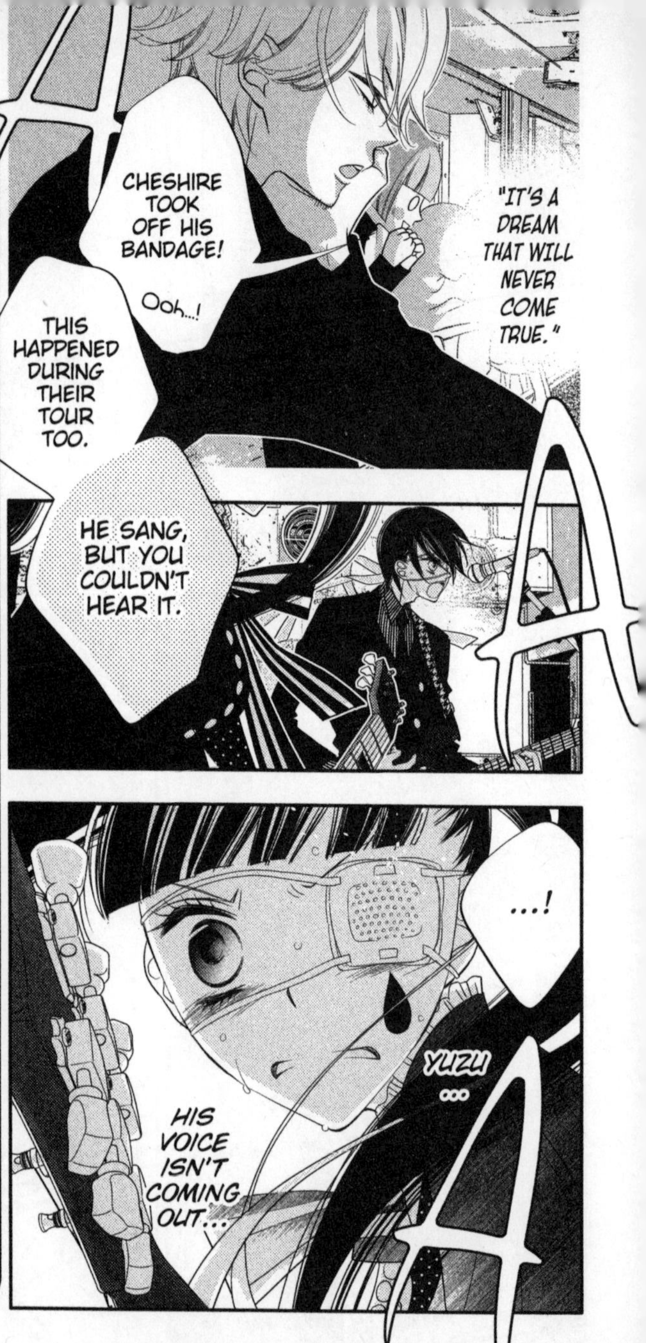
"IT'S A DREAM THAT WILL NEVER COME TRUE."
CHESHIRE TOOK OFF HIS BANDAGE!
Ooh...!
THIS HAPPENED DURING THEIR TOUR TOO.
HE SANG, BUT YOU COULDN'T HEAR IT.
...!
YUZU...
HIS VOICE ISN'T COMING OUT...

1

Hello and welcome! I'm Ryoko Fukuyama. Thank you so much for picking up a copy of *Anonymous Noise* volume 14!

What's that? You've noticed that I'm not actually handwriting this like I promised? I'm afraid you're right, and I'm deeply sorry. Since the new chapter I just submitted was the start of the Rock Horizon arc, I had to draw a ton of difficult panels, and my writing hand is more tired than it's been in a long time. I hope you'll forgive me for giving it a rest before I draw the next chapter. I'm sorry for being so weak!

Anyway, I drew Yuzu for the cover of this volume's regular edition and Cheshire for the limited edition (in Japan). *Hana to Yume* issue 24 comes out at the same time as this volume—it includes a DVD showing how I made the special edition art! (Plug) And I think it's already been announced, but volume 15 is going to have a limited edition too, with a drama CD that has a new song on it! Hurray!

I hope that you enjoy volume 14 of *Anonymous Noise*!

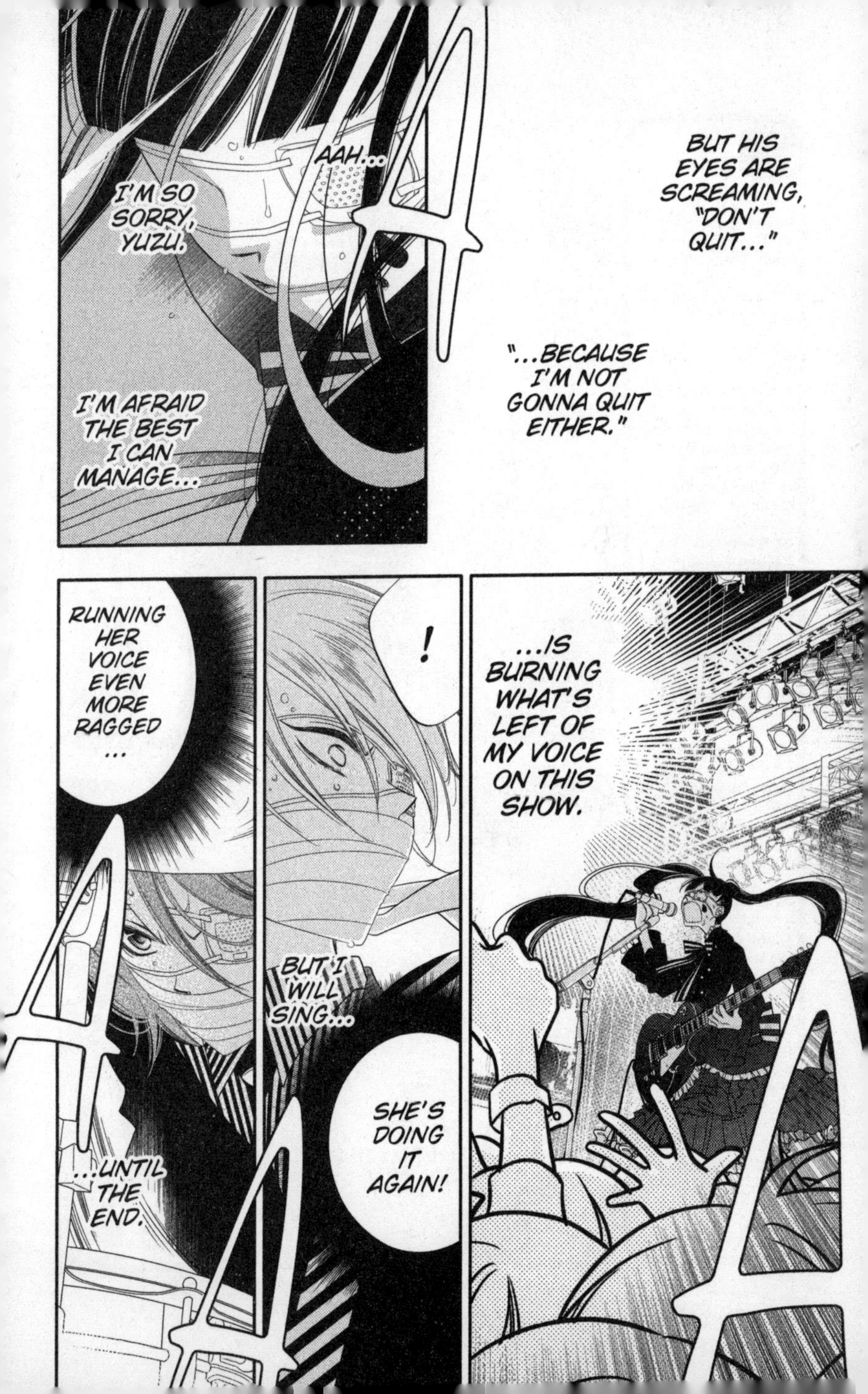
BUT HIS EYES ARE SCREAMING, "DON'T QUIT..."
"...BECAUSE I'M NOT GONNA QUIT EITHER."
AAH...
I'M SO SORRY, YUZU.
I'M AFRAID THE BEST I CAN MANAGE...
...IS BURNING WHAT'S LEFT OF MY VOICE ON THIS SHOW.
!
BUT I WILL SING...
SHE'S DOING IT AGAIN!
RUNNING HER VOICE EVEN MORE RAGGED...
...UNTIL THE END.

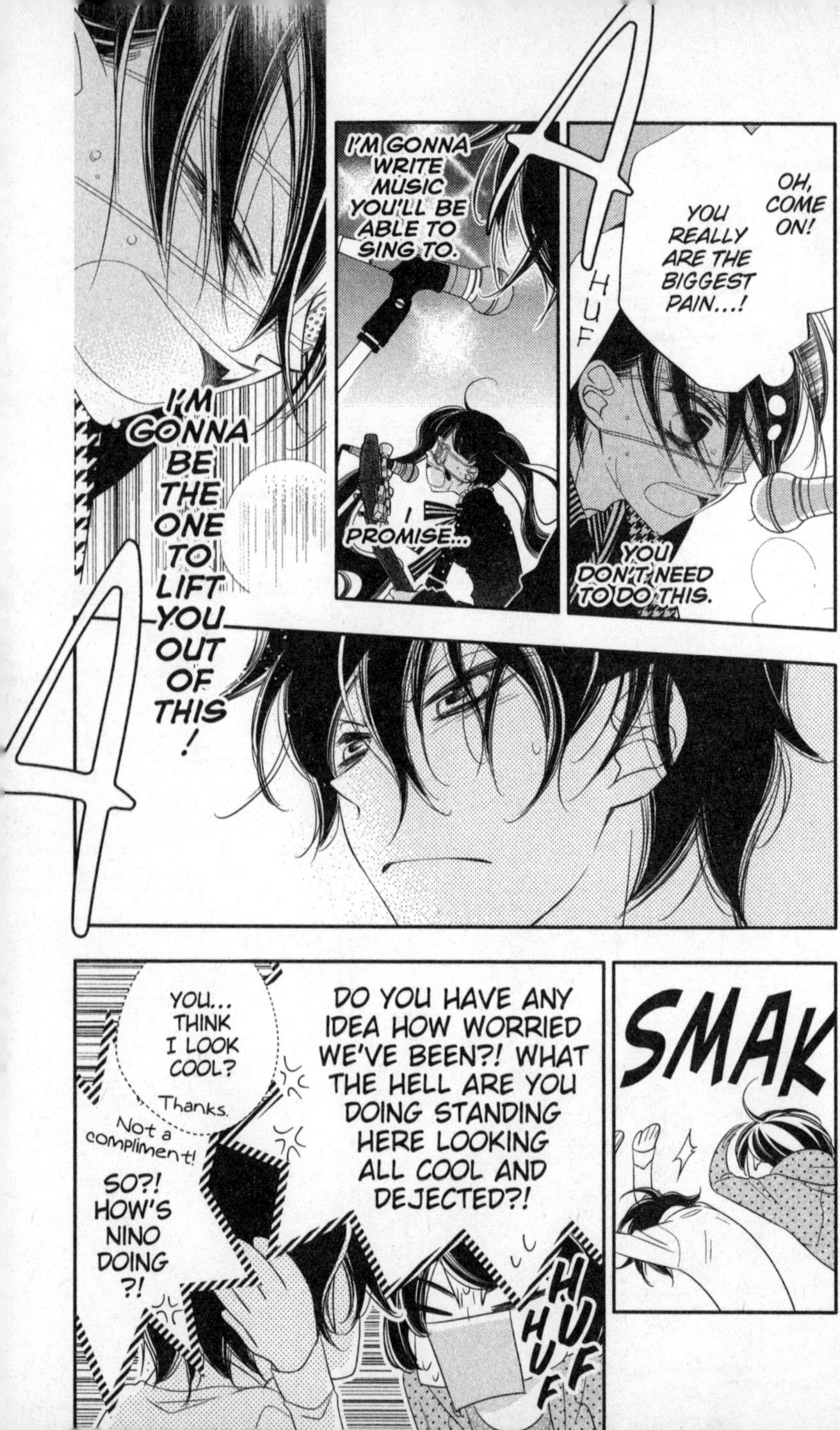
OH, COME ON!
YOU REALLY ARE THE BIGGEST PAIN...!
HUF
YOU DON'T NEED TO DO THIS.
I'M GONNA WRITE MUSIC YOU'LL BE ABLE TO SING TO.
I PROMISE...
I'M GONNA BE THE ONE TO LIFT YOU OUT OF THIS!
SMAK
DO YOU HAVE ANY IDEA HOW WORRIED WE'VE BEEN?! WHAT THE HELL ARE YOU DOING STANDING HERE LOOKING ALL COOL AND DEJECTED?!
YOU... THINK I LOOK COOL?
Thanks.
Not a compliment!
SO?! HOW'S NINO DOING?!
HUF HUF HUF

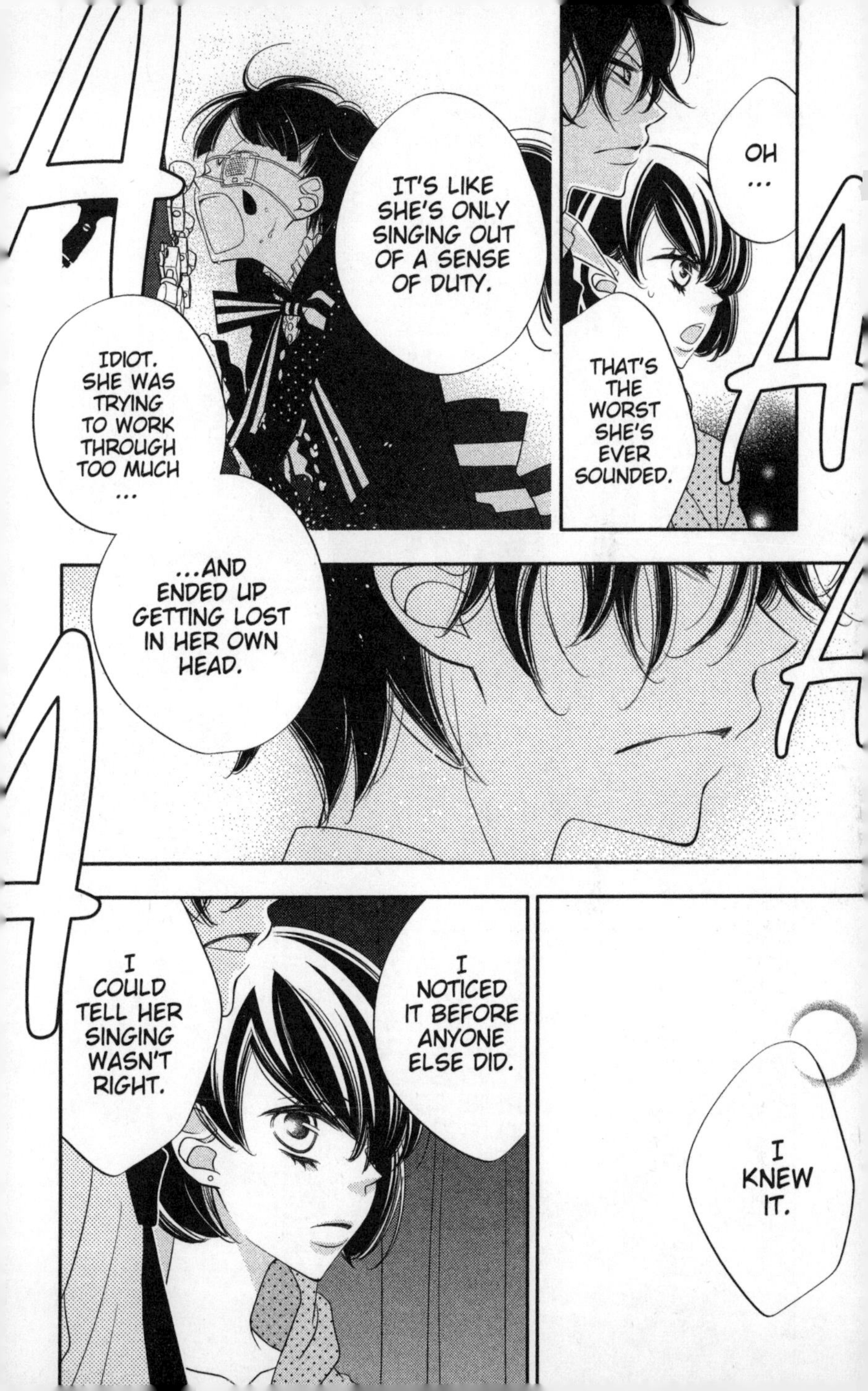
OH ...
THAT'S THE WORST SHE'S EVER SOUNDED.
IT'S LIKE SHE'S ONLY SINGING OUT OF A SENSE OF DUTY.
IDIOT. SHE WAS TRYING TO WORK THROUGH TOO MUCH ...
...AND ENDED UP GETTING LOST IN HER OWN HEAD.
I KNEW IT.
I NOTICED IT BEFORE ANYONE ELSE DID.
I COULD TELL HER SINGING WASN'T RIGHT.

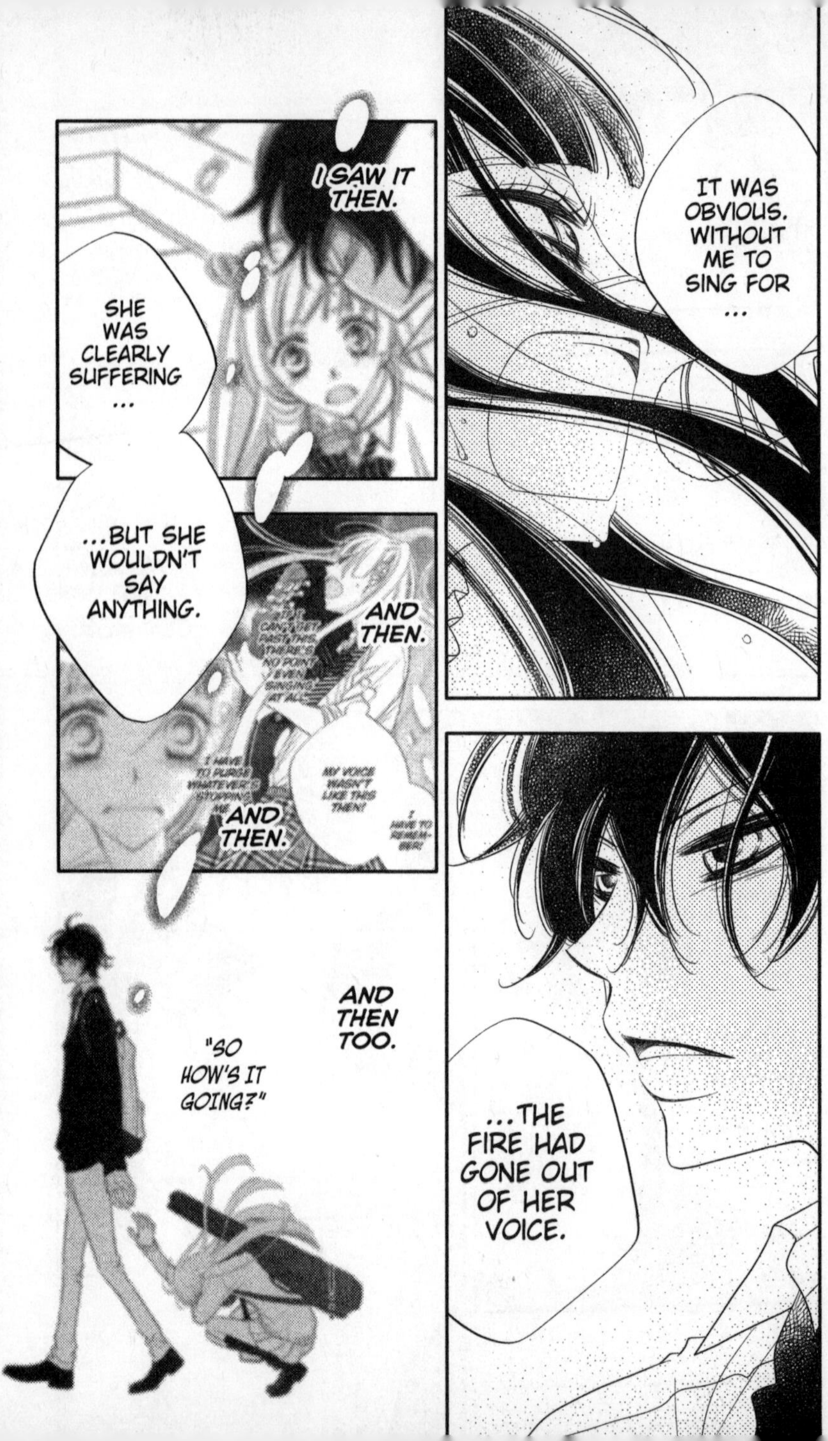
IT WAS OBVIOUS. WITHOUT ME TO SING FOR ...
...THE FIRE HAD GONE OUT OF HER VOICE.
I SAW IT THEN.
SHE WAS CLEARLY SUFFERING ...
...BUT SHE WOULDN'T SAY ANYTHING.
AND THEN.
MY VOICE WASN'T LIKE THIS THEN!
I HAVE TO REMEMBER!
I HAVE TO PURGE WHATEVER'S STOPPING ME
AND THEN.
AND THEN TOO.
"SO HOW'S IT GOING?"

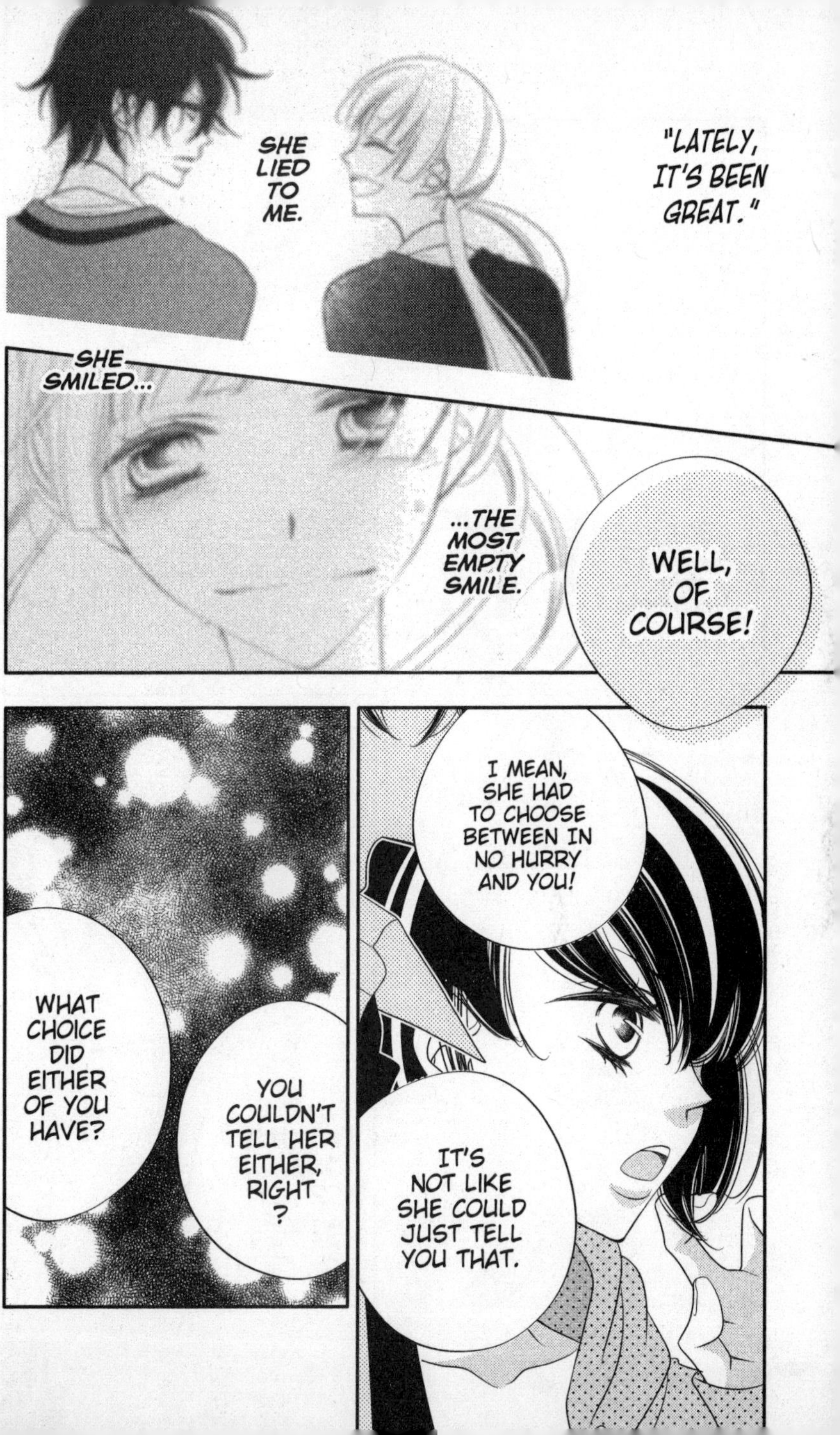
"LATELY, IT'S BEEN GREAT."
SHE LIED TO ME.
SHE SMILED...
...THE MOST EMPTY SMILE.
WELL, OF COURSE!
I MEAN, SHE HAD TO CHOOSE BETWEEN IN NO HURRY AND YOU!
IT'S NOT LIKE SHE COULD JUST TELL YOU THAT.
YOU COULDN'T TELL HER EITHER, RIGHT?
WHAT CHOICE DID EITHER OF YOU HAVE?

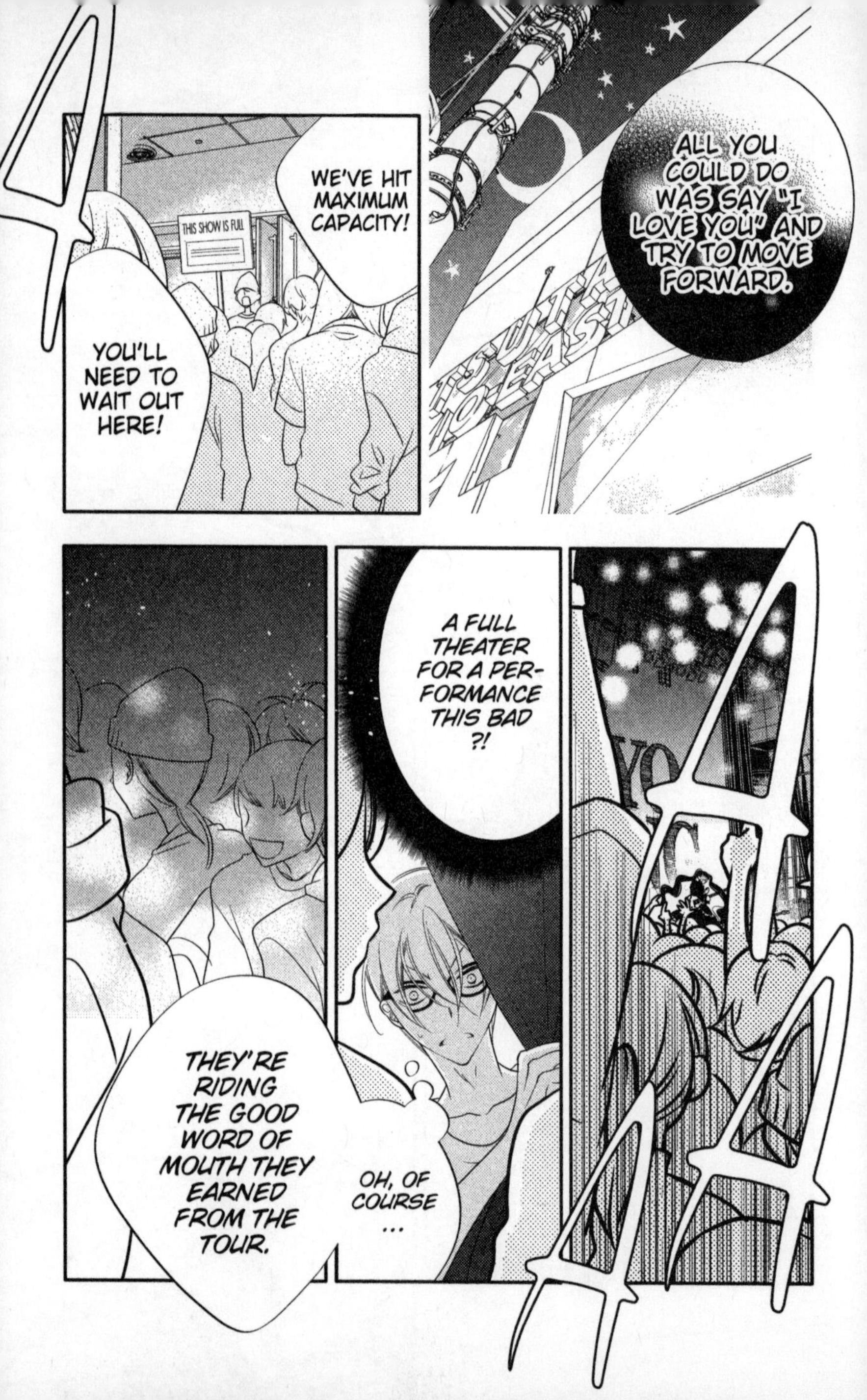
ALL YOU COULD DO WAS SAY "I LOVE YOU" AND TRY TO MOVE FORWARD.
WE'VE HIT MAXIMUM CAPACITY!
THIS SHOW IS FULL
YOU'LL NEED TO WAIT OUT HERE!
A FULL THEATER FOR A PERFORMANCE THIS BAD?!
OH, OF COURSE...
THEY'RE RIDING THE GOOD WORD OF MOUTH THEY EARNED FROM THE TOUR.

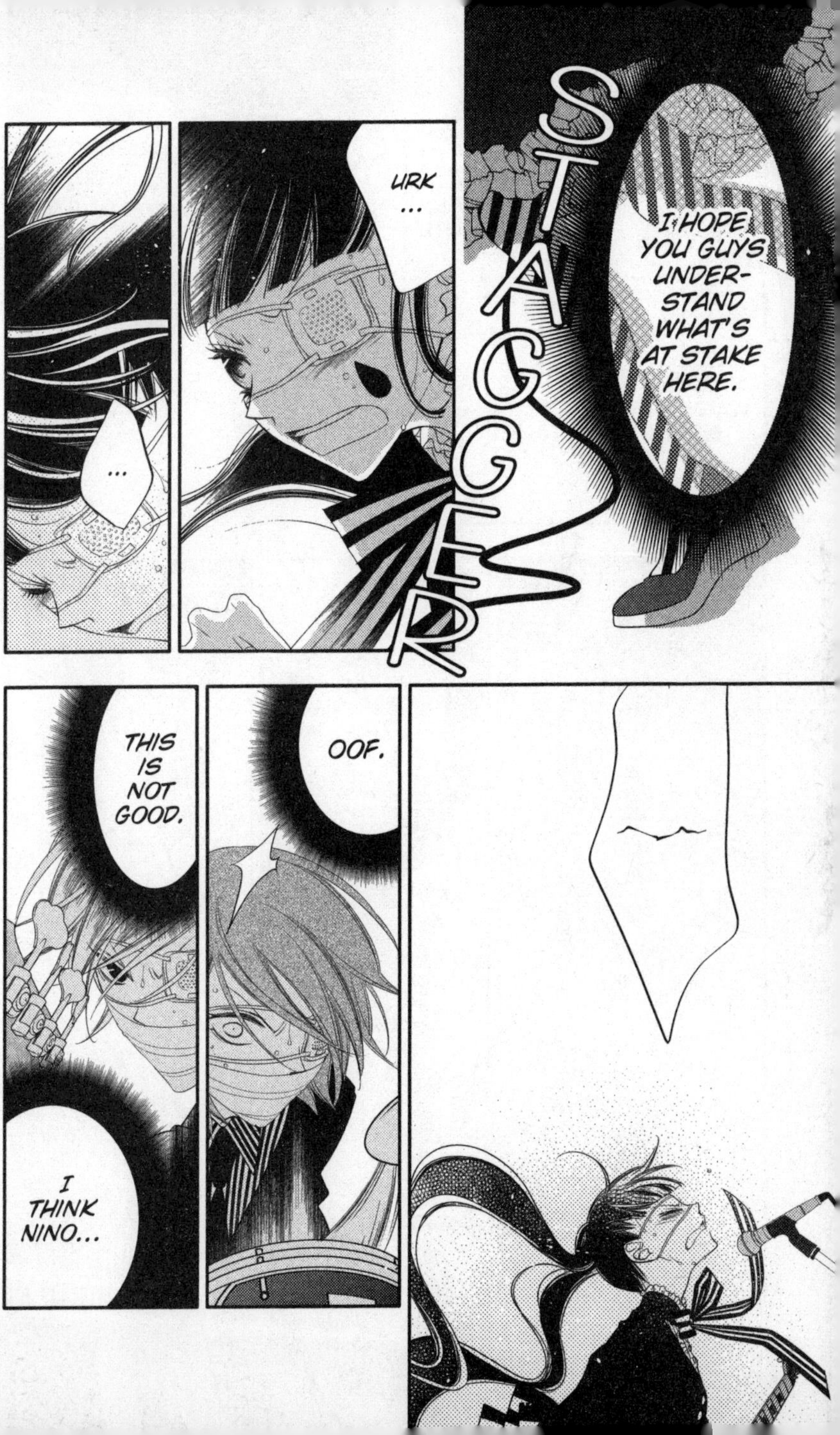
I HOPE YOU GUYS UNDER-STAND WHAT'S AT STAKE HERE.
STAGGER
URK ...
...
OOF.
THIS IS NOT GOOD.
I THINK NINO...

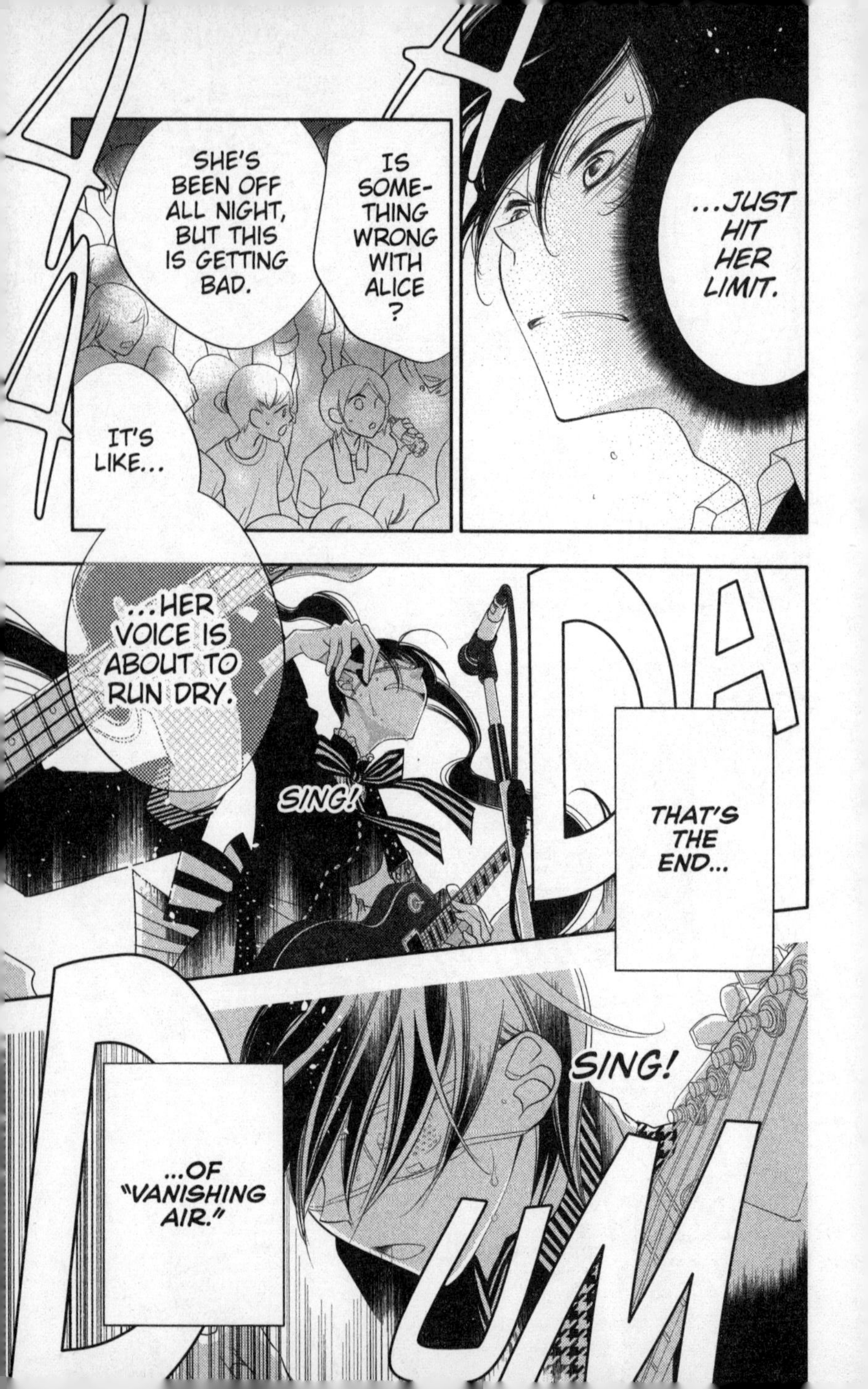
...JUST HIT HER LIMIT.
IS SOME-THING WRONG WITH ALICE?
SHE'S BEEN OFF ALL NIGHT, BUT THIS IS GETTING BAD.
IT'S LIKE...
...HER VOICE IS ABOUT TO RUN DRY.
DA
THAT'S THE END...
SING!
SING!
UM
...OF "VANISHING AIR."

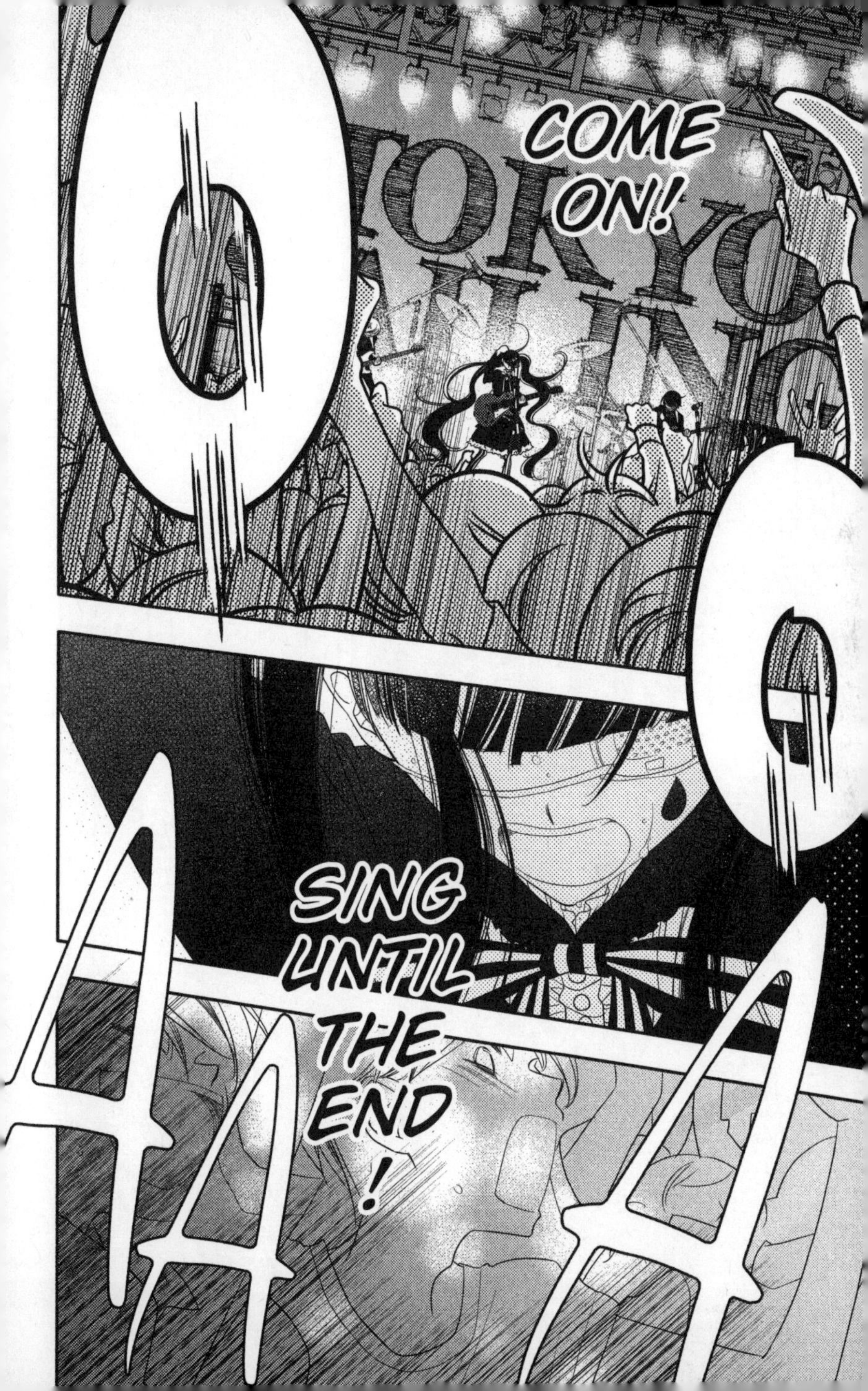
COME ON!
OOAAA
SING UNTIL THE END!

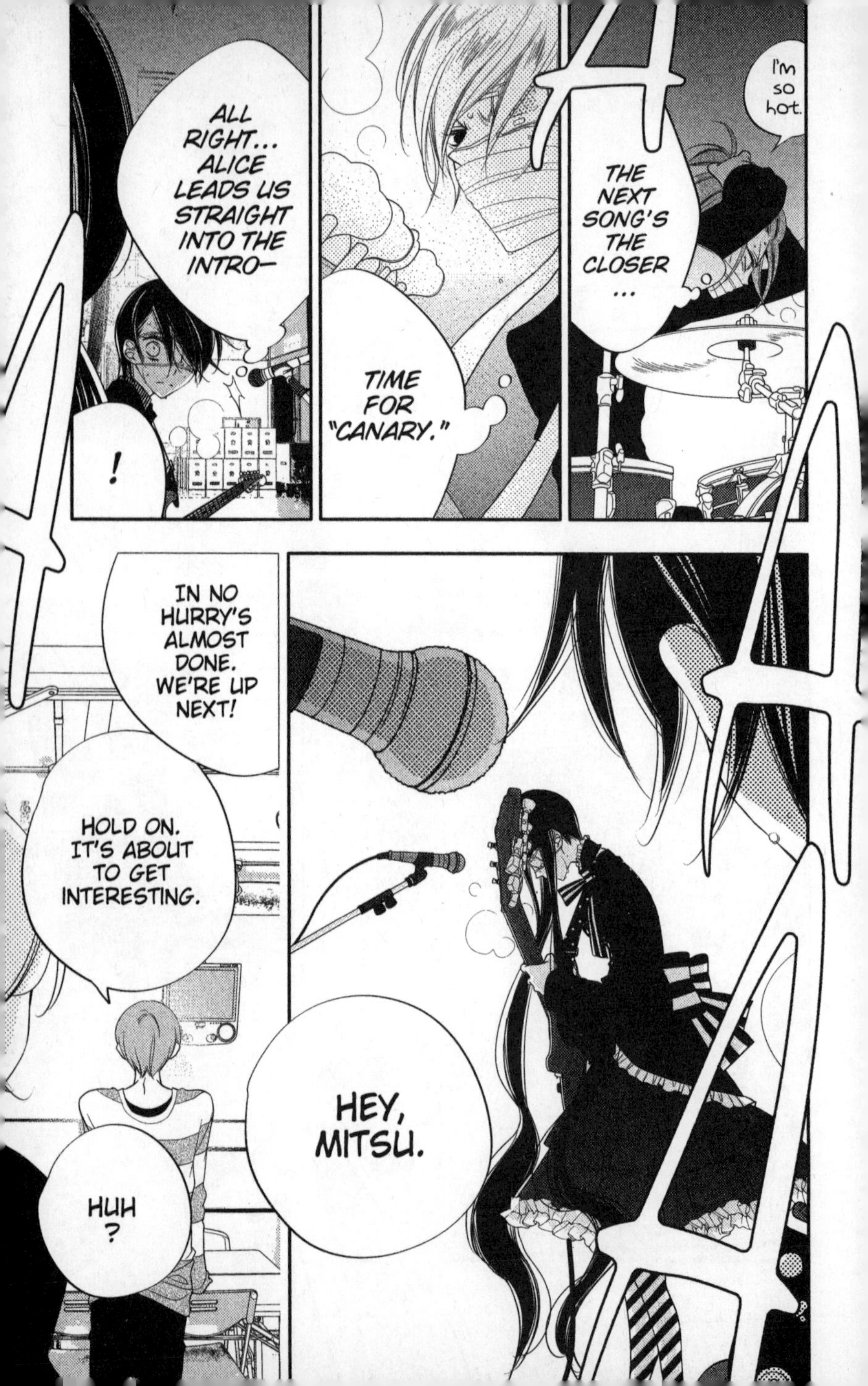
I'm so hot.
THE NEXT SONG'S THE CLOSER ...
TIME FOR "CANARY."
ALL RIGHT... ALICE LEADS US STRAIGHT INTO THE INTRO—
!
HEY, MITSU.
IN NO HURRY'S ALMOST DONE. WE'RE UP NEXT!
HOLD ON. IT'S ABOUT TO GET INTERESTING.
HUH?

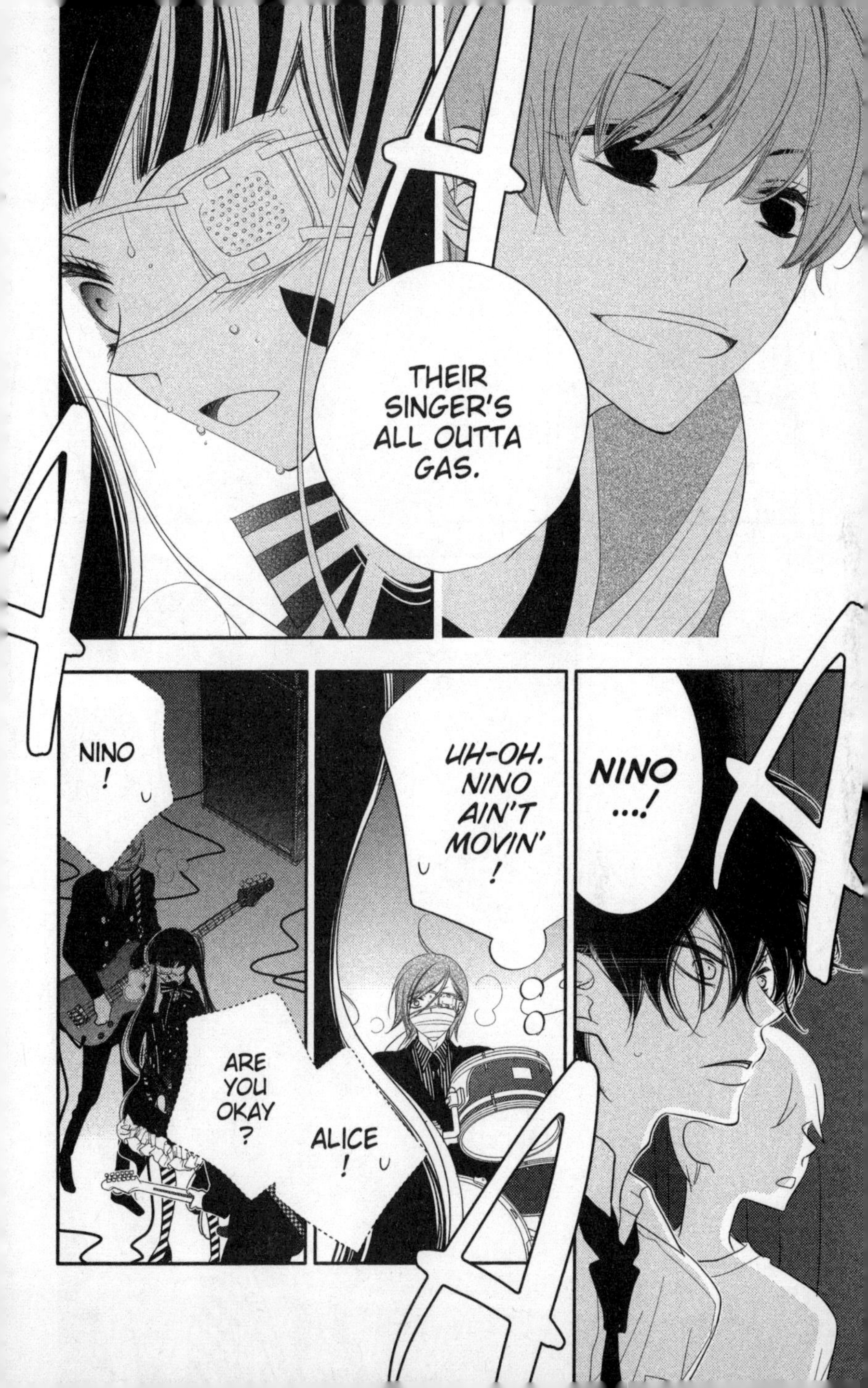
THEIR SINGER'S ALL OUTTA GAS.
NINO ...!
UH-OH. NINO AIN'T MOVIN'!
ALICE!
NINO!
ARE YOU OKAY?

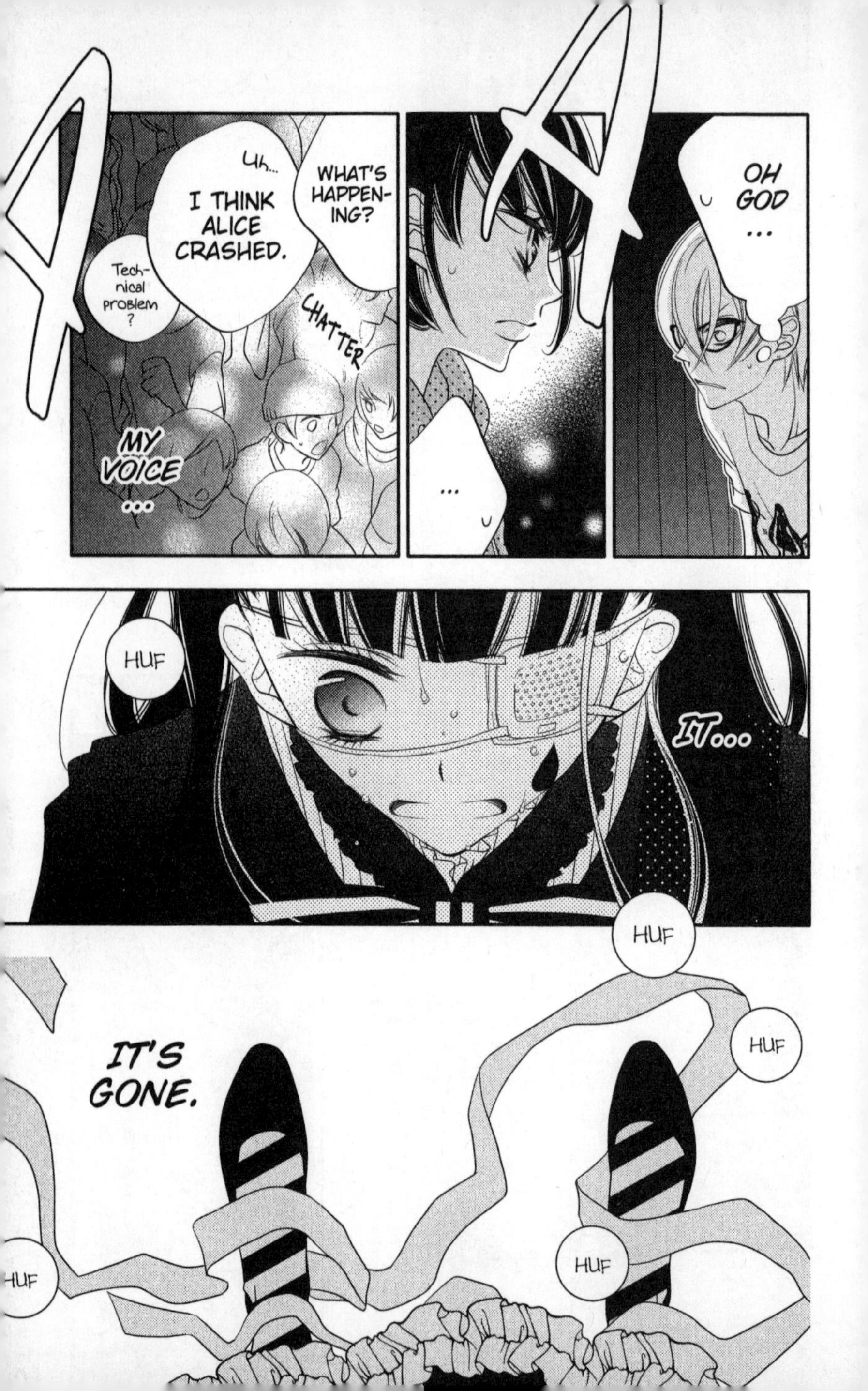
OH GOD ...
...
WHAT'S HAPPEN-ING?
Uh... I THINK ALICE CRASHED.
Tech-nical problem?
CHATTER
MY VOICE ...
IT...
HUF
HUF
HUF
IT'S GONE.
HUF
HUF

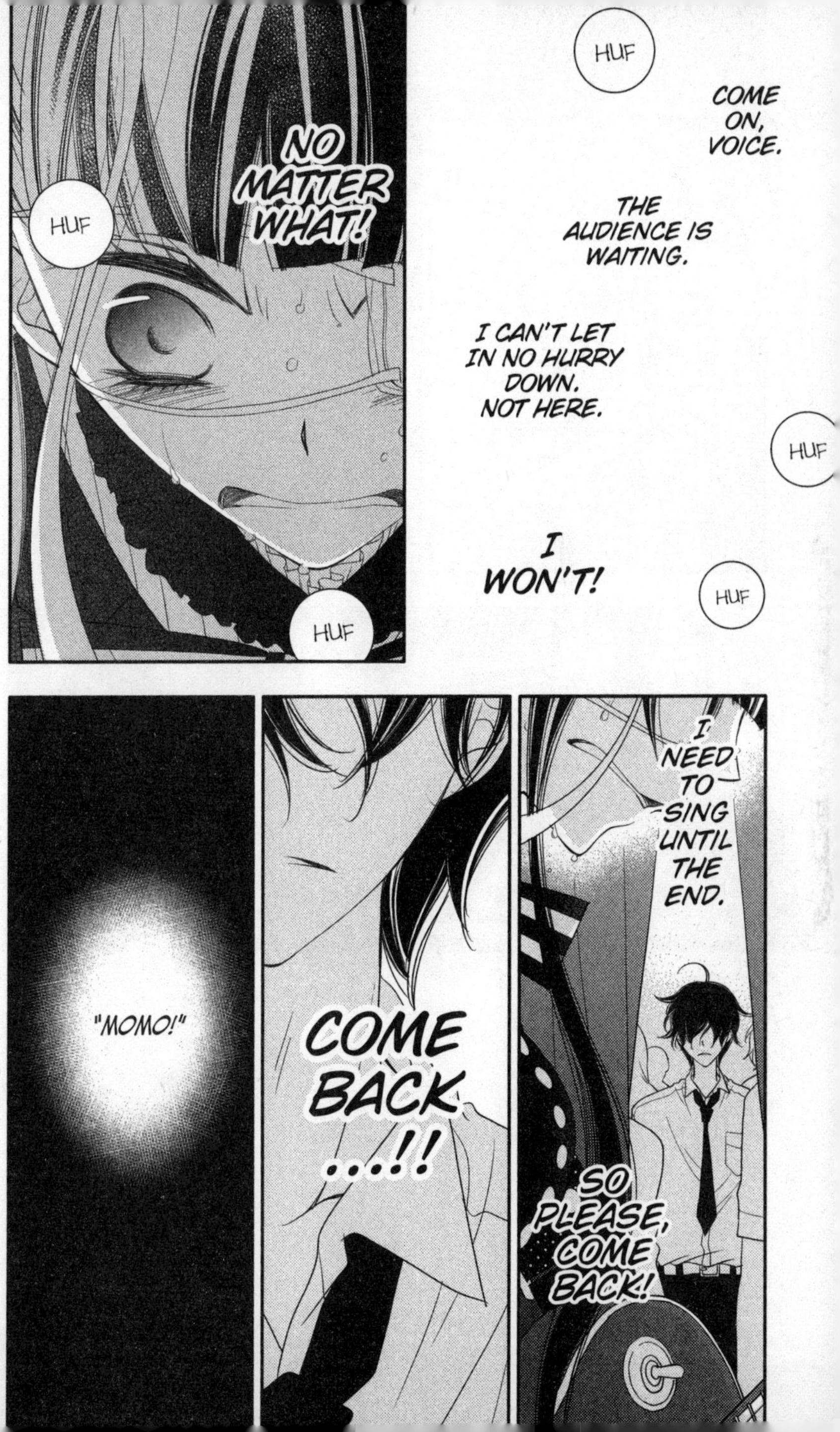
HUF
COME ON, VOICE.
THE AUDIENCE IS WAITING.
I CAN'T LET IN NO HURRY DOWN. NOT HERE.
HUF
I WON'T!
HUF
NO MATTER WHAT!
HUF
HUF
I NEED TO SING UNTIL THE END.
SO PLEASE, COME BACK!
COME BACK ...!!
"MOMO!"

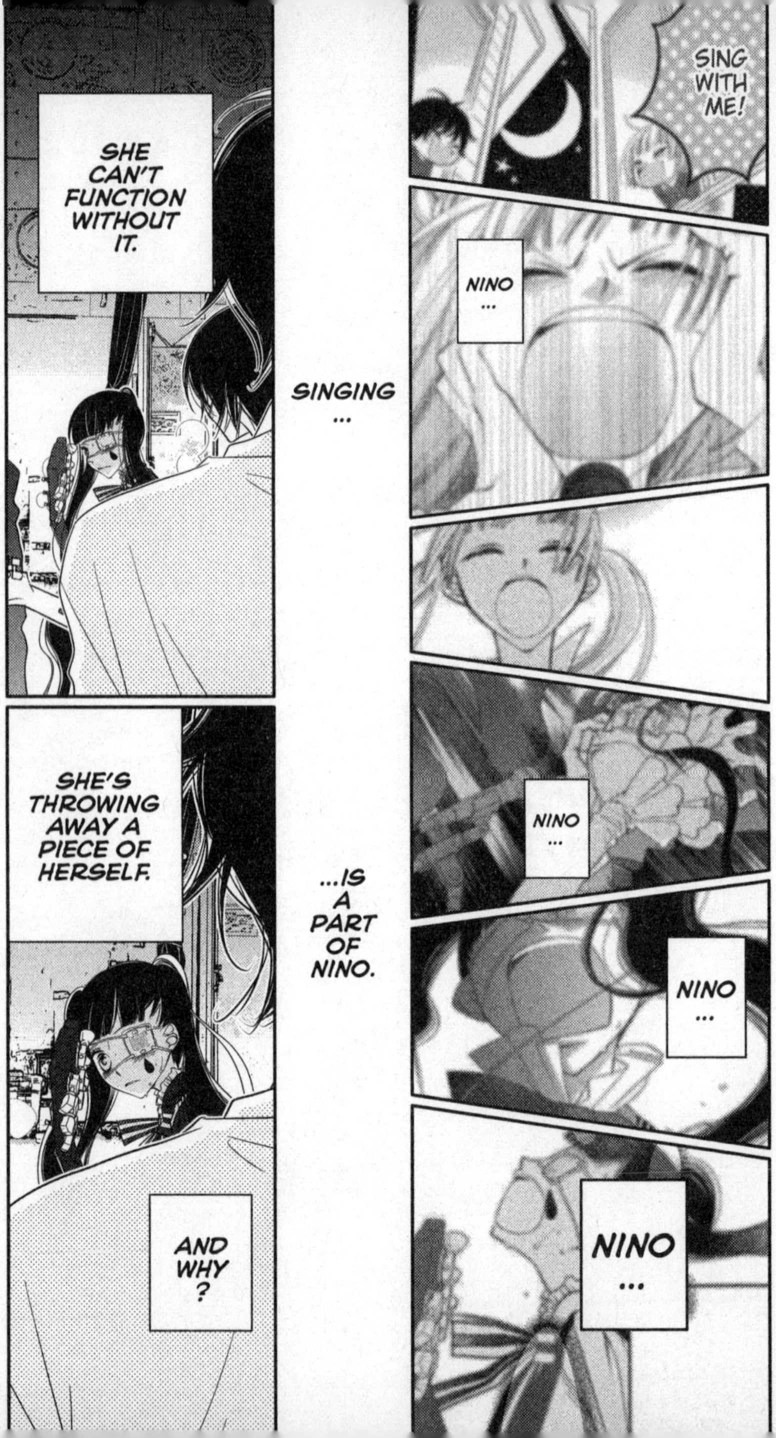
SING WITH ME!
NINO...
NINO...
NINO...
NINO...
SINGING...
...IS A PART OF NINO.
SHE CAN'T FUNCTION WITHOUT IT.
SHE'S THROWING AWAY A PIECE OF HERSELF.
AND WHY?

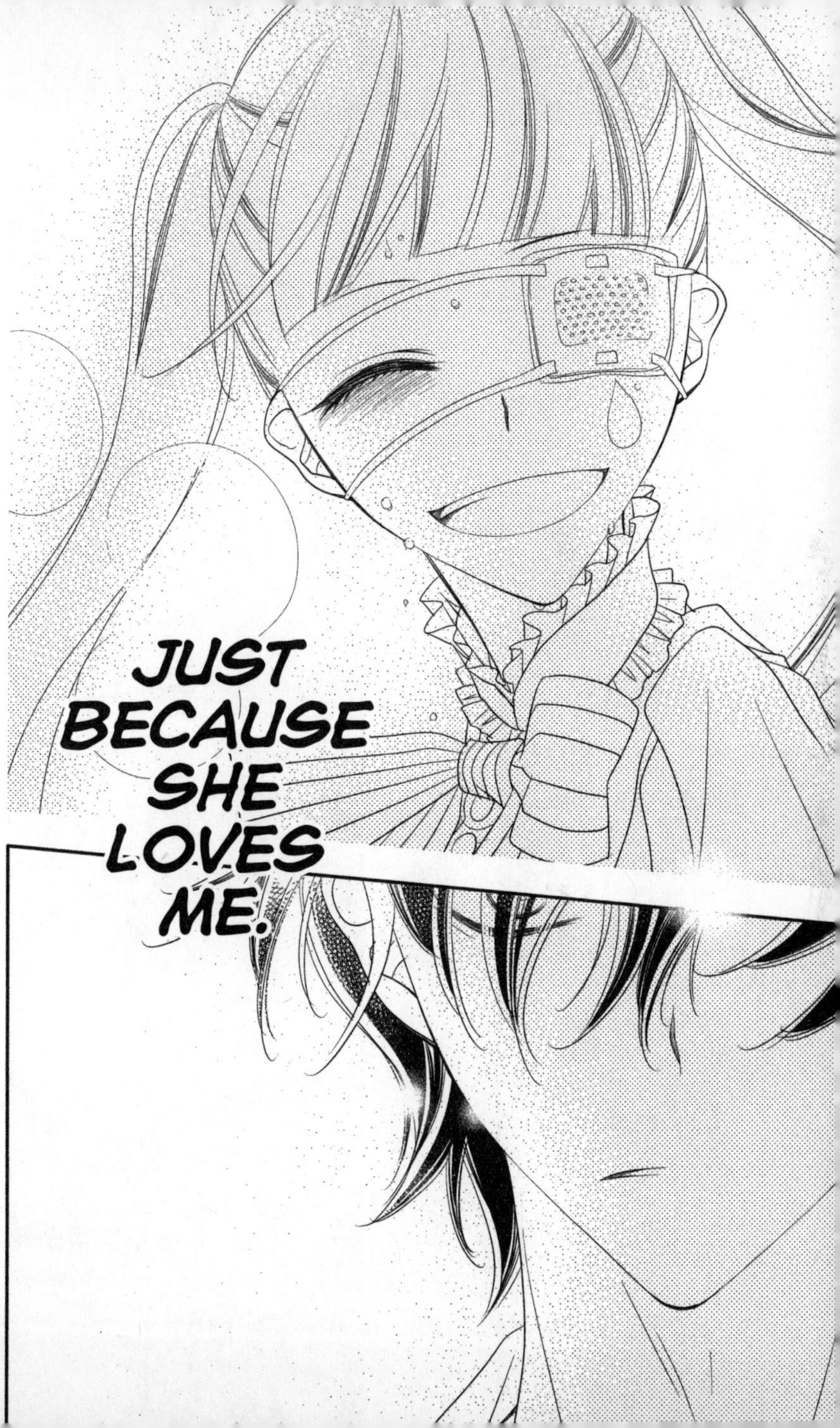
JUST BECAUSE SHE LOVES ME.

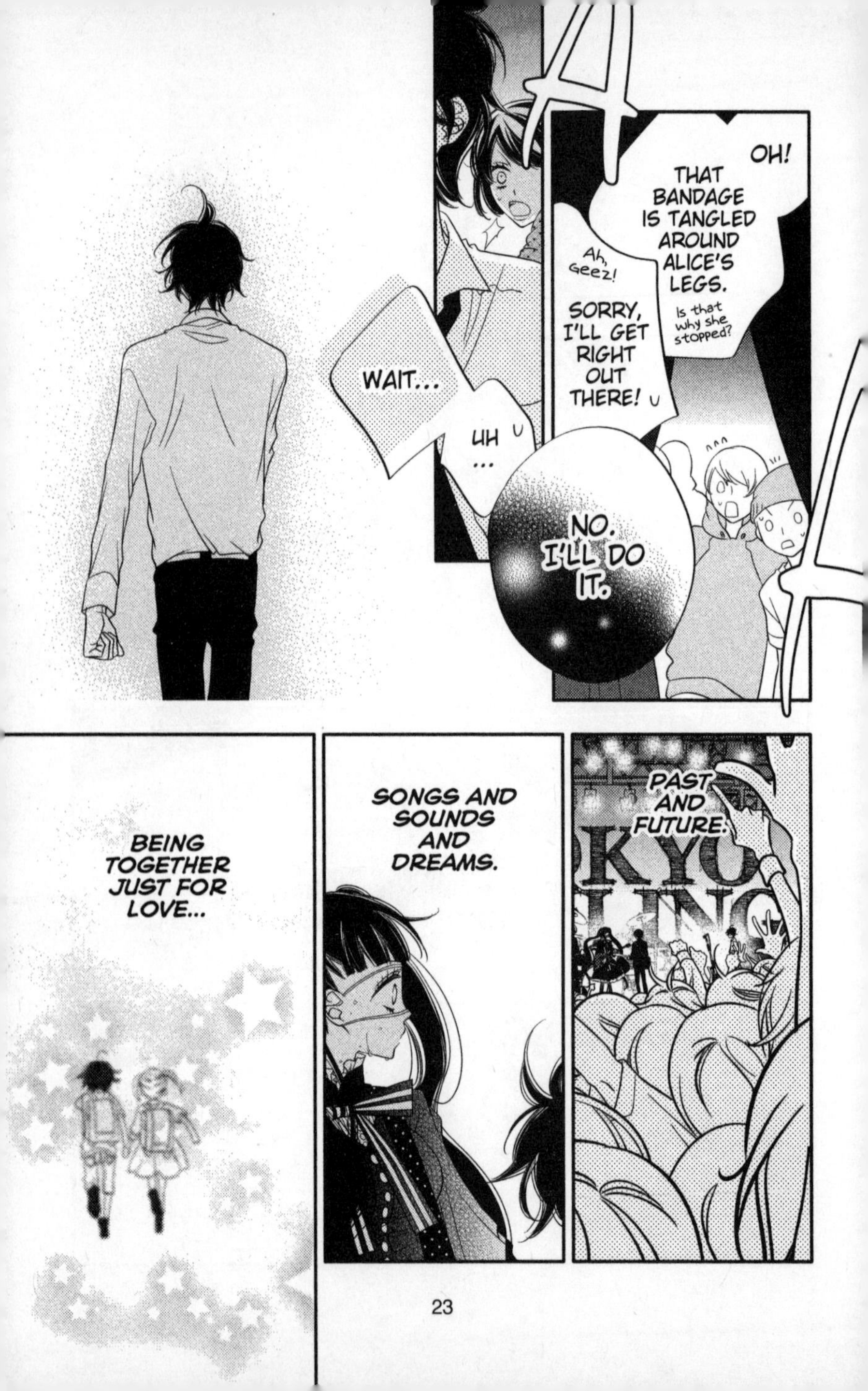
OH!
THAT BANDAGE IS TANGLED AROUND ALICE'S LEGS.
Is that why she stopped?
Ah, Geez!
SORRY, I'LL GET RIGHT OUT THERE!
NO. I'LL DO IT.
WAIT...
UH...
PAST AND FUTURE.
SONGS AND SOUNDS AND DREAMS.
BEING TOGETHER JUST FOR LOVE...

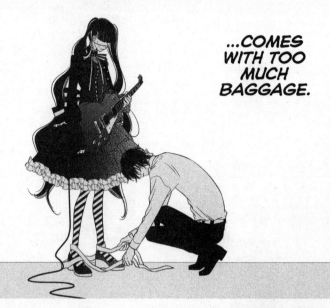

...COMES WITH TOO MUCH BAGGAGE.

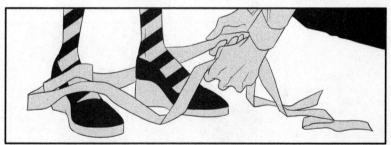

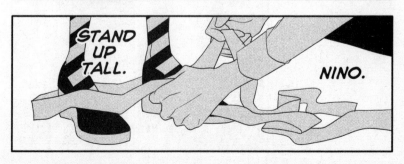

STAND UP TALL.

NINO.

24

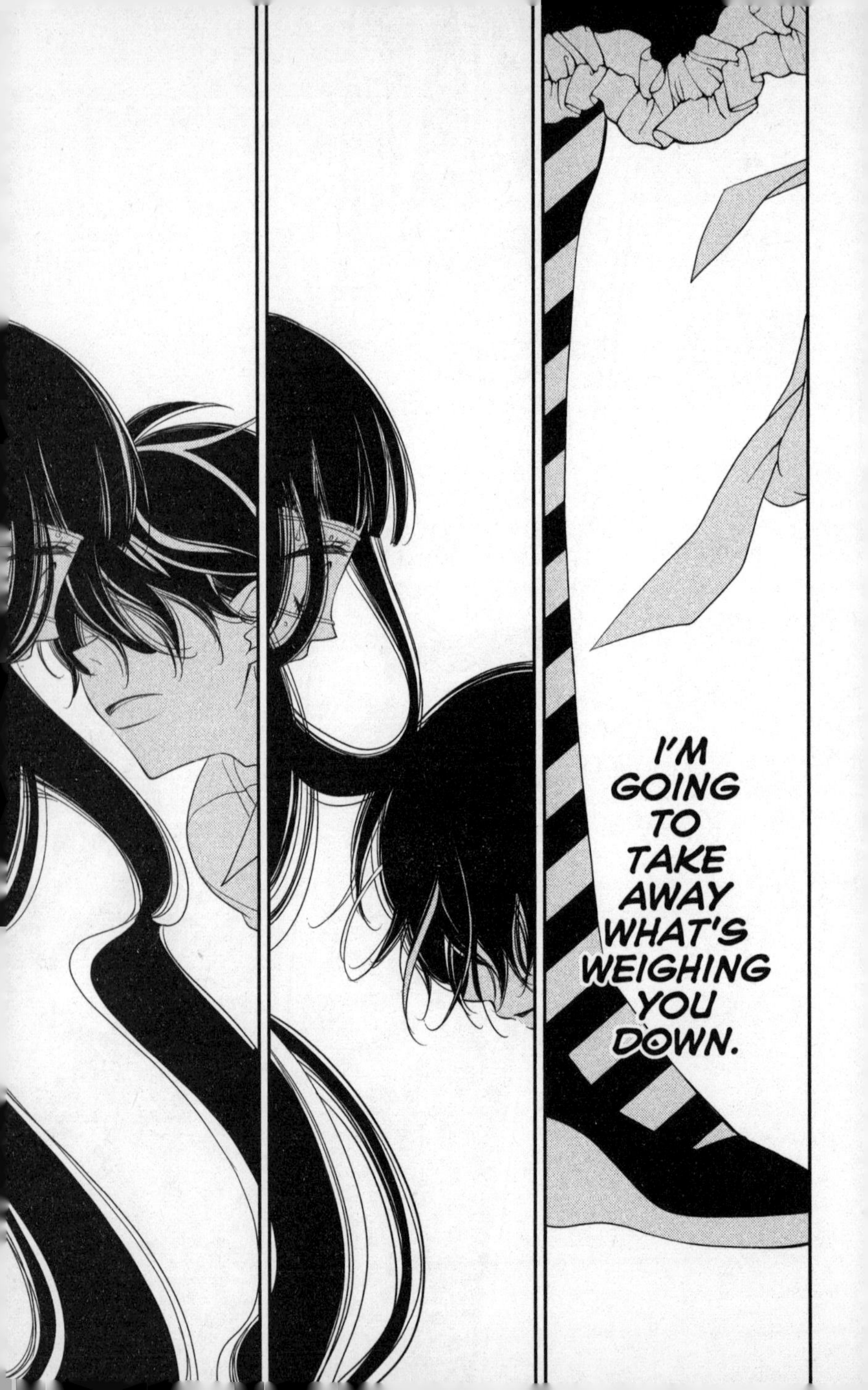
I'M GOING TO TAKE AWAY WHAT'S WEIGHING YOU DOWN.

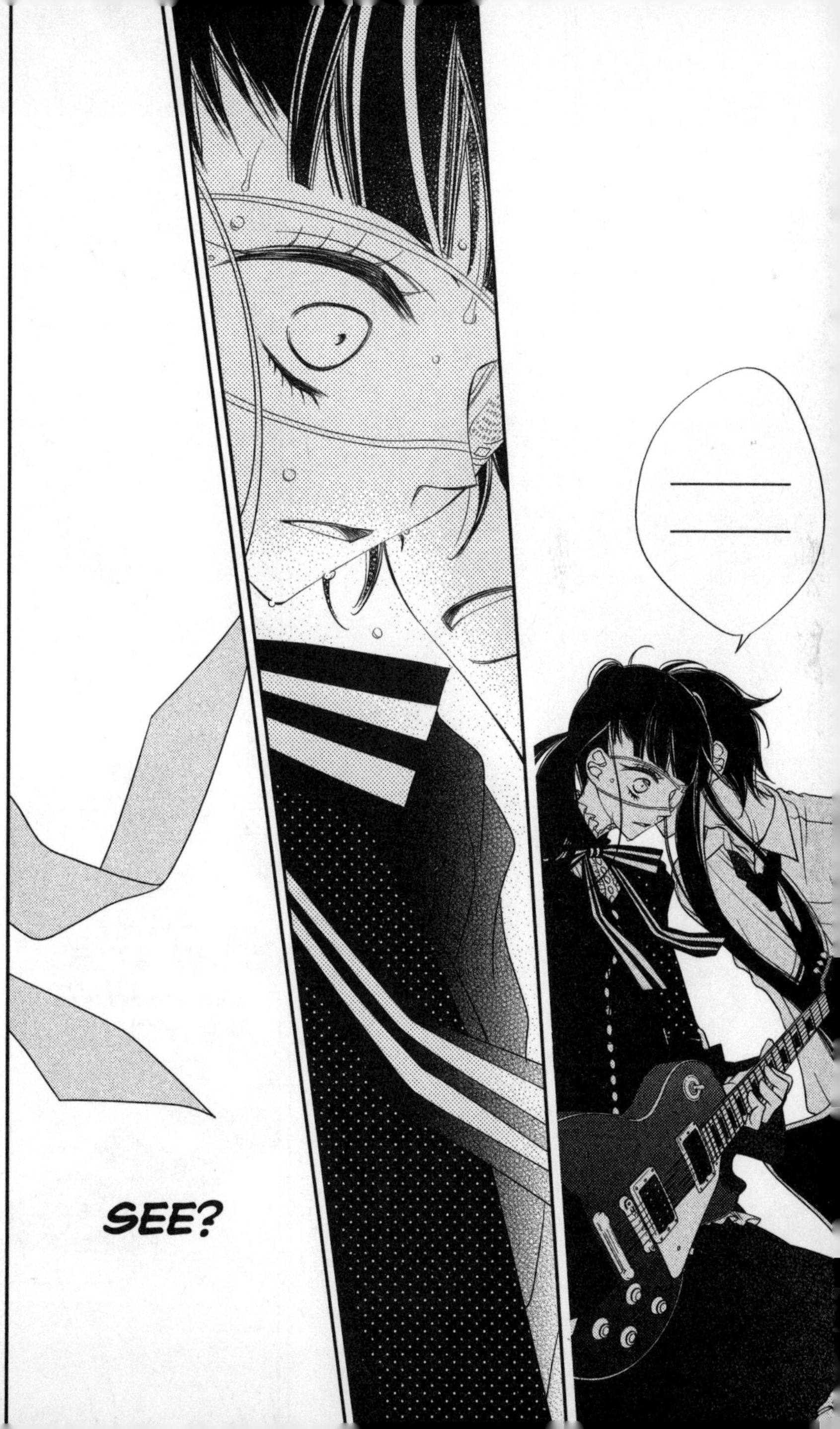
——
——
SEE?

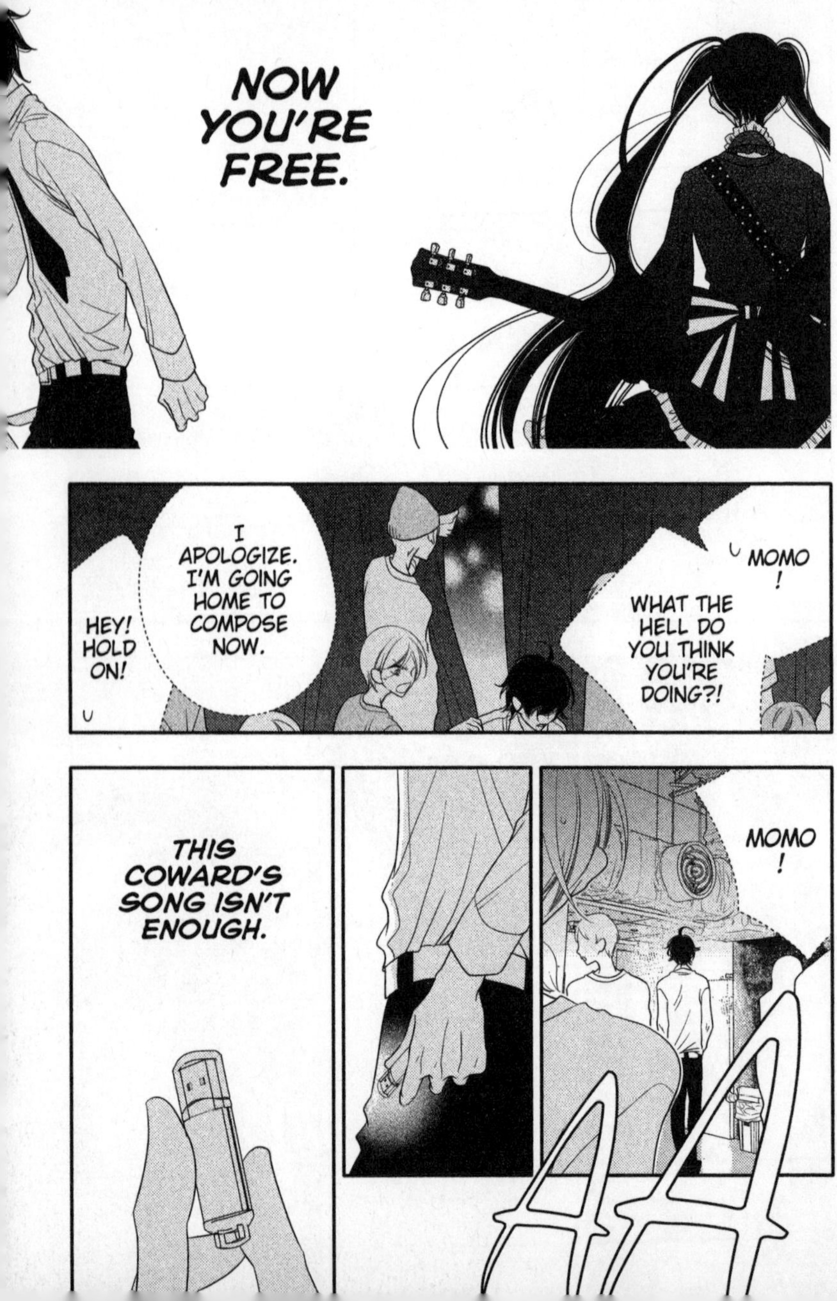
NOW YOU'RE FREE.
MOMO!
WHAT THE HELL DO YOU THINK YOU'RE DOING?!
I APOLOGIZE. I'M GOING HOME TO COMPOSE NOW.
HEY! HOLD ON!
MOMO!
THIS COWARD'S SONG ISN'T ENOUGH.

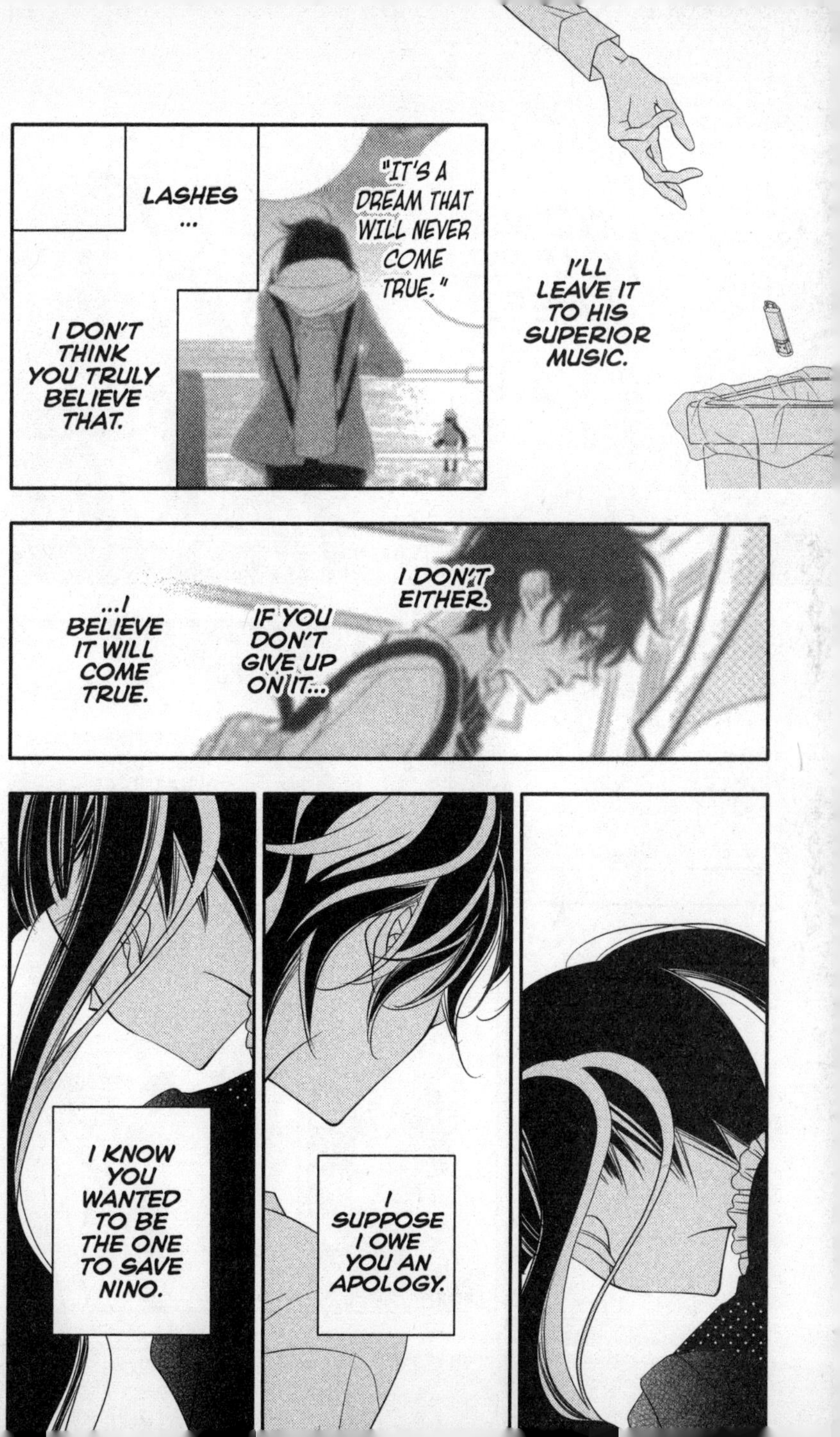
I'LL LEAVE IT TO HIS SUPERIOR MUSIC.
"IT'S A DREAM THAT WILL NEVER COME TRUE."
LASHES ...
I DON'T THINK YOU TRULY BELIEVE THAT.
I DON'T EITHER.
IF YOU DON'T GIVE UP ON IT...
...I BELIEVE IT WILL COME TRUE.
I SUPPOSE I OWE YOU AN APOLOGY.
I KNOW YOU WANTED TO BE THE ONE TO SAVE NINO.

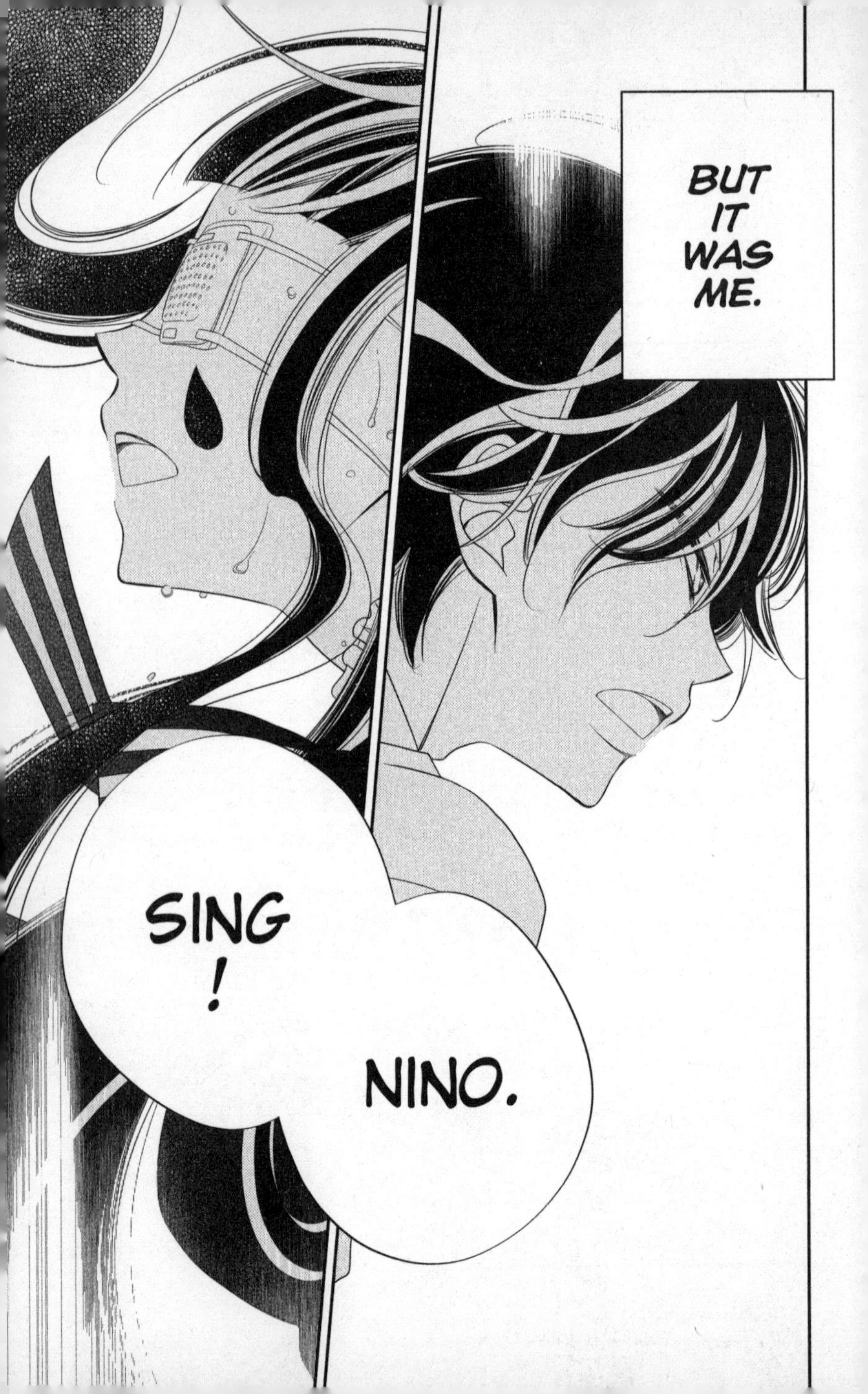
BUT IT WAS ME.
SING!
NINO.

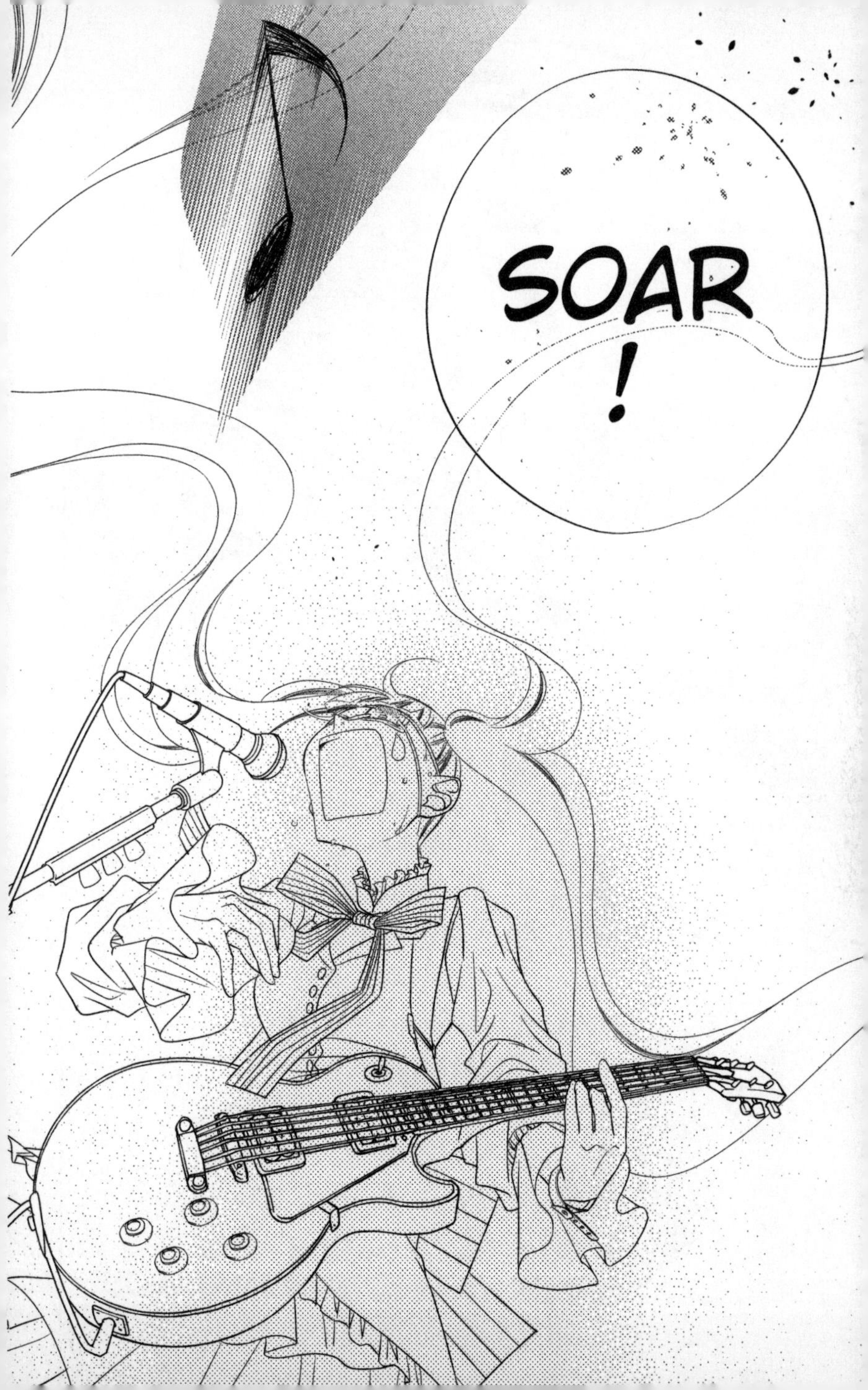
SOAR!

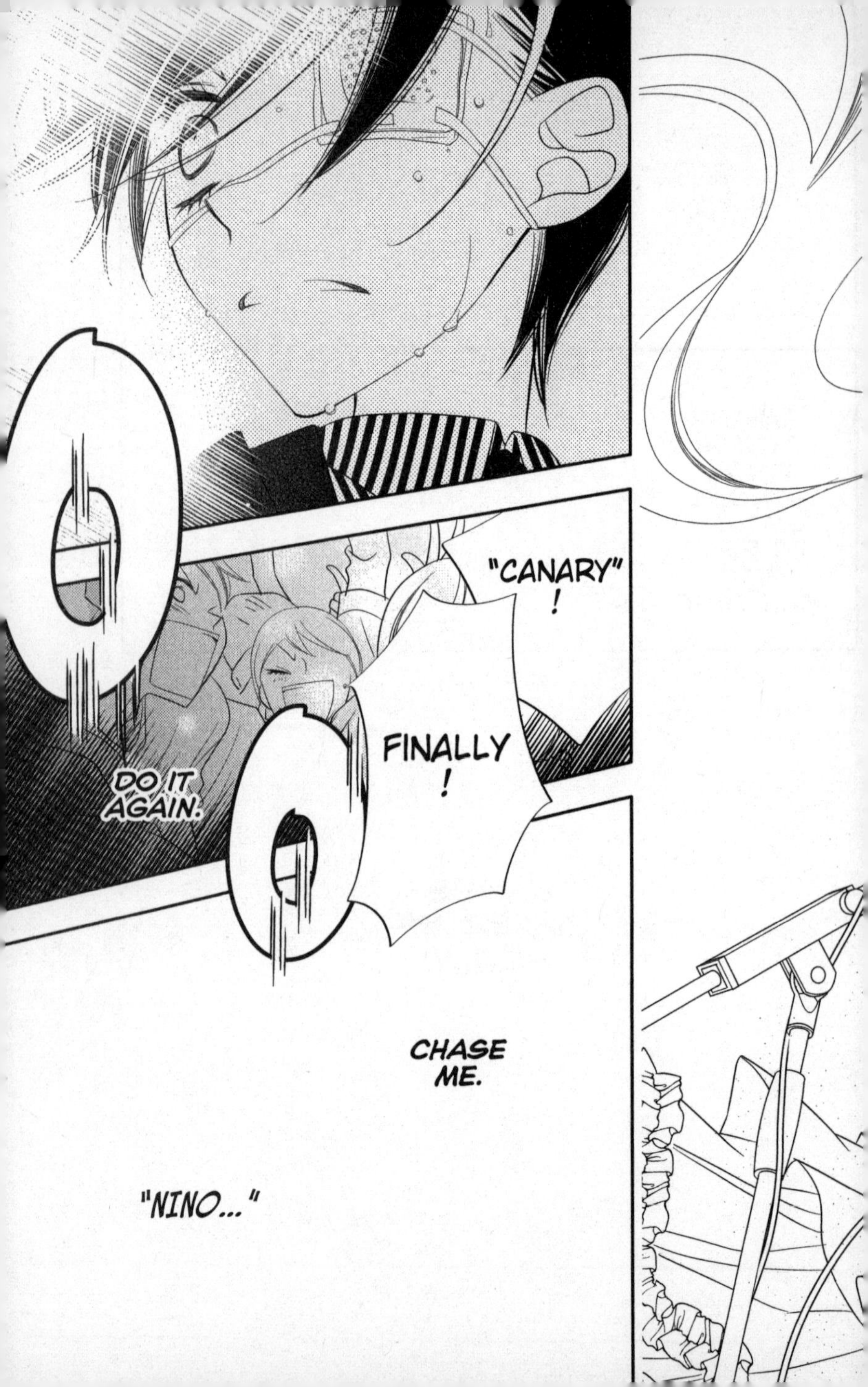
"CANARY"!
FINALLY!
DO IT AGAIN.
CHASE ME.
"NINO..."

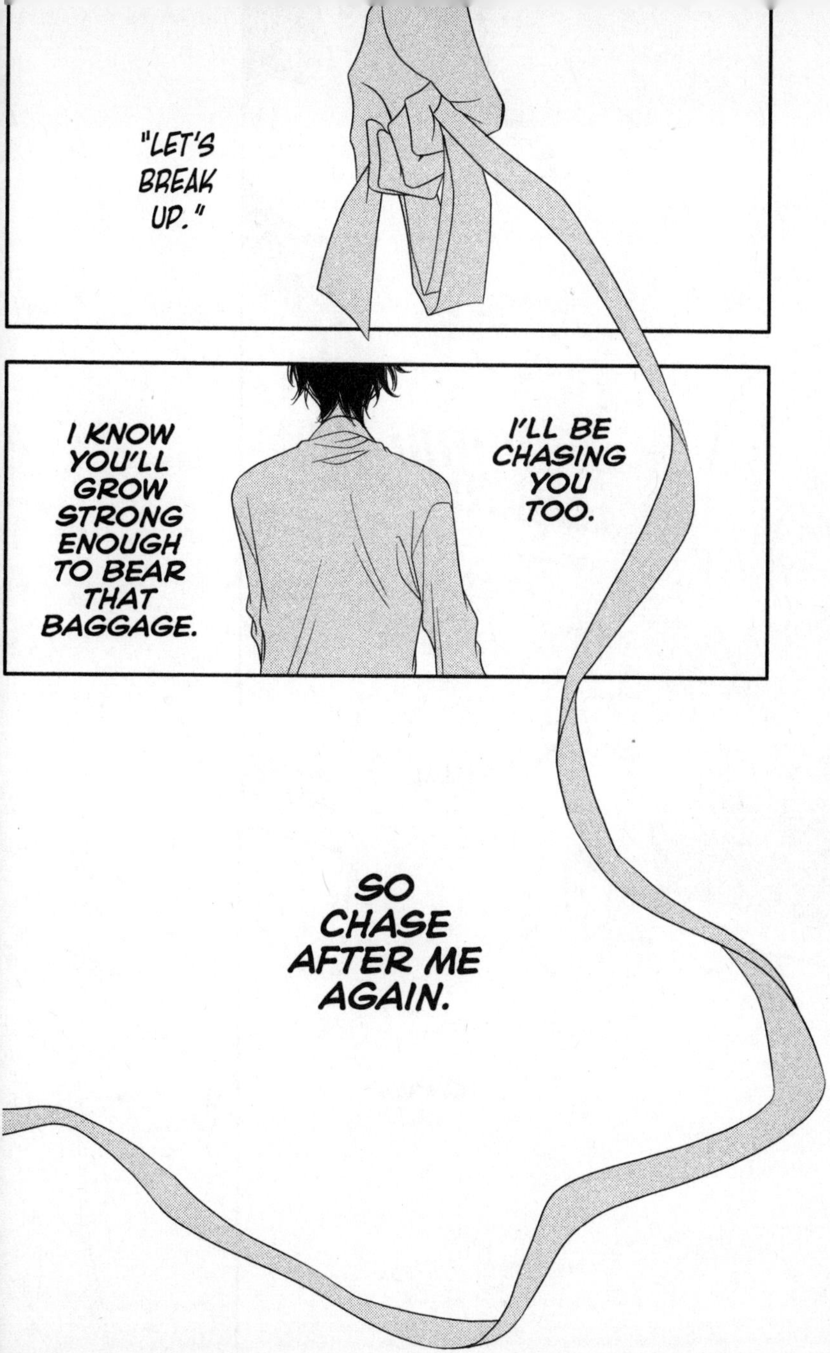
"LET'S BREAK UP."
I'LL BE CHASING YOU TOO.
I KNOW YOU'LL GROW STRONG ENOUGH TO BEAR THAT BAGGAGE.
SO CHASE AFTER ME AGAIN.

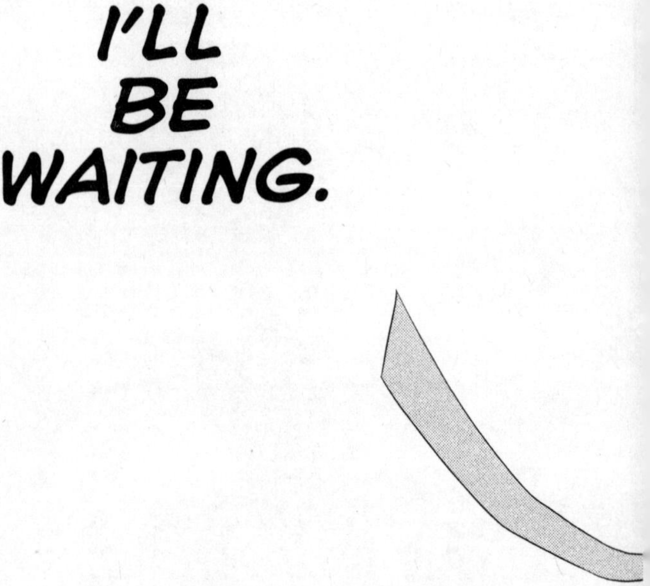

I'LL
BE
WAITING.

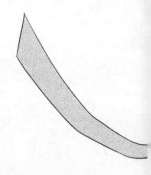

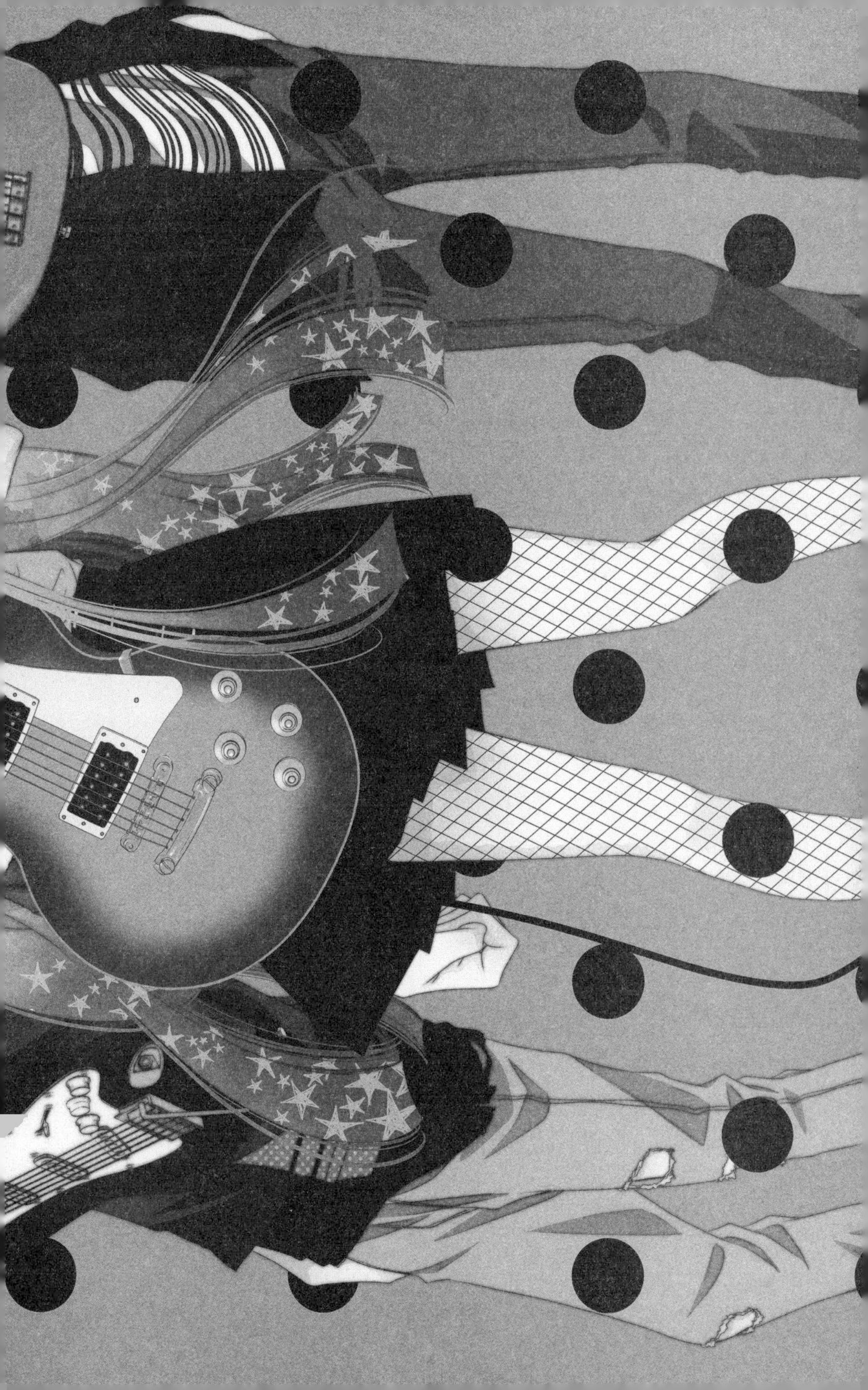

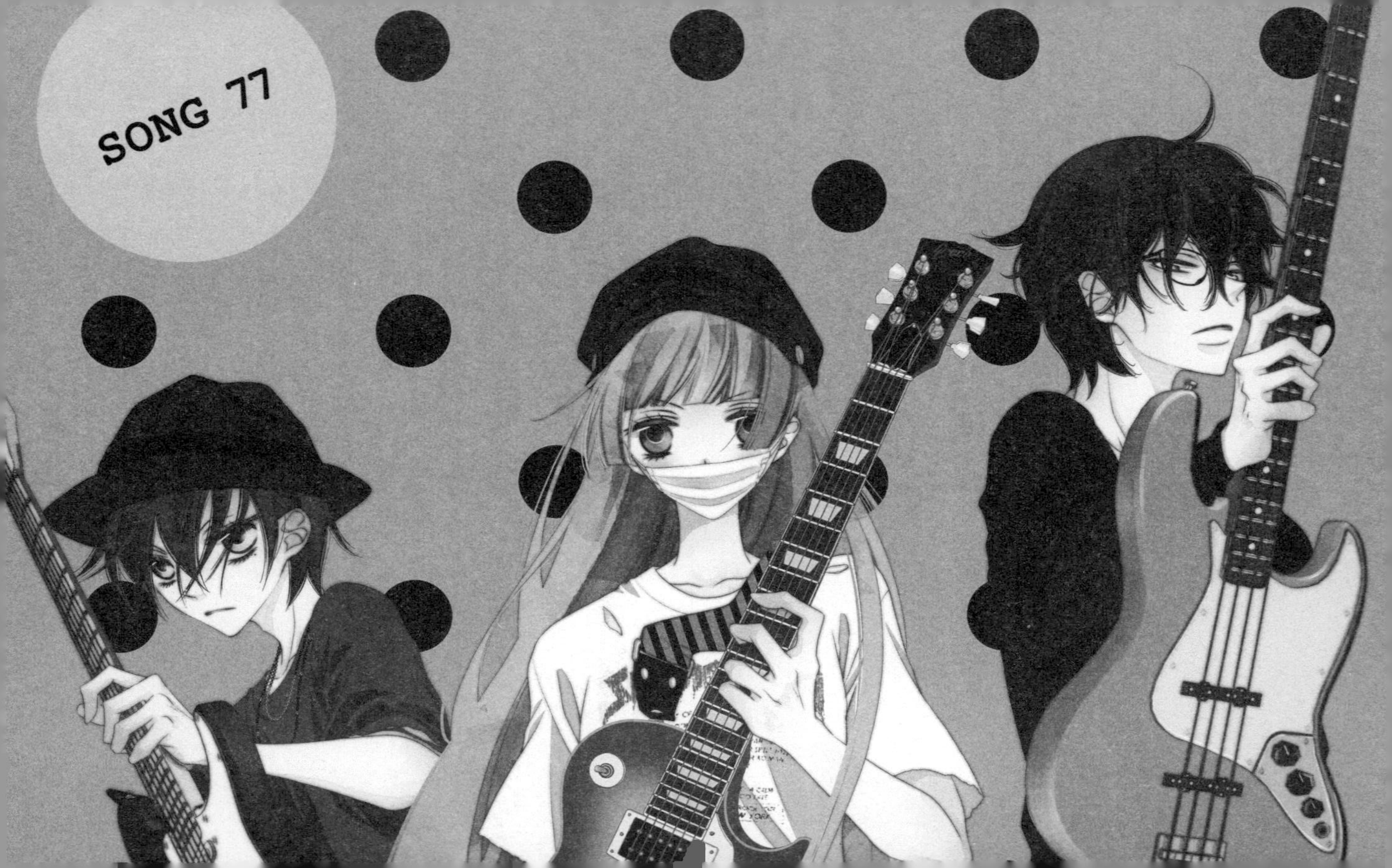
SONG 77

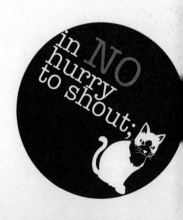
in NO
hurry
to shout;

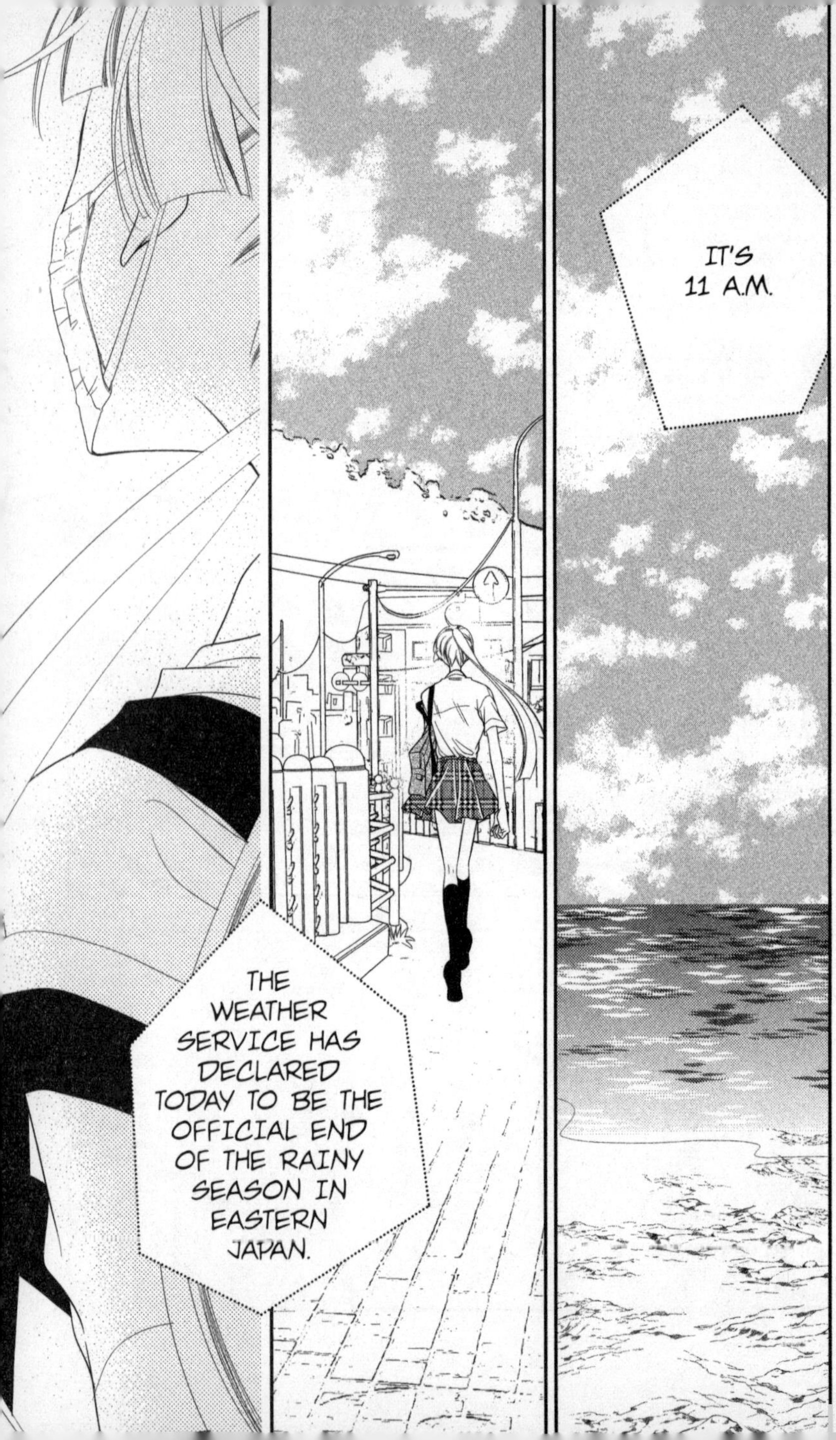
IT'S 11 A.M.
THE WEATHER SERVICE HAS DECLARED TODAY TO BE THE OFFICIAL END OF THE RAINY SEASON IN EASTERN JAPAN.

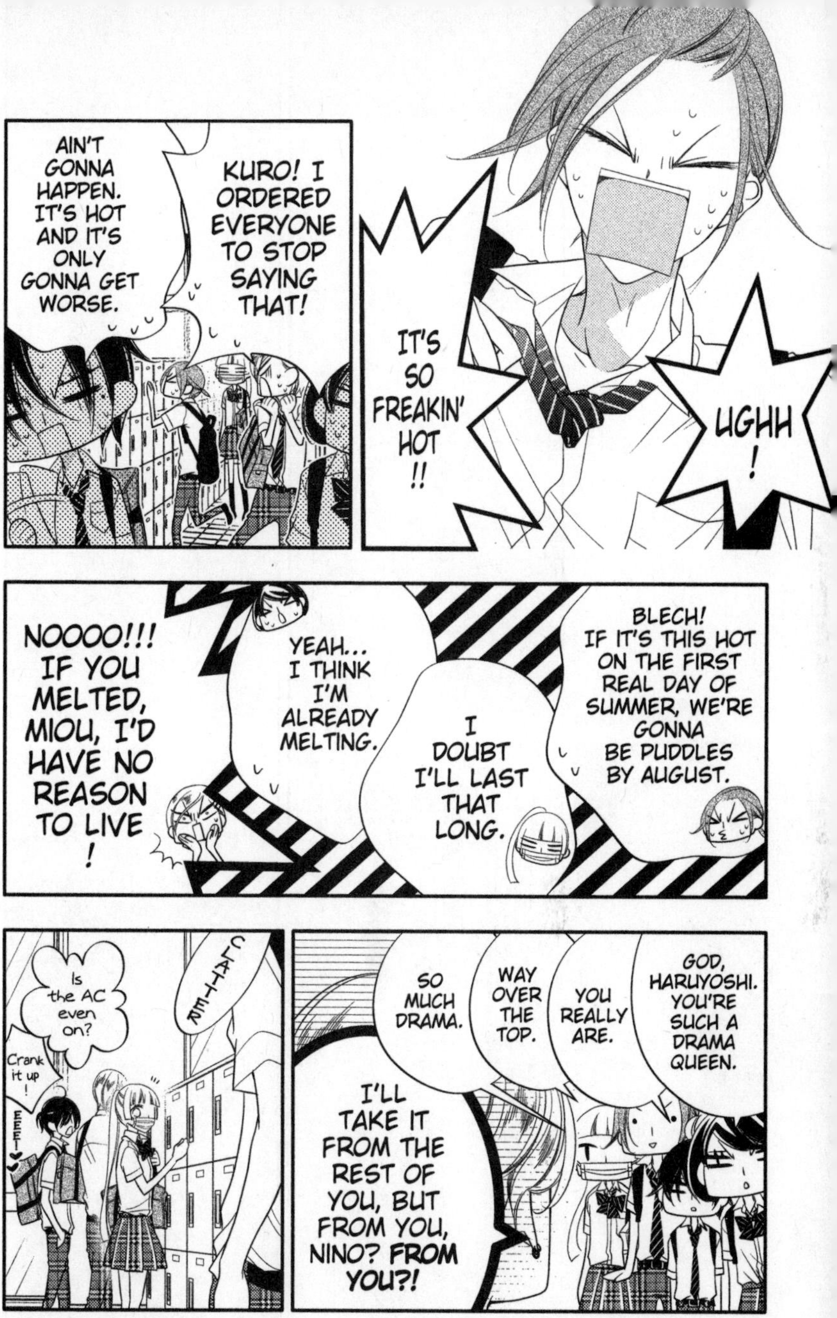
UGHH!
IT'S SO FREAKIN' HOT!!
KURO! I ORDERED EVERYONE TO STOP SAYING THAT!
AIN'T GONNA HAPPEN. IT'S HOT AND IT'S ONLY GONNA GET WORSE.
BLECH! IF IT'S THIS HOT ON THE FIRST REAL DAY OF SUMMER, WE'RE GONNA BE PUDDLES BY AUGUST.
I DOUBT I'LL LAST THAT LONG.
YEAH... I THINK I'M ALREADY MELTING.
NOOOO!!! IF YOU MELTED, MIOU, I'D HAVE NO REASON TO LIVE!
GOD, HARUYOSHI. YOU'RE SUCH A DRAMA QUEEN.
YOU REALLY ARE.
WAY OVER THE TOP.
SO MUCH DRAMA.
I'LL TAKE IT FROM THE REST OF YOU, BUT FROM YOU, NINO? FROM YOU?!
CLATTER
Is the AC even on?
Crank it up!
EEE!

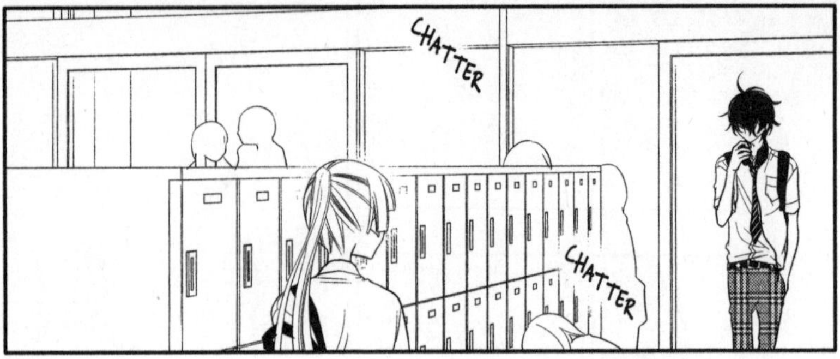
CHATTER
CHATTER

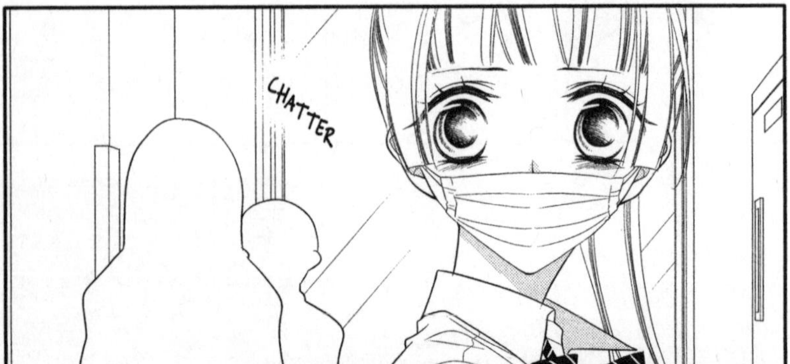
CHATTER

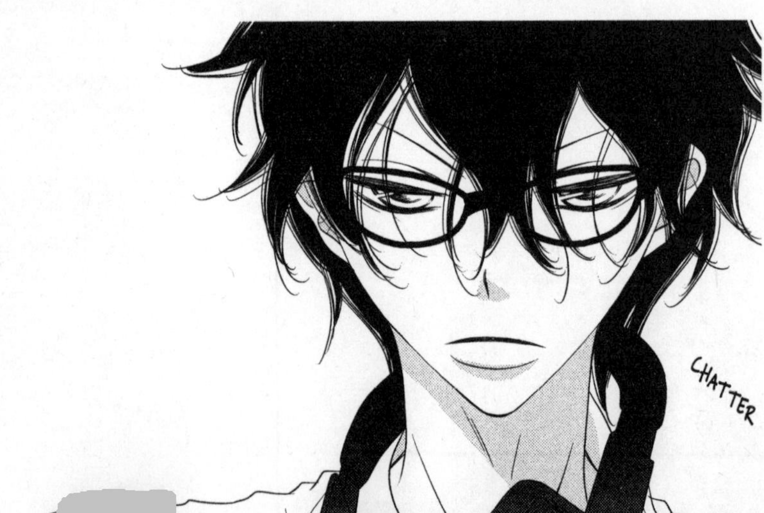
CHATTER

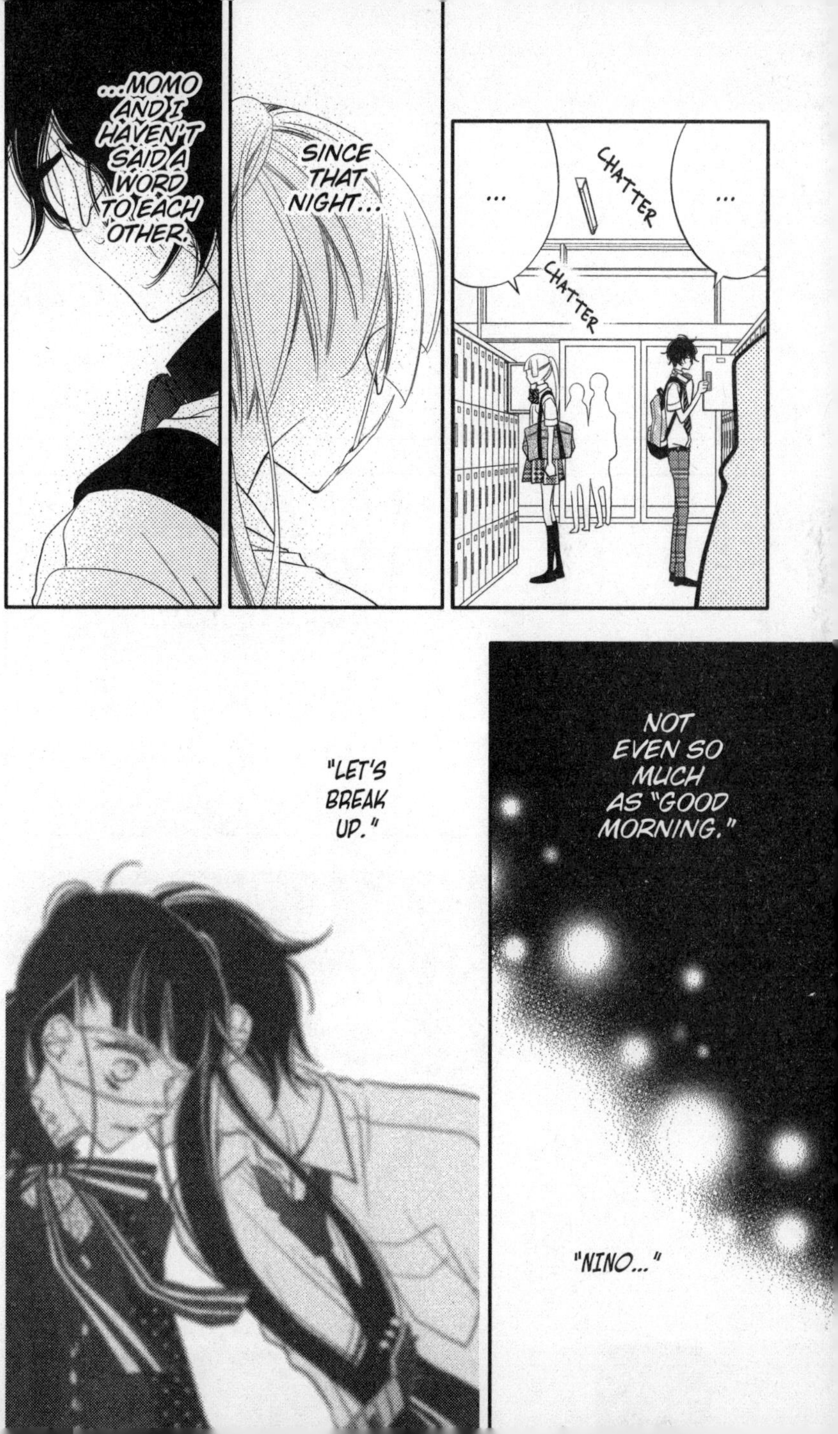
...
CHATTER
...
CHATTER
SINCE THAT NIGHT...
...MOMO AND I HAVEN'T SAID A WORD TO EACH OTHER.
NOT EVEN SO MUCH AS "GOOD MORNING."
"NINO..."
"LET'S BREAK UP."

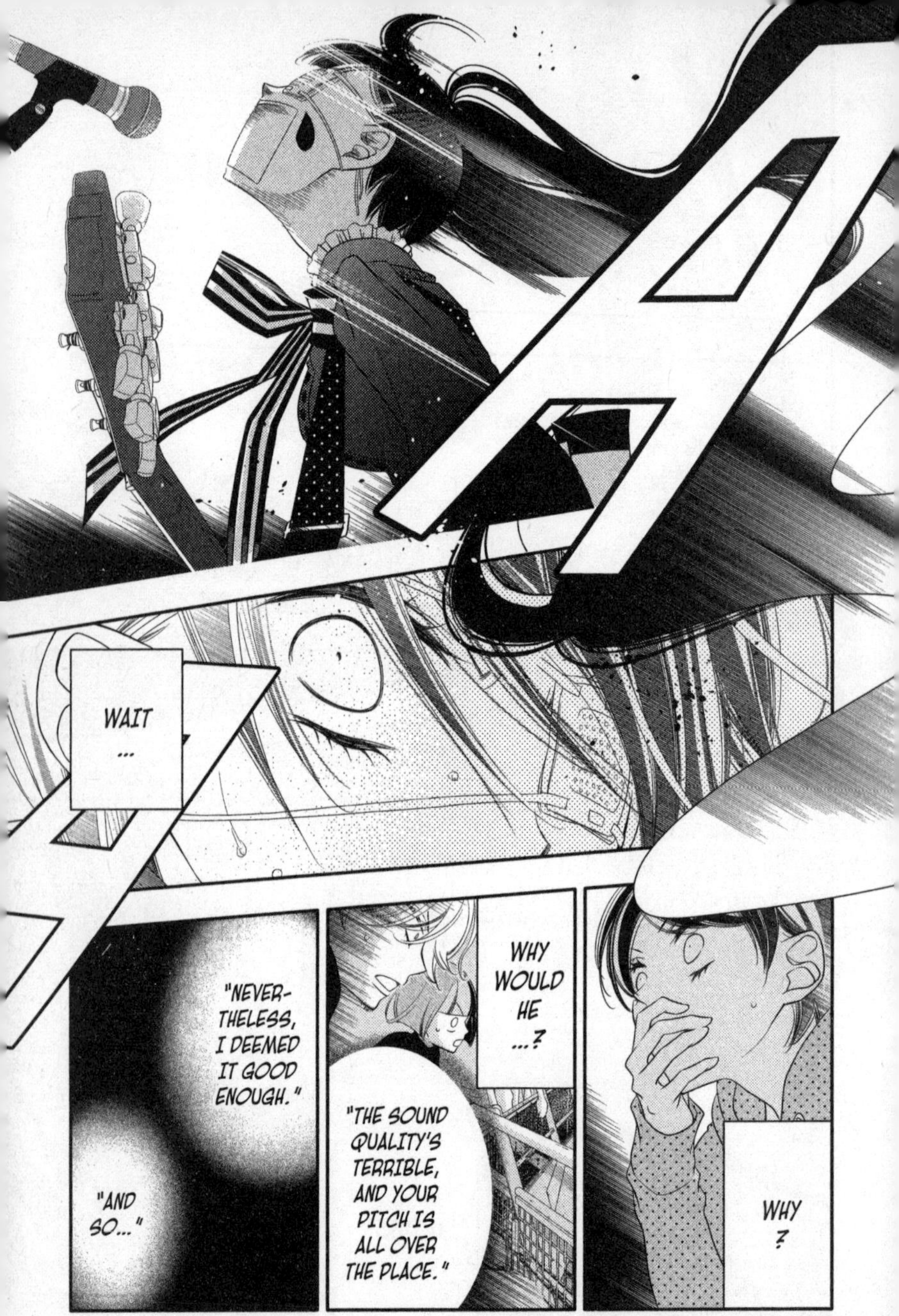
WAIT ...
WHY ?
WHY WOULD HE ...?
"THE SOUND QUALITY'S TERRIBLE, AND YOUR PITCH IS ALL OVER THE PLACE."
"NEVER-THELESS, I DEEMED IT GOOD ENOUGH."
"AND SO..."

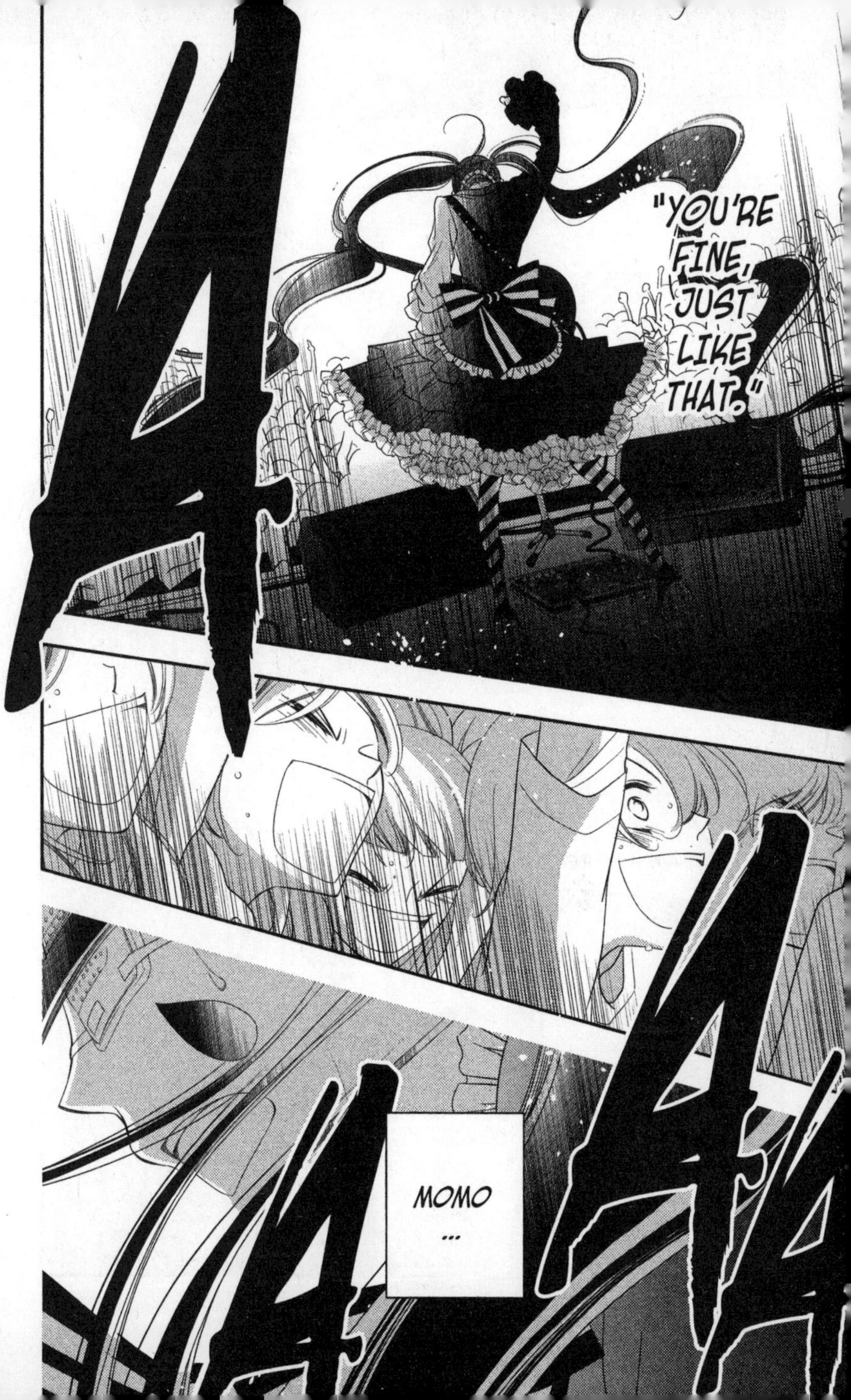
"YOU'RE FINE, JUST LIKE THAT."
MOMO ...

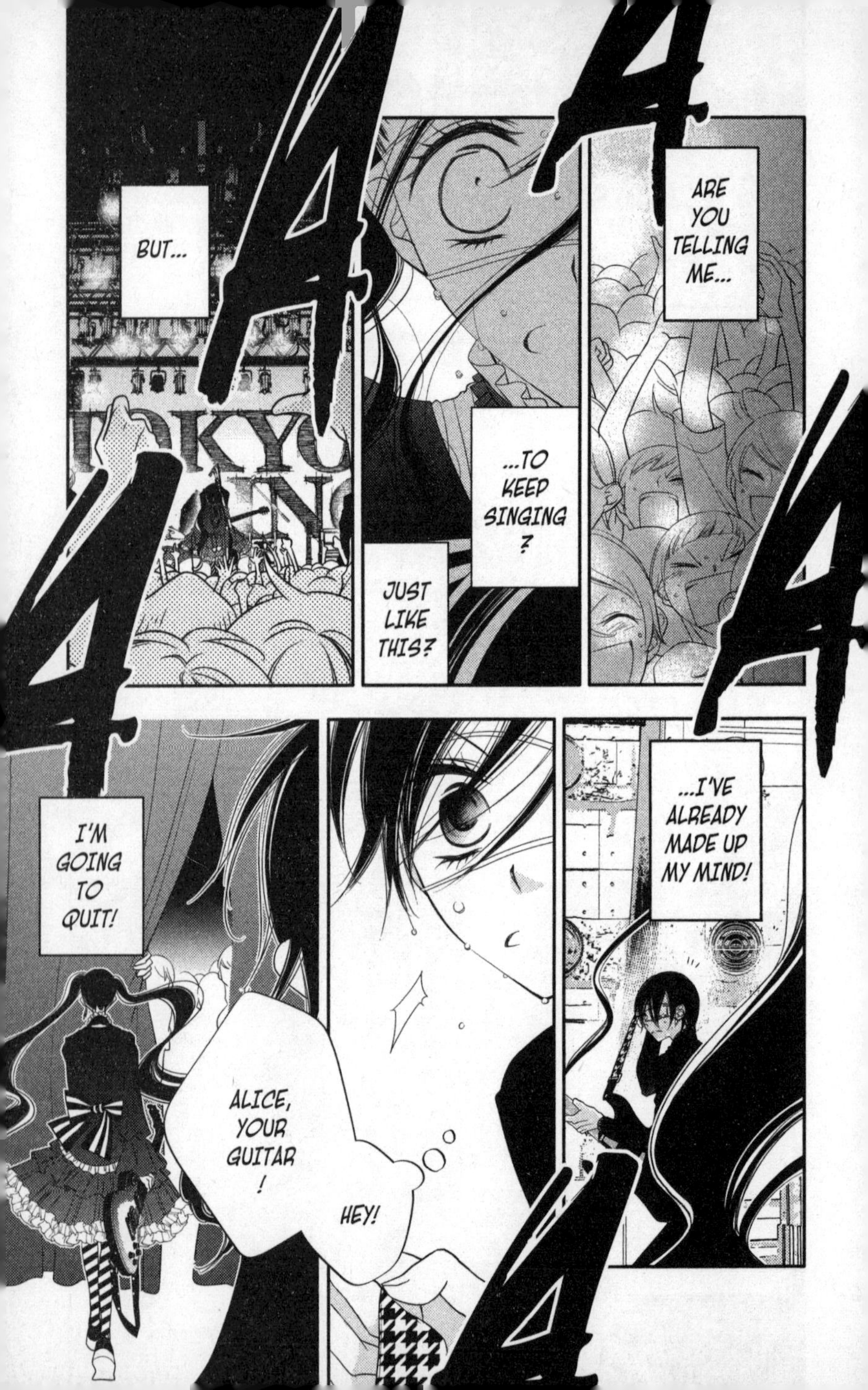
ARE YOU TELLING ME...
...TO KEEP SINGING?
JUST LIKE THIS?
BUT...
...I'VE ALREADY MADE UP MY MIND!
ALICE, YOUR GUITAR!
HEY!
I'M GOING TO QUIT!

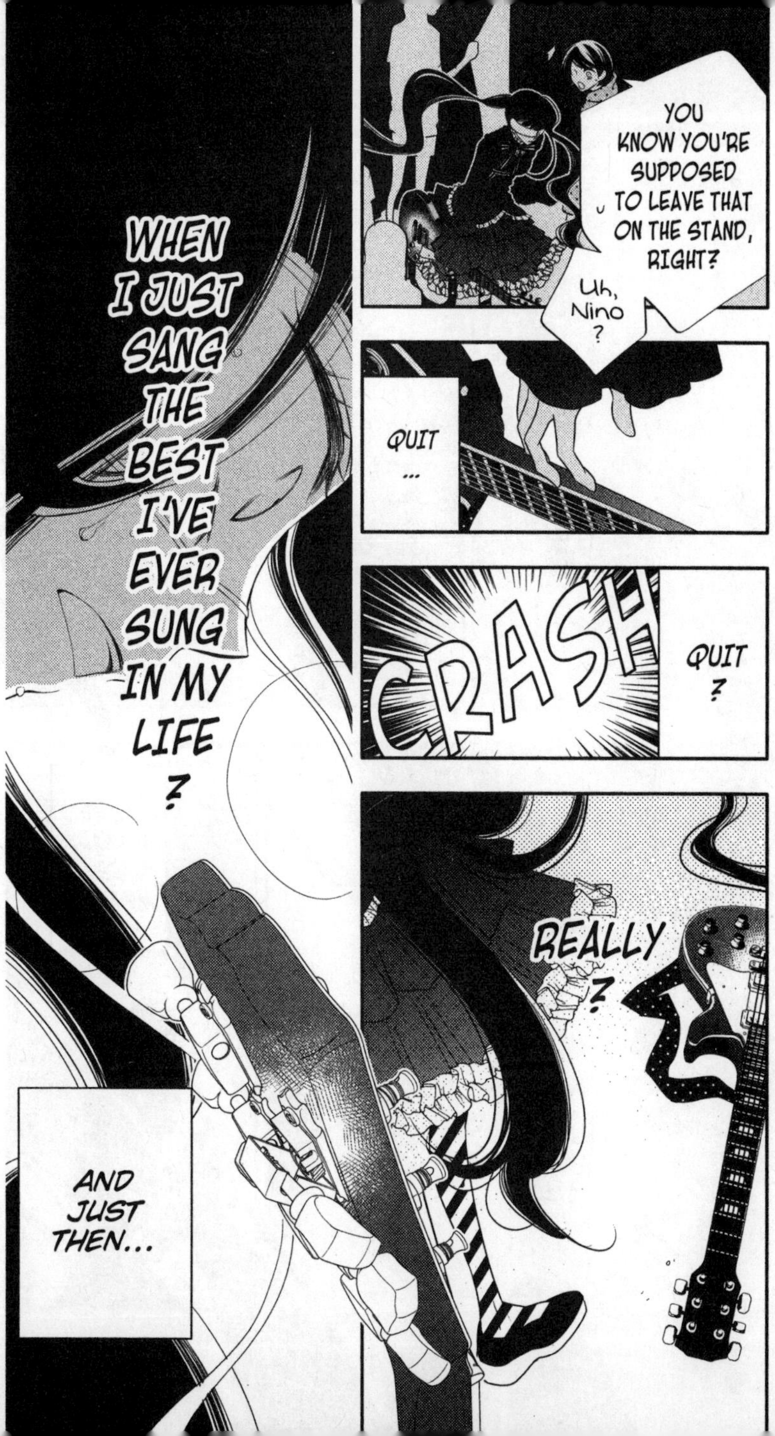
YOU KNOW YOU'RE SUPPOSED TO LEAVE THAT ON THE STAND, RIGHT?
Uh, Nino?
QUIT...
QUIT?
CRASH
REALLY?
WHEN I JUST SANG THE BEST I'VE EVER SUNG IN MY LIFE?
AND JUST THEN...

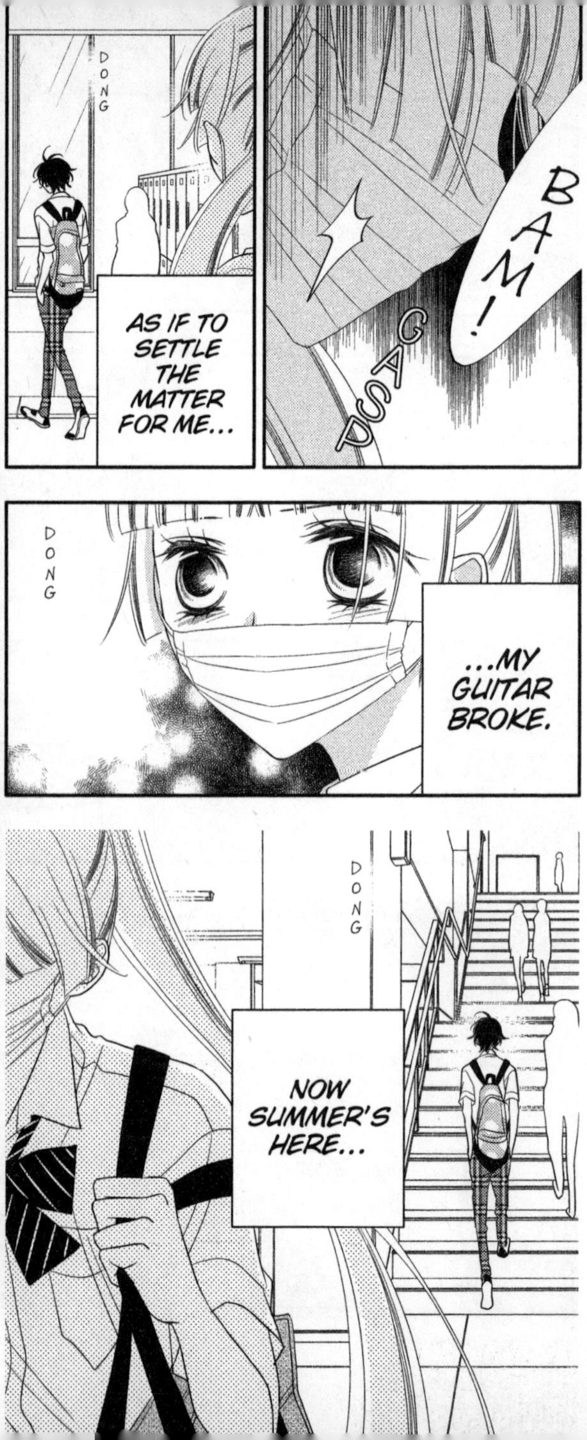
BAM!
GASP
DONG
AS IF TO SETTLE THE MATTER FOR ME...
DONG
...MY GUITAR BROKE.
DONG
NOW SUMMER'S HERE...

2

A little before the release of volume 13 (in June, I think), my editor was reassigned. How I cried! In shock, we met at a bar and cried our eyes out. This editor had been with me since the last year of *Monochrome Kids*, and we've loved each other as colleagues ever since. I still love him today! (Even if I do get email responses late.) However, I learned long ago that working with new editors doesn't affect my manga at all. (In fact, I've had former editors tell me they were a little sad when they read my manga after they'd left and saw that for themselves... *Ha ha*...) What was so valuable to me was the incredible emotional support he provided.
I never would have been able to write this manga for as long as I have otherwise. Thank you, truly, from the bottom of my heart. I hope you'll continue to stay in my life as my drinking buddy from here on out.

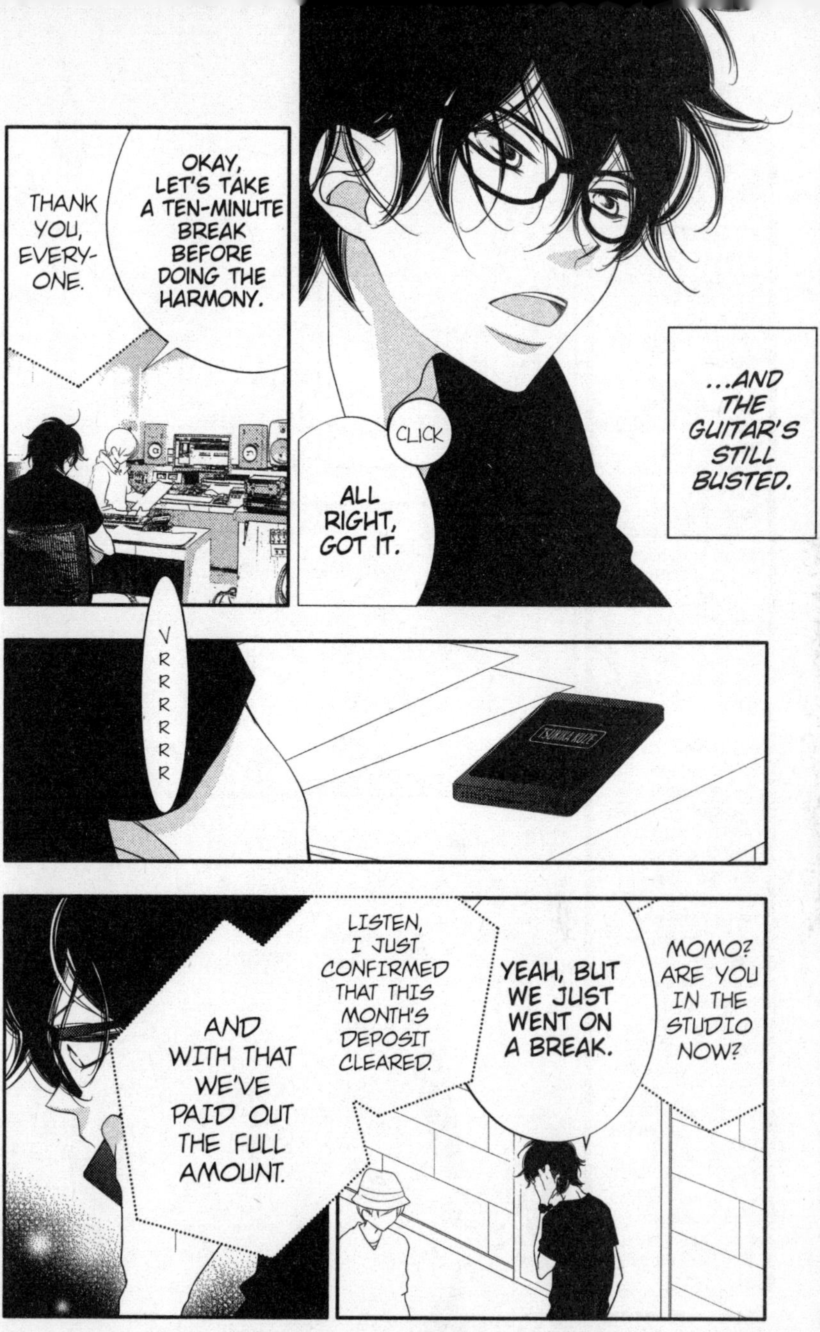
...AND THE GUITAR'S STILL BUSTED.
CLICK
ALL RIGHT, GOT IT.
OKAY, LET'S TAKE A TEN-MINUTE BREAK BEFORE DOING THE HARMONY.
THANK YOU, EVERY-ONE.
VRRRRRR
MOMO? ARE YOU IN THE STUDIO NOW?
YEAH, BUT WE JUST WENT ON A BREAK.
LISTEN, I JUST CONFIRMED THAT THIS MONTH'S DEPOSIT CLEARED.
AND WITH THAT WE'VE PAID OUT THE FULL AMOUNT.

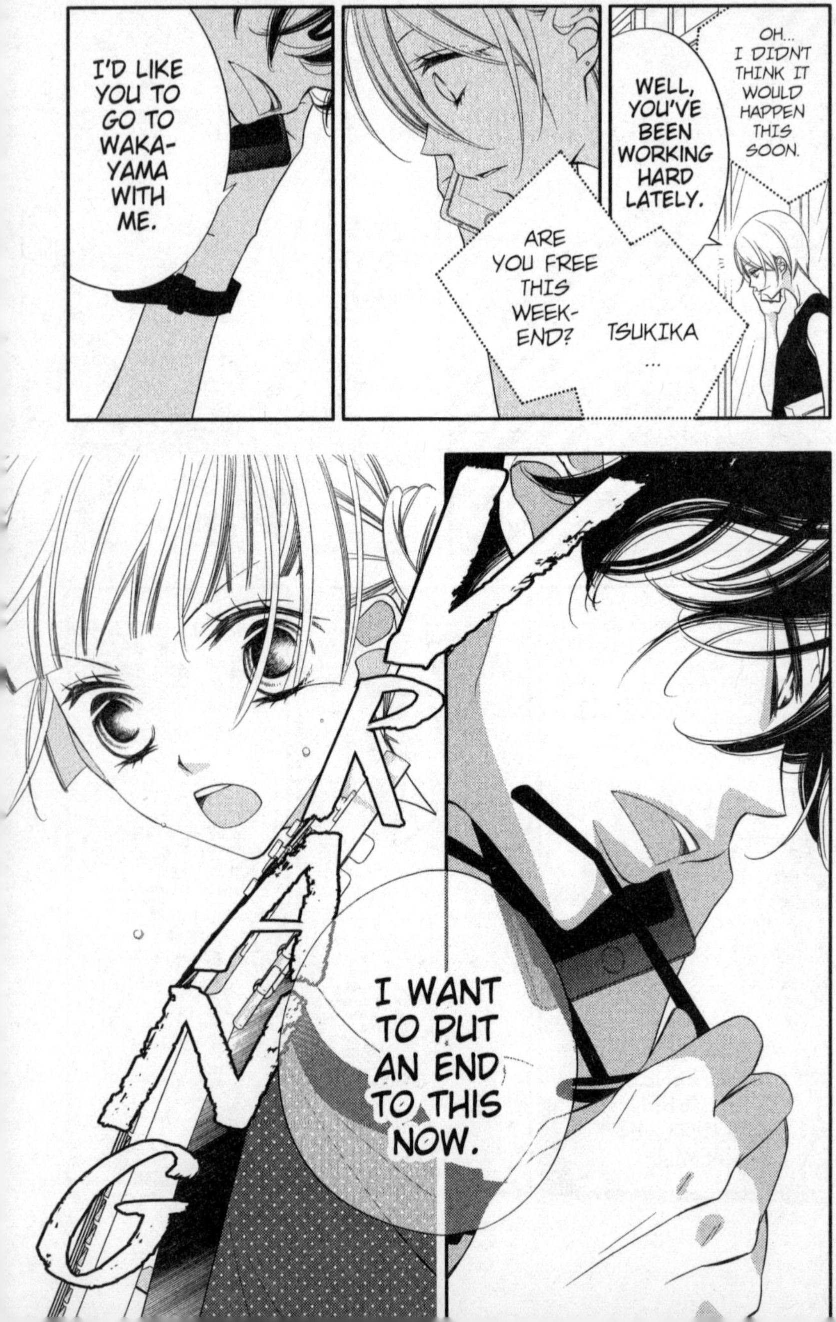
OH... I DIDN'T THINK IT WOULD HAPPEN THIS SOON.
WELL, YOU'VE BEEN WORKING HARD LATELY.
TSUKIKA ...
ARE YOU FREE THIS WEEK-END?
I'D LIKE YOU TO GO TO WAKA-YAMA WITH ME.
I WANT TO PUT AN END TO THIS NOW.

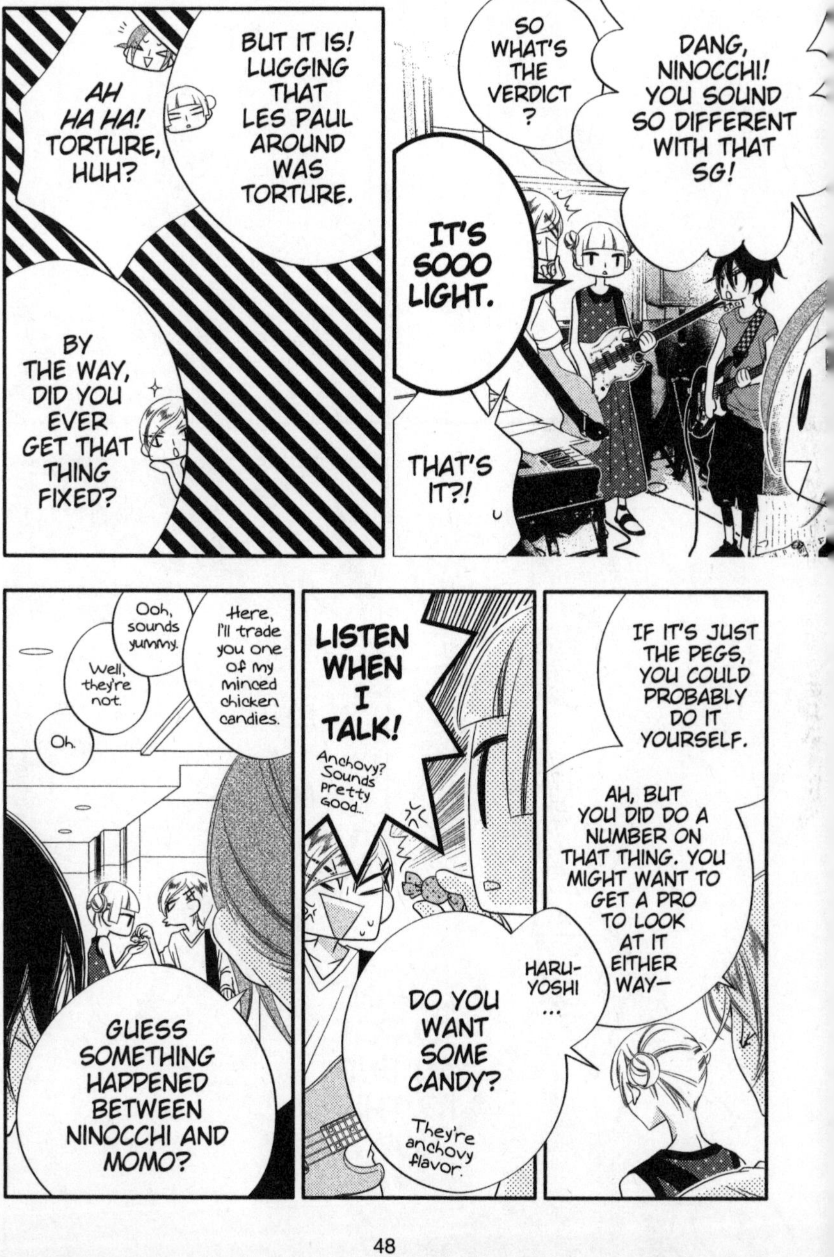
DANG, NINOCCHI! YOU SOUND SO DIFFERENT WITH THAT SG!
SO WHAT'S THE VERDICT?
IT'S SOOO LIGHT.
THAT'S IT?!
BUT IT IS! LUGGING THAT LES PAUL AROUND WAS TORTURE.
AH HA HA! TORTURE, HUH?
BY THE WAY, DID YOU EVER GET THAT THING FIXED?
IF IT'S JUST THE PEGS, YOU COULD PROBABLY DO IT YOURSELF.
AH, BUT YOU DID DO A NUMBER ON THAT THING. YOU MIGHT WANT TO GET A PRO TO LOOK AT IT EITHER WAY—
HARU-YOSHI...
DO YOU WANT SOME CANDY?
They're anchovy flavor.
LISTEN WHEN I TALK!
Anchovy? Sounds pretty good...
Here, I'll trade you one of my minced chicken candies.
Ooh, sounds yummy.
Well, they're not.
Oh.
GUESS SOMETHING HAPPENED BETWEEN NINOCCHI AND MOMO?

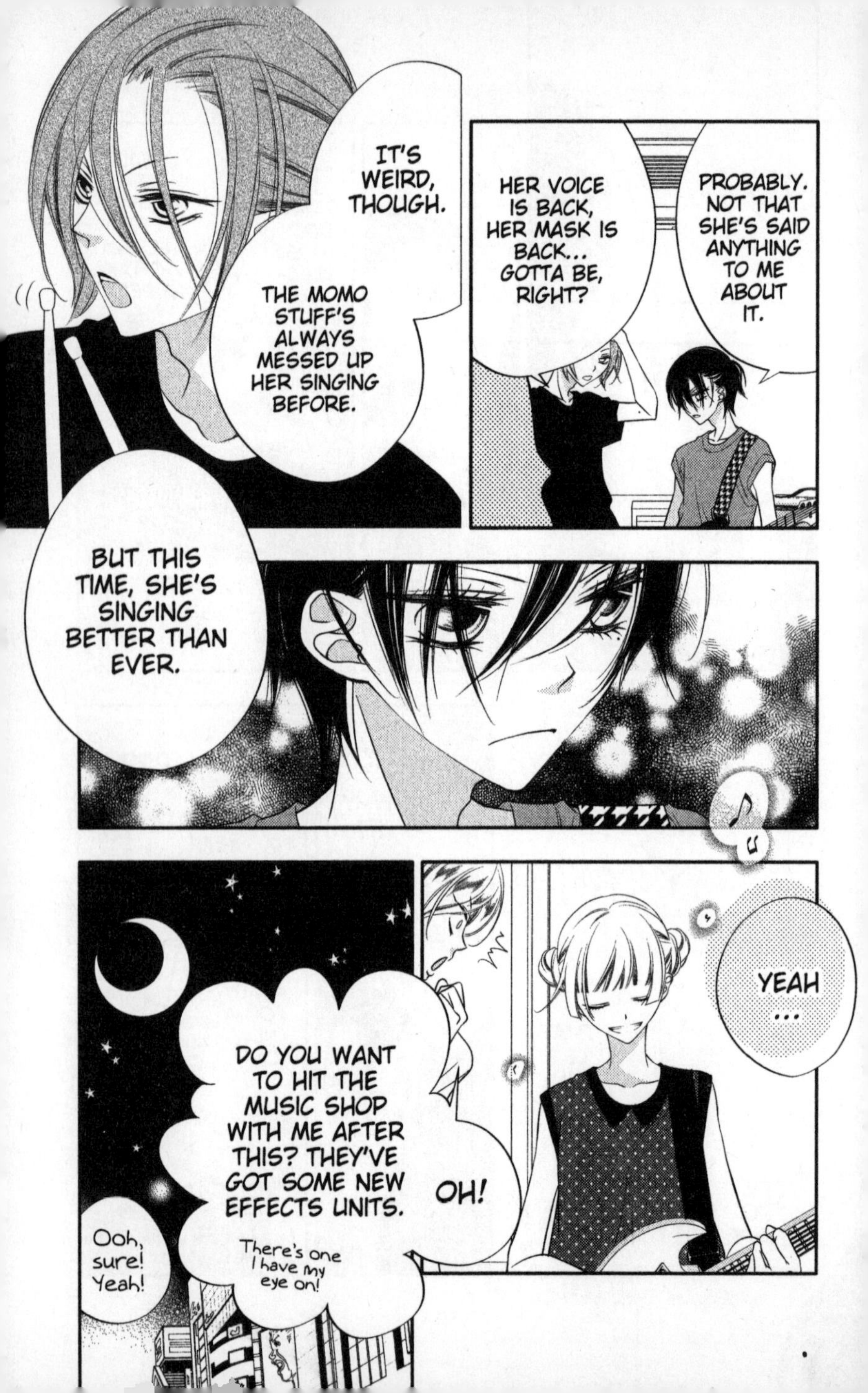
HER VOICE IS BACK, HER MASK IS BACK... GOTTA BE, RIGHT?
PROBABLY. NOT THAT SHE'S SAID ANYTHING TO ME ABOUT IT.
IT'S WEIRD, THOUGH.
THE MOMO STUFF'S ALWAYS MESSED UP HER SINGING BEFORE.
BUT THIS TIME, SHE'S SINGING BETTER THAN EVER.
YEAH ...
OH!
DO YOU WANT TO HIT THE MUSIC SHOP WITH ME AFTER THIS? THEY'VE GOT SOME NEW EFFECTS UNITS.
There's one I have my eye on!
Ooh, sure! Yeah!

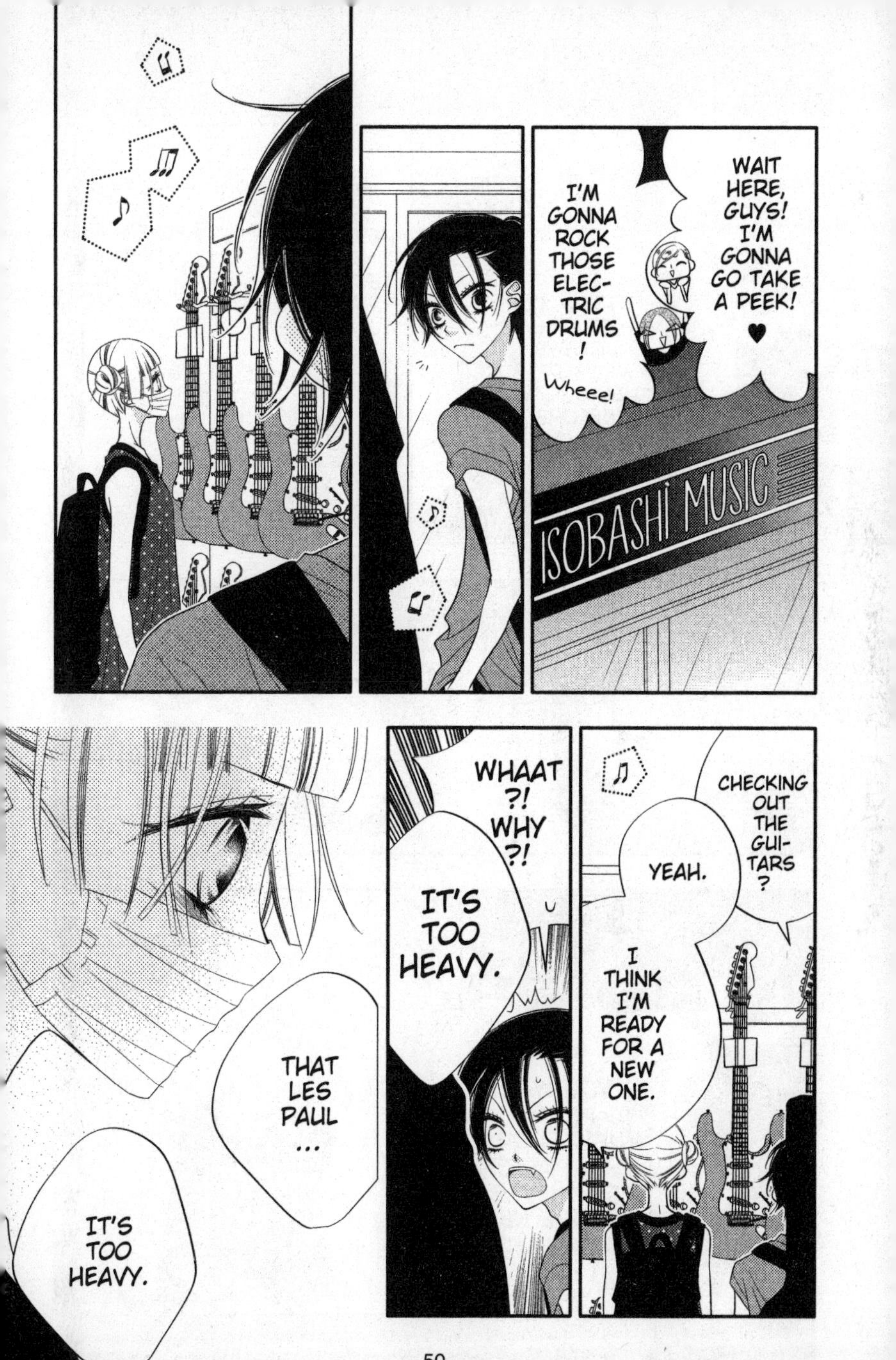
WAIT HERE, GUYS! I'M GONNA GO TAKE A PEEK! ♥
I'M GONNA ROCK THOSE ELECTRIC DRUMS!
Wheee!
ISOBASHI MUSIC
CHECKING OUT THE GUITARS?
YEAH.
I THINK I'M READY FOR A NEW ONE.
WHAAT?! WHY?!
IT'S TOO HEAVY.
THAT LES PAUL...
IT'S TOO HEAVY.

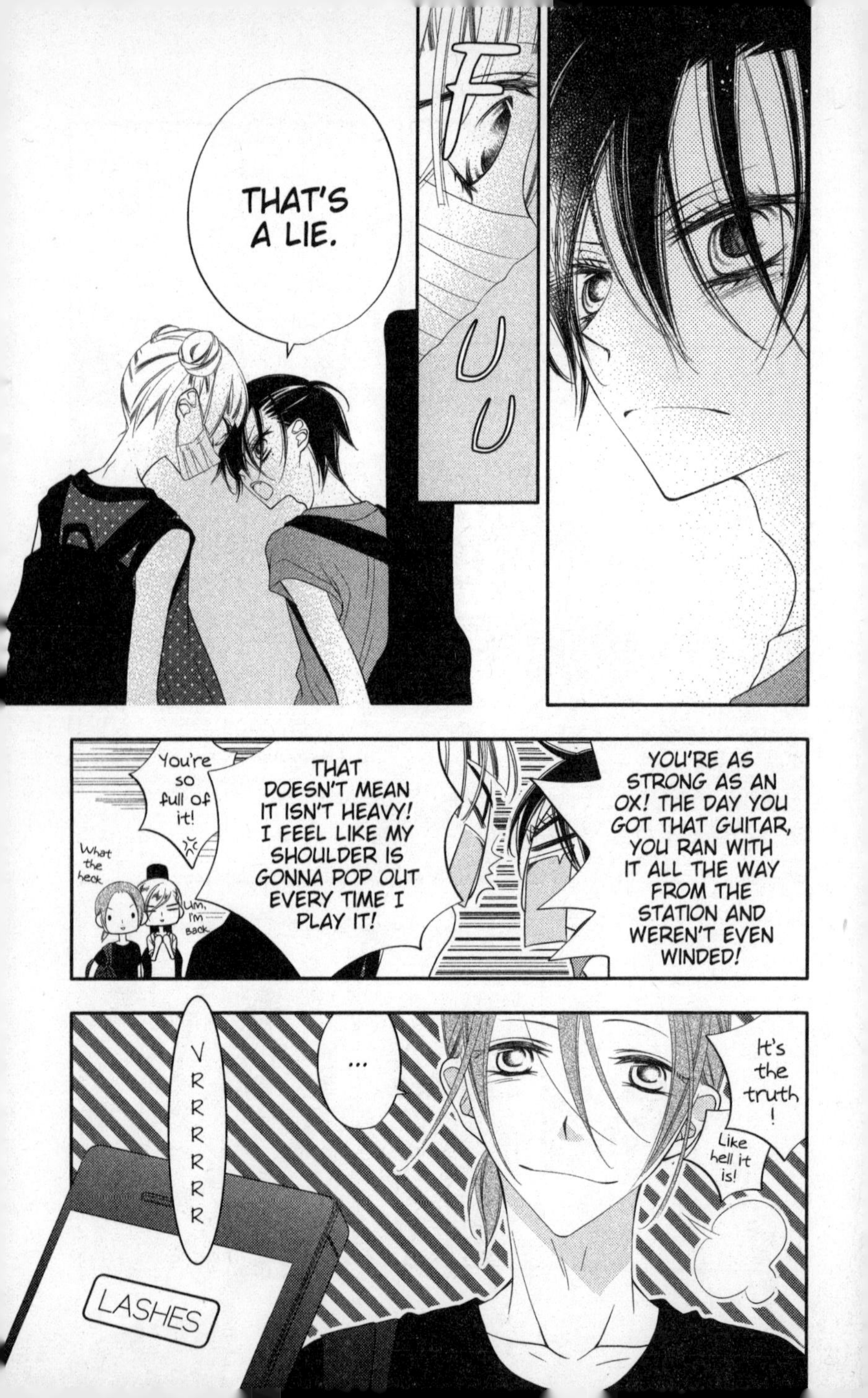
F
UU
THAT'S A LIE.
YOU'RE AS STRONG AS AN OX! THE DAY YOU GOT THAT GUITAR, YOU RAN WITH IT ALL THE WAY FROM THE STATION AND WEREN'T EVEN WINDED!
THAT DOESN'T MEAN IT ISN'T HEAVY! I FEEL LIKE MY SHOULDER IS GONNA POP OUT EVERY TIME I PLAY IT!
You're so full of it!
What the heck.
Um, I'm back.
It's the truth!
Like hell it is!
...
VRRRRRR
LASHES

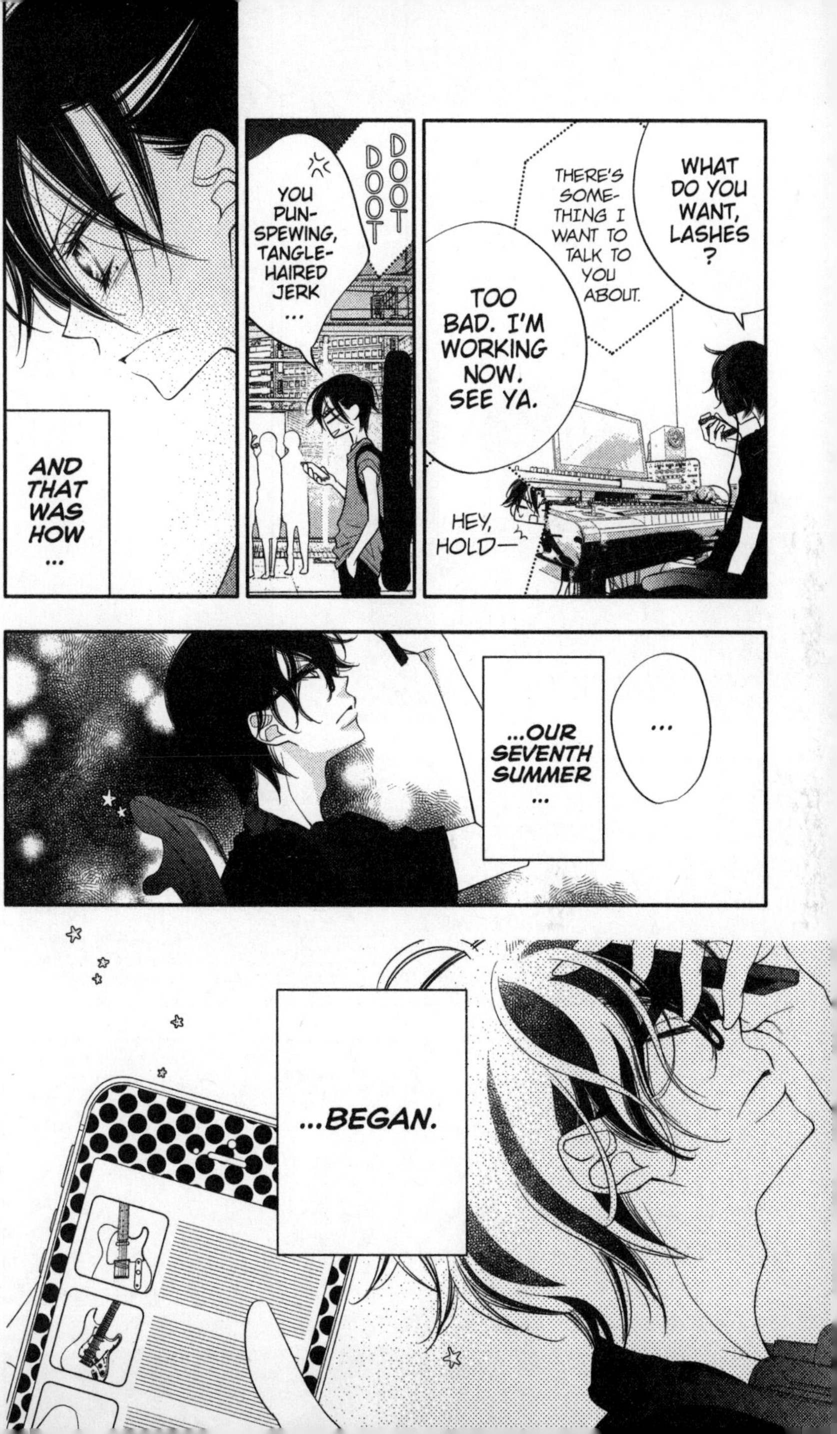
WHAT DO YOU WANT, LASHES?
THERE'S SOME-THING I WANT TO TALK TO YOU ABOUT.
TOO BAD. I'M WORKING NOW. SEE YA.
HEY, HOLD—
DOOT DOOT
YOU PUN-SPEWING, TANGLE-HAIRED JERK...
AND THAT WAS HOW...
...
...OUR SEVENTH SUMMER...
...BEGAN.

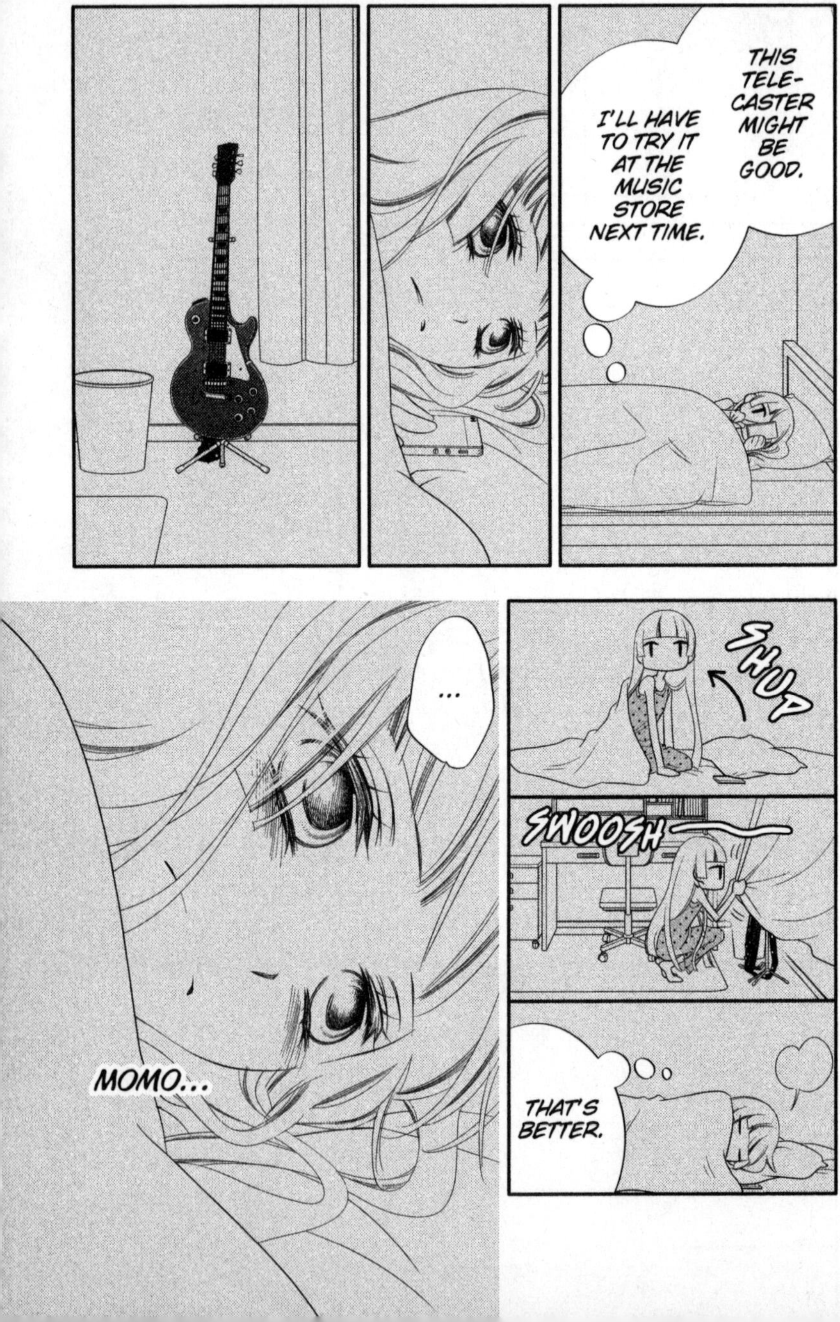
THIS TELE-CASTER MIGHT BE GOOD.
I'LL HAVE TO TRY IT AT THE MUSIC STORE NEXT TIME.
SHUP
SWOOSH
THAT'S BETTER.
...
MOMO...

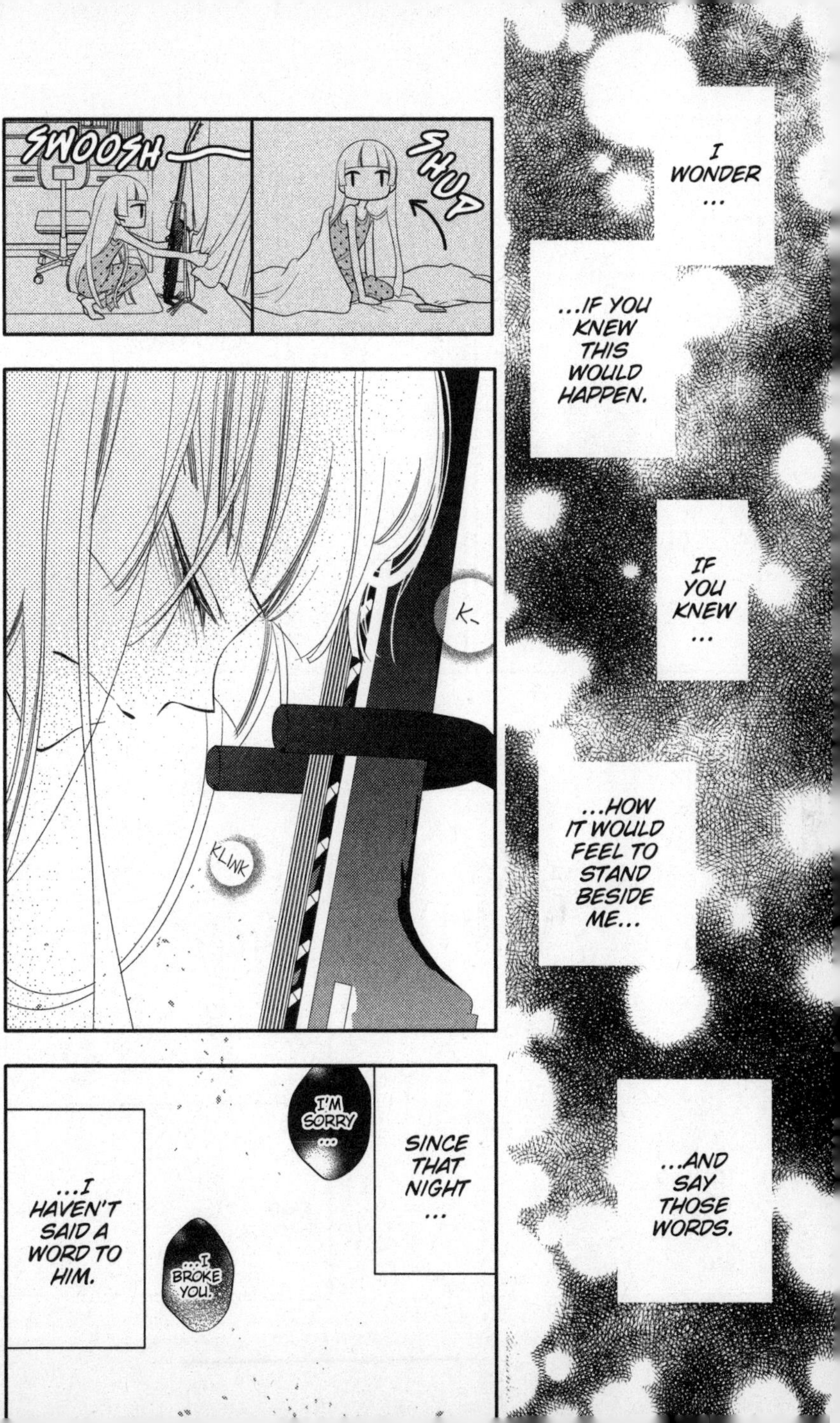
I WONDER ...
...IF YOU KNEW THIS WOULD HAPPEN.
IF YOU KNEW ...
...HOW IT WOULD FEEL TO STAND BESIDE ME...
...AND SAY THOSE WORDS.
SHUP
SWOOSH
K-
KLINK
SINCE THAT NIGHT ...
I'M SORRY ...
...I HAVEN'T SAID A WORD TO HIM.
...I BROKE YOU.

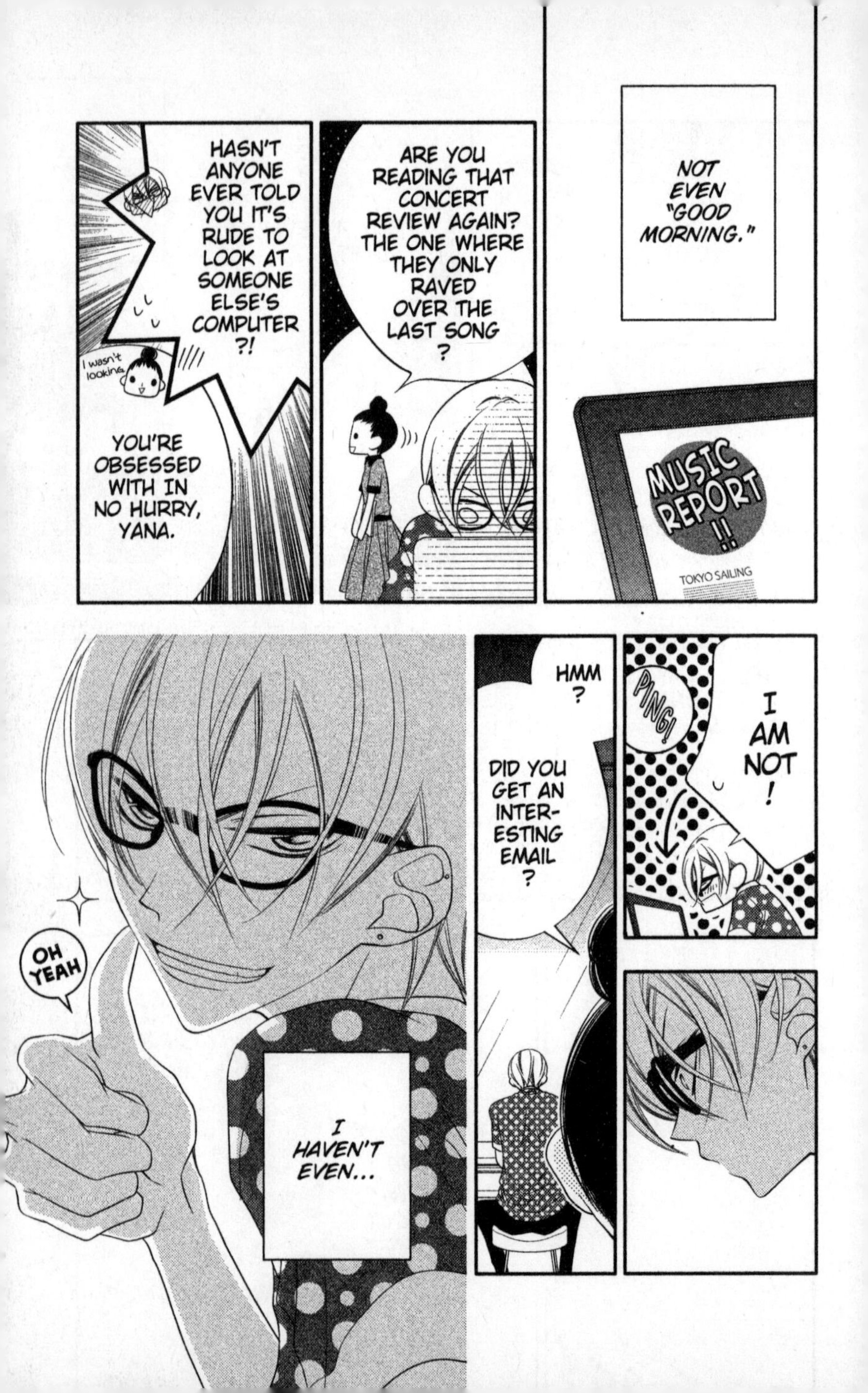
NOT EVEN "GOOD MORNING."
MUSIC REPORT !!
TOKYO SAILING
ARE YOU READING THAT CONCERT REVIEW AGAIN? THE ONE WHERE THEY ONLY RAVED OVER THE LAST SONG?
HASN'T ANYONE EVER TOLD YOU IT'S RUDE TO LOOK AT SOMEONE ELSE'S COMPUTER?!
I wasn't looking
YOU'RE OBSESSED WITH IN NO HURRY, YANA.
PING!
I AM NOT!
HMM?
DID YOU GET AN INTER-ESTING EMAIL?
OH YEAH
I HAVEN'T EVEN...

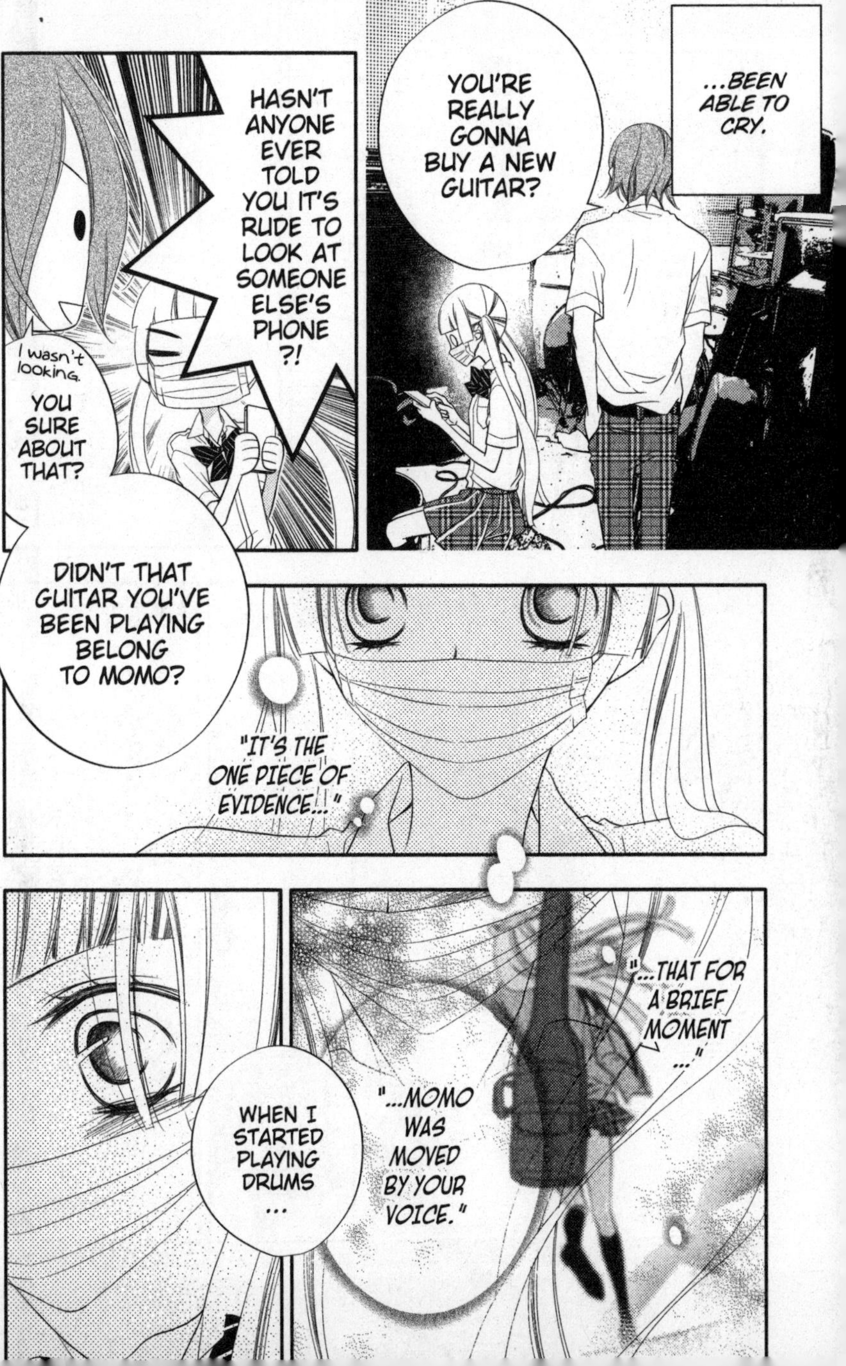
...BEEN ABLE TO CRY.
YOU'RE REALLY GONNA BUY A NEW GUITAR?
HASN'T ANYONE EVER TOLD YOU IT'S RUDE TO LOOK AT SOMEONE ELSE'S PHONE ?!
I wasn't looking.
YOU SURE ABOUT THAT?
DIDN'T THAT GUITAR YOU'VE BEEN PLAYING BELONG TO MOMO?
"IT'S THE ONE PIECE OF EVIDENCE..."
"...THAT FOR A BRIEF MOMENT..."
"...MOMO WAS MOVED BY YOUR VOICE."
WHEN I STARTED PLAYING DRUMS ...

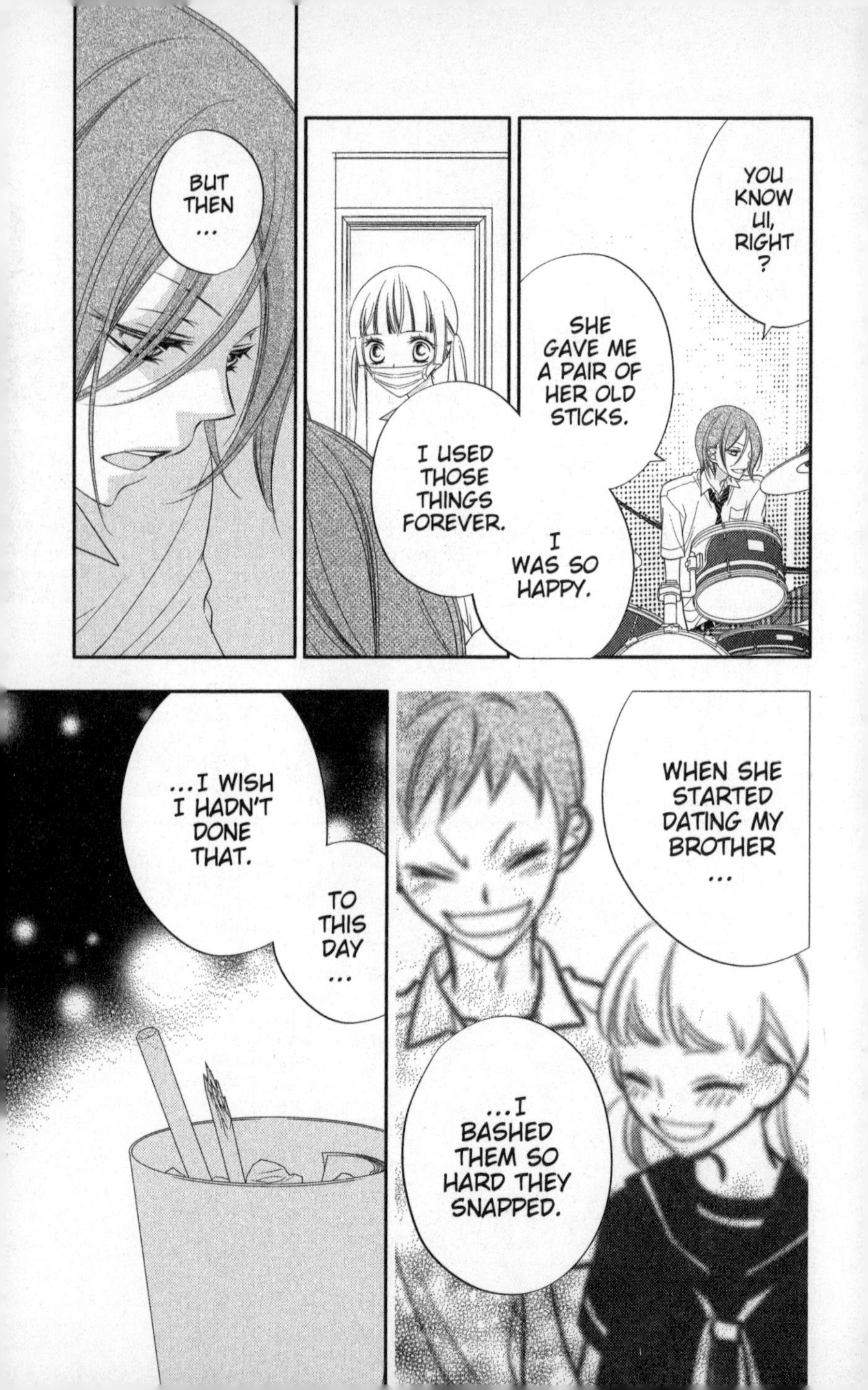
YOU KNOW UI, RIGHT?
SHE GAVE ME A PAIR OF HER OLD STICKS.
I WAS SO HAPPY.
I USED THOSE THINGS FOREVER.
BUT THEN ...
WHEN SHE STARTED DATING MY BROTHER ...
...I BASHED THEM SO HARD THEY SNAPPED.
TO THIS DAY ...
...I WISH I HADN'T DONE THAT.

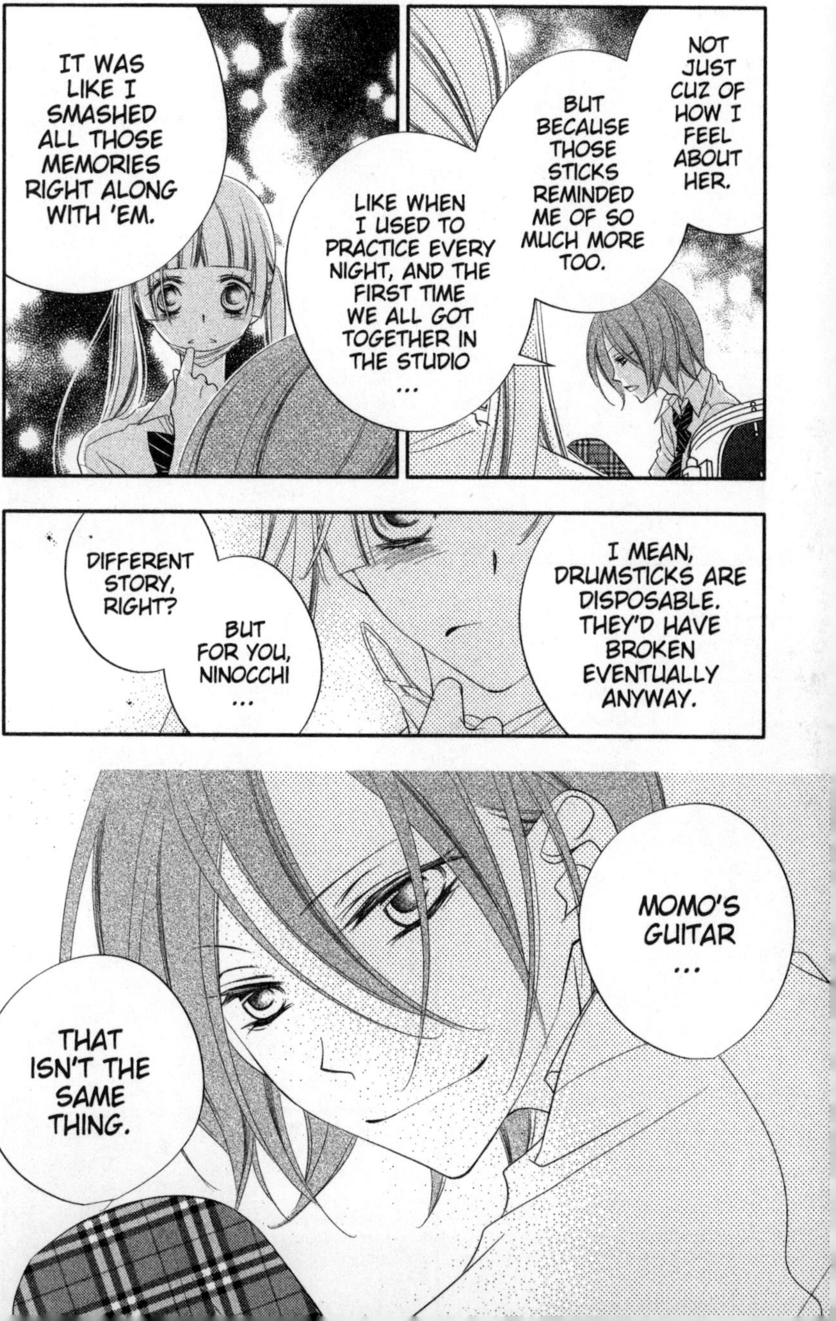
NOT JUST CUZ OF HOW I FEEL ABOUT HER.
BUT BECAUSE THOSE STICKS REMINDED ME OF SO MUCH MORE TOO.
LIKE WHEN I USED TO PRACTICE EVERY NIGHT, AND THE FIRST TIME WE ALL GOT TOGETHER IN THE STUDIO ...
IT WAS LIKE I SMASHED ALL THOSE MEMORIES RIGHT ALONG WITH 'EM.
I MEAN, DRUMSTICKS ARE DISPOSABLE. THEY'D HAVE BROKEN EVENTUALLY ANYWAY.
BUT FOR YOU, NINOCCHI ...
DIFFERENT STORY, RIGHT?
MOMO'S GUITAR ...
THAT ISN'T THE SAME THING.

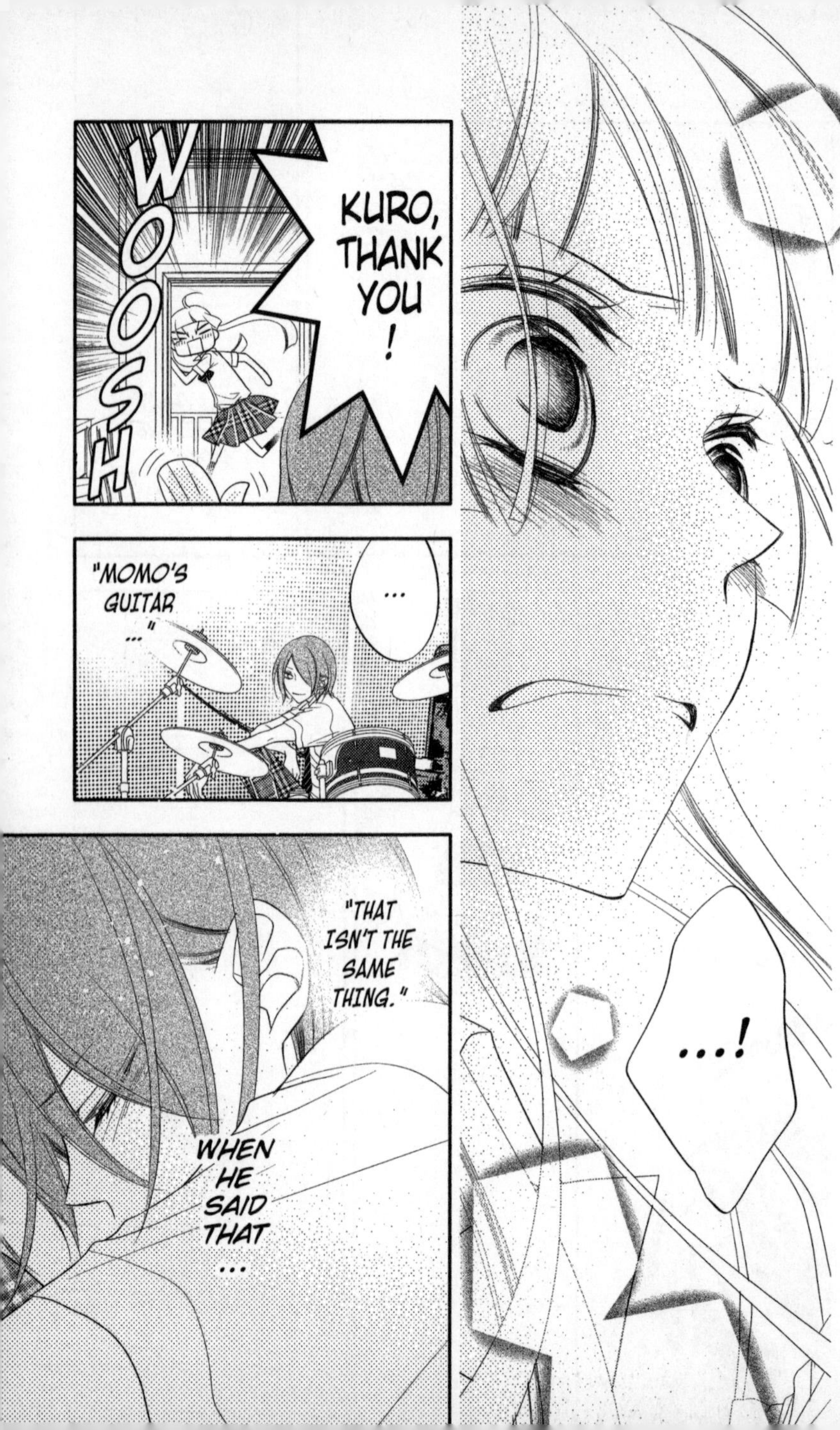
...!
KURO, THANK YOU!
WOOSH
...
"MOMO'S GUITAR ..."
"THAT ISN'T THE SAME THING."
WHEN HE SAID THAT ...

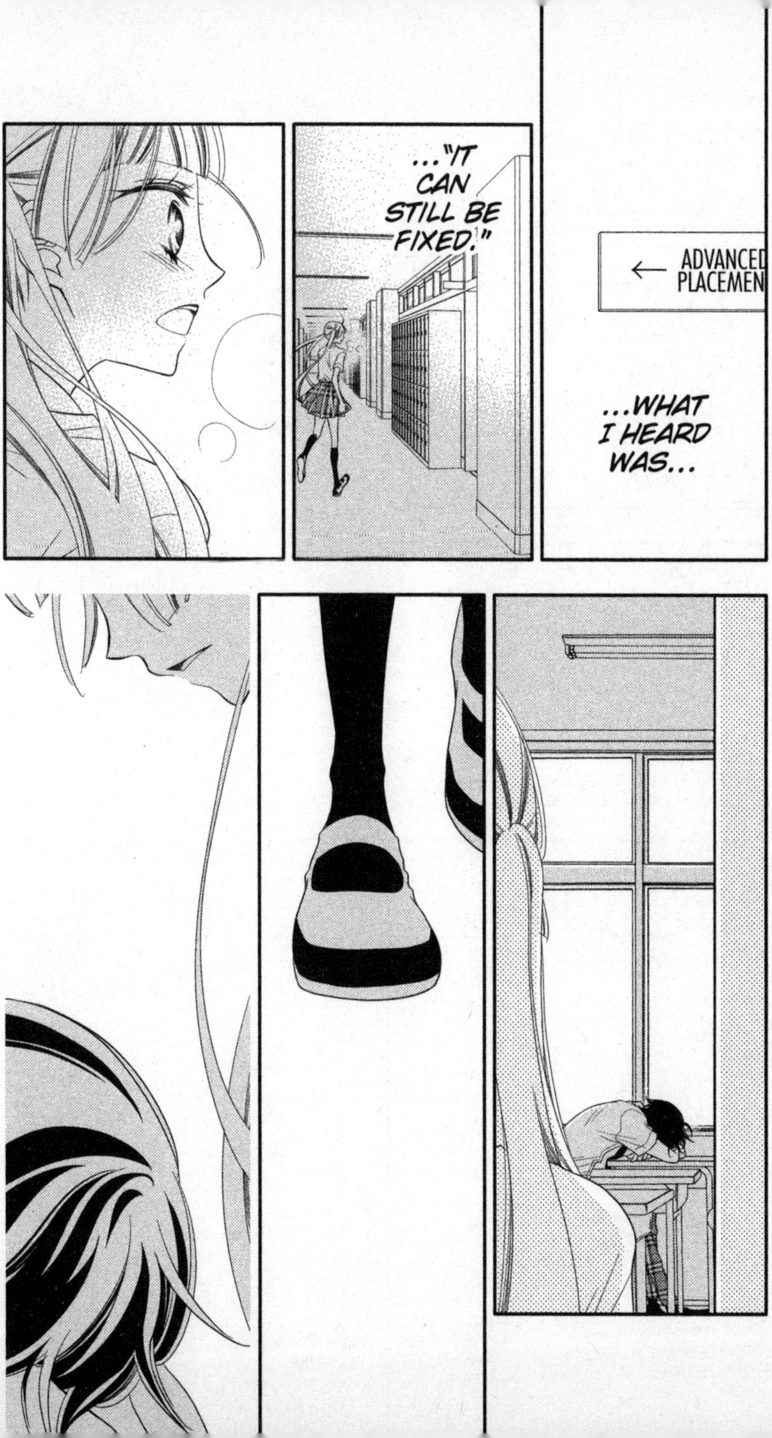
ADVANCED PLACEMEN
...WHAT I HEARD WAS...
..."IT CAN STILL BE FIXED."

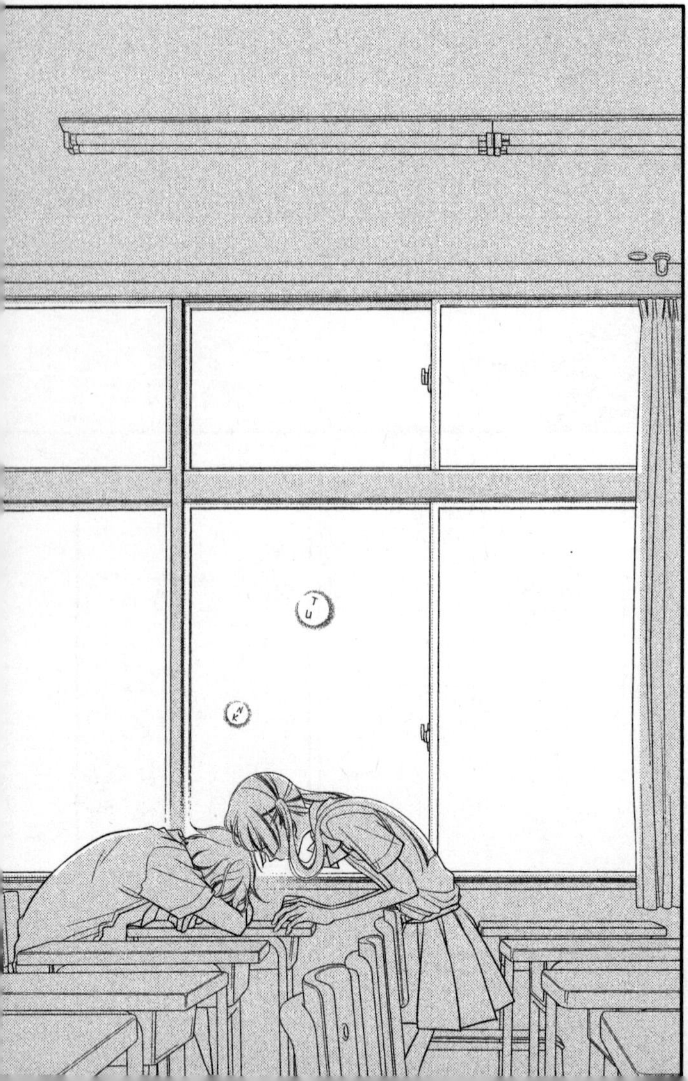
TU
NK

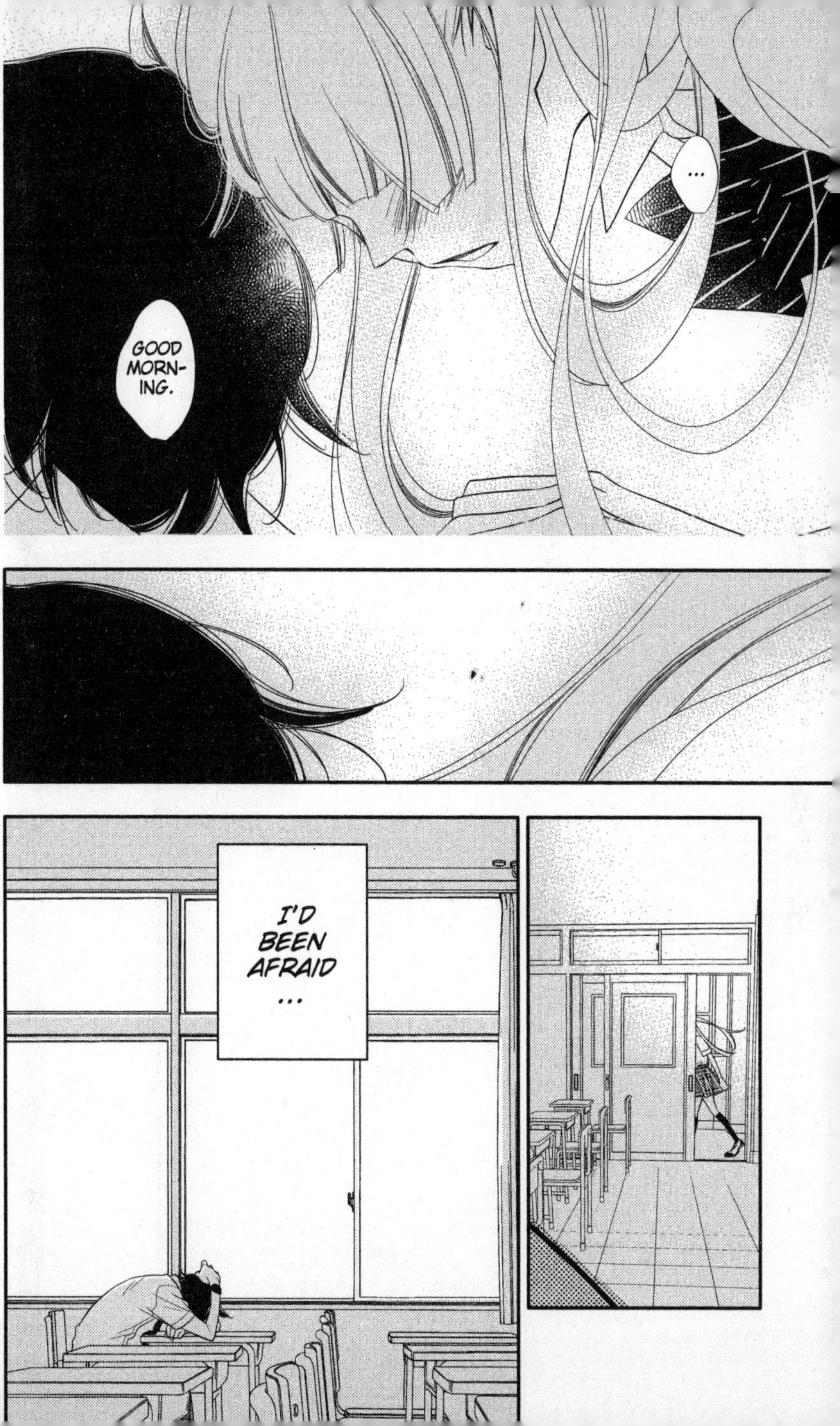
...
GOOD MORNING.
I'D BEEN AFRAID...

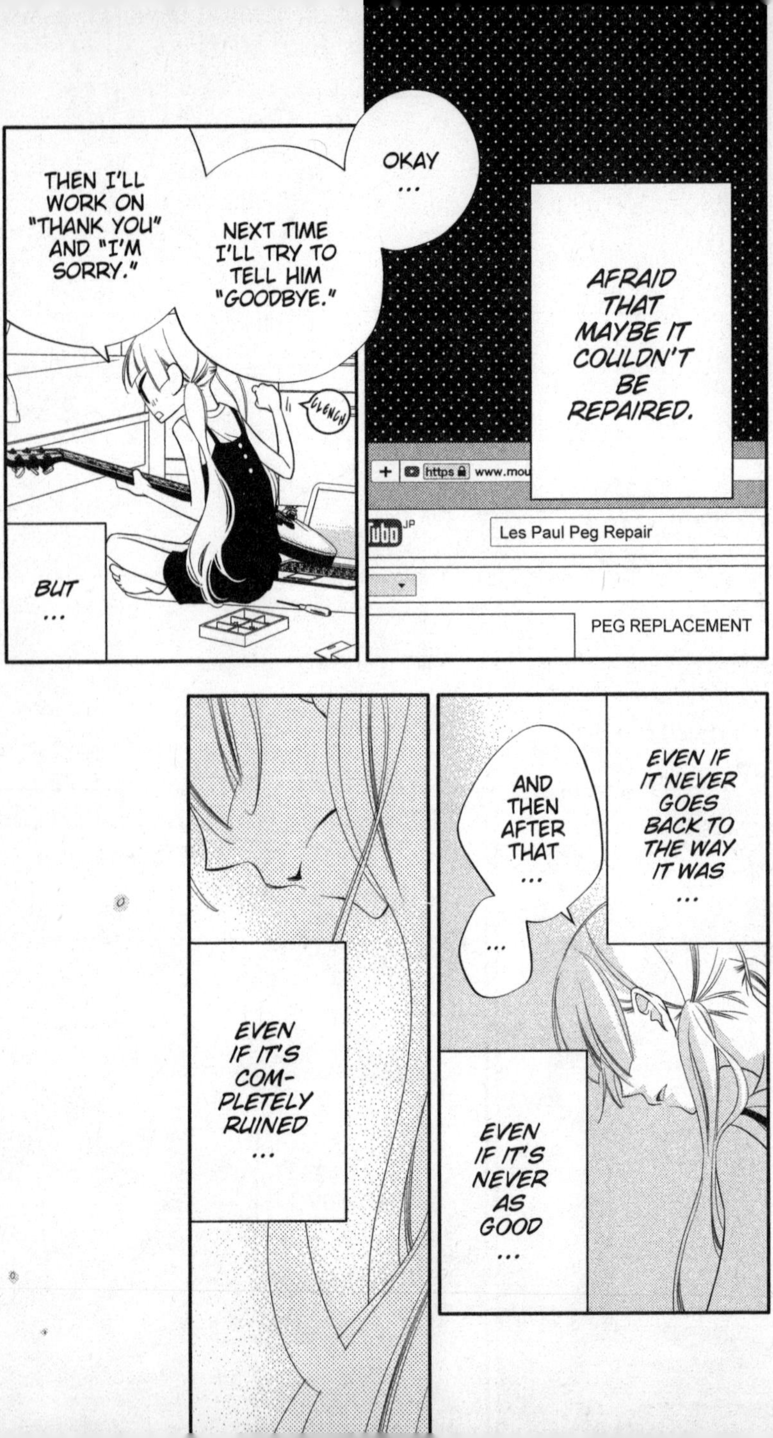
AFRAID THAT MAYBE IT COULDN'T BE REPAIRED.
https www.mou
Les Paul Peg Repair
PEG REPLACEMENT
OKAY ...
NEXT TIME I'LL TRY TO TELL HIM "GOODBYE."
THEN I'LL WORK ON "THANK YOU" AND "I'M SORRY."
CLENCH
BUT ...
EVEN IF IT NEVER GOES BACK TO THE WAY IT WAS ...
AND THEN AFTER THAT ...
...
EVEN IF IT'S NEVER AS GOOD ...
EVEN IF IT'S COM-PLETELY RUINED ...

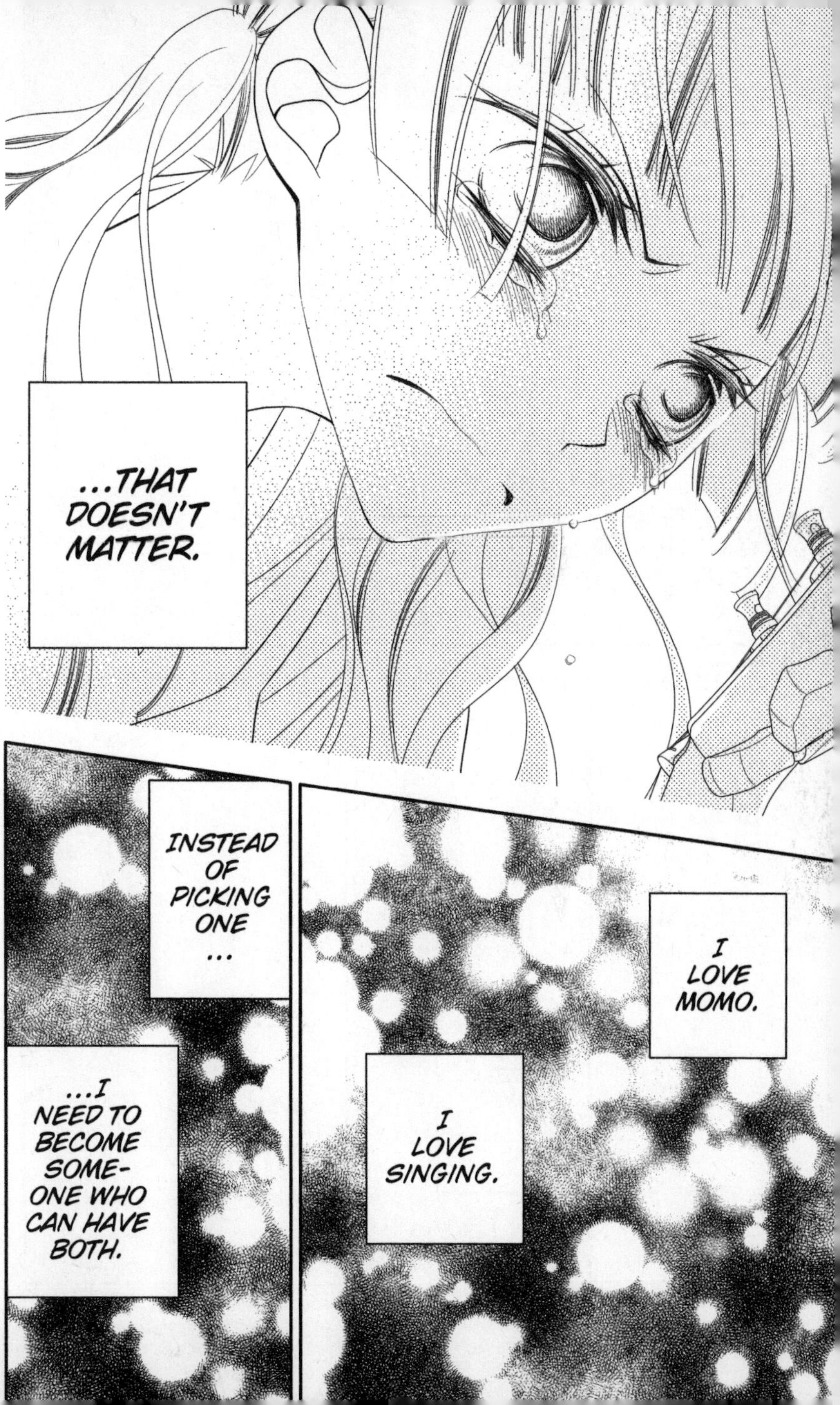
...THAT DOESN'T MATTER.
I LOVE MOMO.
I LOVE SINGING.
INSTEAD OF PICKING ONE ...
...I NEED TO BECOME SOME-ONE WHO CAN HAVE BOTH.

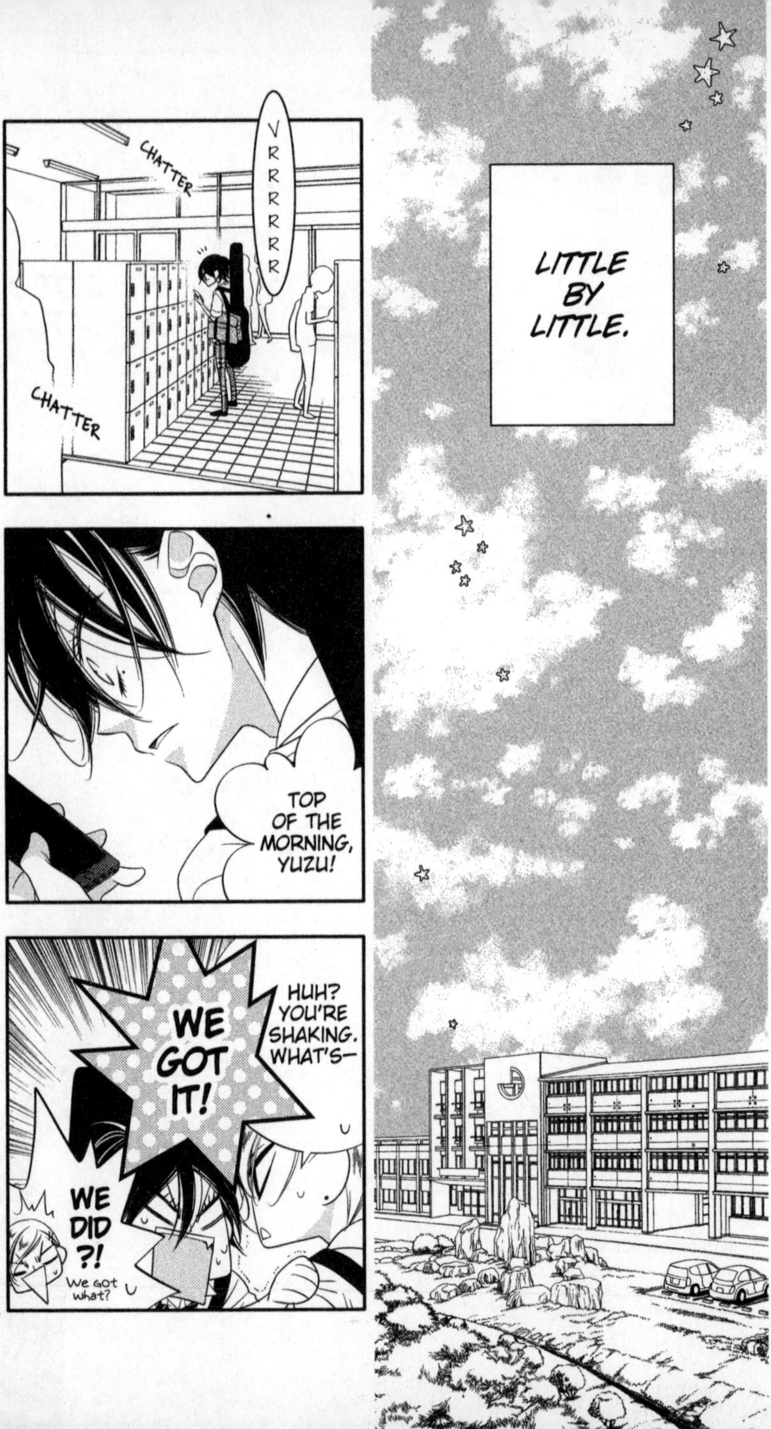
LITTLE BY LITTLE.
VRRRRRRR
CHATTER
CHATTER
TOP OF THE MORNING, YUZU!
HUH? YOU'RE SHAKING. WHAT'S—
WE GOT IT!
WE DID?!
We got what?

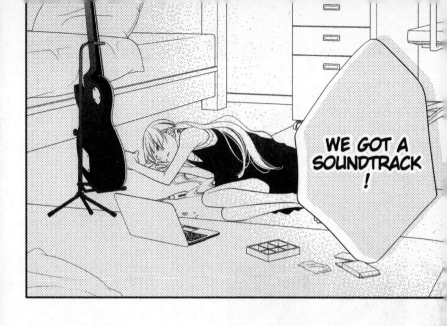

WE GOT A SOUNDTRACK!

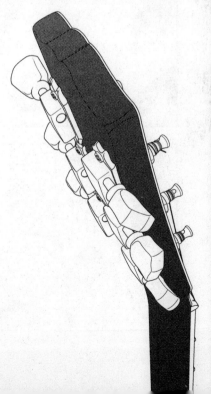

STARTING FROM SQUARE ONE.

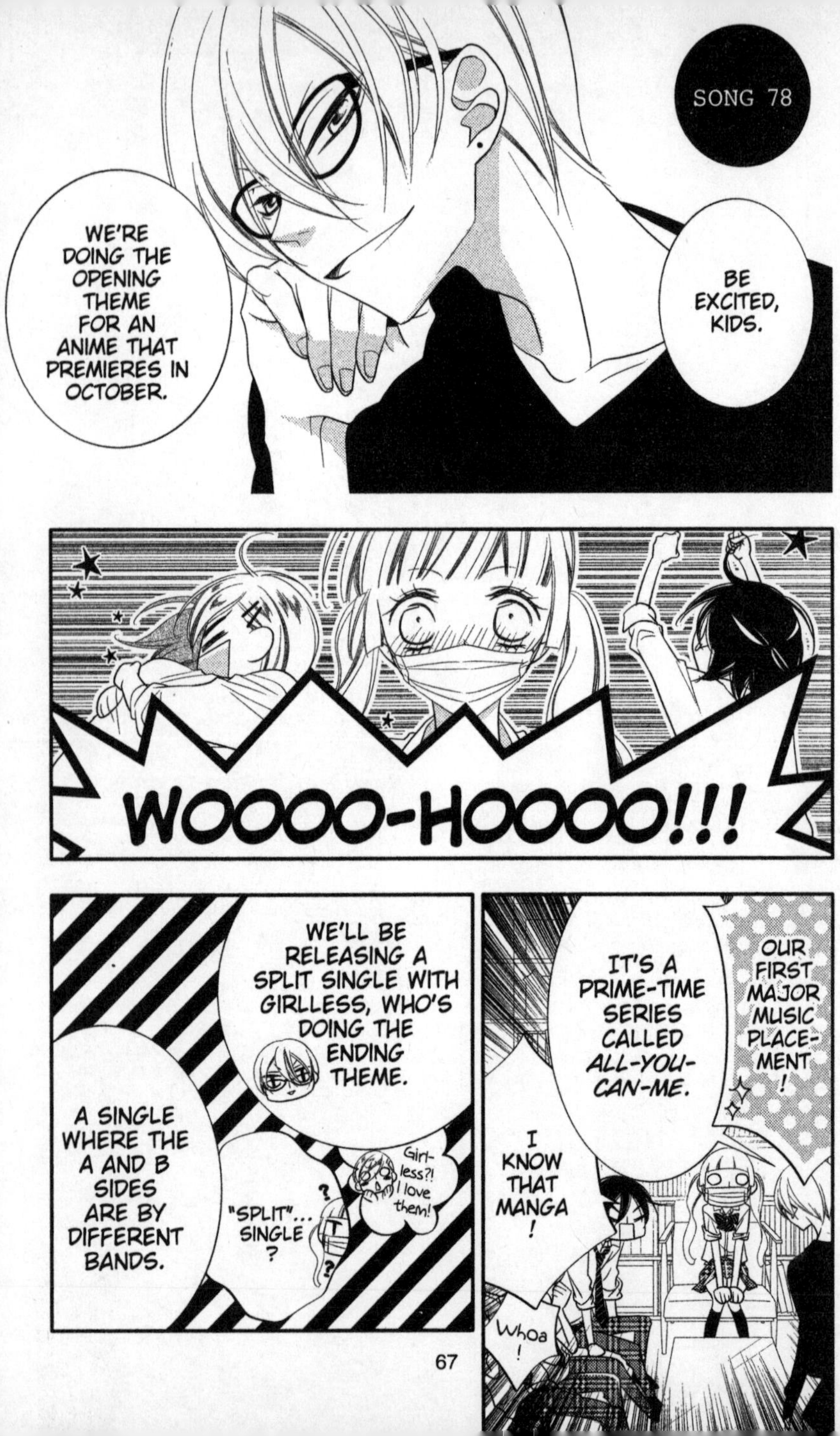
SONG 78
WE'RE DOING THE OPENING THEME FOR AN ANIME THAT PREMIERES IN OCTOBER.
BE EXCITED, KIDS.
WOOOO-HOOOOO!!!
OUR FIRST MAJOR MUSIC PLACE-MENT!
IT'S A PRIME-TIME SERIES CALLED *ALL-YOU-CAN-ME*.
I KNOW THAT MANGA!
Whoa!
WE'LL BE RELEASING A SPLIT SINGLE WITH GIRLLESS, WHO'S DOING THE ENDING THEME.
Girl-less?! I love them!
"SPLIT"... SINGLE?
A SINGLE WHERE THE A AND B SIDES ARE BY DIFFERENT BANDS.

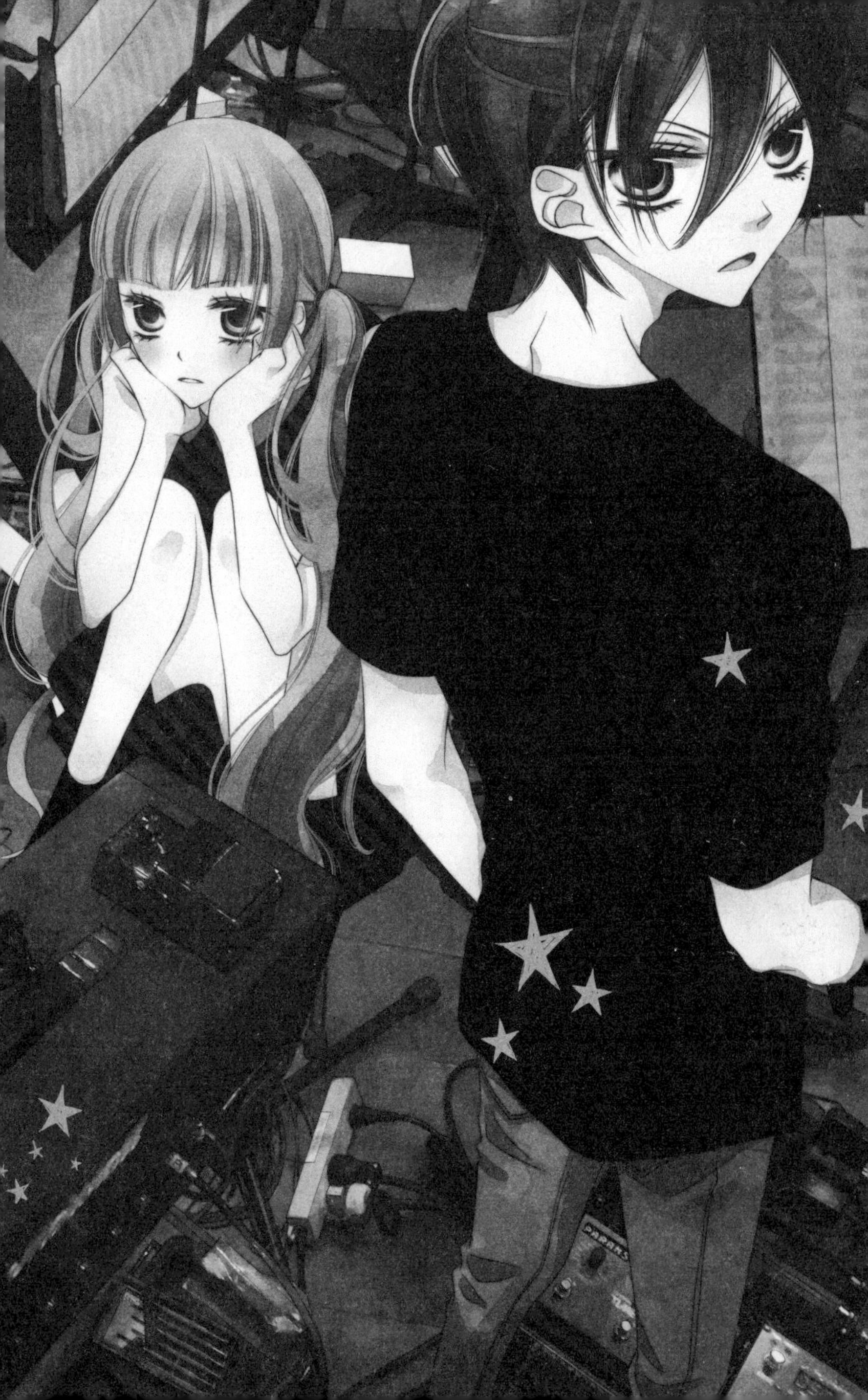

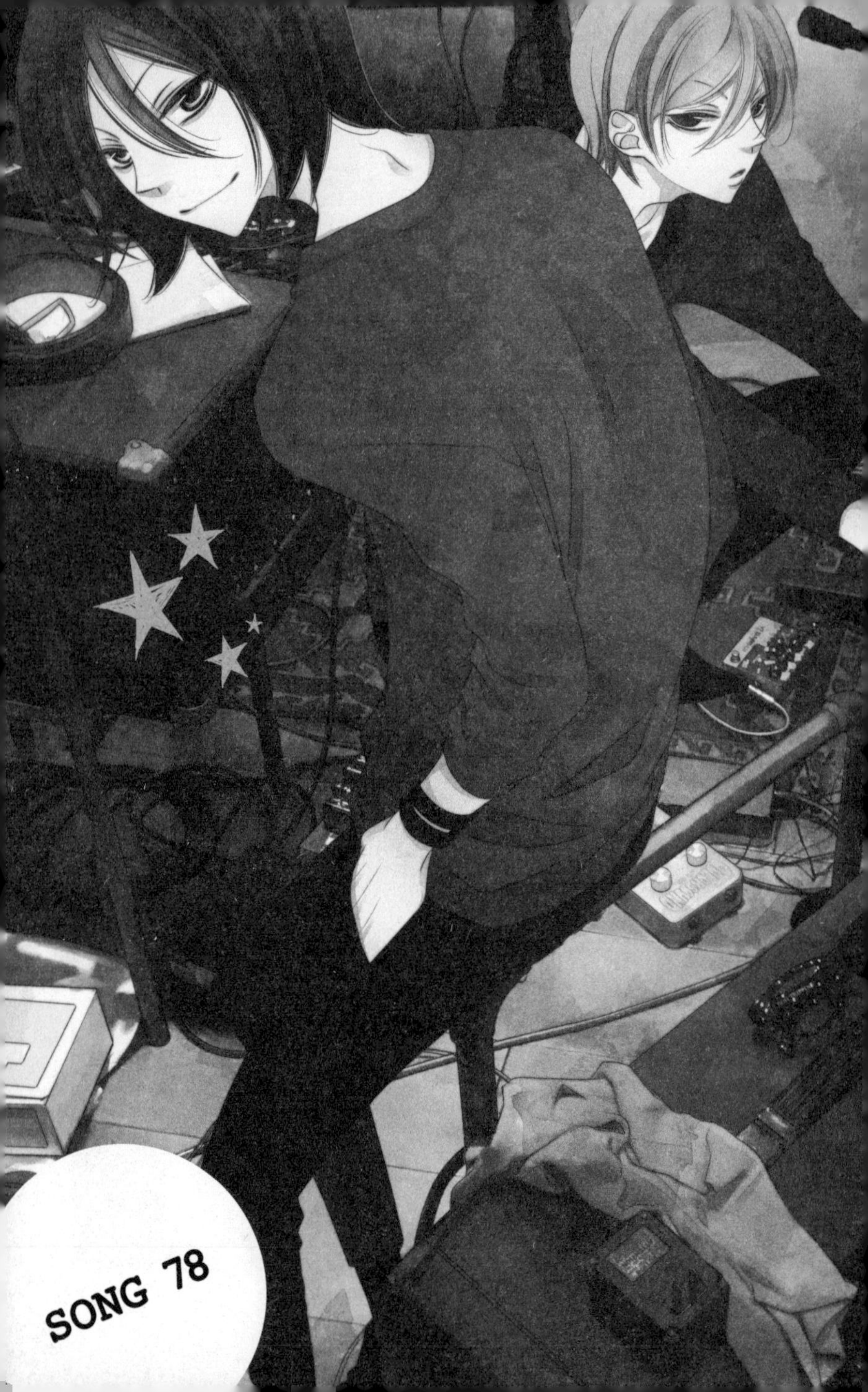
SONG 78

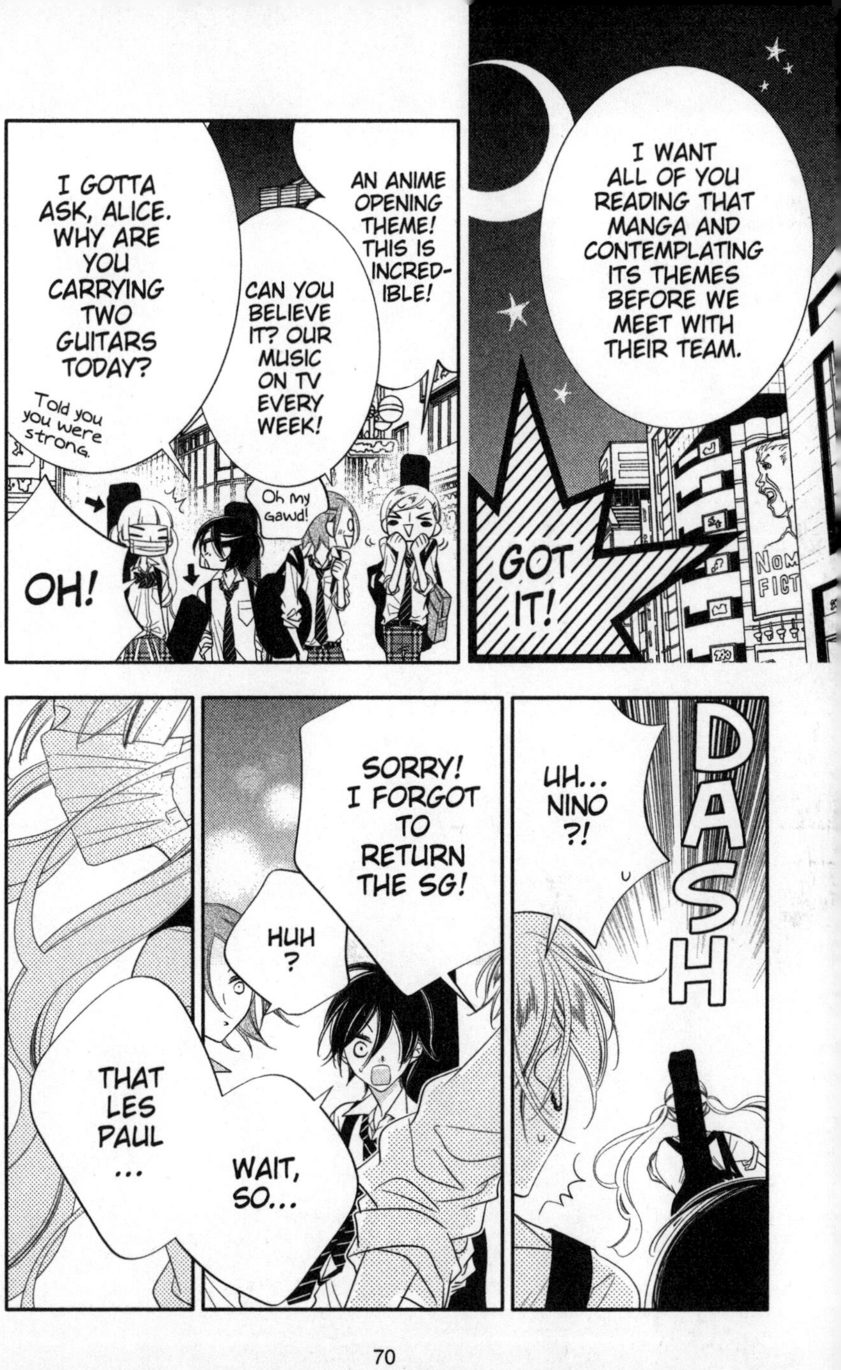
I WANT ALL OF YOU READING THAT MANGA AND CONTEMPLATING ITS THEMES BEFORE WE MEET WITH THEIR TEAM.
GOT IT!
AN ANIME OPENING THEME! THIS IS INCRED-IBLE!
CAN YOU BELIEVE IT? OUR MUSIC ON TV EVERY WEEK!
I GOTTA ASK, ALICE. WHY ARE YOU CARRYING TWO GUITARS TODAY?
Oh my Gawd!
Told you you were strong.
OH!
DASH
UH... NINO ?!
SORRY! I FORGOT TO RETURN THE SG!
HUH ?
WAIT, SO...
THAT LES PAUL ...

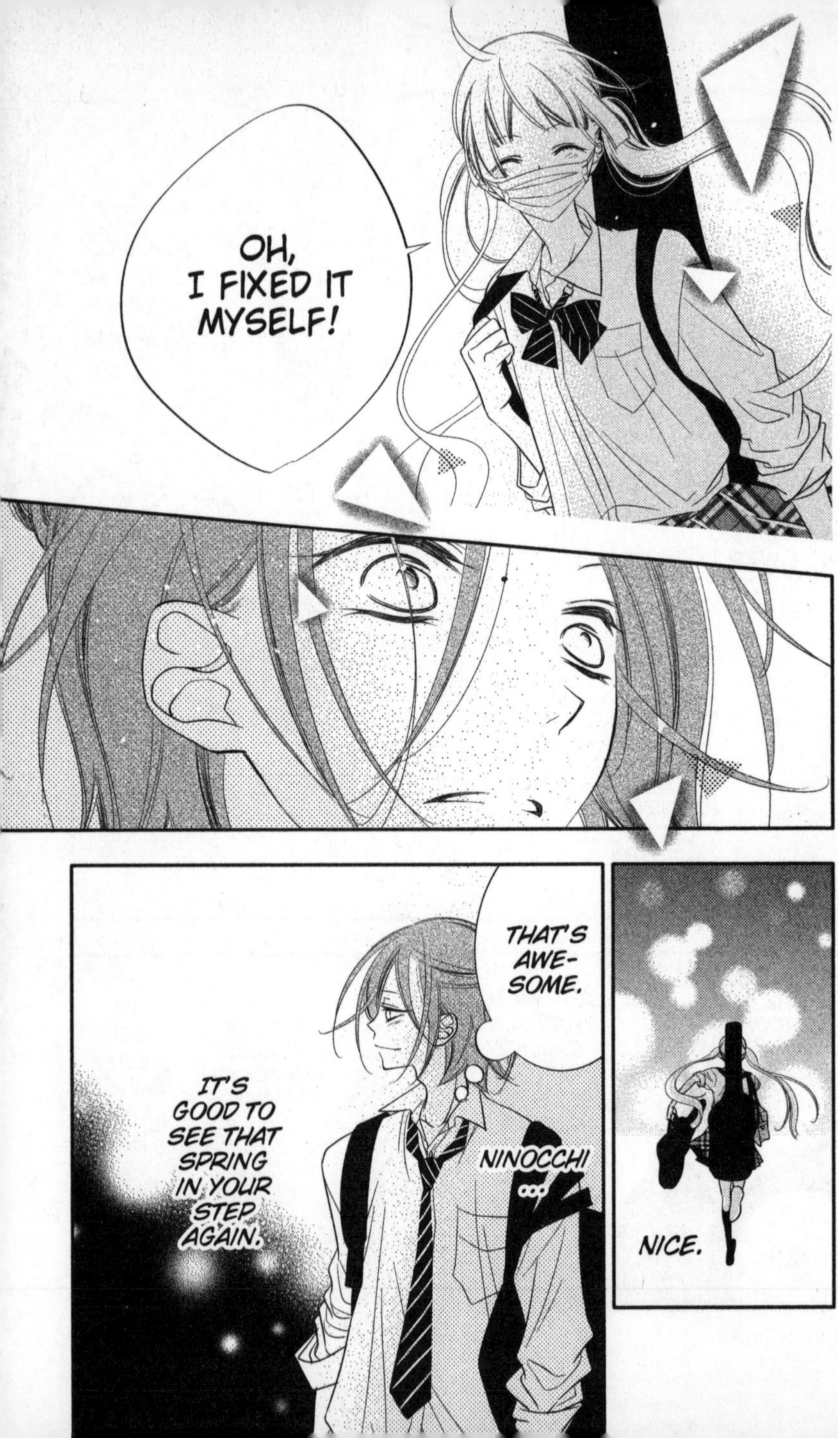
OH, I FIXED IT MYSELF!
NICE.
THAT'S AWE-SOME.
NINOCCHI...
IT'S GOOD TO SEE THAT SPRING IN YOUR STEP AGAIN.

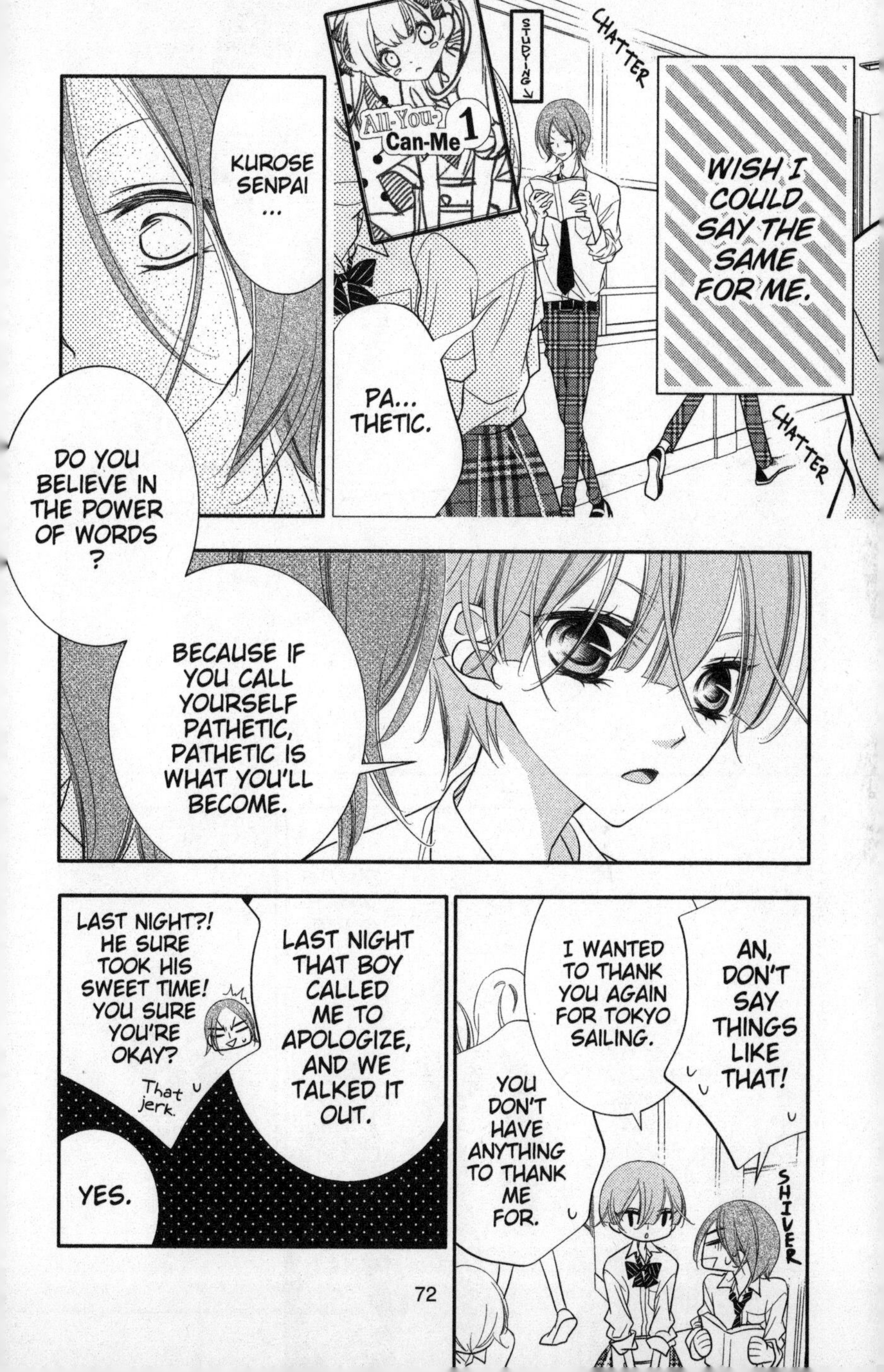
CHATTER
WISH I COULD SAY THE SAME FOR ME.
STUDYING
HOP COMICS
All-You-Can-Me 1
PA... THETIC.
CHATTER
KUROSE SENPAI ...
DO YOU BELIEVE IN THE POWER OF WORDS?
BECAUSE IF YOU CALL YOURSELF PATHETIC, PATHETIC IS WHAT YOU'LL BECOME.
AN, DON'T SAY THINGS LIKE THAT!
I WANTED TO THANK YOU AGAIN FOR TOKYO SAILING.
YOU DON'T HAVE ANYTHING TO THANK ME FOR.
SHIVER
LAST NIGHT THAT BOY CALLED ME TO APOLOGIZE, AND WE TALKED IT OUT.
LAST NIGHT?! HE SURE TOOK HIS SWEET TIME! YOU SURE YOU'RE OKAY?
That jerk.
YES.

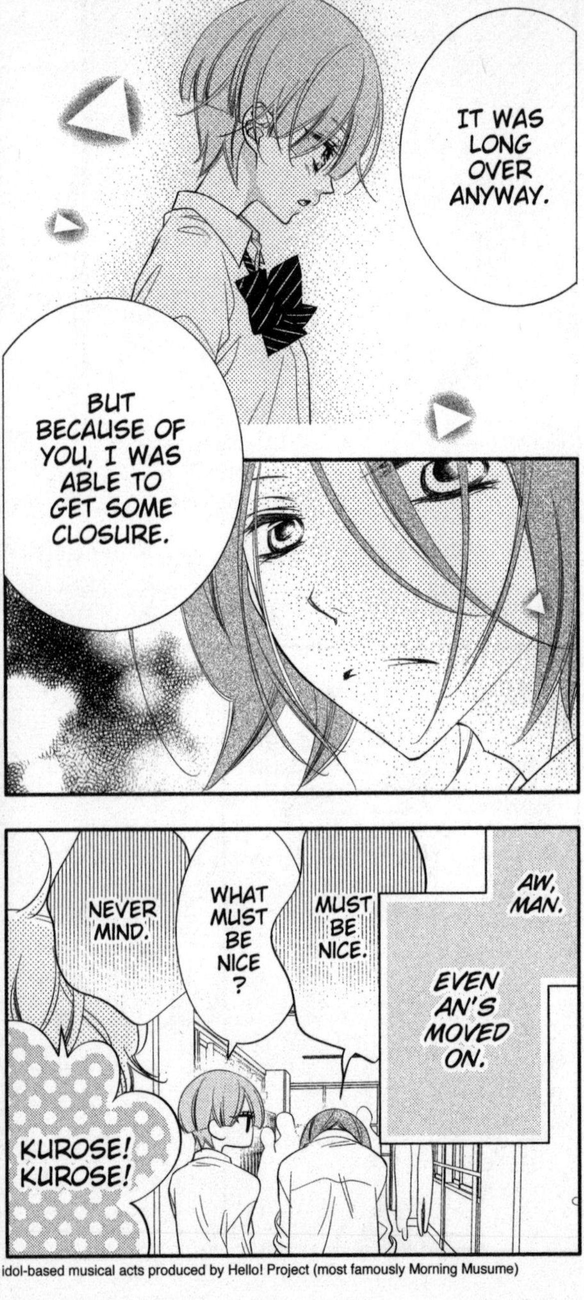
IT WAS LONG OVER ANYWAY.
BUT BECAUSE OF YOU, I WAS ABLE TO GET SOME CLOSURE.
AW, MAN.
EVEN AN'S MOVED ON.
MUST BE NICE.
WHAT MUST BE NICE?
NEVER MIND.
KUROSE! KUROSE!

3

So now I have a new editor! And for the first time in a long time, it's a woman! Like, a real girlie girl! She's adorable! In fact, I actually knew her. She filled in for a previous editor of mine who went on maternity leave a long time ago. So seeing her again was like a reunion of old friends. Even back then she could hold her liquor, but at the time I hadn't yet developed a taste for sake. When I found out we'd be working together again, I wasted no time in inviting her out to a sake bar! *Ha ha!* Incidentally, she's a Hello-Ota!* I've never actually been close to a Hello-Ota before, so it's quite the novelty for me. As my editor, she joined me at Rock in Japan this year, which was a real eye-opener for her since she wasn't very familiar with the Japanese rock scene. I introduced her to a wide variety of bands, and she ended up taking a liking to GEN and Sekaikan Ozaki because of how cute they were. Well, they certainly are! *Tee hee!* I'm looking forward to working with you, Ms. New Editor!

* Passionate fans of the mostly idol-based musical acts produced by Hello! Project (most famously Morning Musume)

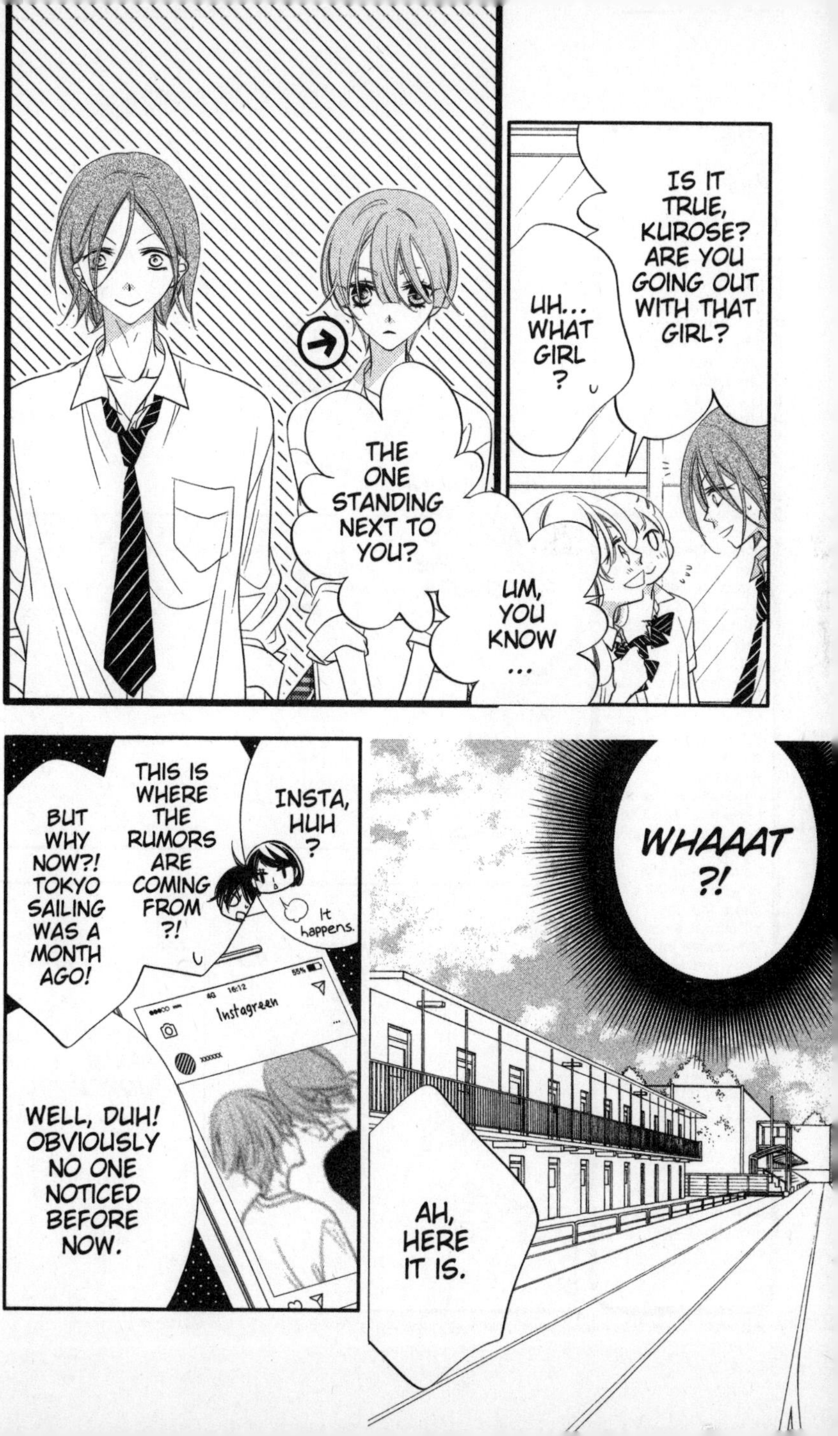
IS IT TRUE, KUROSE? ARE YOU GOING OUT WITH THAT GIRL?
UH... WHAT GIRL?
UM, YOU KNOW...
THE ONE STANDING NEXT TO YOU?
WHAAAT?!
AH, HERE IT IS.
INSTA, HUH?
It happens.
THIS IS WHERE THE RUMORS ARE COMING FROM?!
BUT WHY NOW?! TOKYO SAILING WAS A MONTH AGO!
Instagreen
WELL, DUH! OBVIOUSLY NO ONE NOTICED BEFORE NOW.

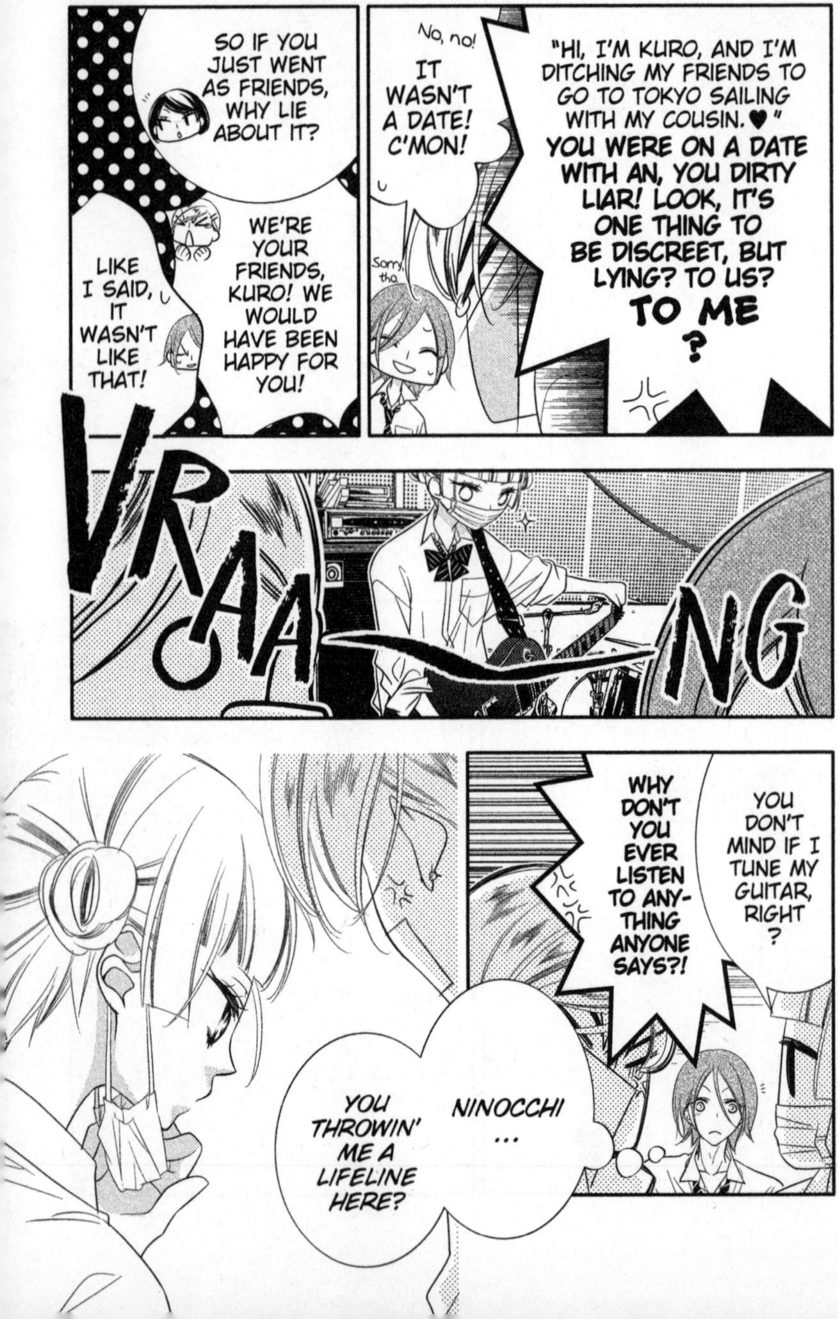
"HI, I'M KURO, AND I'M DITCHING MY FRIENDS TO GO TO TOKYO SAILING WITH MY COUSIN.♥" YOU WERE ON A DATE WITH AN, YOU DIRTY LIAR! LOOK, IT'S ONE THING TO BE DISCREET, BUT LYING? TO US? TO ME?
No, no!
IT WASN'T A DATE! C'MON!
Sorry, tho.
SO IF YOU JUST WENT AS FRIENDS, WHY LIE ABOUT IT?
WE'RE YOUR FRIENDS, KURO! WE WOULD HAVE BEEN HAPPY FOR YOU!
LIKE I SAID, IT WASN'T LIKE THAT!
VRAANG
YOU DON'T MIND IF I TUNE MY GUITAR, RIGHT?
WHY DON'T YOU EVER LISTEN TO ANY-THING ANYONE SAYS?!
NINOCCHI ...
YOU THROWIN' ME A LIFELINE HERE?

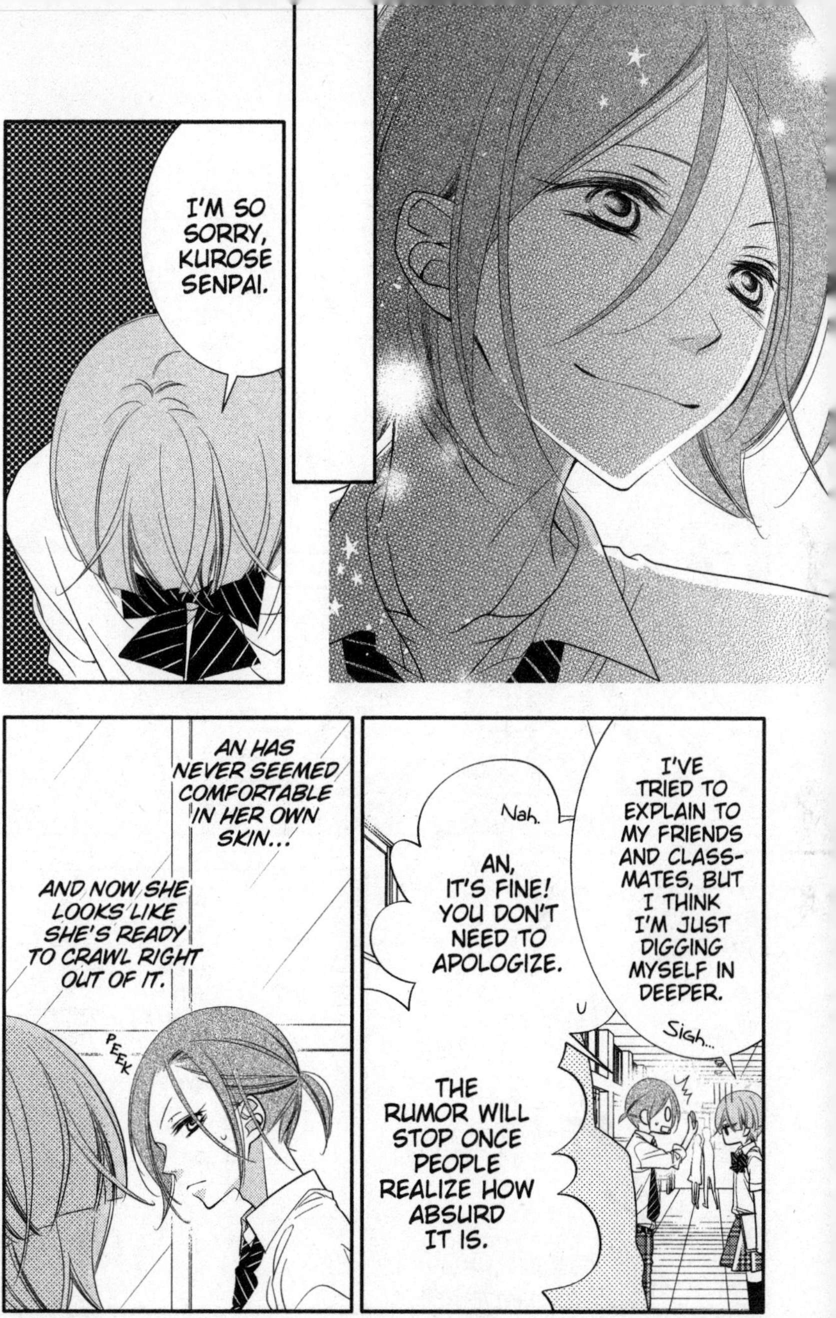
I'M SO SORRY, KUROSE SENPAI.
I'VE TRIED TO EXPLAIN TO MY FRIENDS AND CLASS-MATES, BUT I THINK I'M JUST DIGGING MYSELF IN DEEPER.
Sigh...
Nah.
AN, IT'S FINE! YOU DON'T NEED TO APOLOGIZE.
THE RUMOR WILL STOP ONCE PEOPLE REALIZE HOW ABSURD IT IS.
AN HAS NEVER SEEMED COMFORTABLE IN HER OWN SKIN...
AND NOW SHE LOOKS LIKE SHE'S READY TO CRAWL RIGHT OUT OF IT.
PEEK

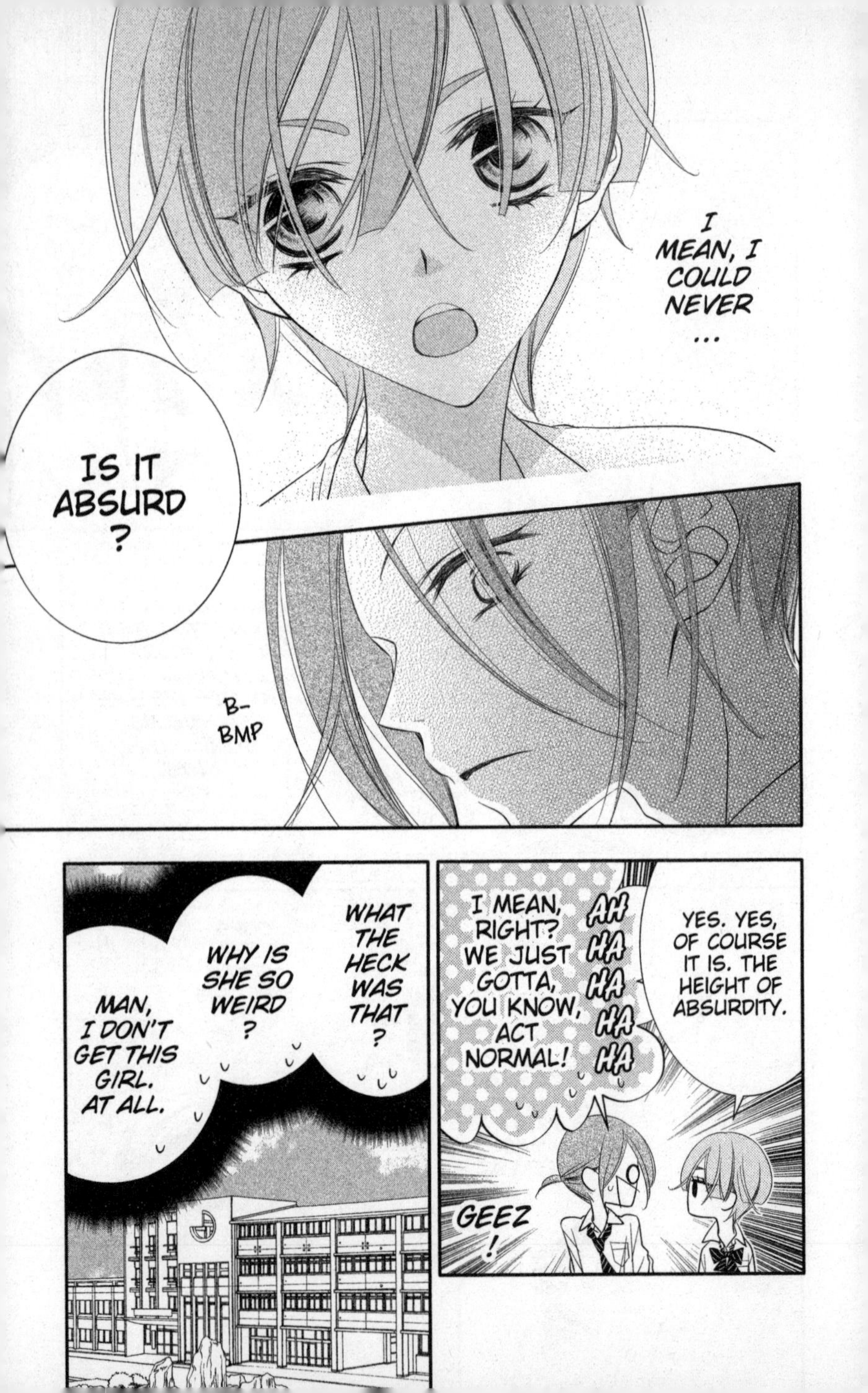
I MEAN, I COULD NEVER ...
IS IT ABSURD?
B-BMP
YES. YES, OF COURSE IT IS. THE HEIGHT OF ABSURDITY.
AH HA HA HA HA
I MEAN, RIGHT? WE JUST GOTTA, YOU KNOW, ACT NORMAL!
GEEZ!
WHAT THE HECK WAS THAT?
WHY IS SHE SO WEIRD?
MAN, I DON'T GET THIS GIRL. AT ALL.

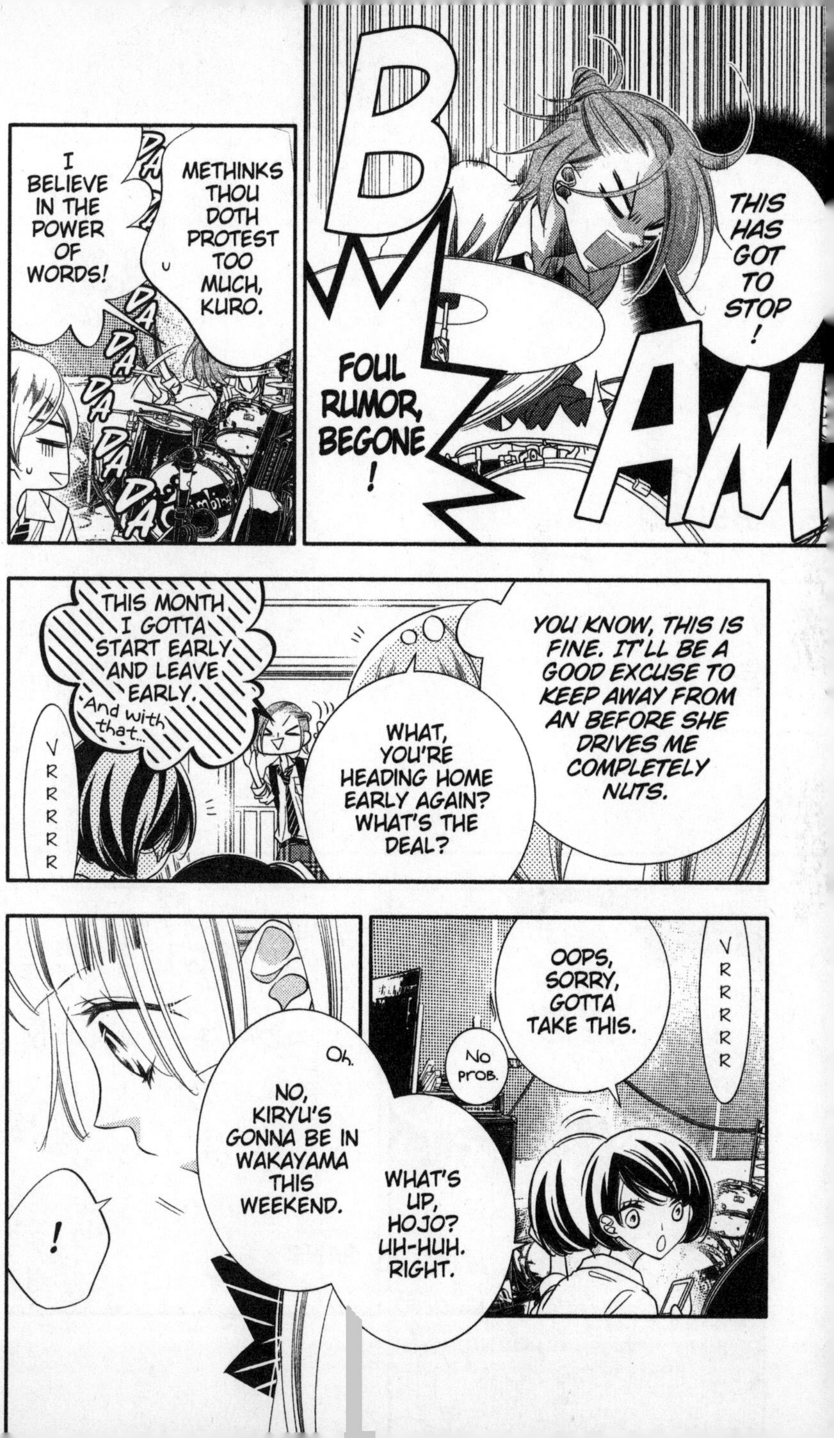
BWAM
THIS HAS GOT TO STOP!
FOUL RUMOR, BEGONE!
METHINKS THOU DOTH PROTEST TOO MUCH, KURO.
I BELIEVE IN THE POWER OF WORDS!
DA DA DA DA DA DA DA DA
YOU KNOW, THIS IS FINE. IT'LL BE A GOOD EXCUSE TO KEEP AWAY FROM AN BEFORE SHE DRIVES ME COMPLETELY NUTS.
WHAT, YOU'RE HEADING HOME EARLY AGAIN? WHAT'S THE DEAL?
THIS MONTH I GOTTA START EARLY AND LEAVE EARLY.
And with that...
VRRRRR
VRRRRR
OOPS, SORRY, GOTTA TAKE THIS.
No prob.
WHAT'S UP, HOJO? UH-HUH. RIGHT.
Oh.
NO, KIRYU'S GONNA BE IN WAKAYAMA THIS WEEKEND.
!

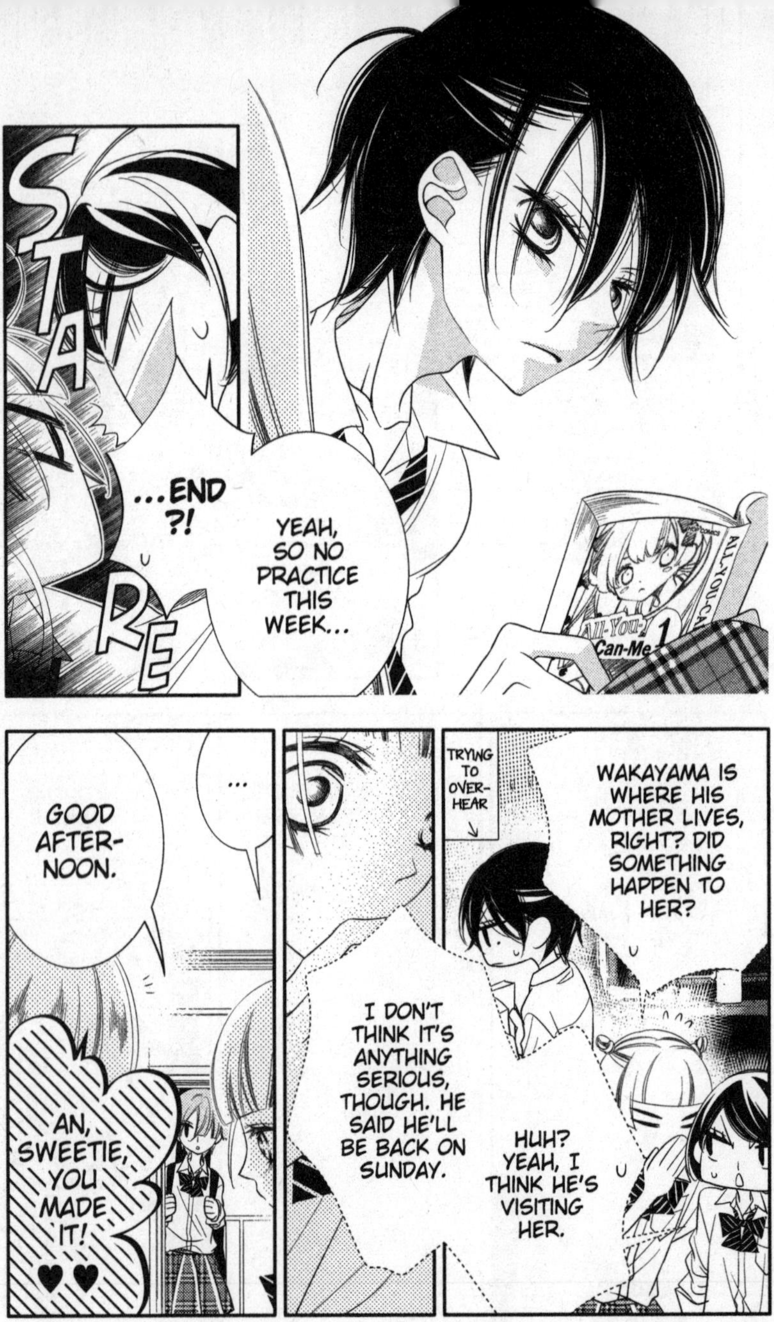
YEAH, SO NO PRACTICE THIS WEEK...
STARE
...END ?!
TRYING TO OVER-HEAR
WAKAYAMA IS WHERE HIS MOTHER LIVES, RIGHT? DID SOMETHING HAPPEN TO HER?
HUH? YEAH, I THINK HE'S VISITING HER.
I DON'T THINK IT'S ANYTHING SERIOUS, THOUGH. HE SAID HE'LL BE BACK ON SUNDAY.
...
GOOD AFTER-NOON.
AN, SWEETIE, YOU MADE IT! ♥♥

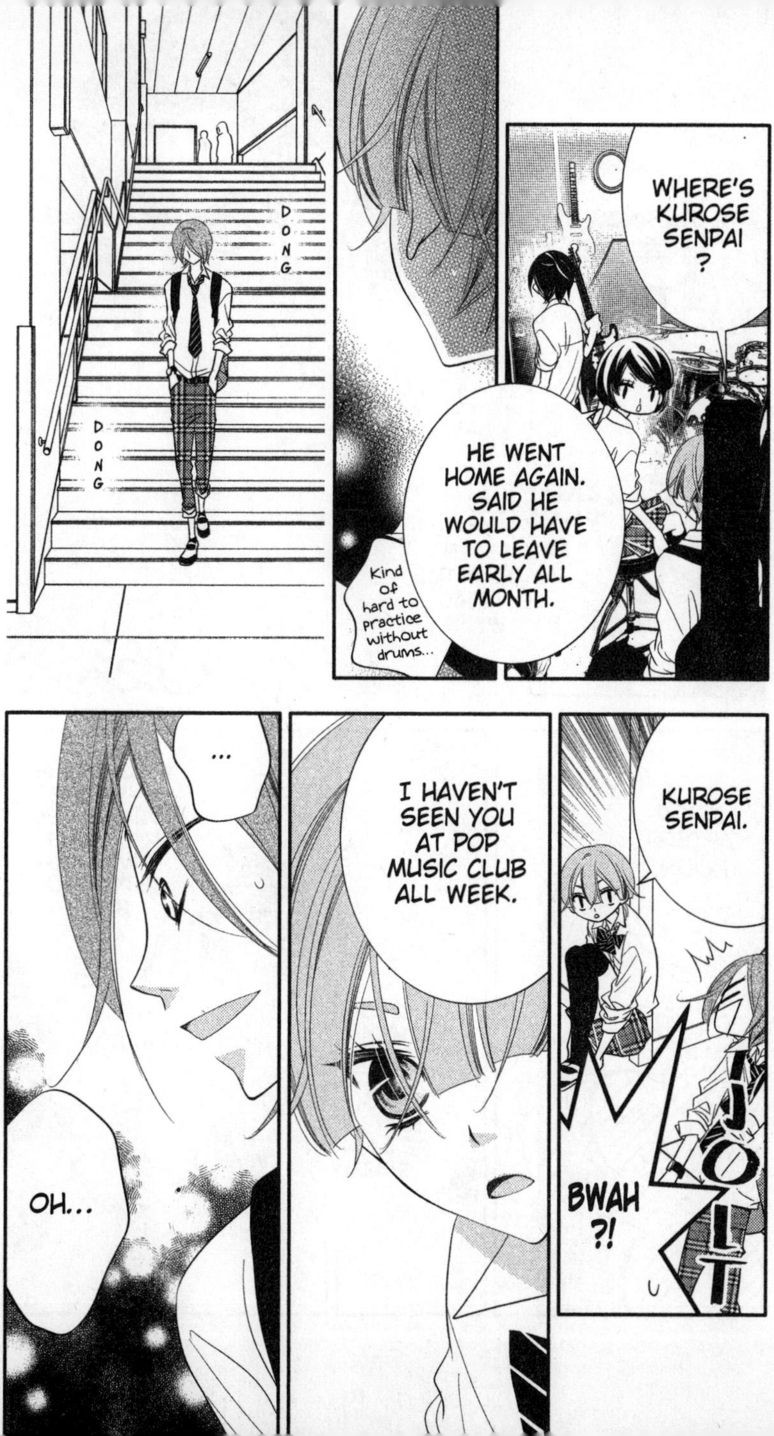
WHERE'S KUROSE SENPAI?
HE WENT HOME AGAIN. SAID HE WOULD HAVE TO LEAVE EARLY ALL MONTH.
Kind of hard to practice without drums...
DONG
DONG
KUROSE SENPAI.
JOLT
BWAH?!
I HAVEN'T SEEN YOU AT POP MUSIC CLUB ALL WEEK.
...
OH...

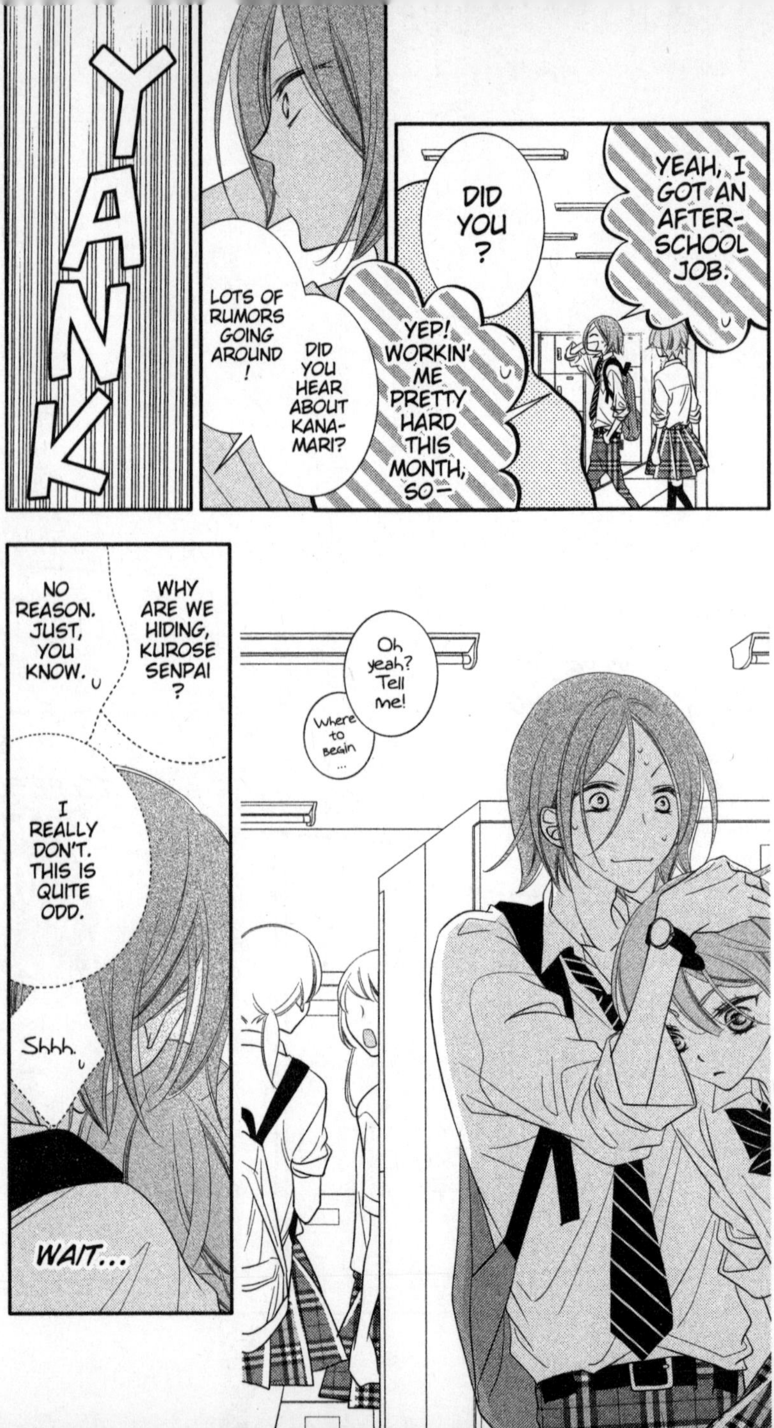

YEAH, I GOT AN AFTER-SCHOOL JOB.
DID YOU?
YEP! WORKIN' ME PRETTY HARD THIS MONTH, SO—
DID YOU HEAR ABOUT KANAMARI?
LOTS OF RUMORS GOING AROUND!
YANK
Oh yeah? Tell me!
Where to begin...
WHY ARE WE HIDING, KUROSE SENPAI?
NO REASON. JUST, YOU KNOW.
I REALLY DON'T. THIS IS QUITE ODD.
Shhh.
WAIT...

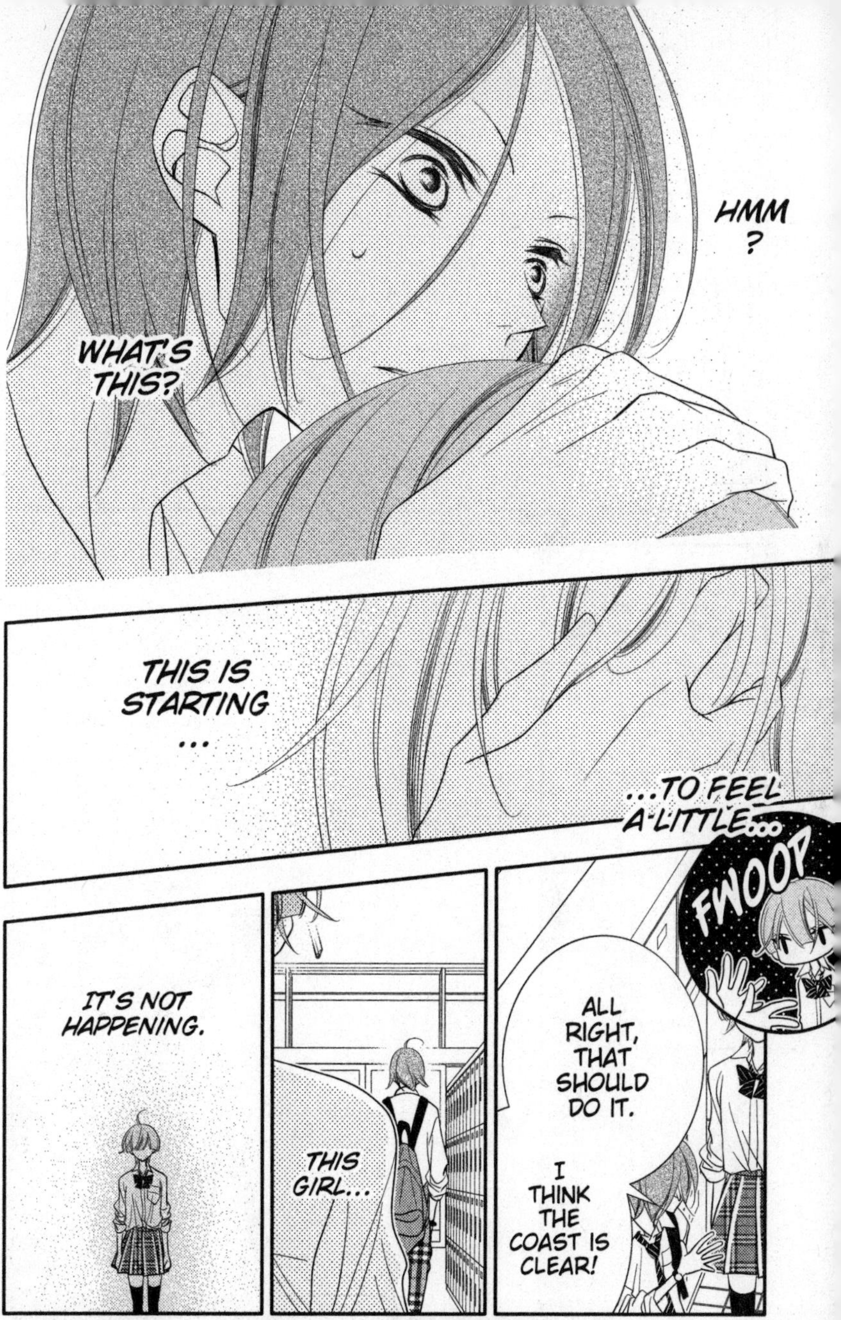
HMM ?
WHAT'S THIS?
THIS IS STARTING ...
...TO FEEL A LITTLE...
FWOOP
ALL RIGHT, THAT SHOULD DO IT.
I THINK THE COAST IS CLEAR!
THIS GIRL...
IT'S NOT HAPPENING.

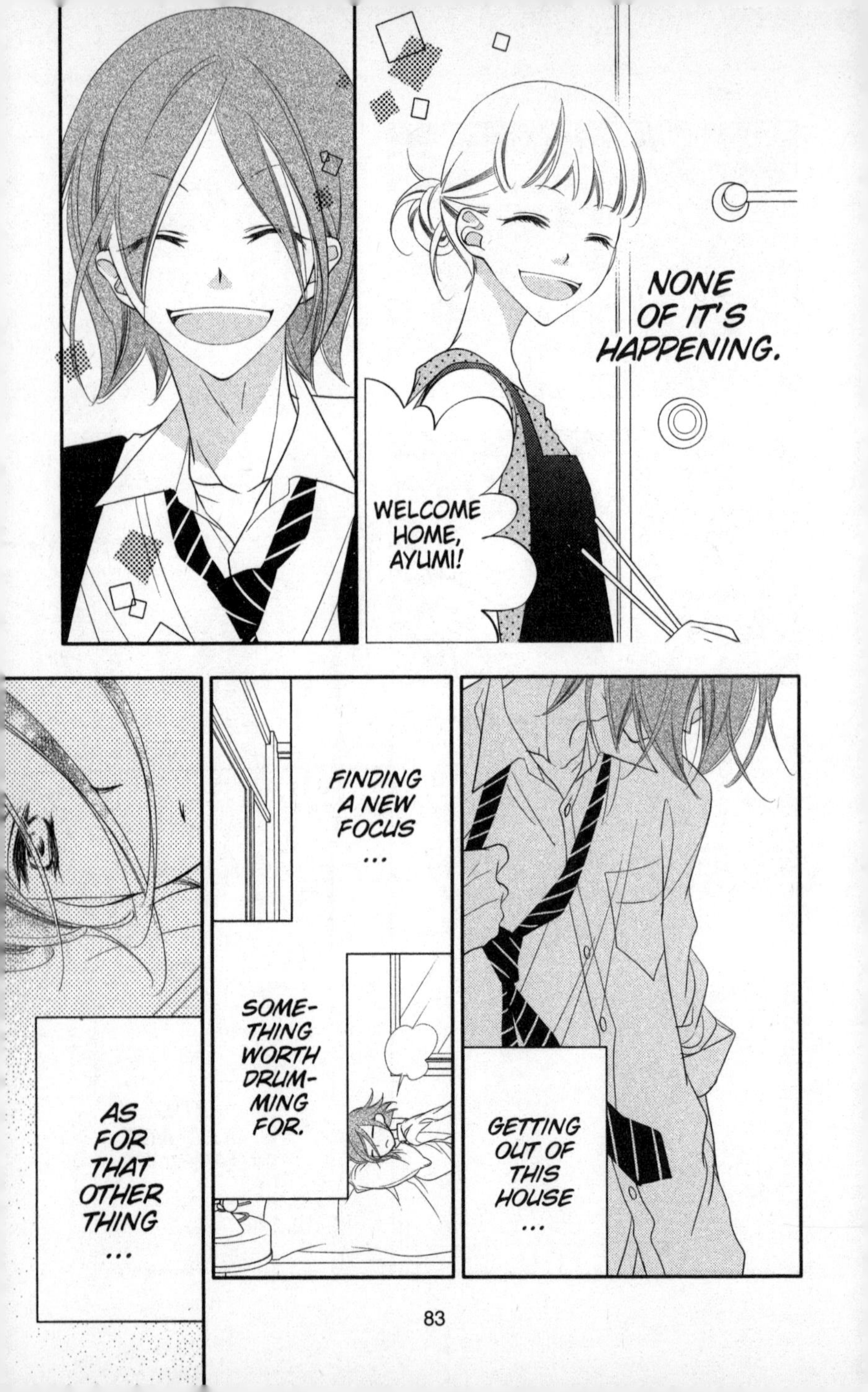
NONE OF IT'S HAPPENING.
WELCOME HOME, AYUMI!
GETTING OUT OF THIS HOUSE ...
FINDING A NEW FOCUS ...
SOME-THING WORTH DRUM-MING FOR.
AS FOR THAT OTHER THING ...

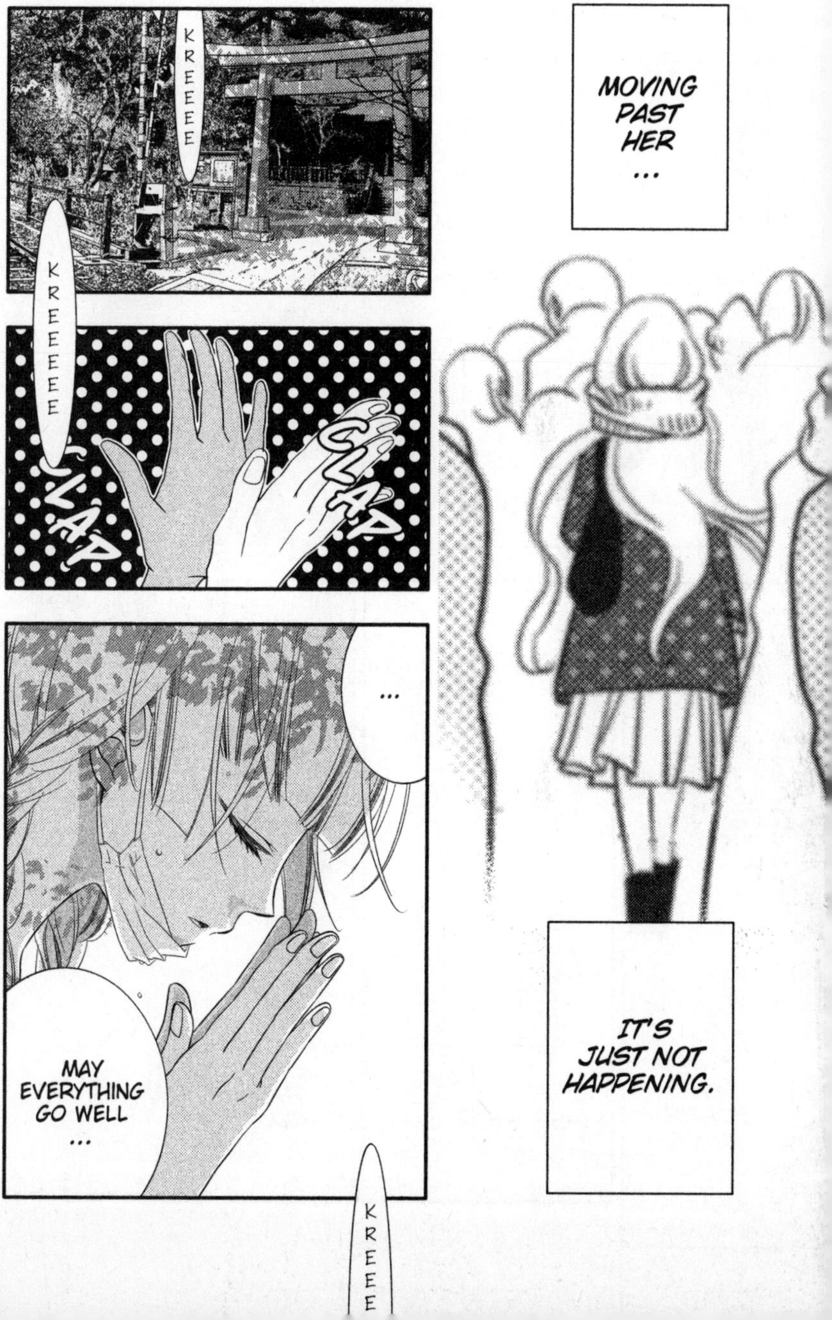
MOVING PAST HER ...
IT'S JUST NOT HAPPENING.
KREEEE
KREEEEE
CLAP
CLAP
...
MAY EVERYTHING GO WELL ...
KREEE

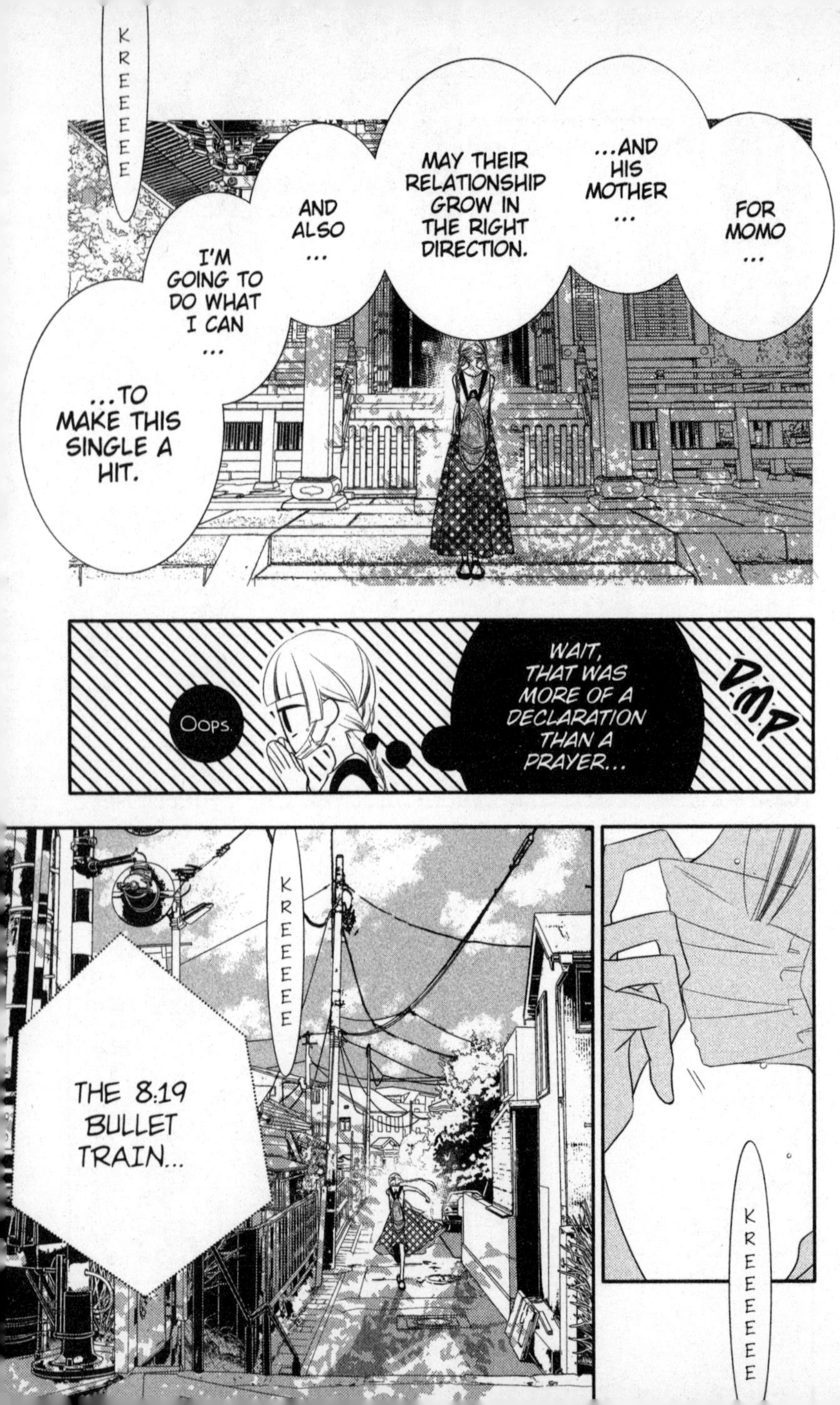
FOR MOMO ...
...AND HIS MOTHER ...
MAY THEIR RELATIONSHIP GROW IN THE RIGHT DIRECTION.
AND ALSO ...
I'M GOING TO DO WHAT I CAN ...
...TO MAKE THIS SINGLE A HIT.
KREEEEEE
DMP
WAIT, THAT WAS MORE OF A DECLARATION THAN A PRAYER...
Oops.
KREEEEEEE
KREEEEEEE
THE 8:19 BULLET TRAIN...

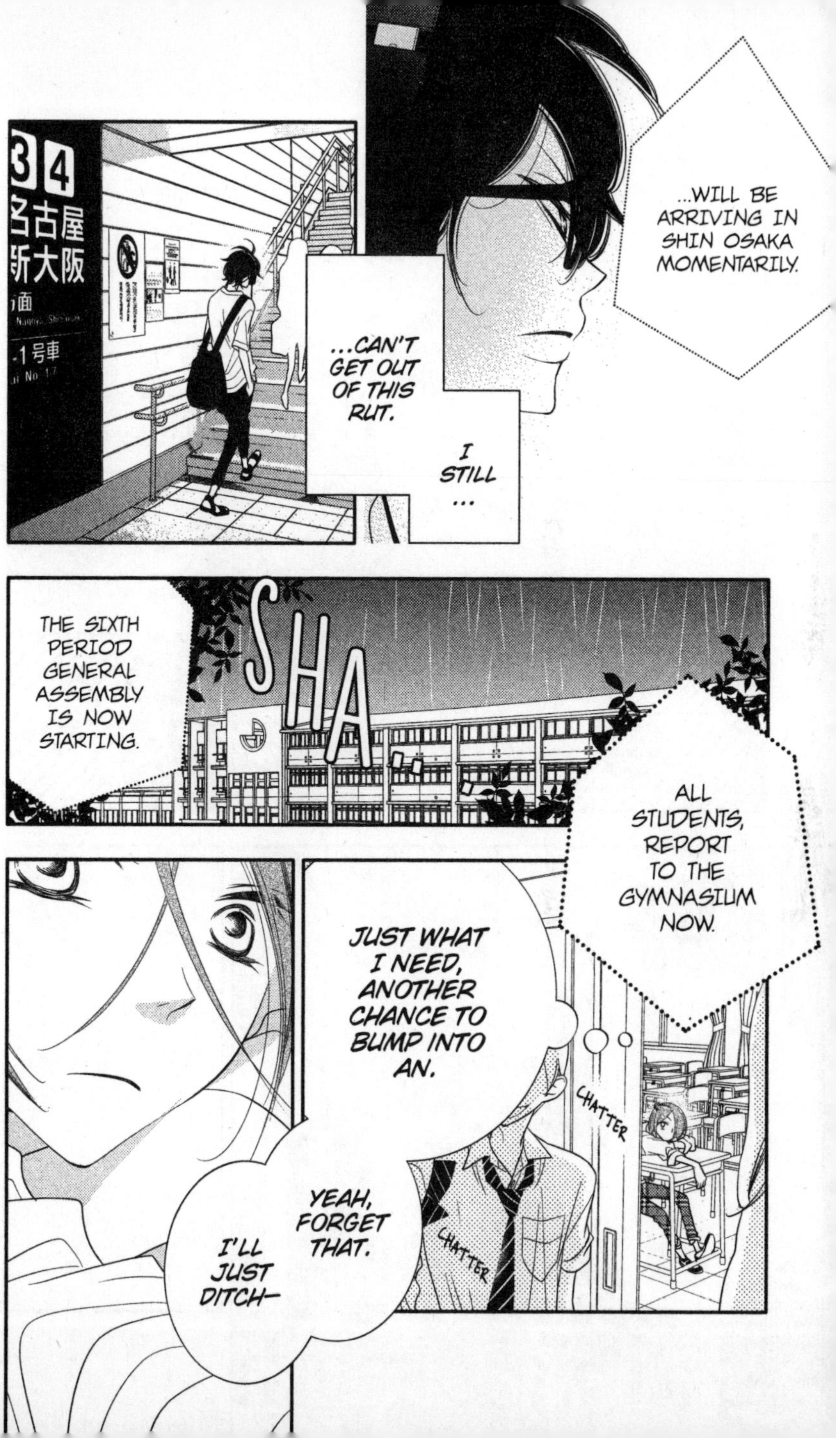

...WILL BE ARRIVING IN SHIN OSAKA MOMENTARILY.
I STILL ...
...CAN'T GET OUT OF THIS RUT.
3 4
名古屋
SHA
THE SIXTH PERIOD GENERAL ASSEMBLY IS NOW STARTING.
ALL STUDENTS, REPORT TO THE GYMNASIUM NOW.
JUST WHAT I NEED, ANOTHER CHANCE TO BUMP INTO AN.
CHATTER
CHATTER
YEAH, FORGET THAT.
I'LL JUST DITCH—

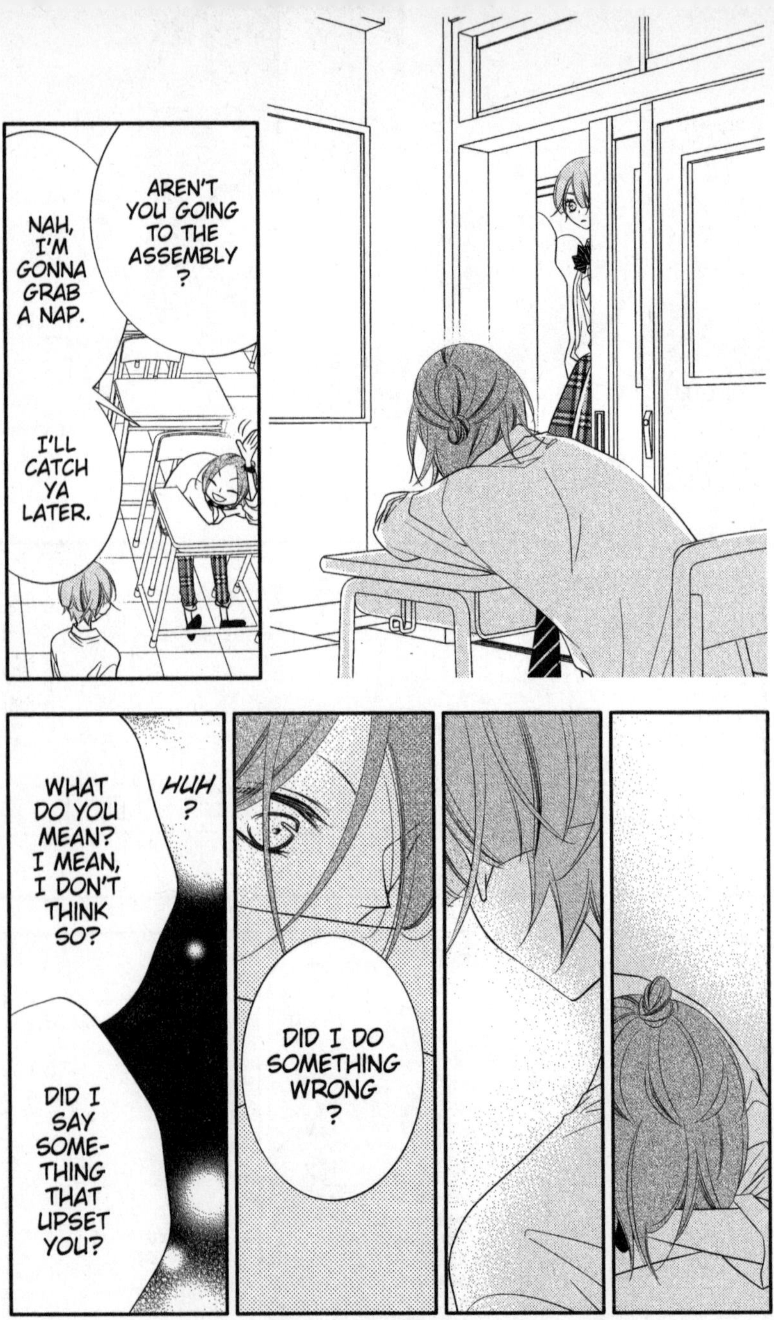
AREN'T YOU GOING TO THE ASSEMBLY?
NAH, I'M GONNA GRAB A NAP.
I'LL CATCH YA LATER.
DID I DO SOMETHING WRONG?
HUH?
WHAT DO YOU MEAN? I MEAN, I DON'T THINK SO?
DID I SAY SOMETHING THAT UPSET YOU?

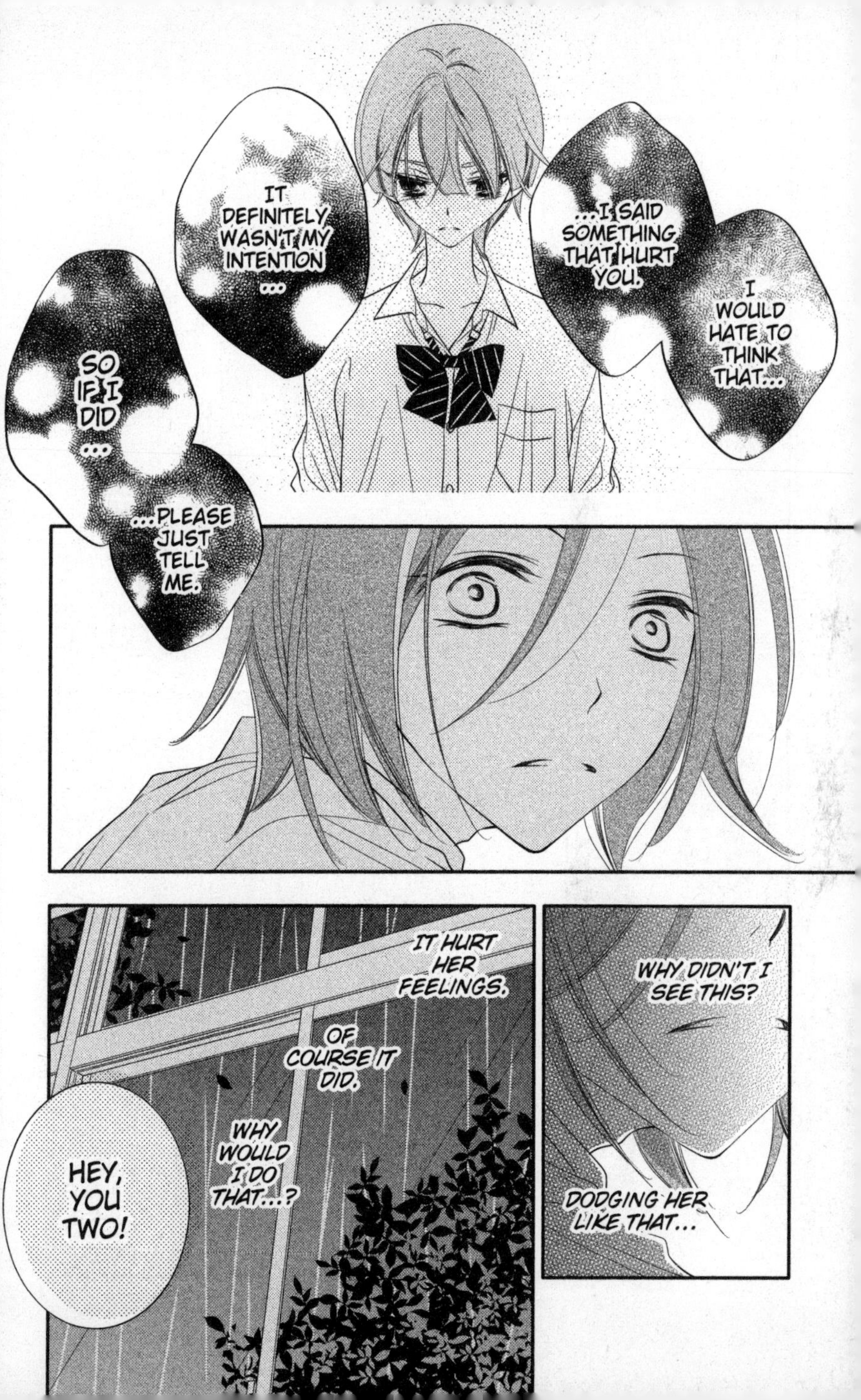

...I SAID SOMETHING THAT HURT YOU.
I WOULD HATE TO THINK THAT...
IT DEFINITELY WASN'T MY INTENTION...
SO IF I DID...
...PLEASE JUST TELL ME.
WHY DIDN'T I SEE THIS?
DODGING HER LIKE THAT...
IT HURT HER FEELINGS.
OF COURSE IT DID.
WHY WOULD I DO THAT...?
HEY, YOU TWO!

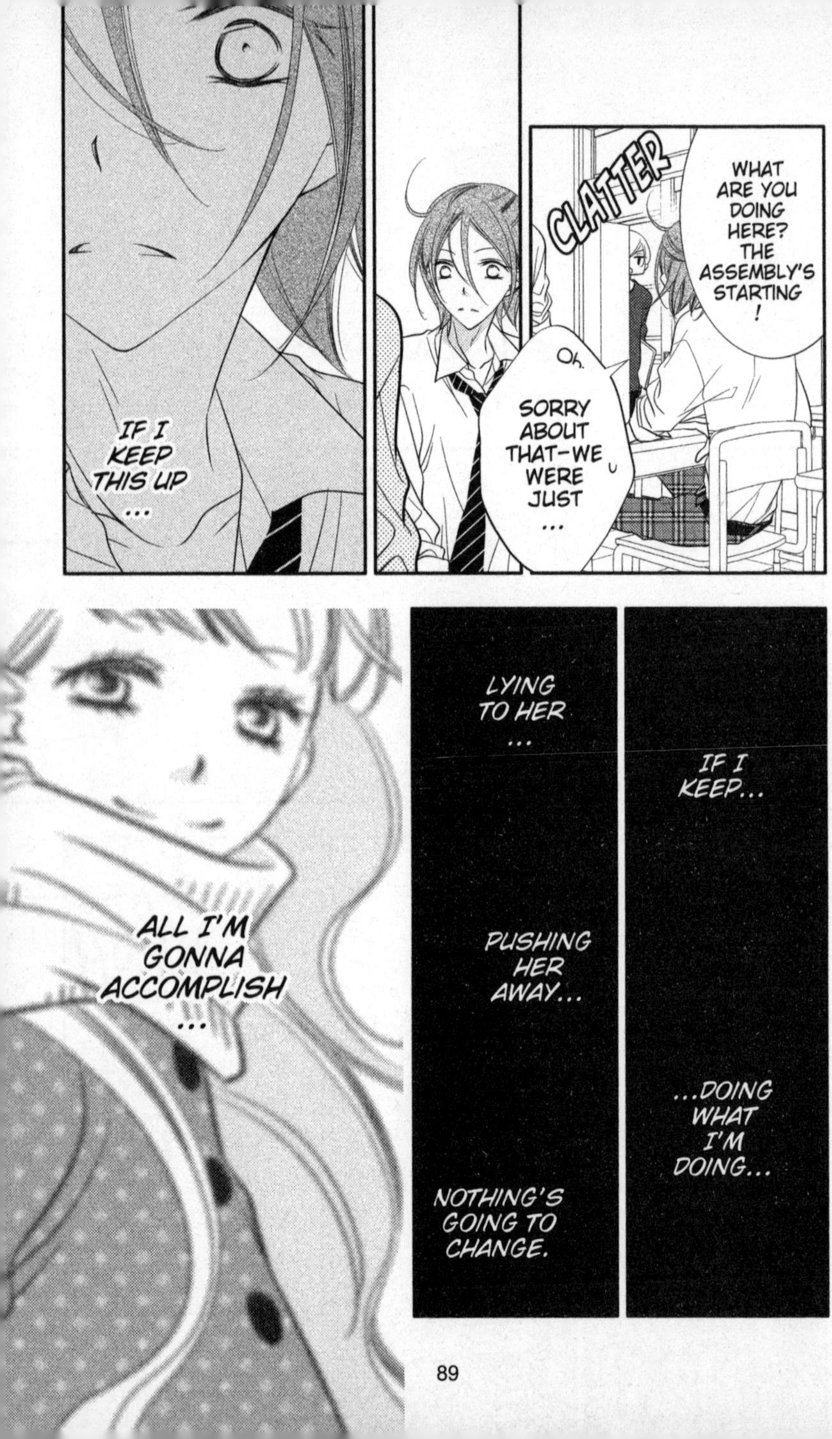
CLATTER
WHAT ARE YOU DOING HERE? THE ASSEMBLY'S STARTING!
Oh.
SORRY ABOUT THAT—WE WERE JUST...
IF I KEEP THIS UP...
IF I KEEP...
...DOING WHAT I'M DOING...
LYING TO HER...
PUSHING HER AWAY...
NOTHING'S GOING TO CHANGE.
ALL I'M GONNA ACCOMPLISH...

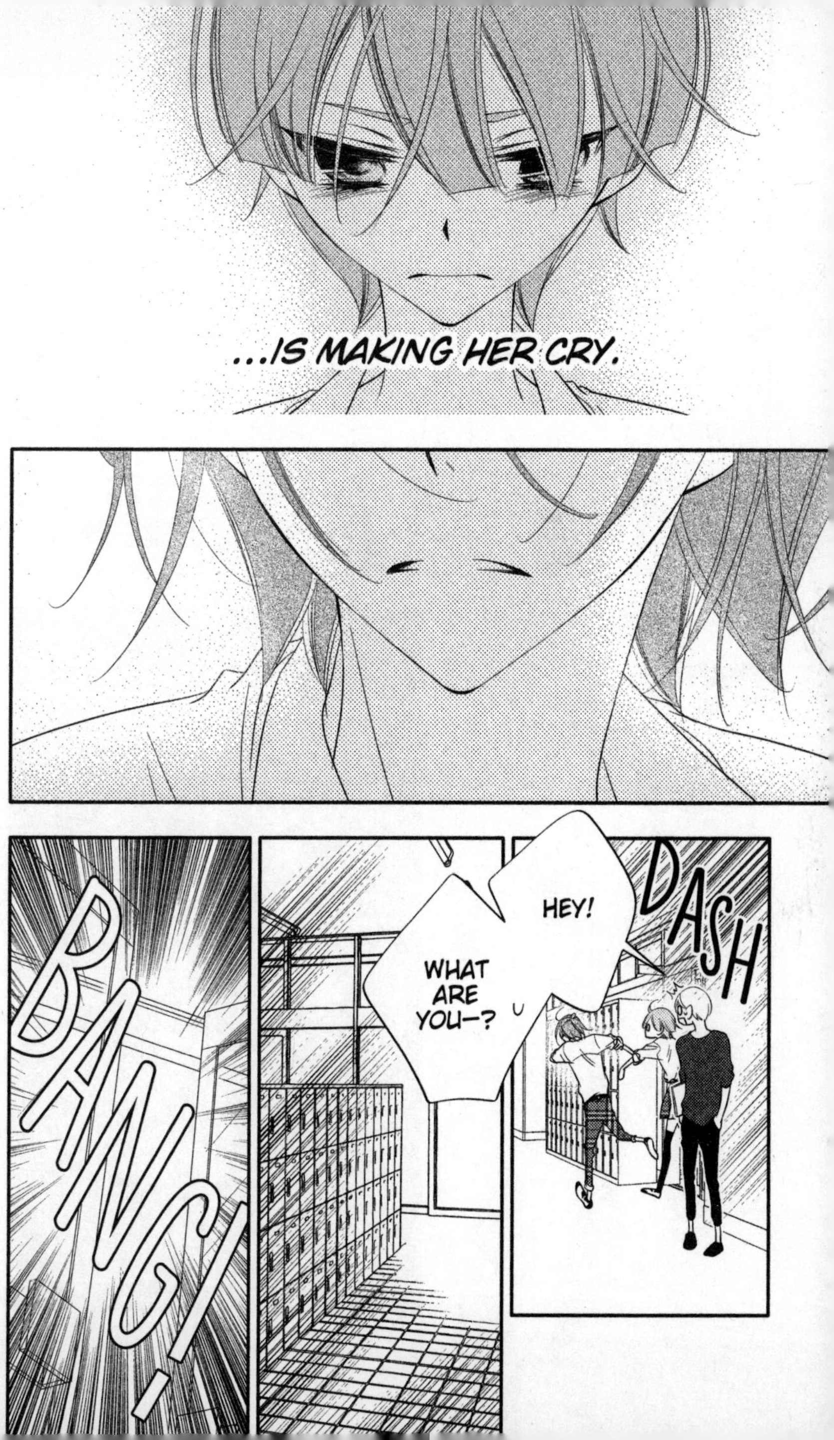
...IS MAKING HER CRY.
DASH
HEY!
WHAT ARE YOU—?
BANG!

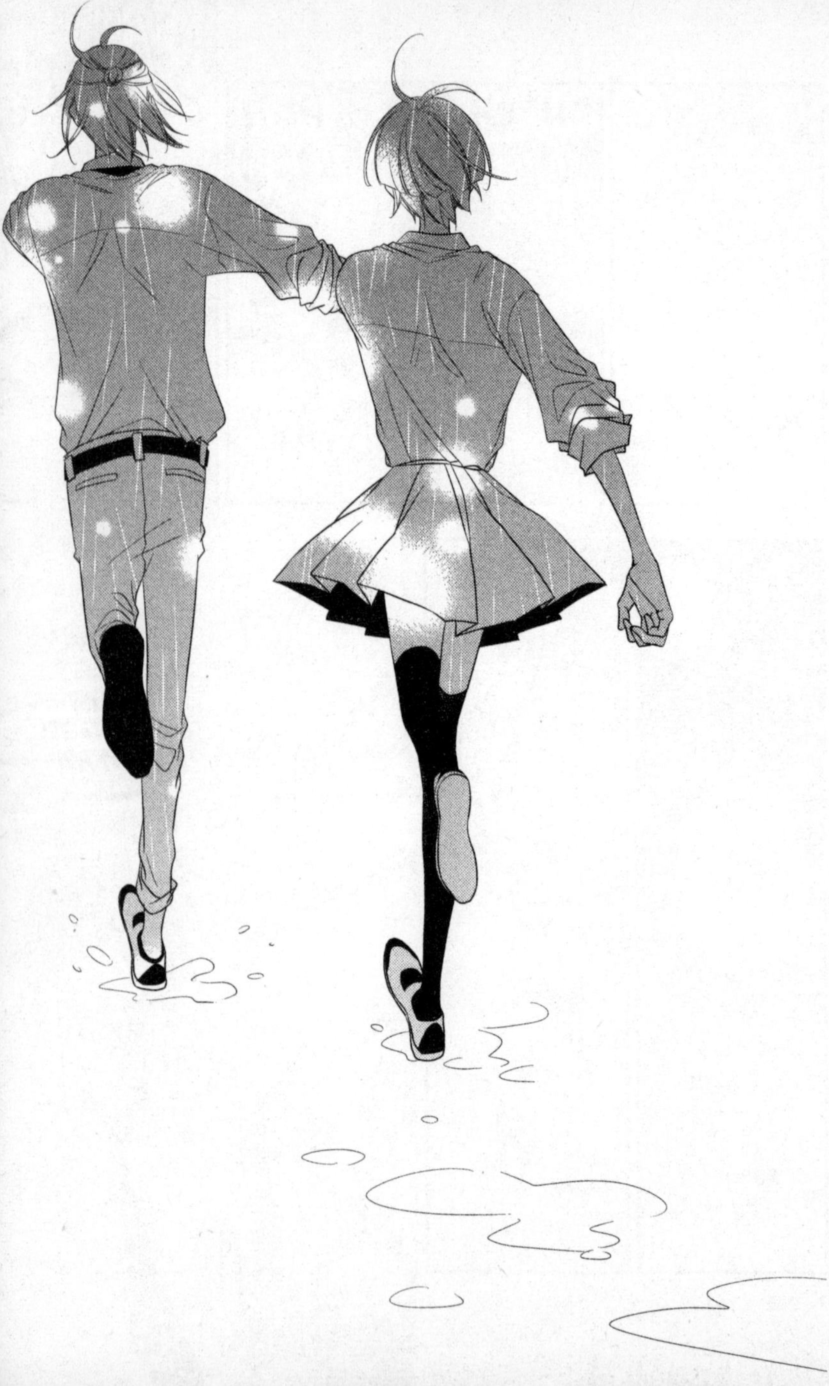

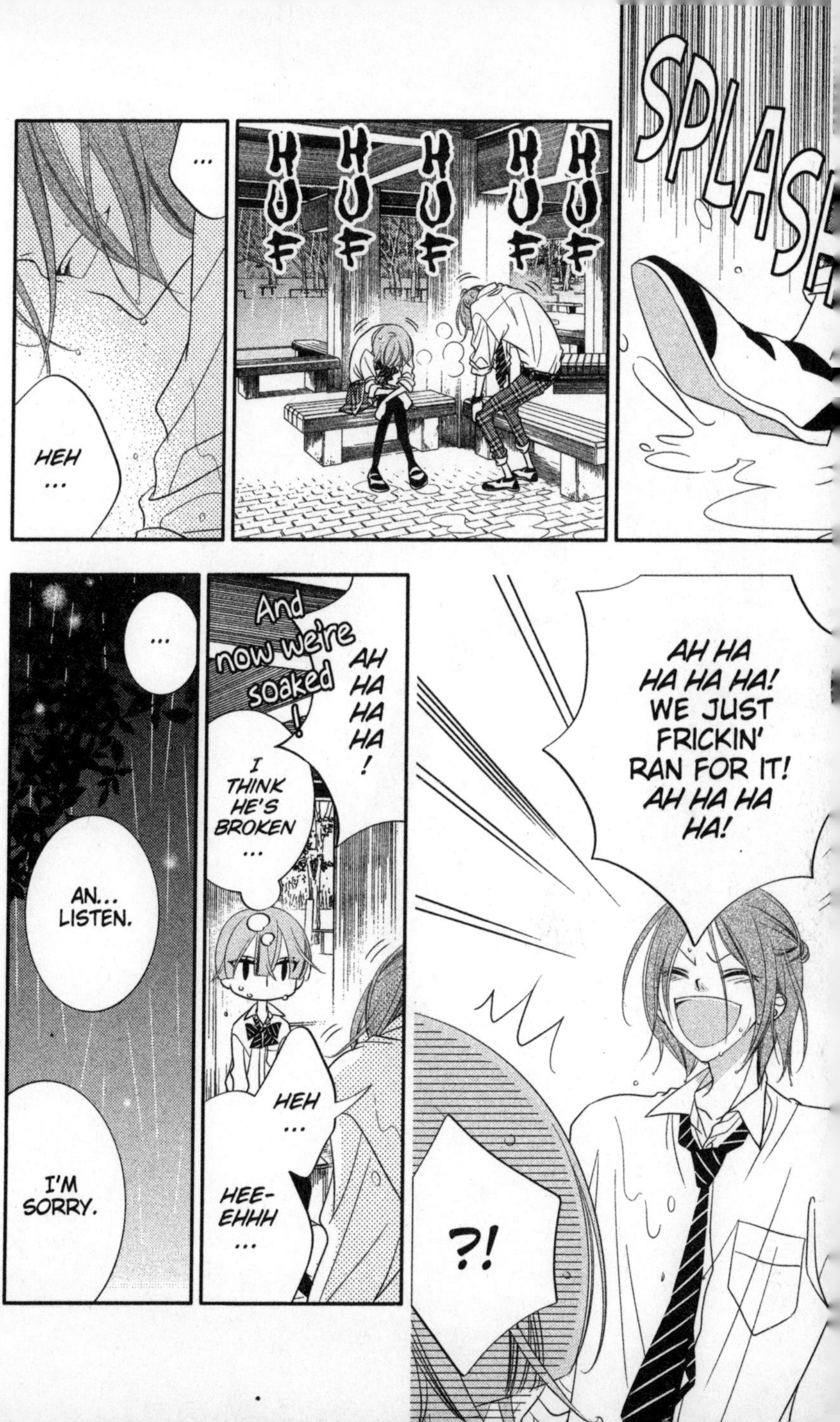
SPLASH
HUFF HUFF HUFF HUFF HUFF
...
HEH ...
AH HA HA HA HA! WE JUST FRICKIN' RAN FOR IT! AH HA HA HA HA!
?!
And now we're soaked!
AH HA HA HA!
I THINK HE'S BROKEN ...
HEH ...
HEE-EHHH ...
...
AN... LISTEN.
I'M SORRY.

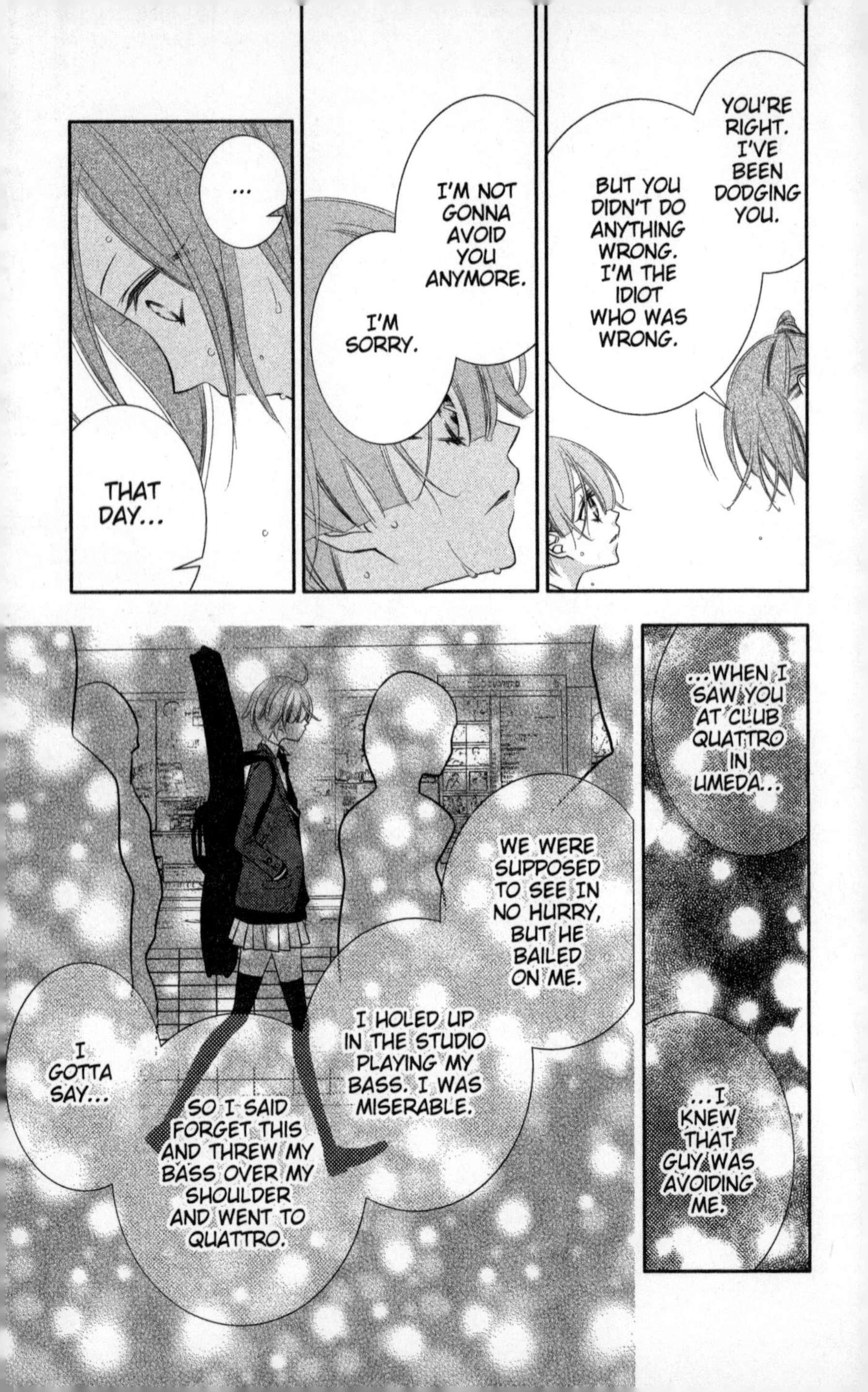
YOU'RE RIGHT. I'VE BEEN DODGING YOU.
BUT YOU DIDN'T DO ANYTHING WRONG. I'M THE IDIOT WHO WAS WRONG.
I'M NOT GONNA AVOID YOU ANYMORE.
I'M SORRY.
...
THAT DAY...
...WHEN I SAW YOU AT CLUB QUATTRO IN UMEDA...
...I KNEW THAT GUY WAS AVOIDING ME.
WE WERE SUPPOSED TO SEE IN NO HURRY, BUT HE BAILED ON ME.
I HOLED UP IN THE STUDIO PLAYING MY BASS. I WAS MISERABLE.
SO I SAID FORGET THIS AND THREW MY BASS OVER MY SHOULDER AND WENT TO QUATTRO.
I GOTTA SAY...

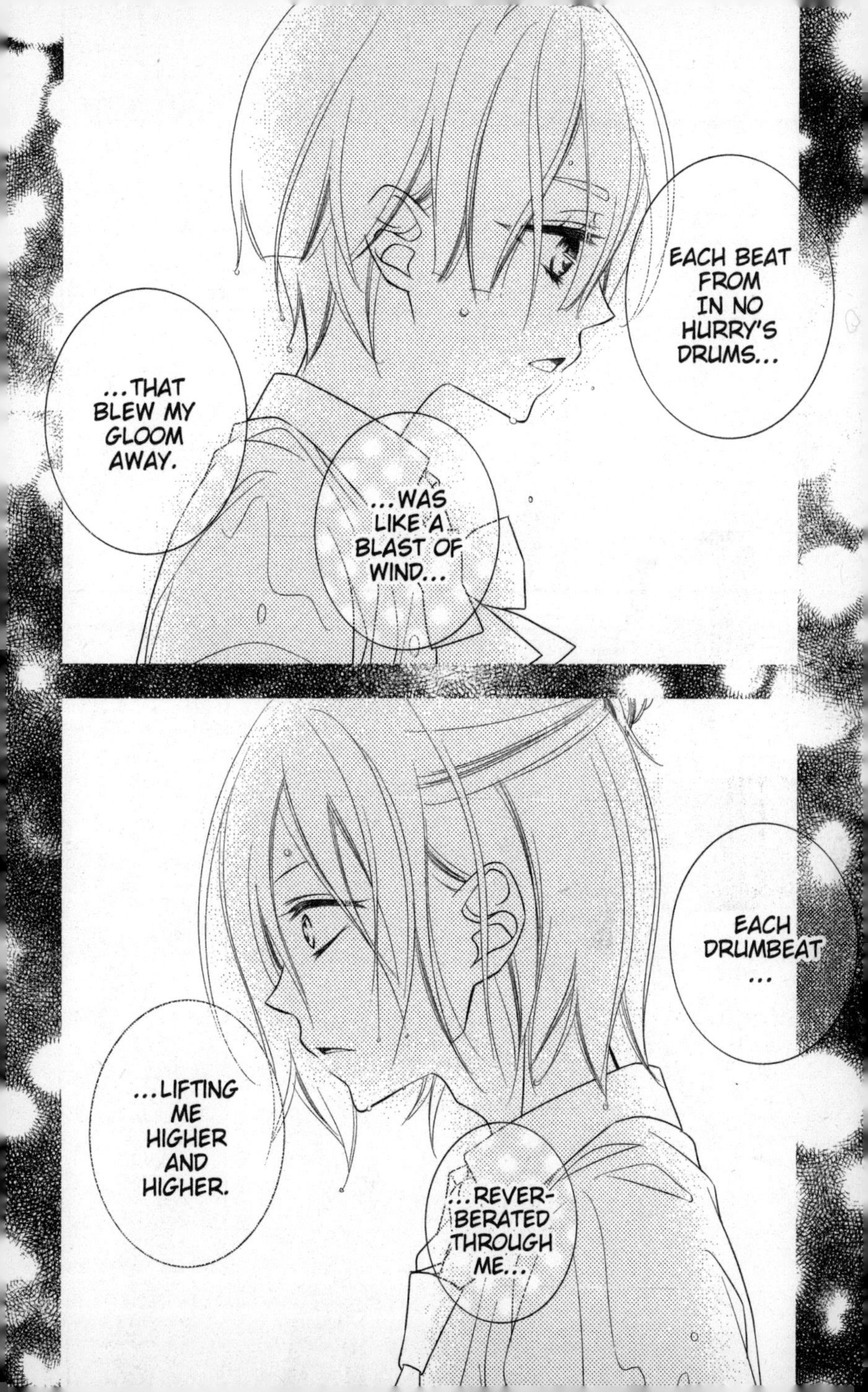
EACH BEAT FROM IN NO HURRY'S DRUMS...
...WAS LIKE A BLAST OF WIND...
...THAT BLEW MY GLOOM AWAY.
EACH DRUMBEAT ...
...REVER-BERATED THROUGH ME...
...LIFTING ME HIGHER AND HIGHER.

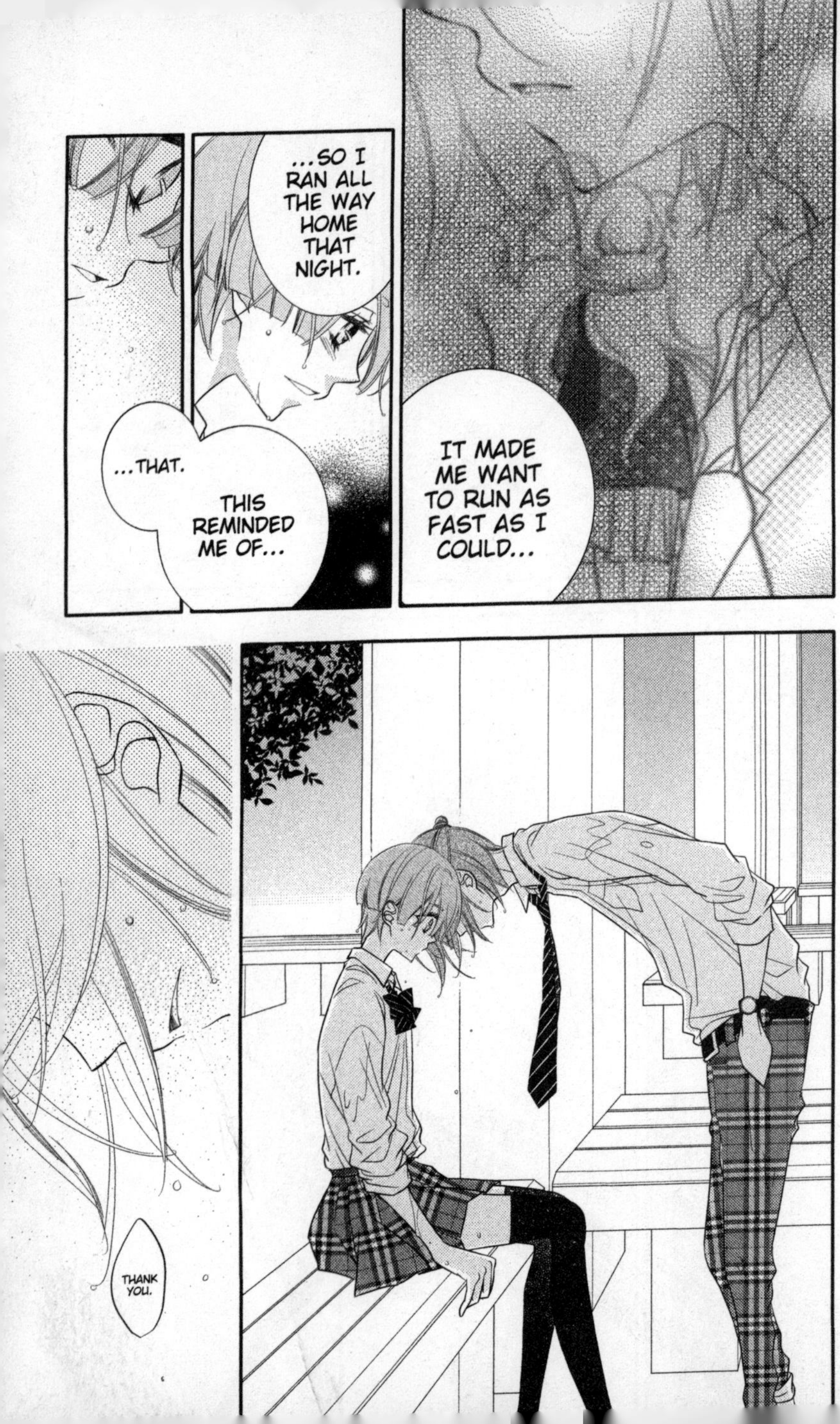
IT MADE ME WANT TO RUN AS FAST AS I COULD...
...SO I RAN ALL THE WAY HOME THAT NIGHT.
THIS REMINDED ME OF...
...THAT.
THANK YOU.

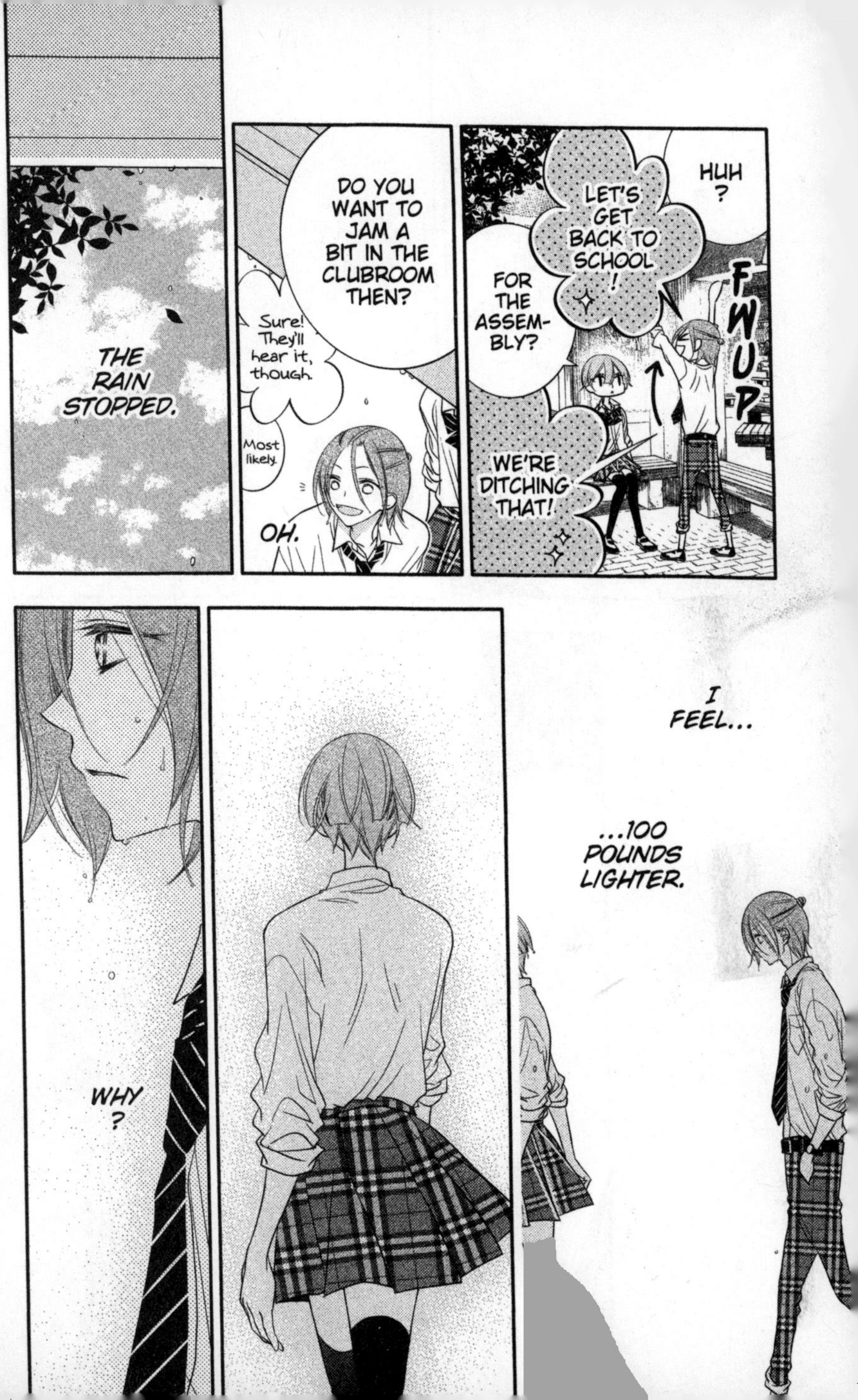
HUH?
LET'S GET BACK TO SCHOOL!
FWUP
FOR THE ASSEMBLY?
WE'RE DITCHING THAT!
DO YOU WANT TO JAM A BIT IN THE CLUBROOM THEN?
Sure! They'll hear it, though.
Most likely.
OH.
THE RAIN STOPPED.
I FEEL...
...100 POUNDS LIGHTER.
WHY?

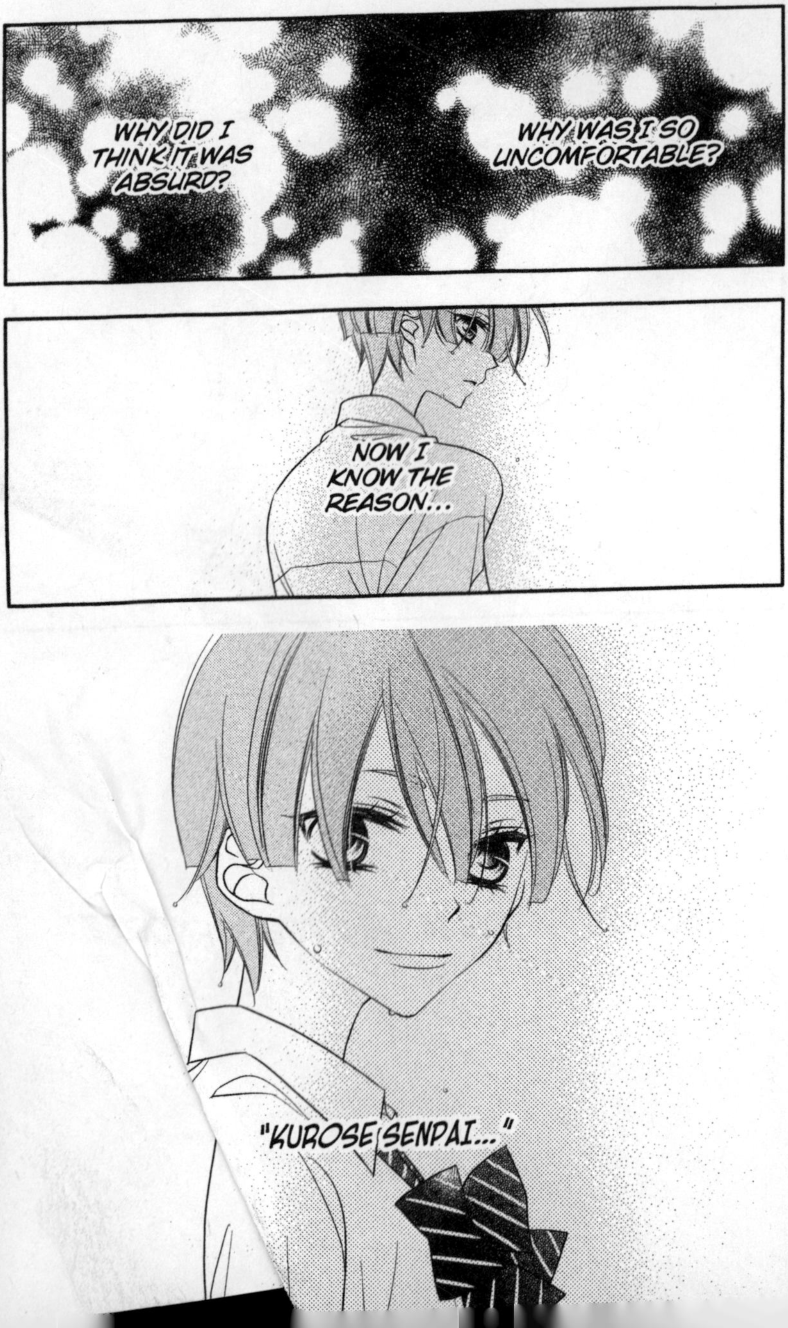
WHY WAS I SO UNCOMFORTABLE?
WHY DID I THINK IT WAS ABSURD?
NOW I KNOW THE REASON...
"KUROSE SENPAI..."

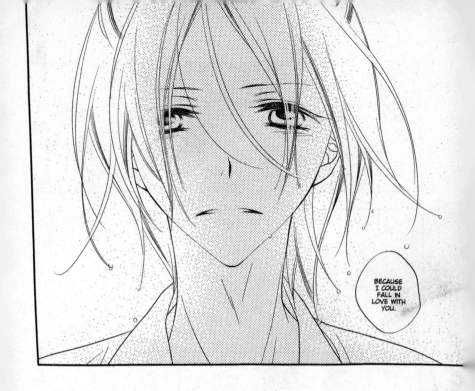

BECAUSE I COULD FALL IN LOVE WITH YOU.

"DO YOU BELIEVE IN THE POWER OF WORDS?"

SONG 79

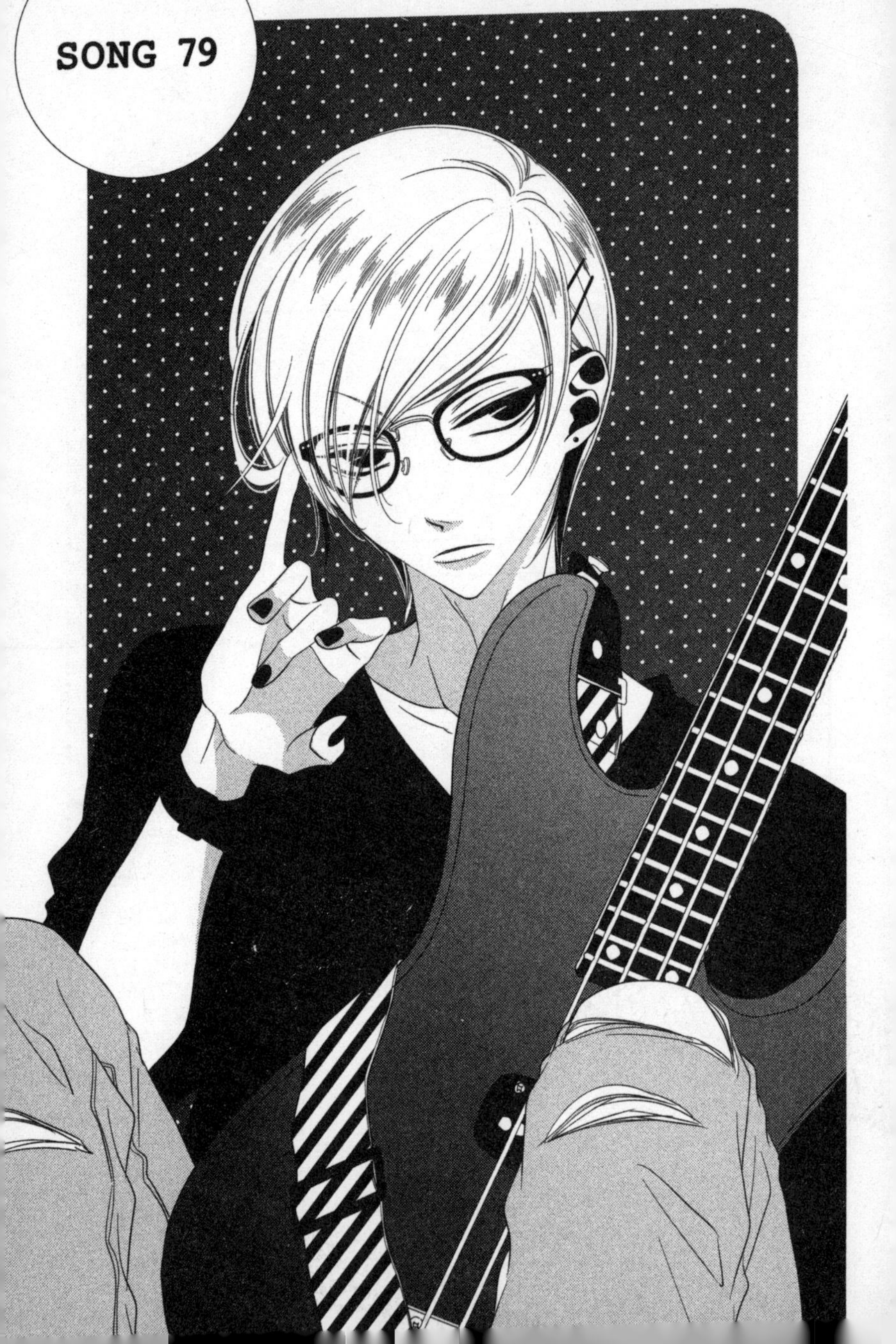

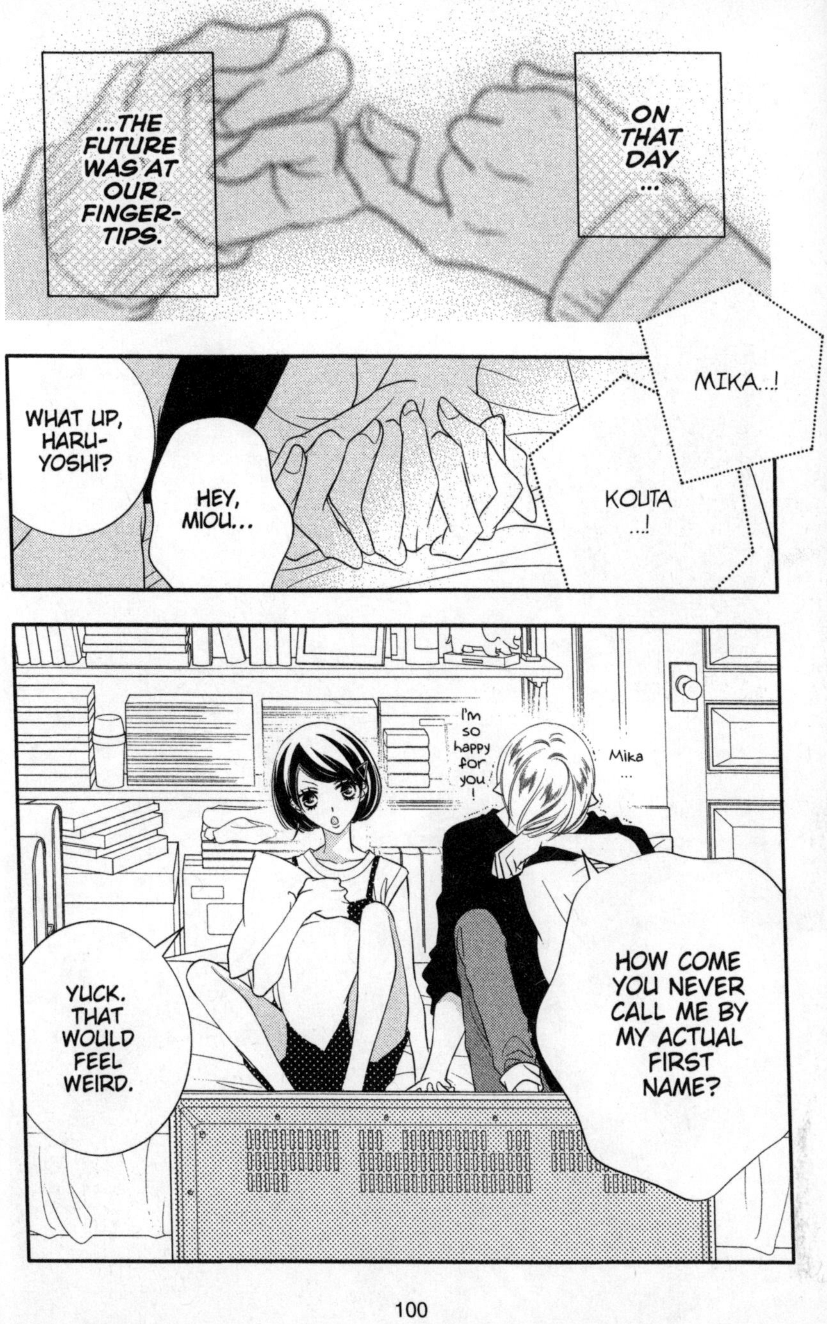
ON THAT DAY...
...THE FUTURE WAS AT OUR FINGER-TIPS.
MIKA...!
KOUTA...!
HEY, MIOU...
WHAT UP, HARU-YOSHI?
Mika...
I'm so happy for you!
HOW COME YOU NEVER CALL ME BY MY ACTUAL FIRST NAME?
YUCK. THAT WOULD FEEL WEIRD.

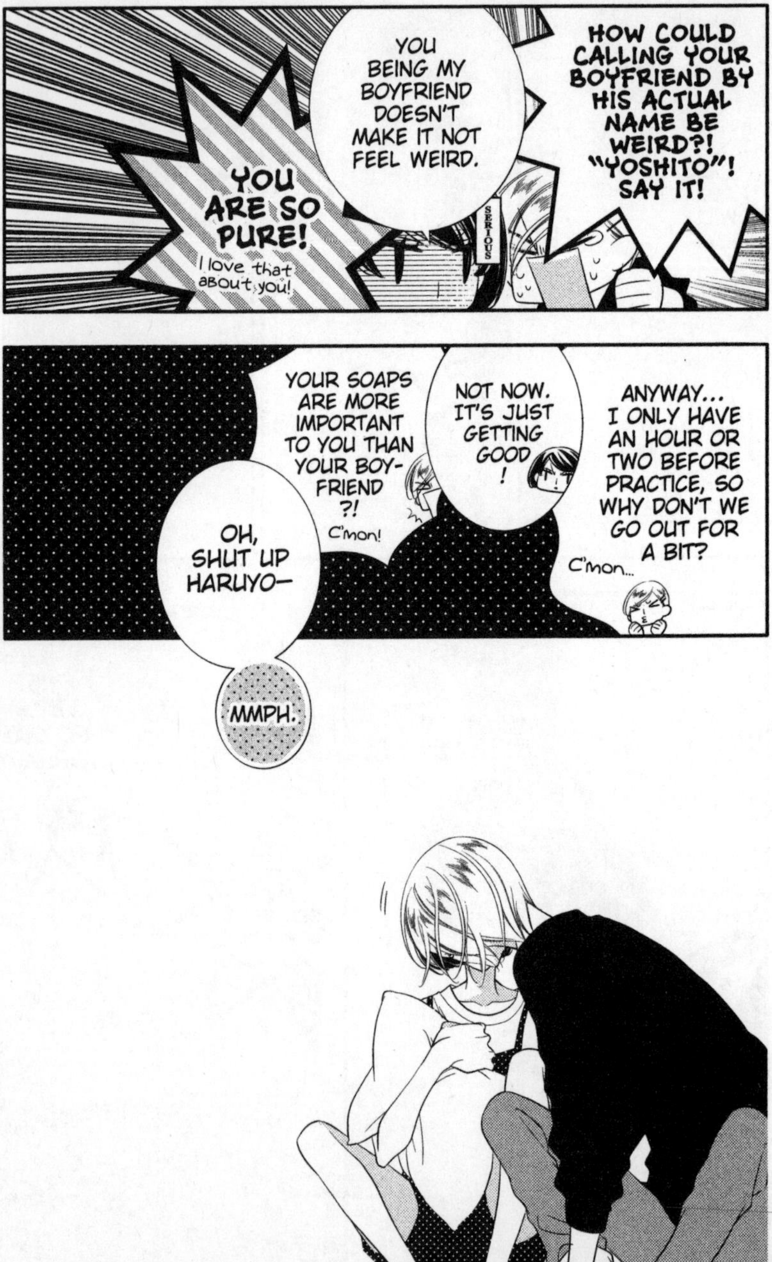
HOW COULD CALLING YOUR BOYFRIEND BY HIS ACTUAL NAME BE WEIRD?! "YOSHITO"! SAY IT!
SERIOUS
YOU BEING MY BOYFRIEND DOESN'T MAKE IT NOT FEEL WEIRD.
YOU ARE SO PURE!
I love that about you!
ANYWAY... I ONLY HAVE AN HOUR OR TWO BEFORE PRACTICE, SO WHY DON'T WE GO OUT FOR A BIT?
C'mon...
NOT NOW. IT'S JUST GETTING GOOD!
YOUR SOAPS ARE MORE IMPORTANT TO YOU THAN YOUR BOY-FRIEND?!
C'mon!
OH, SHUT UP HARUYO—
MMPH.

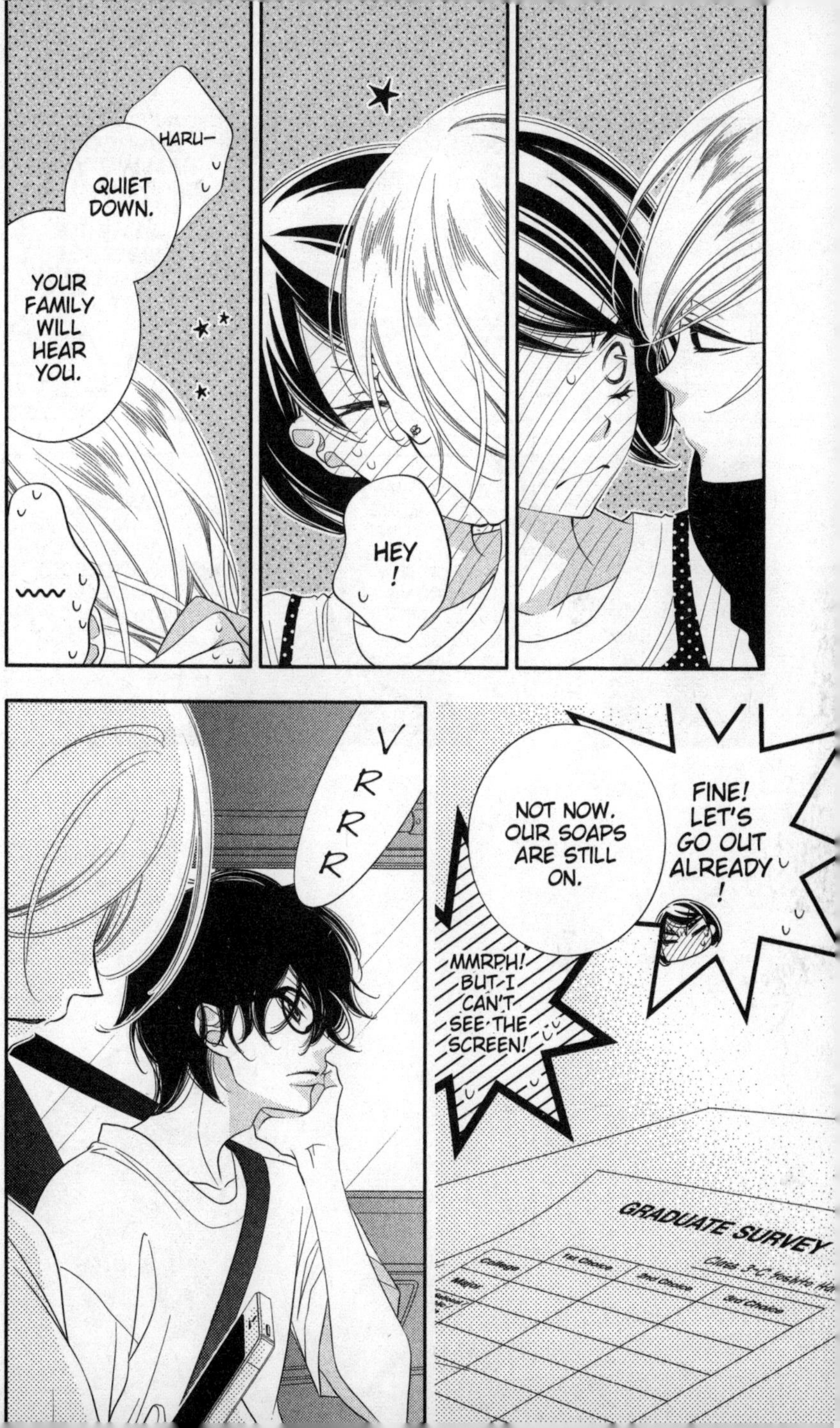
HEY!
HARU—
QUIET DOWN.
YOUR FAMILY WILL HEAR YOU.
FINE! LET'S GO OUT ALREADY!
NOT NOW. OUR SOAPS ARE STILL ON.
MMRPH! BUT I CAN'T SEE THE SCREEN!
GRADUATE SURVEY
College
1st Choice
2nd Choice
3rd Choice
Major
VRRR

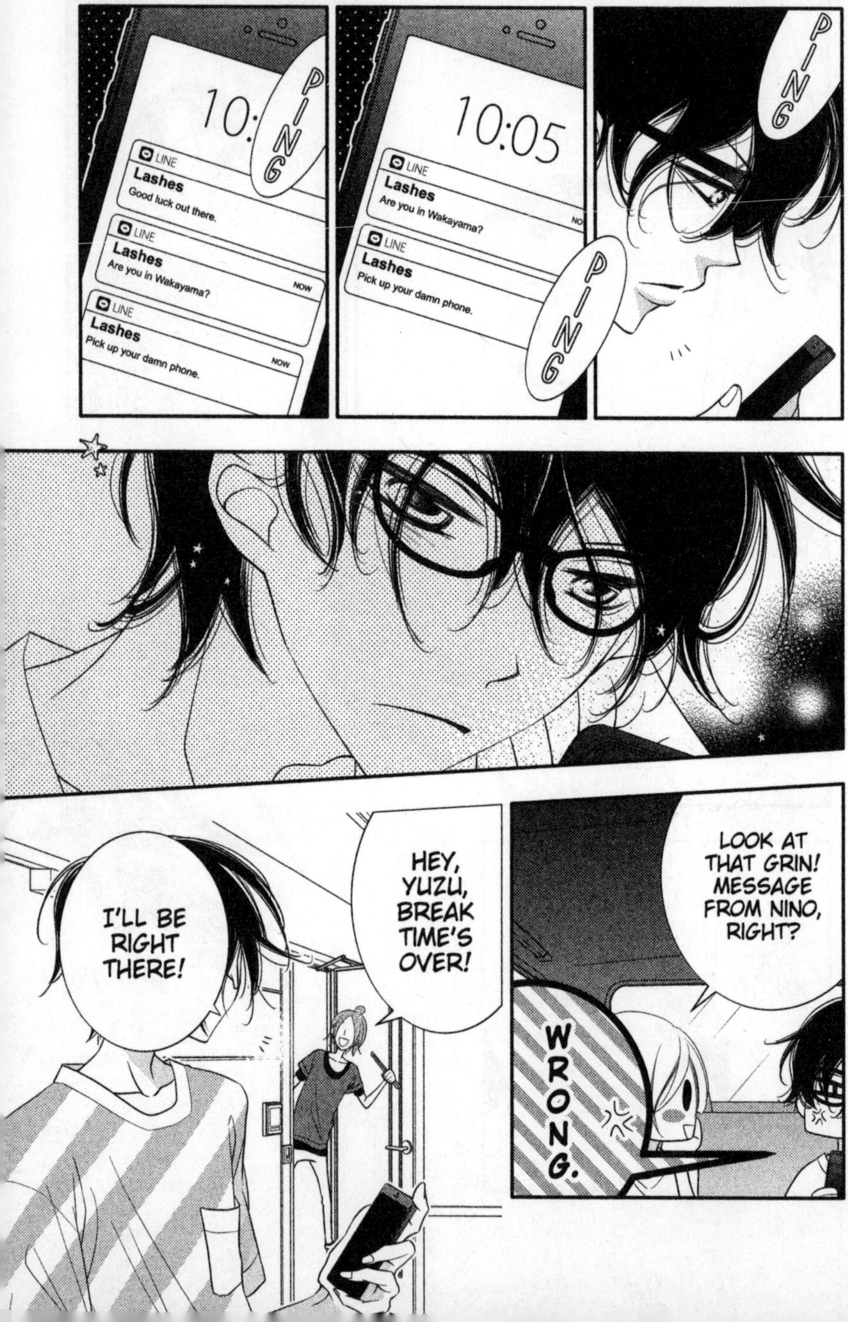

PING
PING
10:05
LINE
Lashes
Are you in Wakayama?
LINE
Lashes
Pick up your damn phone.
10:
PING
LINE
Lashes
Good luck out there.
LINE
Lashes
Are you in Wakayama?
NOW
LINE
Lashes
Pick up your damn phone.
NOW
LOOK AT THAT GRIN! MESSAGE FROM NINO, RIGHT?
WRONG.
HEY, YUZU, BREAK TIME'S OVER!
I'LL BE RIGHT THERE!

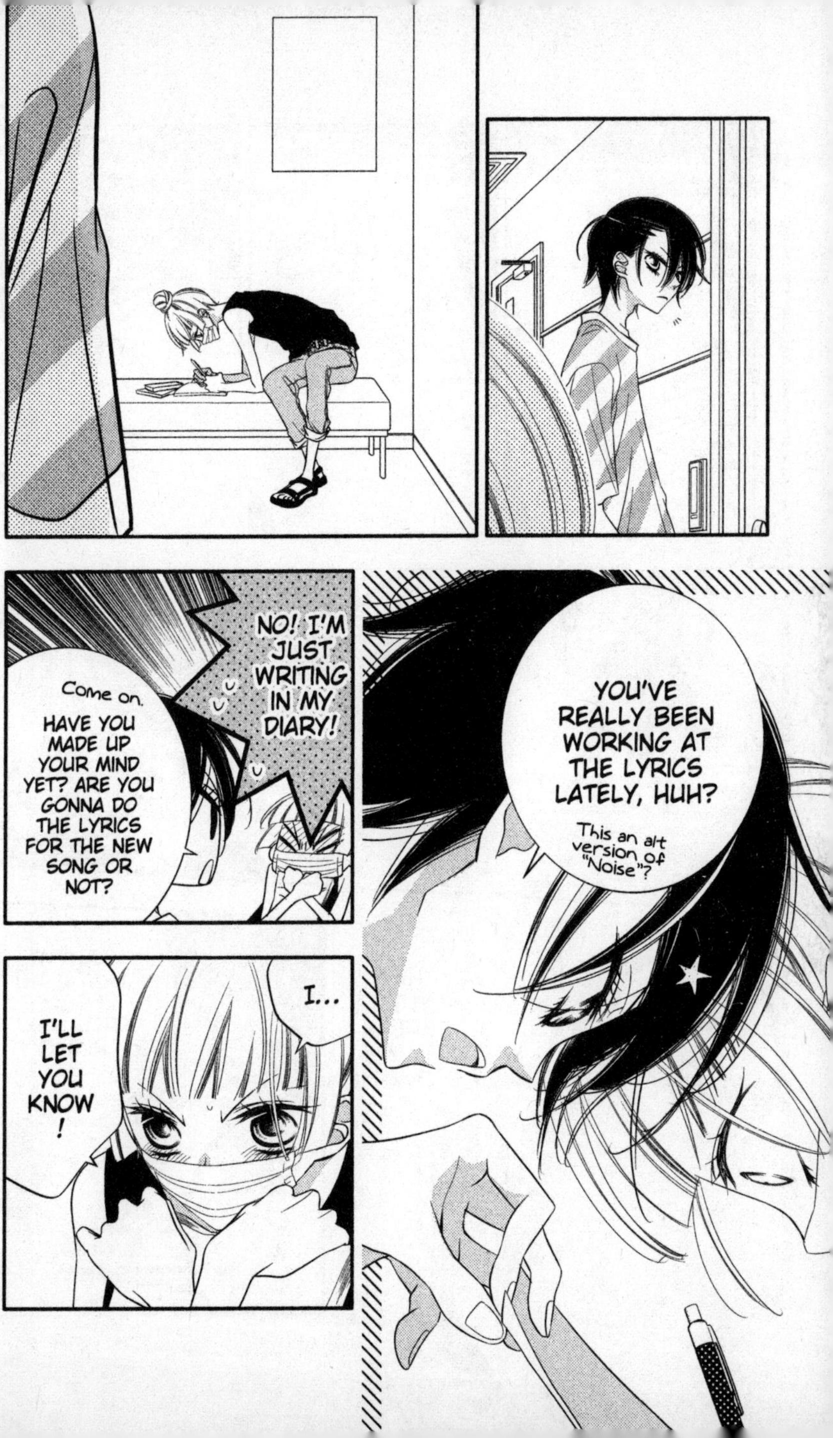
YOU'VE REALLY BEEN WORKING AT THE LYRICS LATELY, HUH?
This an alt version of "Noise"?
NO! I'M JUST WRITING IN MY DIARY!
Come on.
HAVE YOU MADE UP YOUR MIND YET? ARE YOU GONNA DO THE LYRICS FOR THE NEW SONG OR NOT?
I...
I'LL LET YOU KNOW!

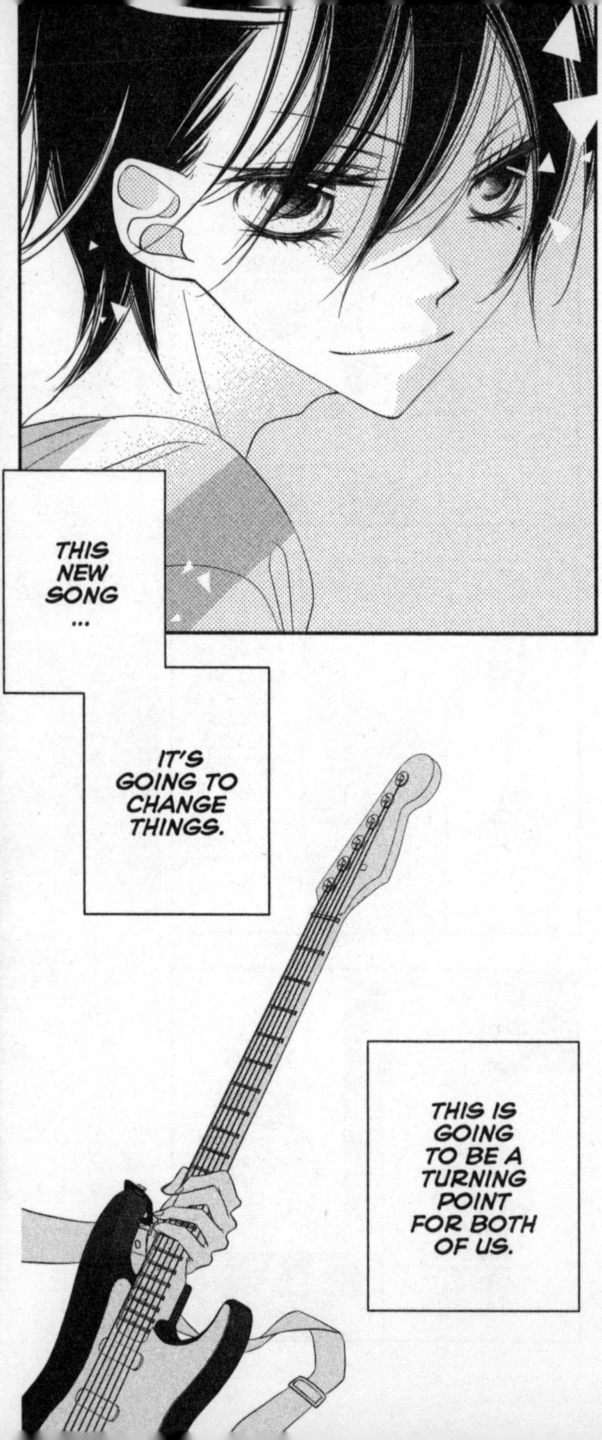
THIS NEW SONG ...
IT'S GOING TO CHANGE THINGS.
THIS IS GOING TO BE A TURNING POINT FOR BOTH OF US.

4

With the Tokyo Sailing arc coming to an end in this volume, I wanted to thank all of the clubs that agreed to my requests for reference materials and permission to use their names.

So to the Shibuya Milkyway, Shibuya Star Lounge, Shibuya Take Off 7, Shibuya Duo Music Exchange, Shibuya Chelsea Hotel and Tsutaya O-East, I extend my deepest gratitude.

Everyone I spoke to conveyed such affection for and pride in their clubs that I can't help but share in the obvious love they hold for their establishments.

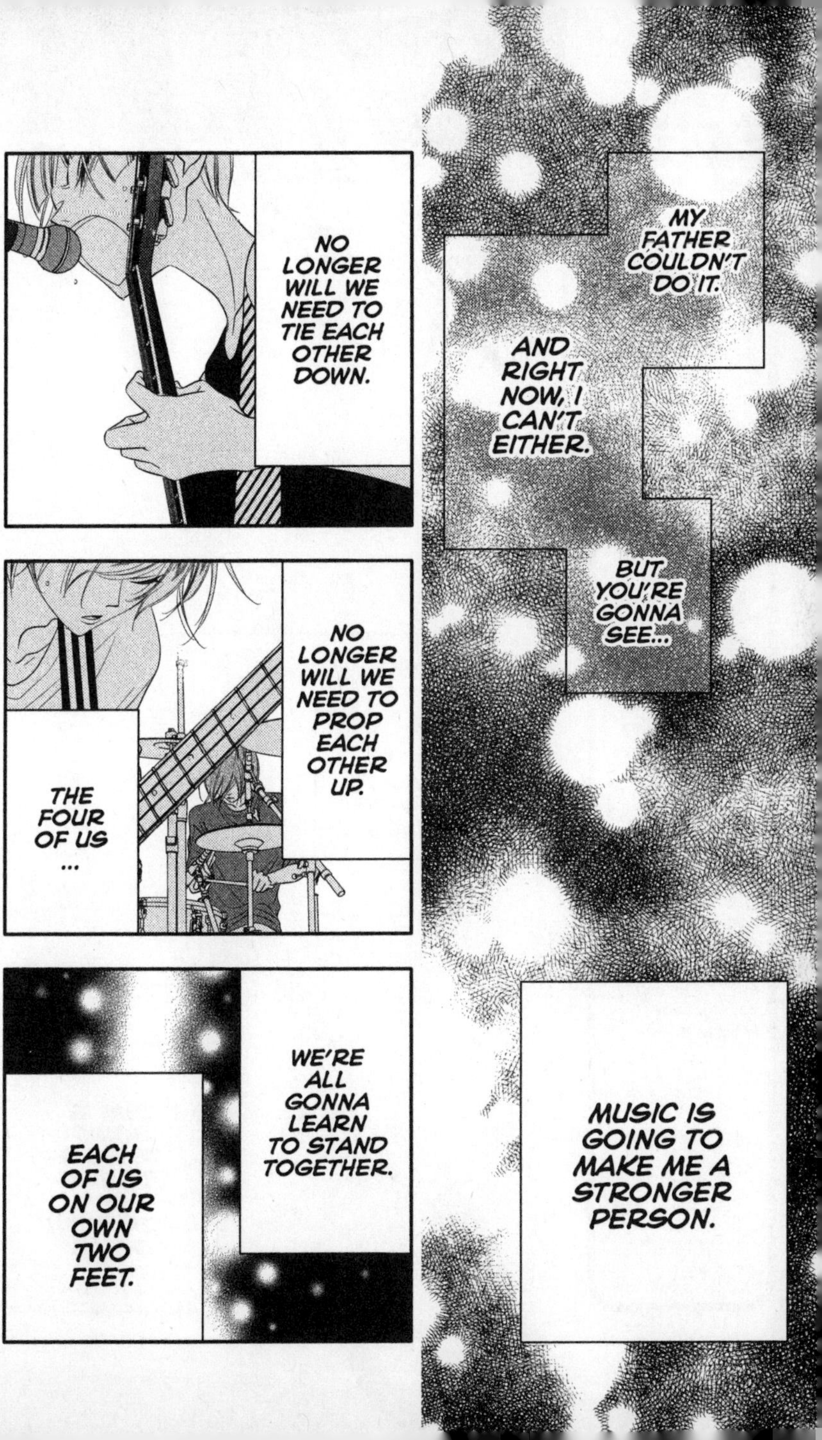
MY FATHER COULDN'T DO IT.
AND RIGHT NOW, I CAN'T EITHER.
BUT YOU'RE GONNA SEE...
MUSIC IS GOING TO MAKE ME A STRONGER PERSON.
NO LONGER WILL WE NEED TO TIE EACH OTHER DOWN.
NO LONGER WILL WE NEED TO PROP EACH OTHER UP.
THE FOUR OF US ...
WE'RE ALL GONNA LEARN TO STAND TOGETHER.
EACH OF US ON OUR OWN TWO FEET.

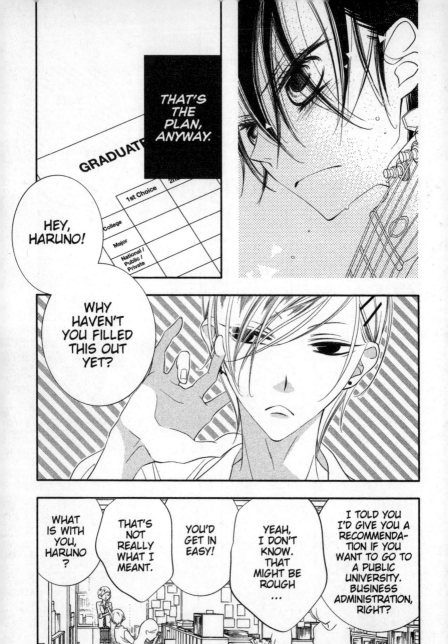

THAT'S THE PLAN, ANYWAY.

GRADUAT

	1st Choice	2nd
College		
Major		
National / Public / Private		

HEY, HARUNO!

WHY HAVEN'T YOU FILLED THIS OUT YET?

WHAT IS WITH YOU, HARUNO?

THAT'S NOT REALLY WHAT I MEANT.

YOU'D GET IN EASY!

YEAH, I DON'T KNOW. THAT MIGHT BE ROUGH...

I TOLD YOU I'D GIVE YOU A RECOMMENDA- TION IF YOU WANT TO GO TO A PUBLIC UNIVERSITY. BUSINESS ADMINISTRATION, RIGHT?

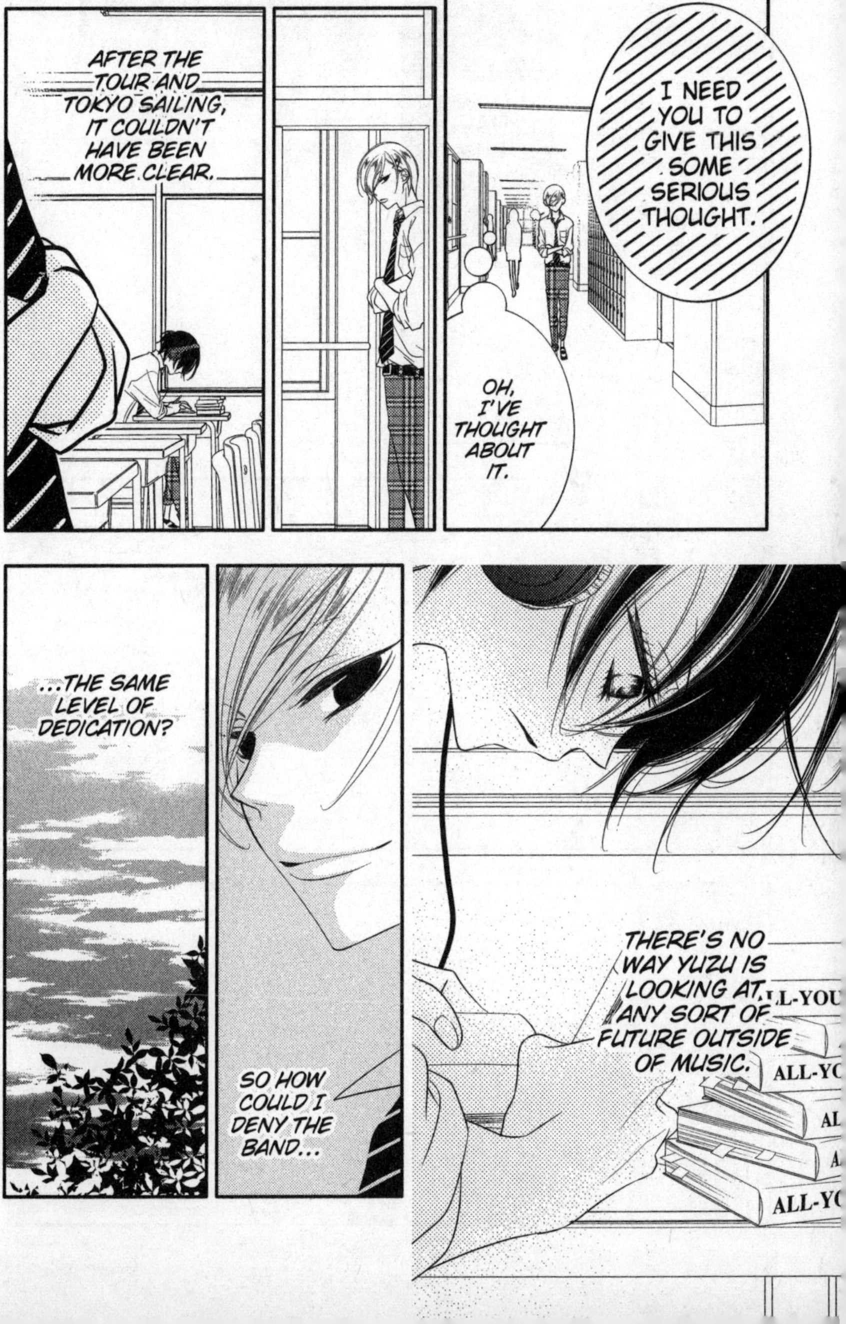
I NEED YOU TO GIVE THIS SOME SERIOUS THOUGHT.
OH, I'VE THOUGHT ABOUT IT.
AFTER THE TOUR AND TOKYO SAILING, IT COULDN'T HAVE BEEN MORE CLEAR.
THERE'S NO WAY YUZU IS LOOKING AT ANY SORT OF FUTURE OUTSIDE OF MUSIC.
SO HOW COULD I DENY THE BAND...
...THE SAME LEVEL OF DEDICATION?

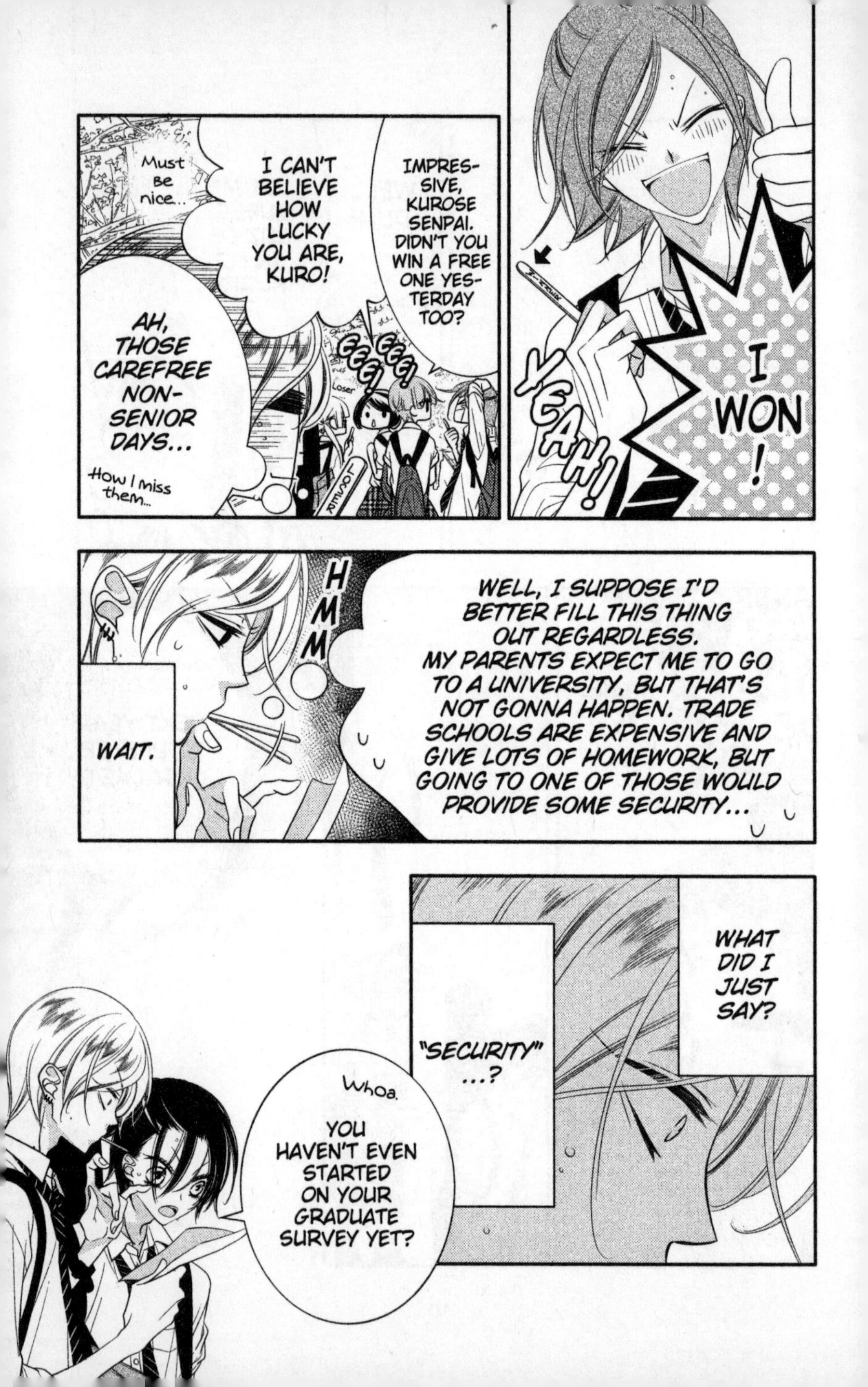
I WON!
YEAH!
IMPRESSIVE, KUROSE SENPAI. DIDN'T YOU WIN A FREE ONE YESTERDAY TOO?
I CAN'T BELIEVE HOW LUCKY YOU ARE, KURO!
Must be nice...
AH, THOSE CAREFREE NON-SENIOR DAYS...
How I miss them...
HMM
WELL, I SUPPOSE I'D BETTER FILL THIS THING OUT REGARDLESS. MY PARENTS EXPECT ME TO GO TO A UNIVERSITY, BUT THAT'S NOT GONNA HAPPEN. TRADE SCHOOLS ARE EXPENSIVE AND GIVE LOTS OF HOMEWORK, BUT GOING TO ONE OF THOSE WOULD PROVIDE SOME SECURITY...
WAIT.
WHAT DID I JUST SAY?
"SECURITY" ...?
Whoa.
YOU HAVEN'T EVEN STARTED ON YOUR GRADUATE SURVEY YET?

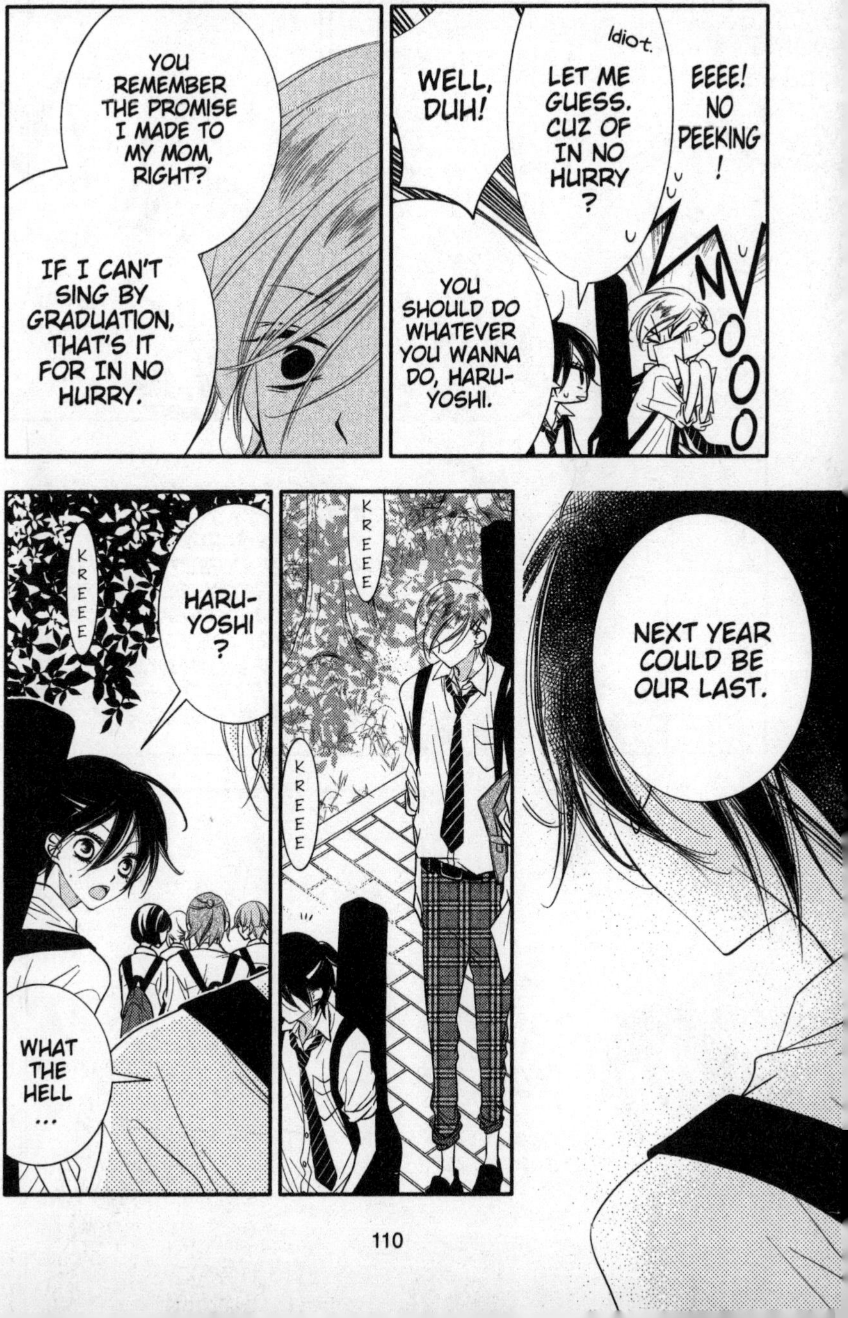
EEEE! NO PEEKING!
NNOOOO
Idiot.
LET ME GUESS. CUZ OF IN NO HURRY?
WELL, DUH!
YOU SHOULD DO WHATEVER YOU WANNA DO, HARU-YOSHI.
YOU REMEMBER THE PROMISE I MADE TO MY MOM, RIGHT?
IF I CAN'T SING BY GRADUATION, THAT'S IT FOR IN NO HURRY.
NEXT YEAR COULD BE OUR LAST.
KREEE
KREEE
HARU-YOSHI?
KREEE
WHAT THE HELL...

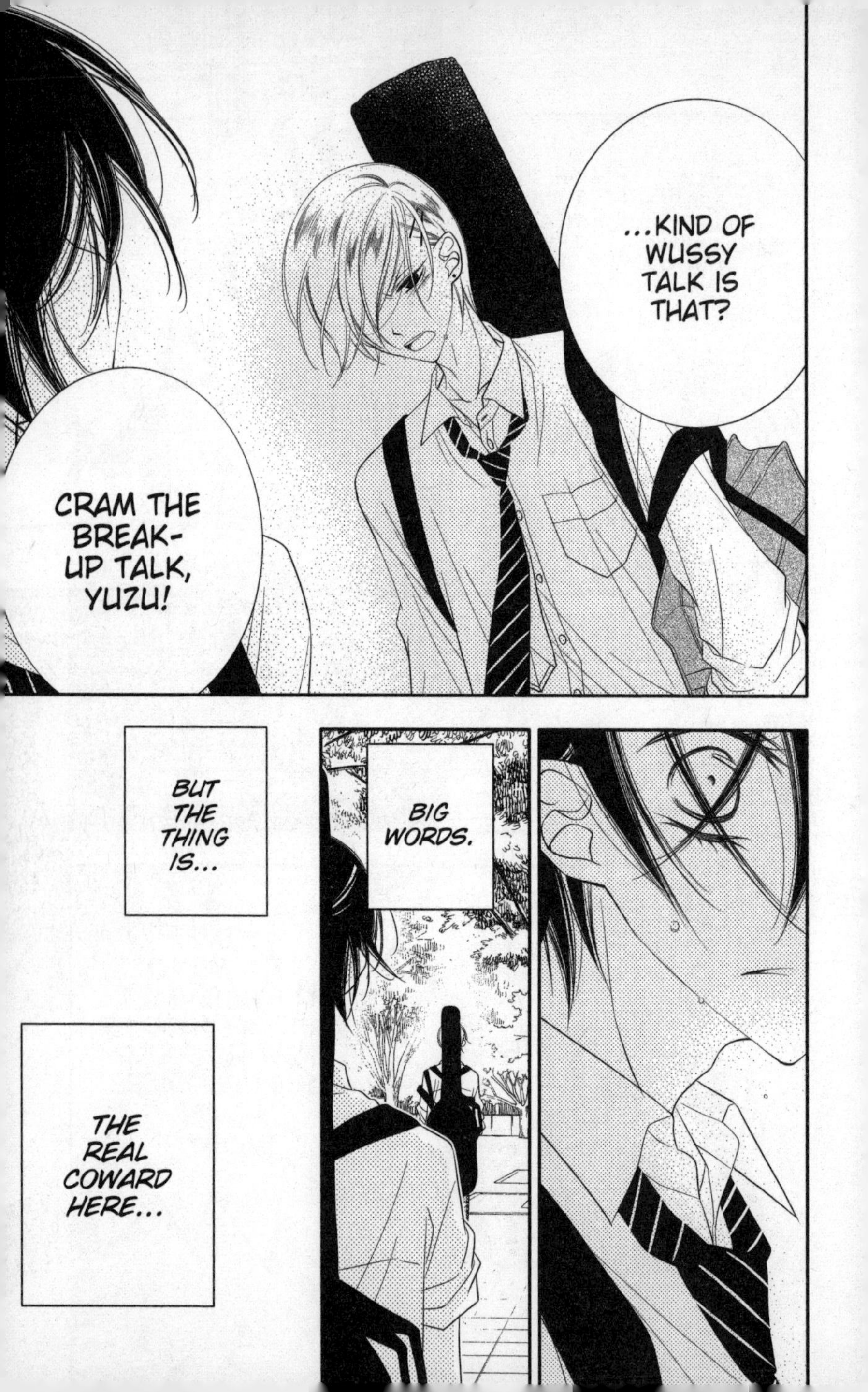
...KIND OF WUSSY TALK IS THAT?
CRAM THE BREAK-UP TALK, YUZU!
BIG WORDS.
BUT THE THING IS...
THE REAL COWARD HERE...

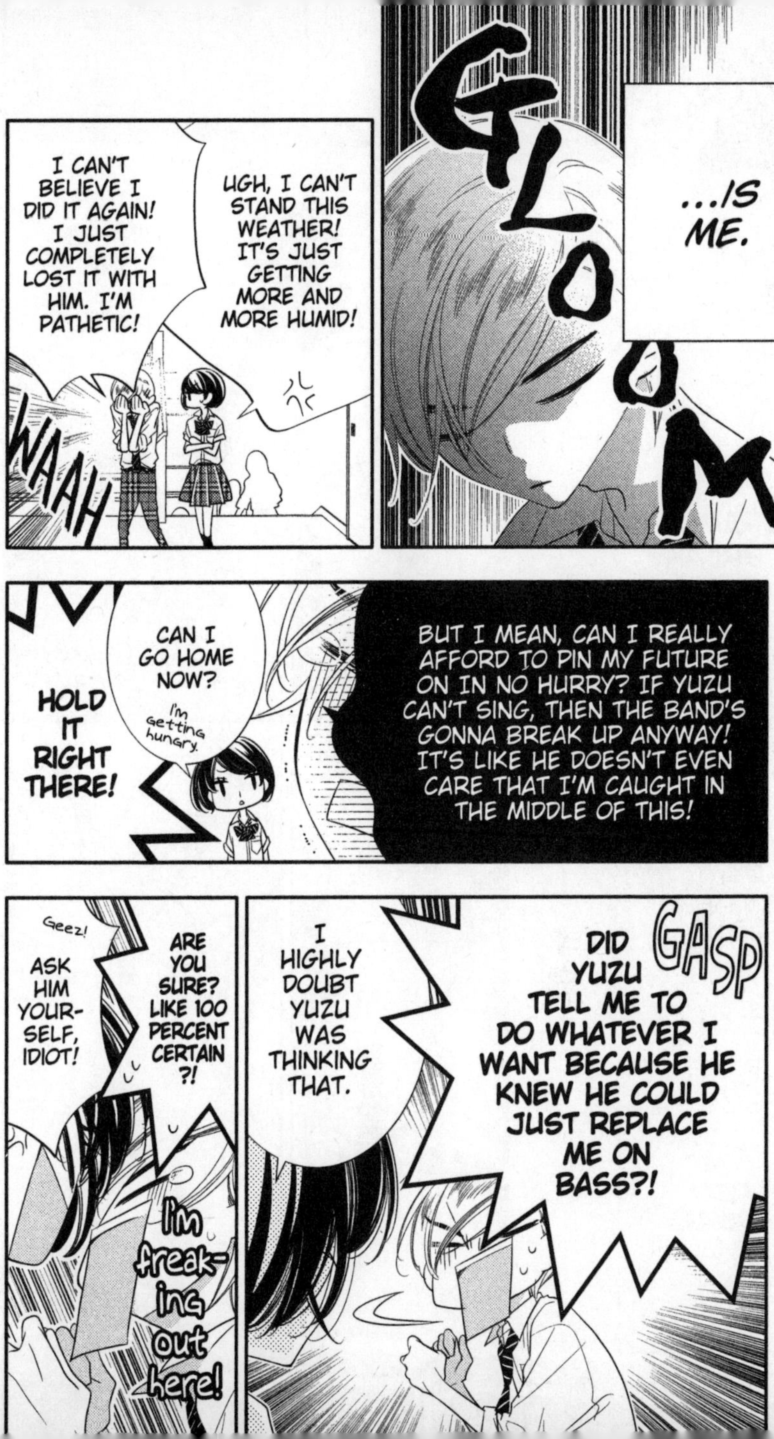
GLOOM
...IS ME.
UGH, I CAN'T STAND THIS WEATHER! IT'S JUST GETTING MORE AND MORE HUMID!
I CAN'T BELIEVE I DID IT AGAIN! I JUST COMPLETELY LOST IT WITH HIM. I'M PATHETIC!
WAAH
BUT I MEAN, CAN I REALLY AFFORD TO PIN MY FUTURE ON IN NO HURRY? IF YUZU CAN'T SING, THEN THE BAND'S GONNA BREAK UP ANYWAY! IT'S LIKE HE DOESN'T EVEN CARE THAT I'M CAUGHT IN THE MIDDLE OF THIS!
CAN I GO HOME NOW?
I'm getting hungry.
HOLD IT RIGHT THERE!
GASP
DID YUZU TELL ME TO DO WHATEVER I WANT BECAUSE HE KNEW HE COULD JUST REPLACE ME ON BASS?!
I HIGHLY DOUBT YUZU WAS THINKING THAT.
ARE YOU SURE? LIKE 100 PERCENT CERTAIN?!
Geez!
ASK HIM YOURSELF, IDIOT!
I'm freaking out here!

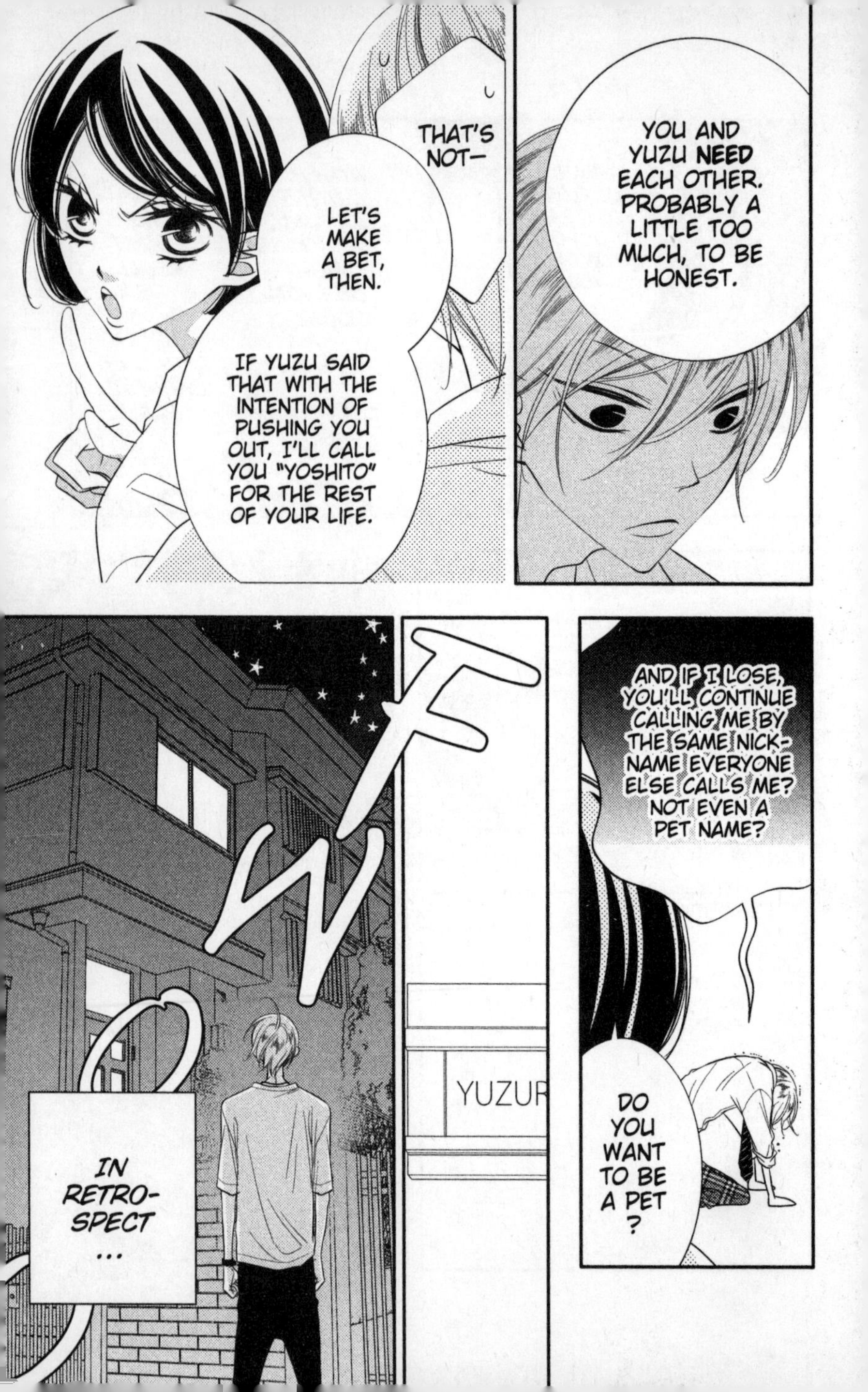
YOU AND YUZU **NEED** EACH OTHER. PROBABLY A LITTLE TOO MUCH, TO BE HONEST.
THAT'S NOT—
LET'S MAKE A BET, THEN.
IF YUZU SAID THAT WITH THE INTENTION OF PUSHING YOU OUT, I'LL CALL YOU "YOSHITO" FOR THE REST OF YOUR LIFE.
AND IF I LOSE, YOU'LL CONTINUE CALLING ME BY THE SAME NICK-NAME EVERYONE ELSE CALLS ME? NOT EVEN A PET NAME?
DO YOU WANT TO BE A PET?
YUZUR
FWO
IN RETRO-SPECT ...

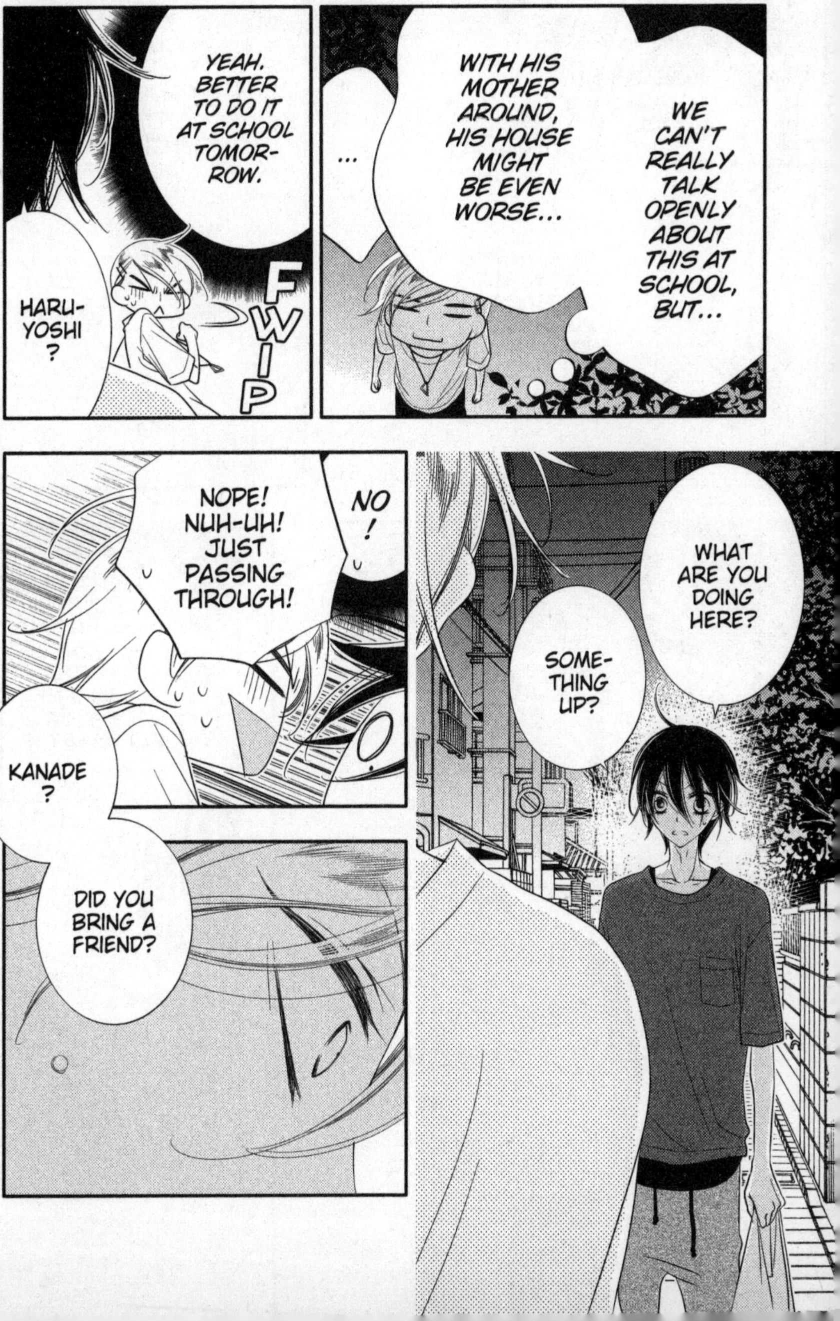
WE CAN'T REALLY TALK OPENLY ABOUT THIS AT SCHOOL, BUT...
WITH HIS MOTHER AROUND, HIS HOUSE MIGHT BE EVEN WORSE...
...
YEAH. BETTER TO DO IT AT SCHOOL TOMORROW.
FWIP
HARUYOSHI?
WHAT ARE YOU DOING HERE?
SOMETHING UP?
NO!
NOPE! NUH-UH! JUST PASSING THROUGH!
KANADE?
DID YOU BRING A FRIEND?

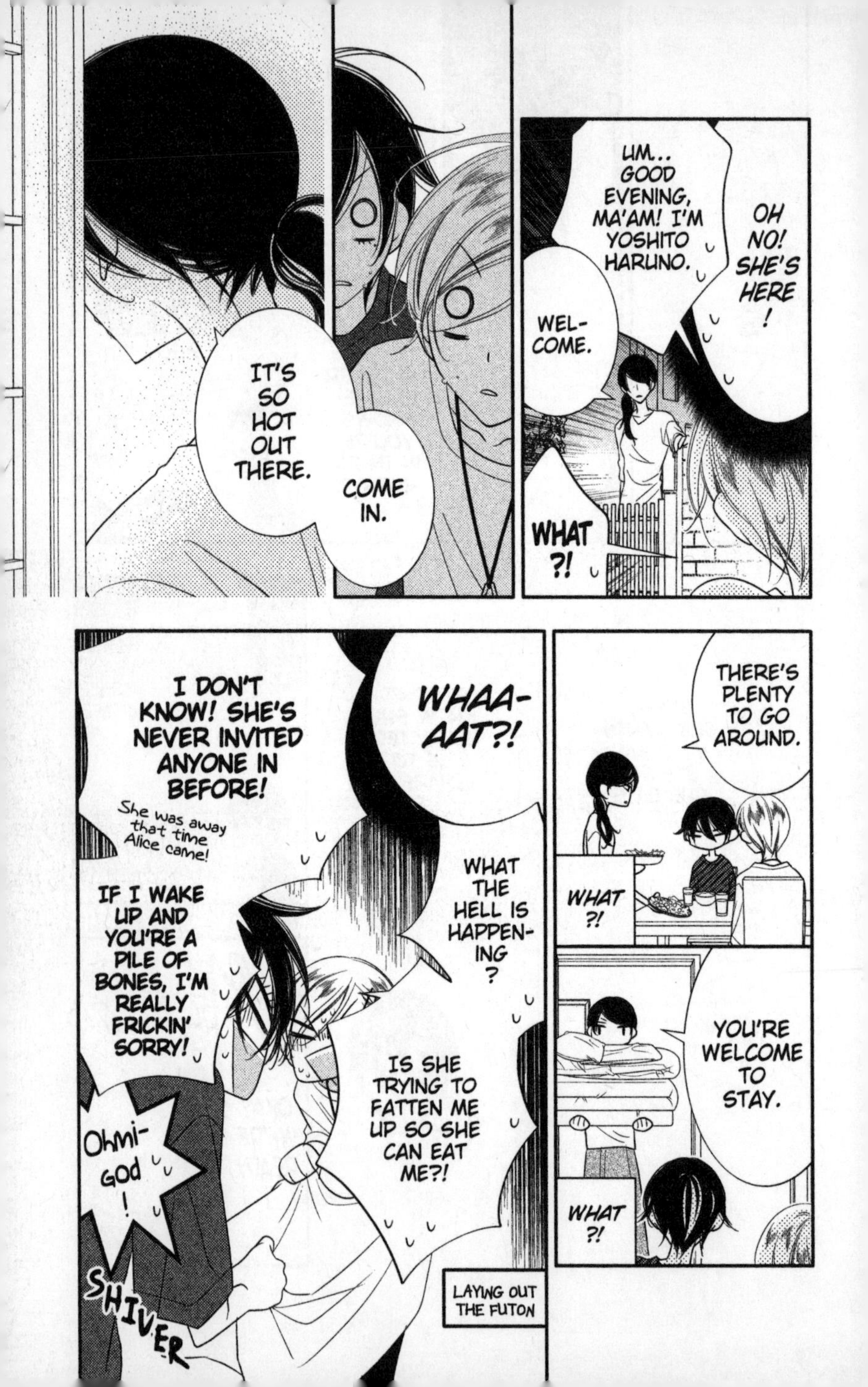
OH NO! SHE'S HERE!
UM... GOOD EVENING, MA'AM! I'M YOSHITO HARUNO.
WEL-COME.
WHAT?!
IT'S SO HOT OUT THERE.
COME IN.
THERE'S PLENTY TO GO AROUND.
WHAT?!
YOU'RE WELCOME TO STAY.
WHAT?!
WHAA-AAT?!
I DON'T KNOW! SHE'S NEVER INVITED ANYONE IN BEFORE!
She was away that time Alice came!
WHAT THE HELL IS HAPPEN-ING?
IF I WAKE UP AND YOU'RE A PILE OF BONES, I'M REALLY FRICKIN' SORRY!
IS SHE TRYING TO FATTEN ME UP SO SHE CAN EAT ME?!
Ohmi-god!
SHIVER
LAYING OUT THE FUTON

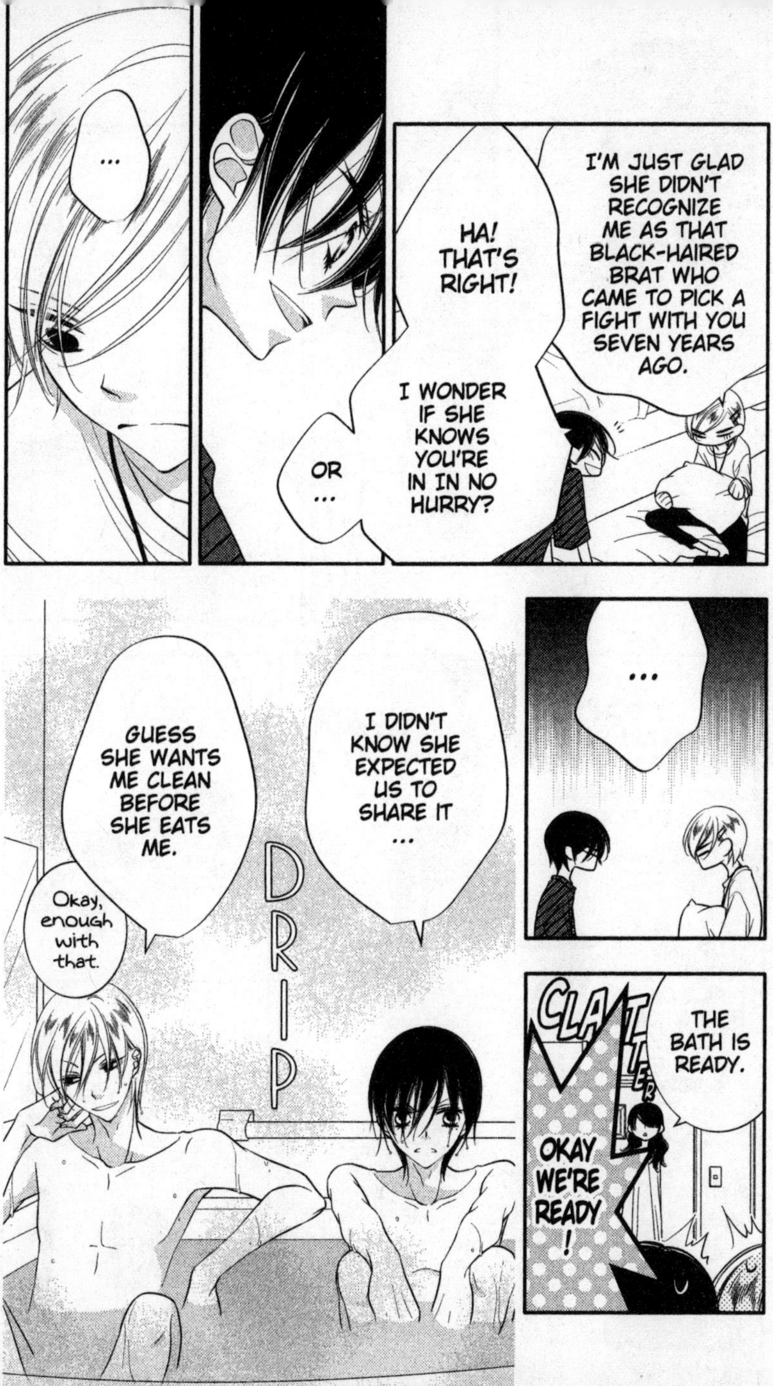

I'M JUST GLAD SHE DIDN'T RECOGNIZE ME AS THAT BLACK-HAIRED BRAT WHO CAME TO PICK A FIGHT WITH YOU SEVEN YEARS AGO.
HA! THAT'S RIGHT!
I WONDER IF SHE KNOWS YOU'RE IN IN NO HURRY?
OR ...
...
...
CLATTER
THE BATH IS READY.
OKAY WE'RE READY!
I DIDN'T KNOW SHE EXPECTED US TO SHARE IT ...
DRIP
GUESS SHE WANTS ME CLEAN BEFORE SHE EATS ME.
Okay, enough with that.

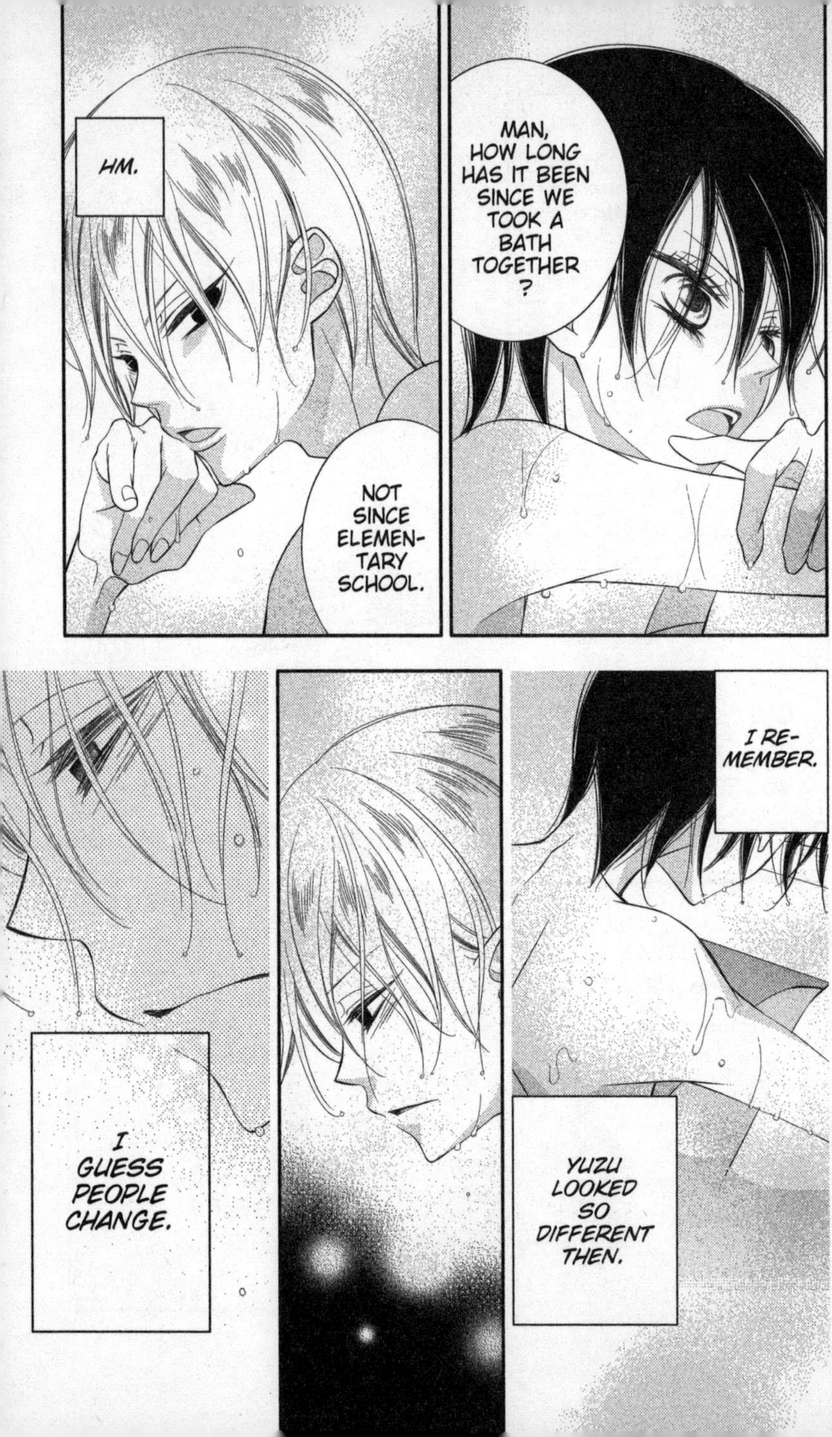
MAN, HOW LONG HAS IT BEEN SINCE WE TOOK A BATH TOGETHER?
HM.
NOT SINCE ELEMEN-TARY SCHOOL.
I RE-MEMBER.
YUZU LOOKED SO DIFFERENT THEN.
I GUESS PEOPLE CHANGE.

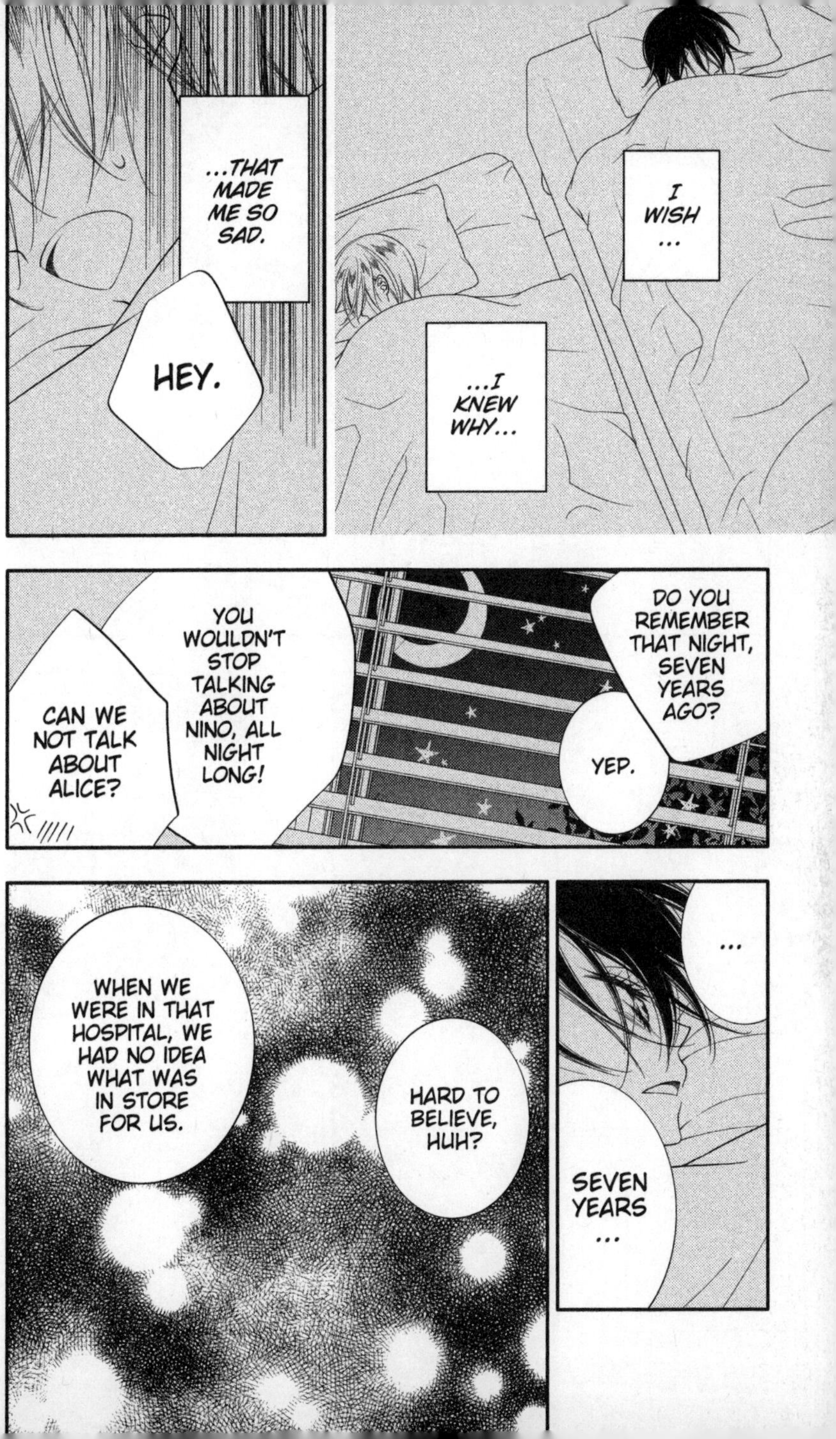
I WISH...
...I KNEW WHY...
...THAT MADE ME SO SAD.
HEY.
DO YOU REMEMBER THAT NIGHT, SEVEN YEARS AGO?
YEP.
YOU WOULDN'T STOP TALKING ABOUT NINO, ALL NIGHT LONG!
CAN WE NOT TALK ABOUT ALICE?
...
SEVEN YEARS...
WHEN WE WERE IN THAT HOSPITAL, WE HAD NO IDEA WHAT WAS IN STORE FOR US.
HARD TO BELIEVE, HUH?

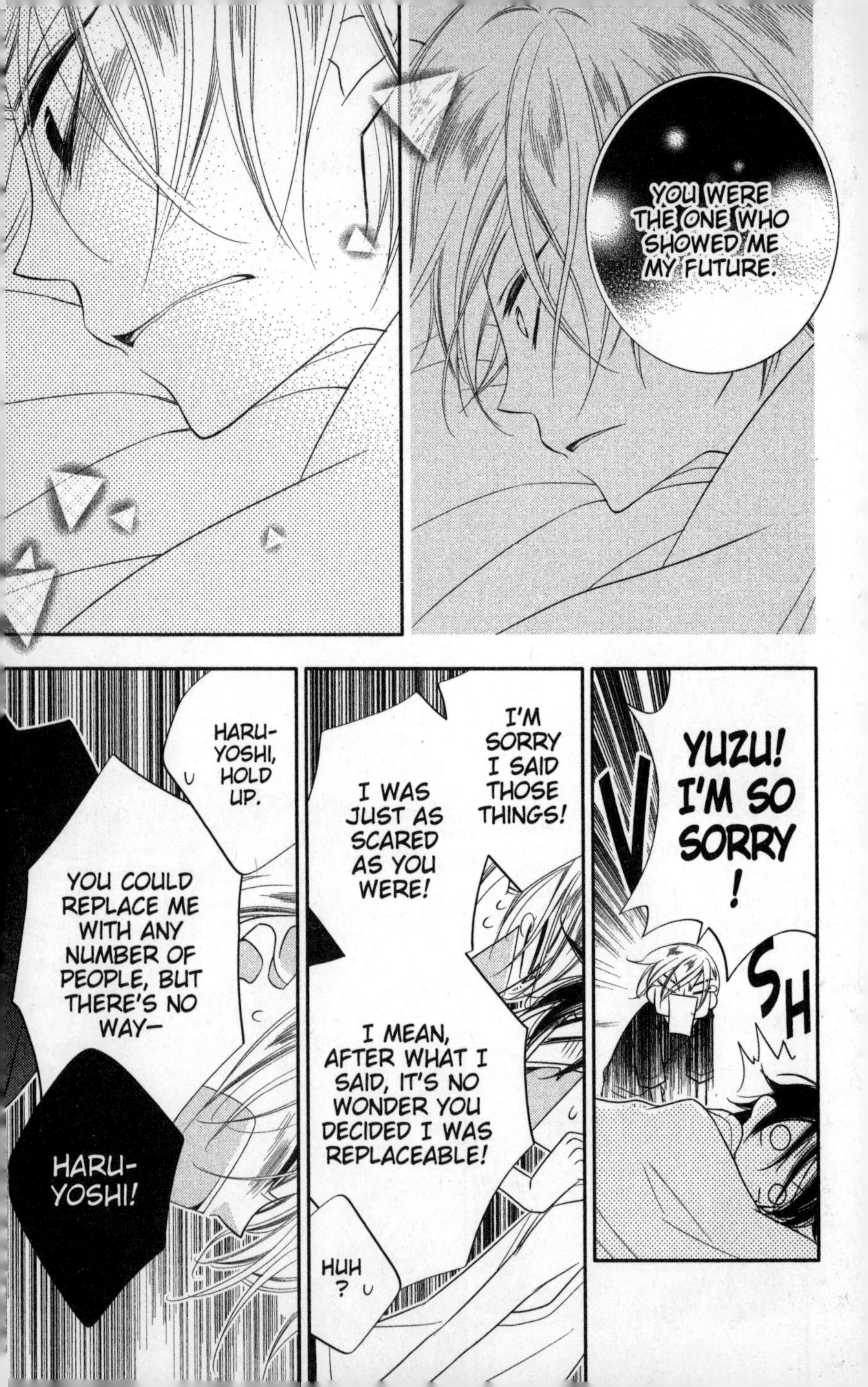
YOU WERE THE ONE WHO SHOWED ME MY FUTURE.
YUZU! I'M SO SORRY!
SH
I'M SORRY I SAID THOSE THINGS!
I WAS JUST AS SCARED AS YOU WERE!
I MEAN, AFTER WHAT I SAID, IT'S NO WONDER YOU DECIDED I WAS REPLACEABLE!
HUH?
HARU-YOSHI, HOLD UP.
YOU COULD REPLACE ME WITH ANY NUMBER OF PEOPLE, BUT THERE'S NO WAY–
HARU-YOSHI!

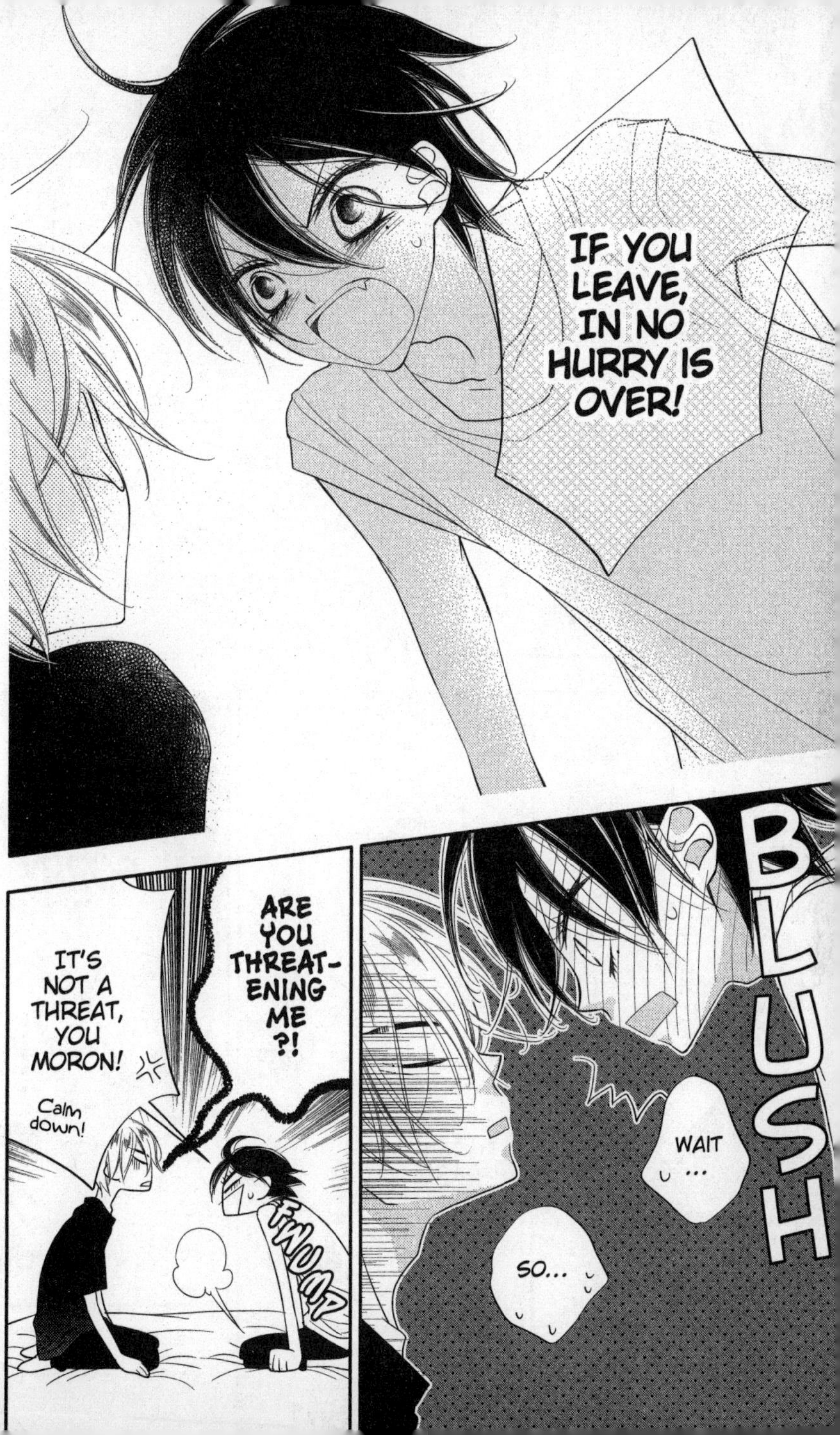
IF YOU LEAVE, IN NO HURRY IS OVER!
BLUSH
WAIT...
SO...
ARE YOU THREAT-ENING ME?!
IT'S NOT A THREAT, YOU MORON!
Calm down!
FWUMP

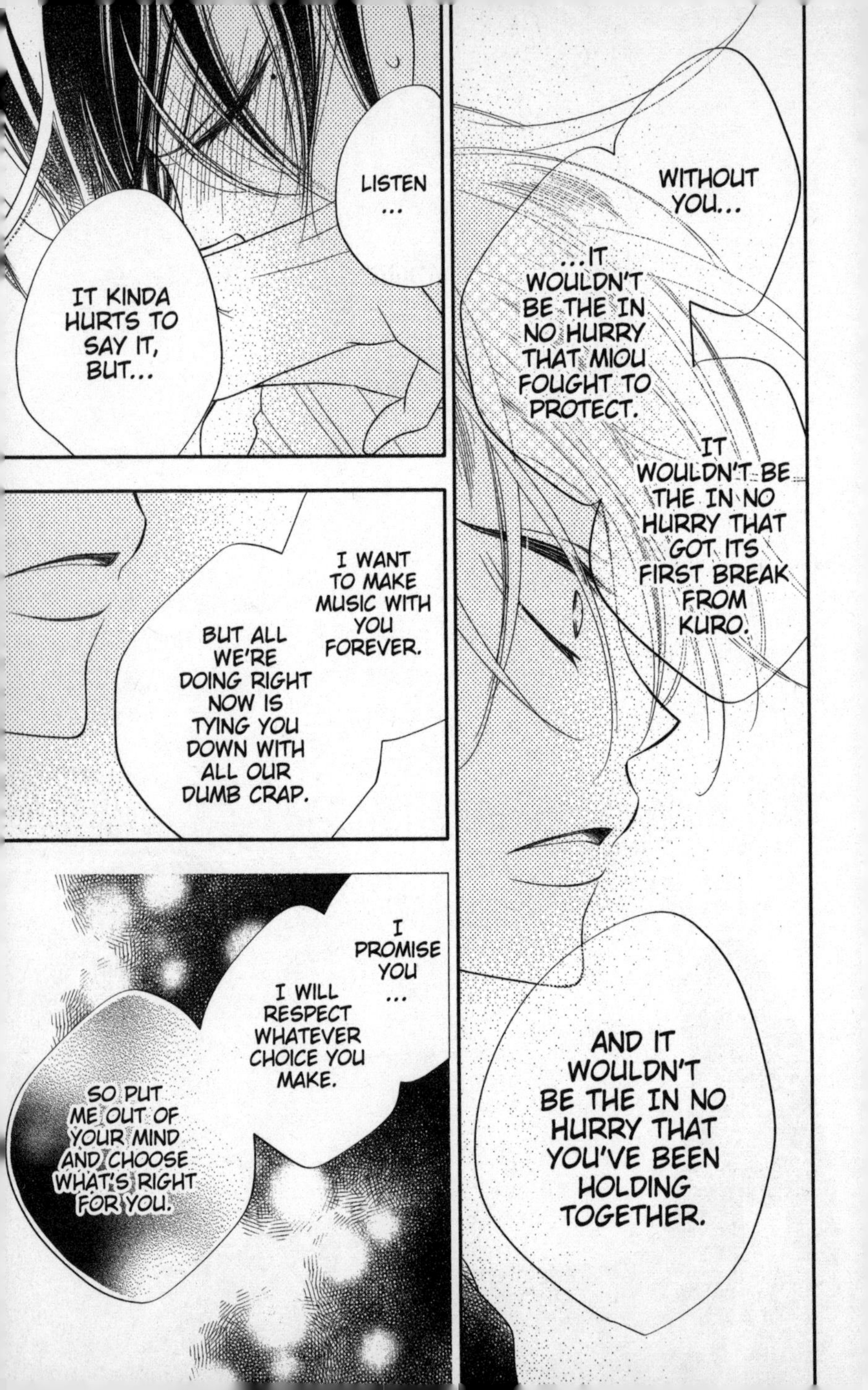
WITHOUT YOU...
...IT WOULDN'T BE THE IN NO HURRY THAT MIOU FOUGHT TO PROTECT.
IT WOULDN'T BE THE IN NO HURRY THAT GOT ITS FIRST BREAK FROM KURO.
AND IT WOULDN'T BE THE IN NO HURRY THAT YOU'VE BEEN HOLDING TOGETHER.
LISTEN ...
IT KINDA HURTS TO SAY IT, BUT...
I WANT TO MAKE MUSIC WITH YOU FOREVER.
BUT ALL WE'RE DOING RIGHT NOW IS TYING YOU DOWN WITH ALL OUR DUMB CRAP.
I PROMISE YOU ...
I WILL RESPECT WHATEVER CHOICE YOU MAKE.
SO PUT ME OUT OF YOUR MIND AND CHOOSE WHAT'S RIGHT FOR YOU.

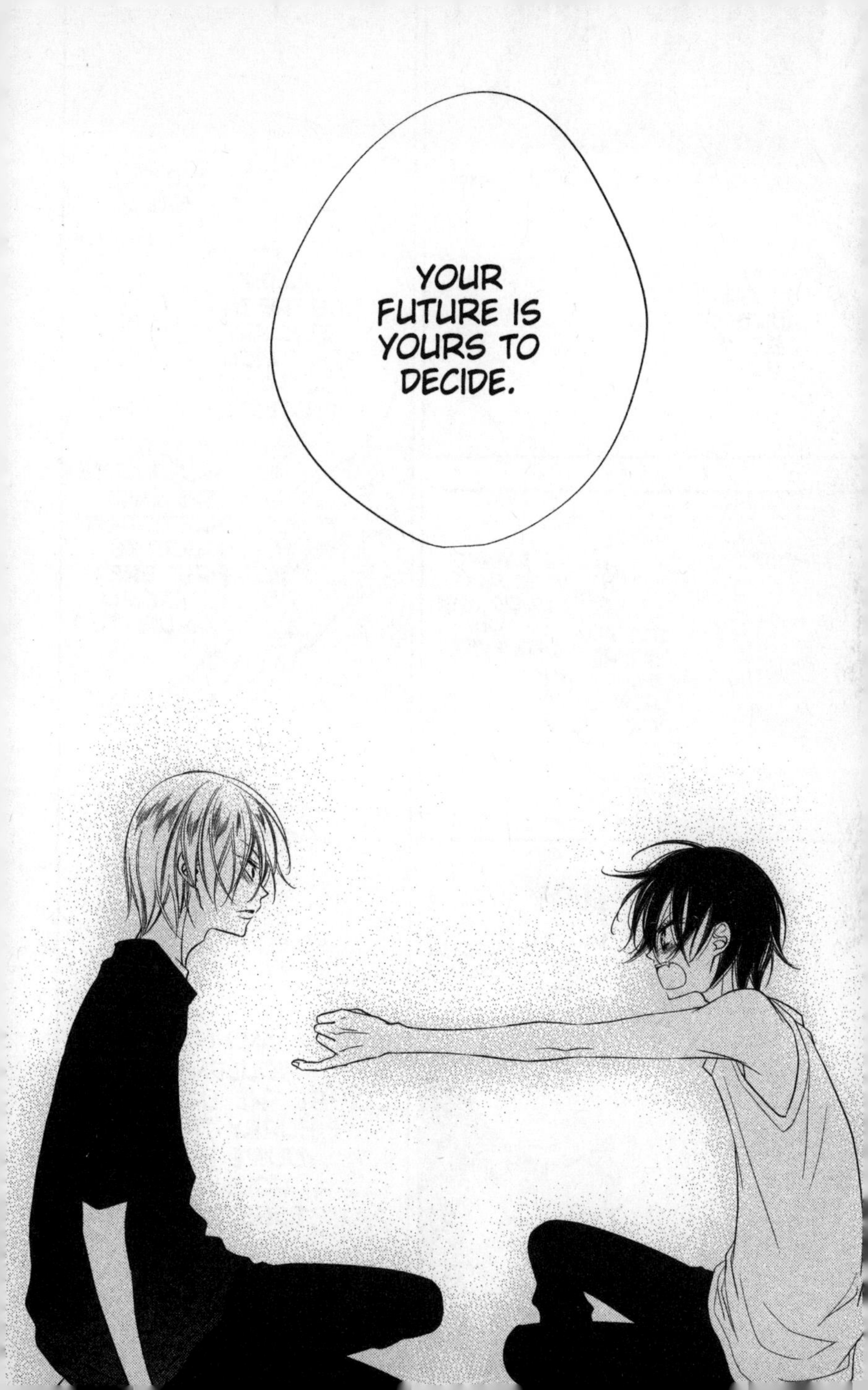
YOUR FUTURE IS YOURS TO DECIDE.

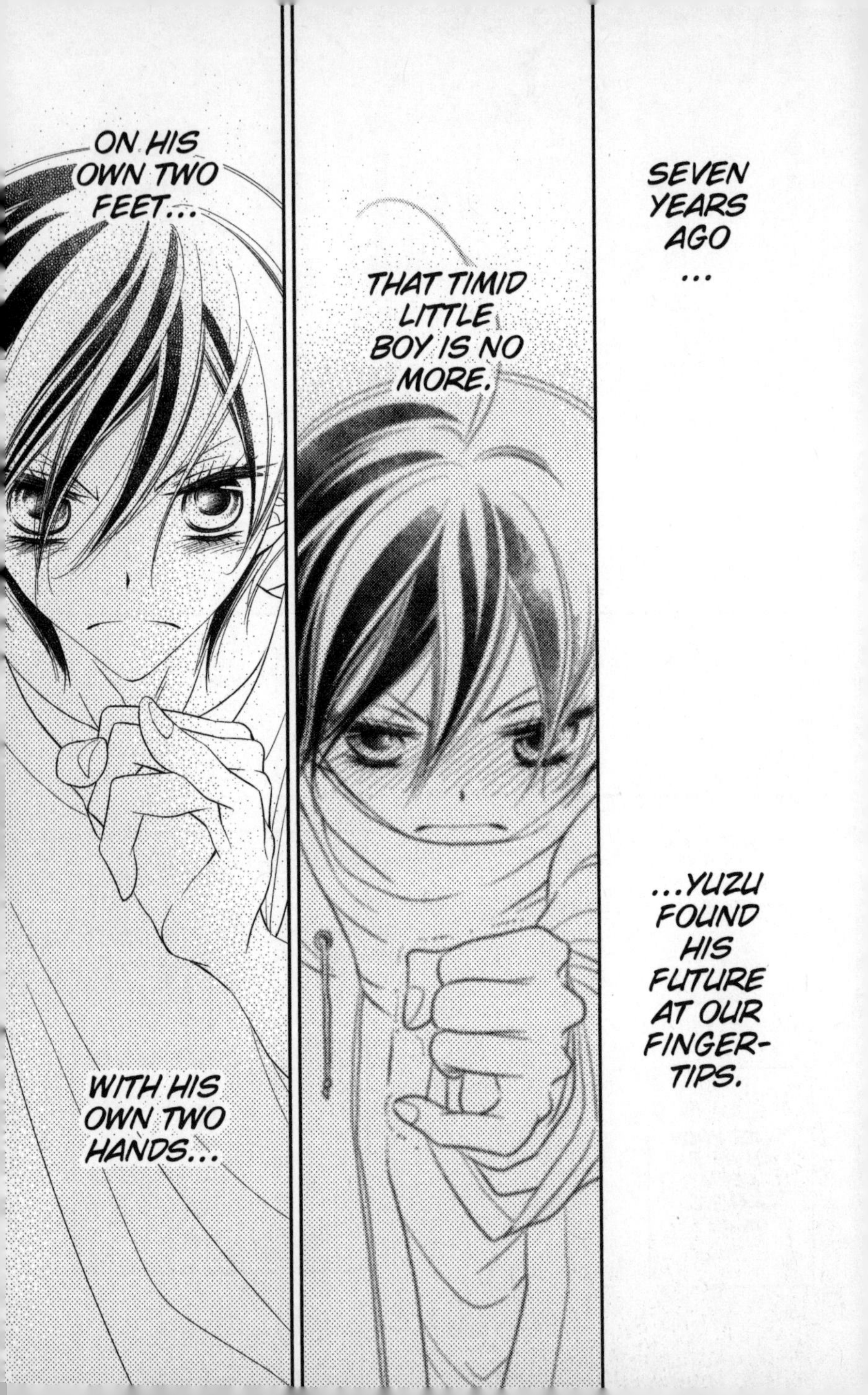
SEVEN YEARS AGO ...
...YUZU FOUND HIS FUTURE AT OUR FINGER-TIPS.
THAT TIMID LITTLE BOY IS NO MORE.
ON HIS OWN TWO FEET...
WITH HIS OWN TWO HANDS...

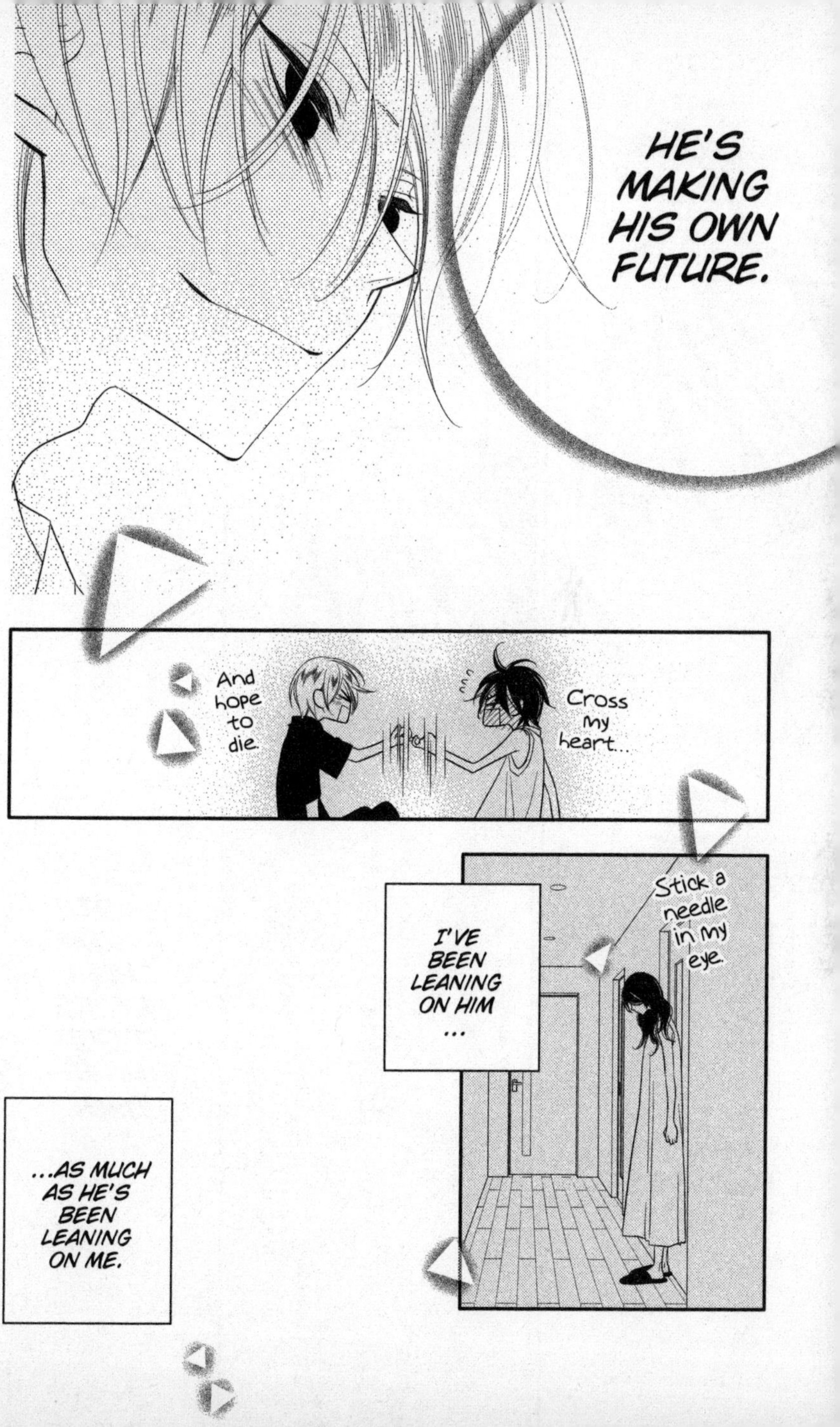
HE'S MAKING HIS OWN FUTURE.
Cross my heart...
And hope to die.
Stick a needle in my eye.
I'VE BEEN LEANING ON HIM ...
...AS MUCH AS HE'S BEEN LEANING ON ME.

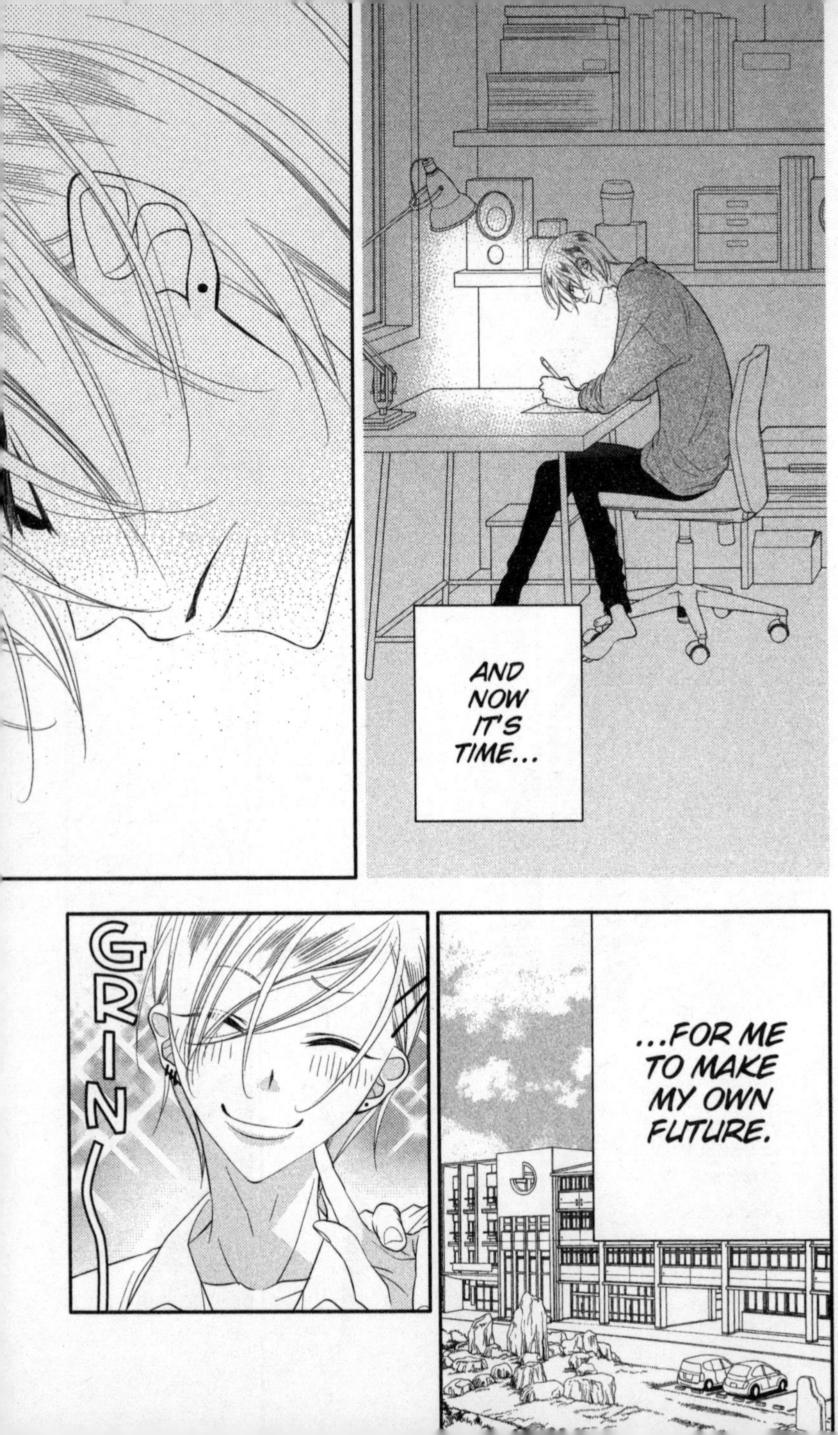
AND NOW IT'S TIME...
...FOR ME TO MAKE MY OWN FUTURE.
GRIN

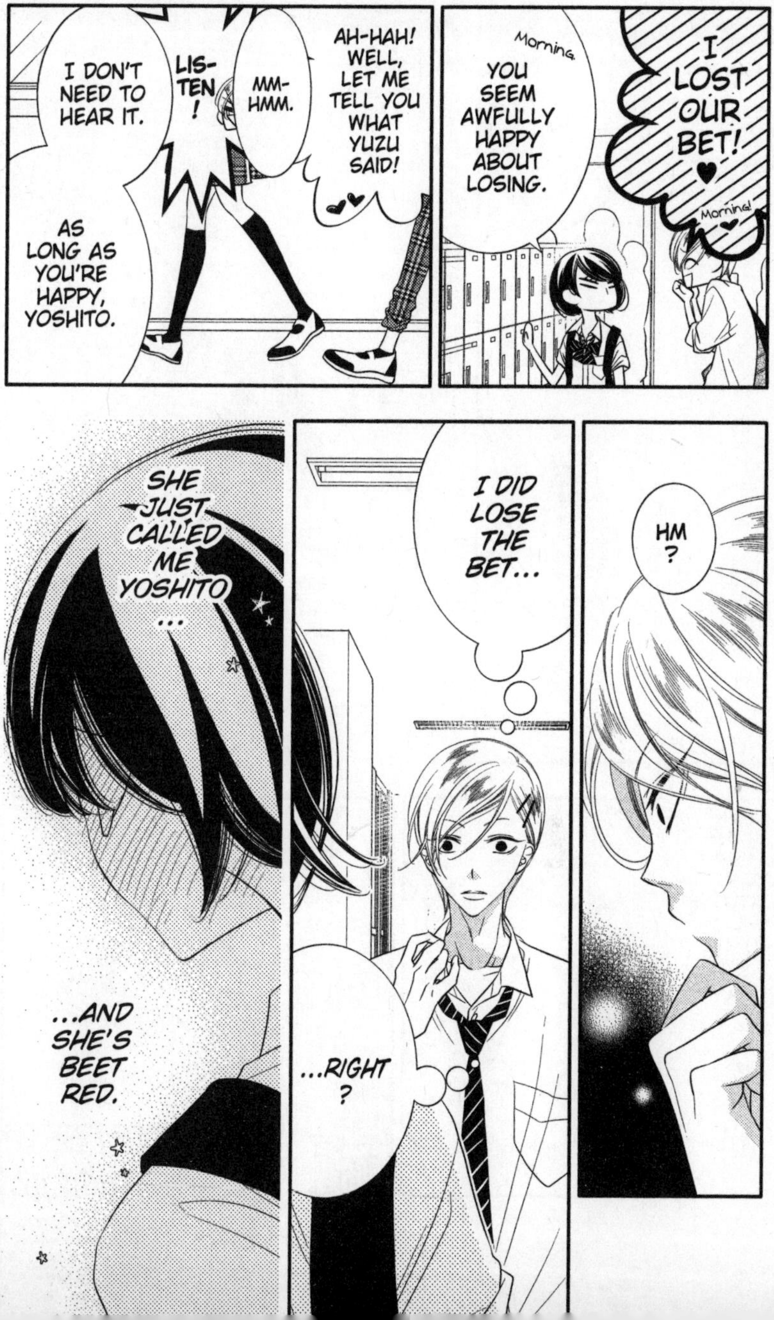

I LOST OUR BET! ♥
Morning! ♥
Morning.
YOU SEEM AWFULLY HAPPY ABOUT LOSING.
AH-HAH! WELL, LET ME TELL YOU WHAT YUZU SAID!
MM-HMM.
LIS-TEN!
I DON'T NEED TO HEAR IT.
AS LONG AS YOU'RE HAPPY, YOSHITO.
HM?
I DID LOSE THE BET...
...RIGHT?
SHE JUST CALLED ME YOSHITO...
...AND SHE'S BEET RED.

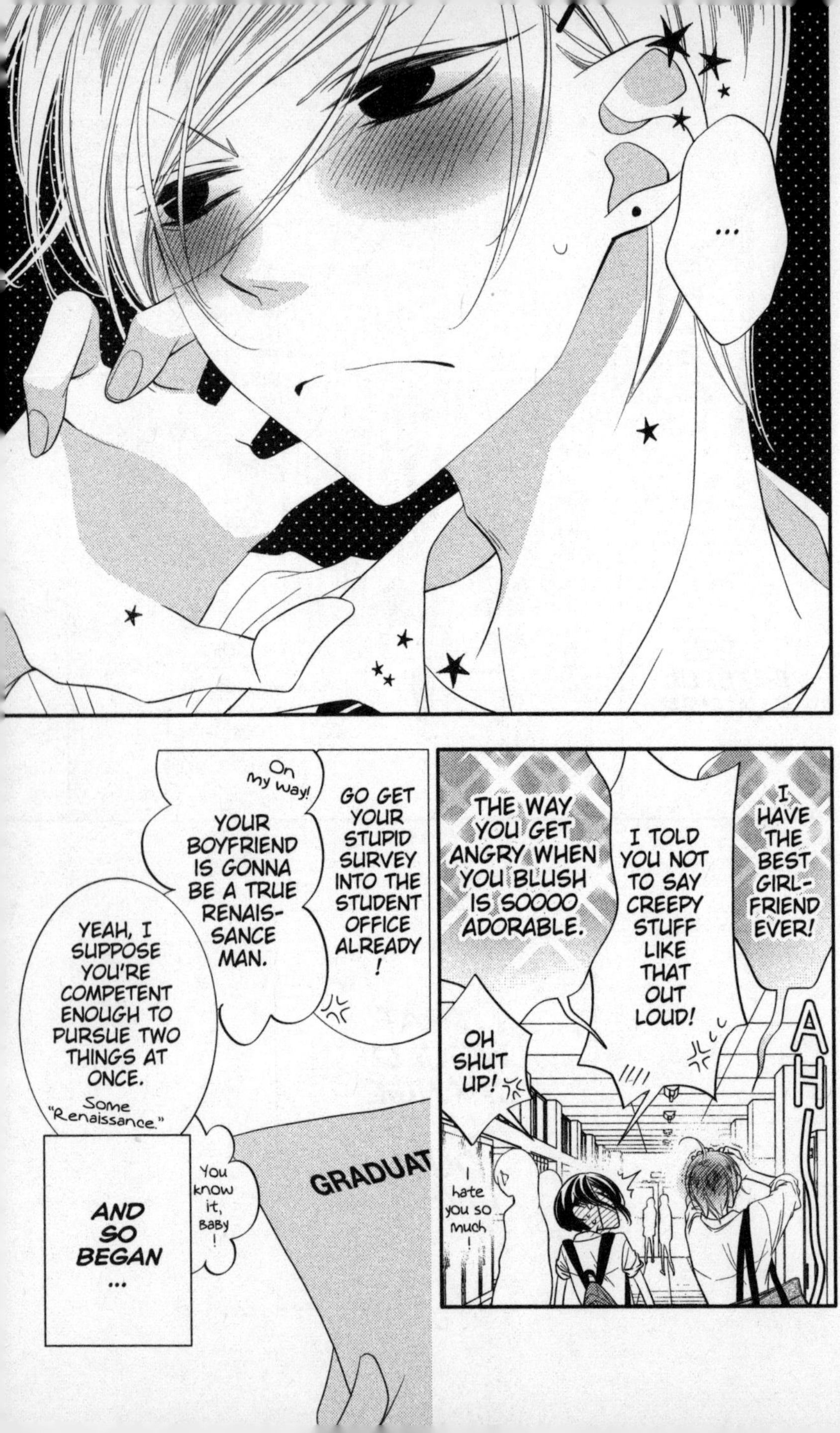
...
I HAVE THE BEST GIRLFRIEND EVER!
AH!
I TOLD YOU NOT TO SAY CREEPY STUFF LIKE THAT OUT LOUD!
THE WAY YOU GET ANGRY WHEN YOU BLUSH IS SOOOO ADORABLE.
OH SHUT UP!
I hate you so much!
GO GET YOUR STUPID SURVEY INTO THE STUDENT OFFICE ALREADY!
On my way!
YOUR BOYFRIEND IS GONNA BE A TRUE RENAISSANCE MAN.
YEAH, I SUPPOSE YOU'RE COMPETENT ENOUGH TO PURSUE TWO THINGS AT ONCE.
Some "Renaissance."
You know it, baby!
GRADUAT
AND SO BEGAN ...

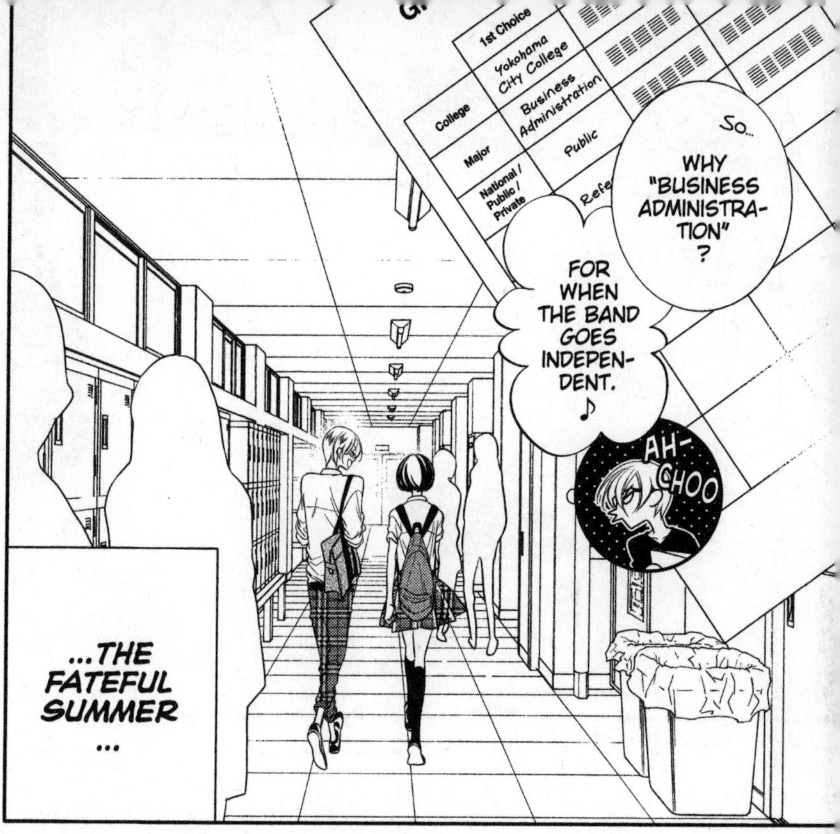
1st Choice
College
Yokohama City College
Major
Business Administration
National / Public / Private
Public
So...
WHY "BUSINESS ADMINISTRATION"?
FOR WHEN THE BAND GOES INDEPENDENT. ♪
AH-CHOO
...THE FATEFUL SUMMER...

...THAT WOULD CHANGE ALL OF OUR LIVES.

SONG 80

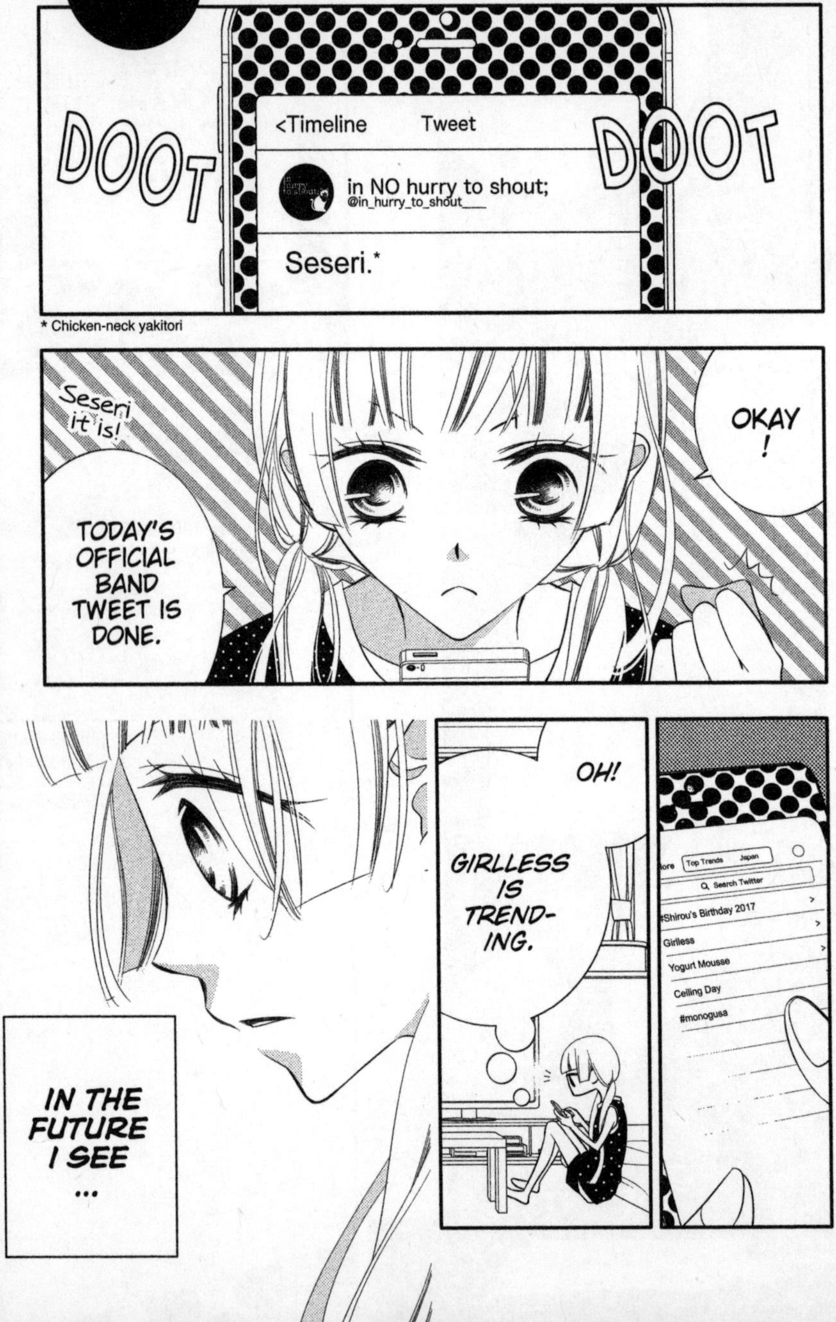
DOOT
DOOT
<Timeline Tweet
in NO hurry to shout;
@in_hurry_to_shout___
Seseri.*
OKAY!
Seseri it is!
TODAY'S OFFICIAL BAND TWEET IS DONE.
Top Trends Japan
Search Twitter
#Shirou's Birthday 2017
Girlless
Yogurt Mousse
Ceiling Day
#monogusa
OH!
GIRLLESS IS TRENDING.
IN THE FUTURE I SEE ...

* Chicken-neck yakitori

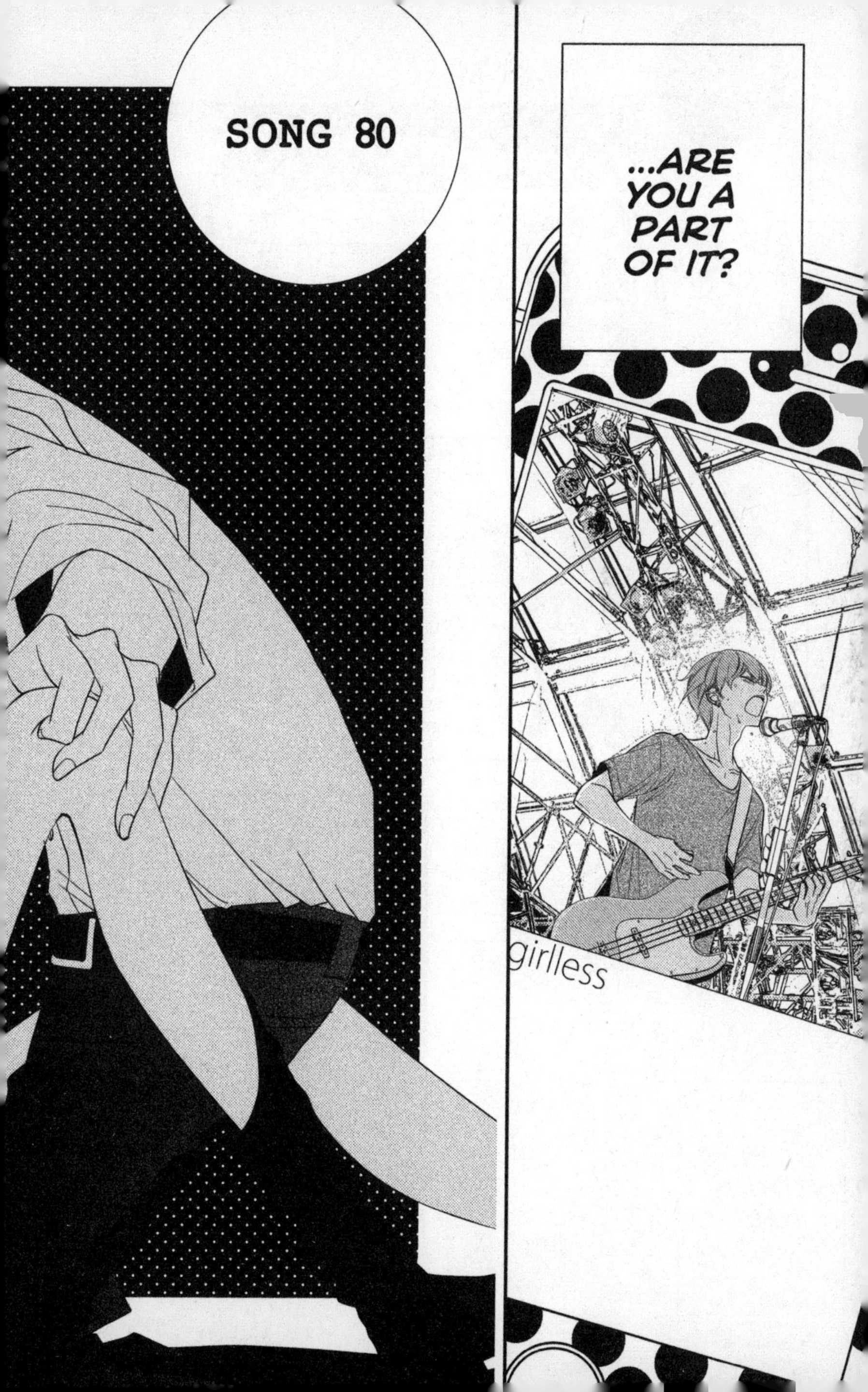
...ARE YOU A PART OF IT?
girlless
SONG 80

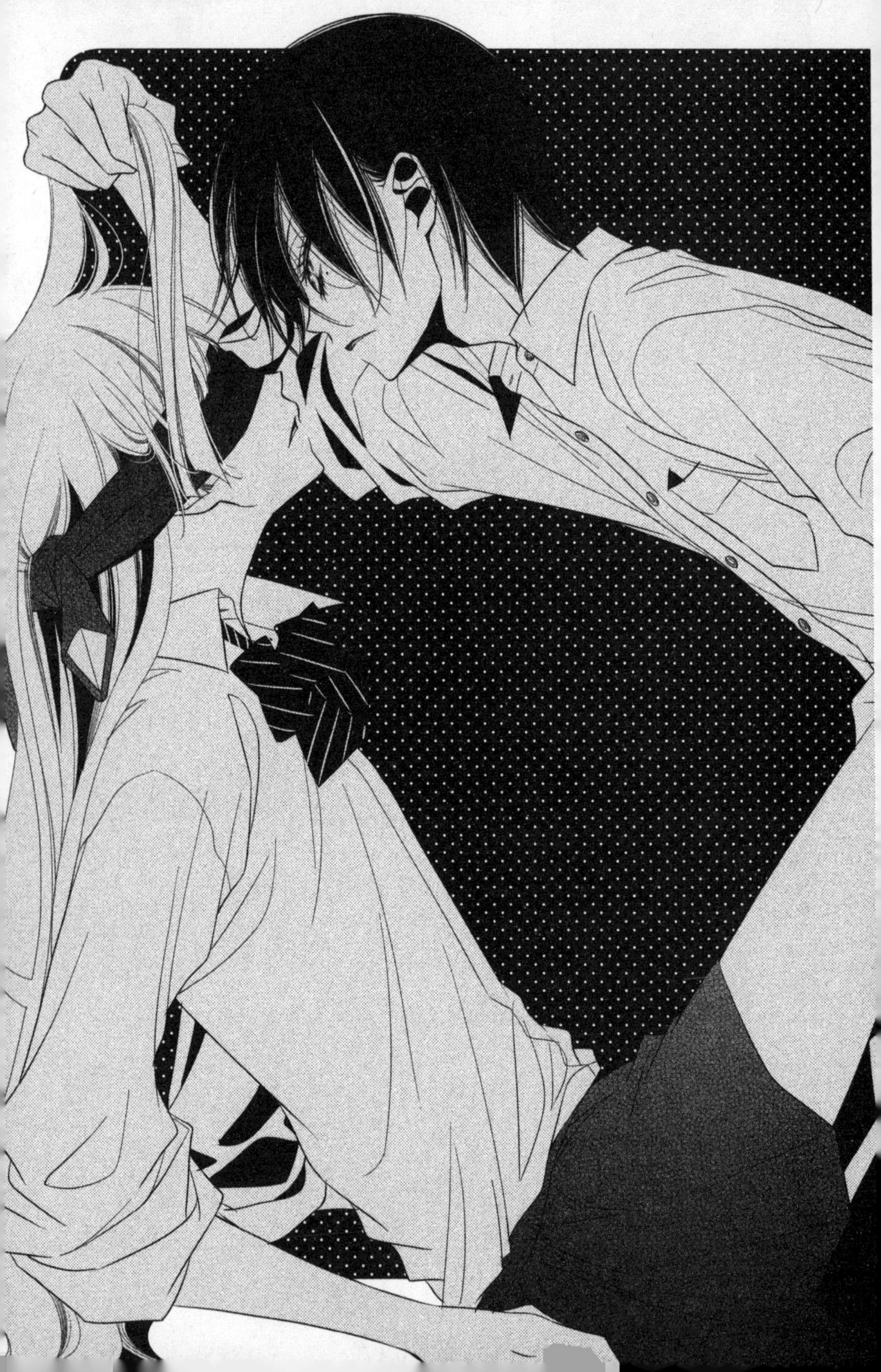

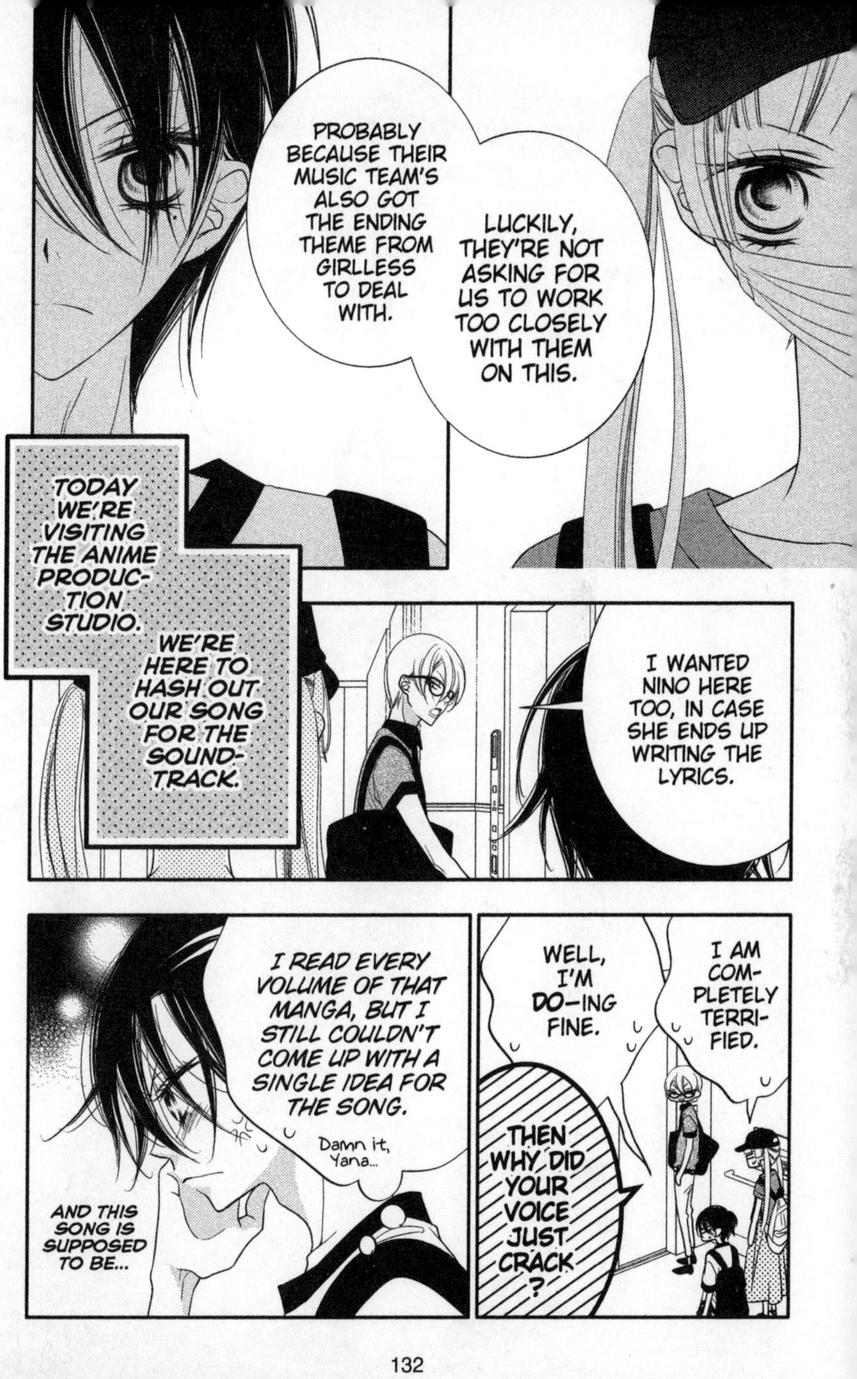
LUCKILY, THEY'RE NOT ASKING FOR US TO WORK TOO CLOSELY WITH THEM ON THIS.
PROBABLY BECAUSE THEIR MUSIC TEAM'S ALSO GOT THE ENDING THEME FROM GIRLLESS TO DEAL WITH.
TODAY WE'RE VISITING THE ANIME PRODUC-TION STUDIO.
WE'RE HERE TO HASH OUT OUR SONG FOR THE SOUND-TRACK.
I WANTED NINO HERE TOO, IN CASE SHE ENDS UP WRITING THE LYRICS.
I AM COM-PLETELY TERRI-FIED.
WELL, I'M DO-ING FINE.
THEN WHY DID YOUR VOICE JUST CRACK?
I READ EVERY VOLUME OF THAT MANGA, BUT I STILL COULDN'T COME UP WITH A SINGLE IDEA FOR THE SONG.
Damn it, Yana...
AND THIS SONG IS SUPPOSED TO BE...

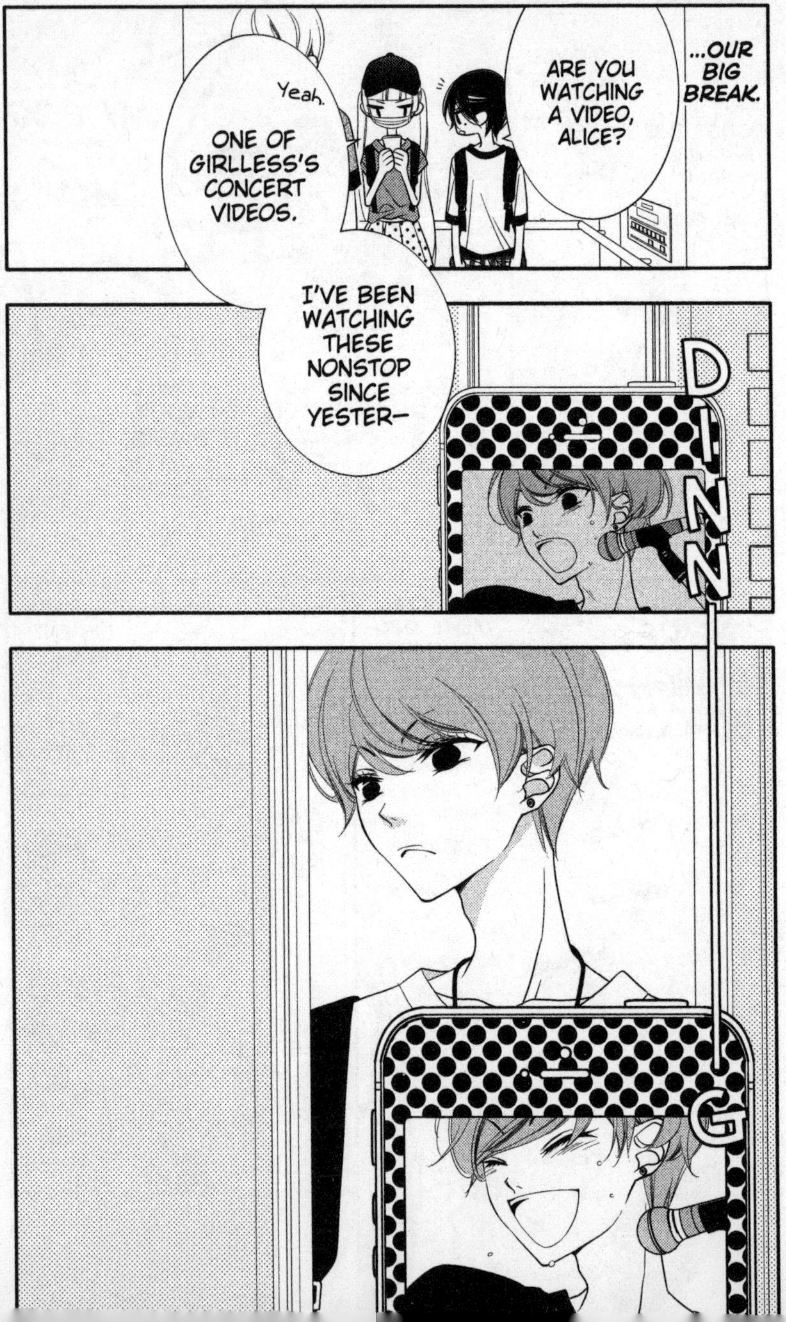
...OUR BIG BREAK.
ARE YOU WATCHING A VIDEO, ALICE?
Yeah.
ONE OF GIRLLESS'S CONCERT VIDEOS.
I'VE BEEN WATCHING THESE NONSTOP SINCE YESTER—
DINNG

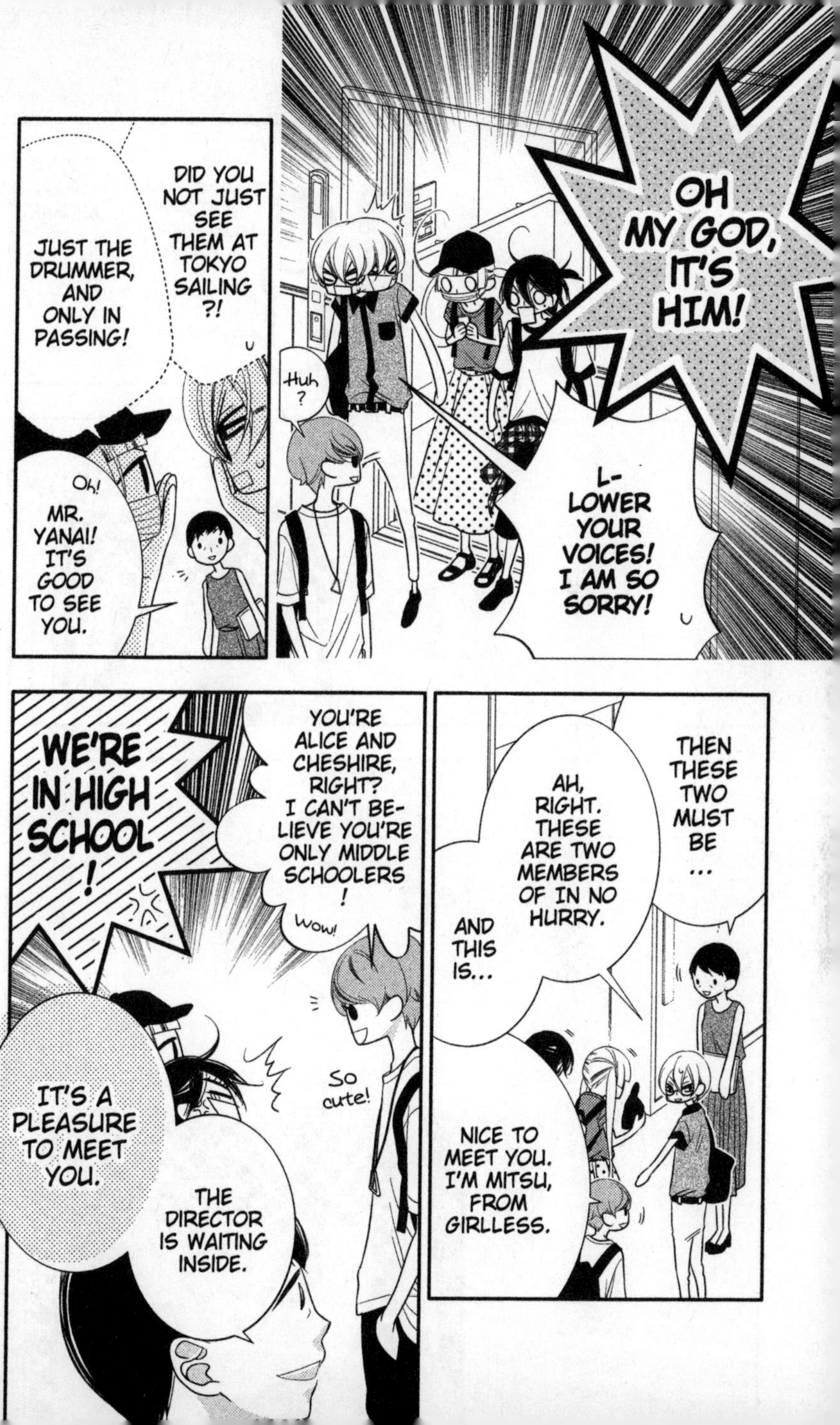
OH MY GOD, IT'S HIM!
Huh?
L-LOWER YOUR VOICES! I AM SO SORRY!
DID YOU NOT JUST SEE THEM AT TOKYO SAILING?!
JUST THE DRUMMER, AND ONLY IN PASSING!
Oh!
MR. YANAI! IT'S GOOD TO SEE YOU.
THEN THESE TWO MUST BE ...
AH, RIGHT. THESE ARE TWO MEMBERS OF IN NO HURRY.
AND THIS IS...
NICE TO MEET YOU. I'M MITSU, FROM GIRLLESS.
YOU'RE ALICE AND CHESHIRE, RIGHT? I CAN'T BELIEVE YOU'RE ONLY MIDDLE SCHOOLERS!
Wow!
WE'RE IN HIGH SCHOOL!
So cute!
THE DIRECTOR IS WAITING INSIDE.
IT'S A PLEASURE TO MEET YOU.

TWO HOURS LATER
GLOOM
I STILL HAVE SOME BUSINESS HERE, SO YOU GUYS HEAD ON BACK.
Okay.
YEAH.
YOU LOOK LIKE DEATH. DID YOU DRINK TOO MUCH MILK?
Tummy hurt?
NOT TAKING THE BAIT
I'VE NEVER HAD TO WRITE AN IN NO HURRY SONG BASED ON A PREDETERMINED THEME BEFORE! IT'S TOO MUCH PRESSURE!
I mean, the deadline's set in stone!
SIGH
AND I HAVEN'T WRITTEN ANYTHING IN MONTHS.

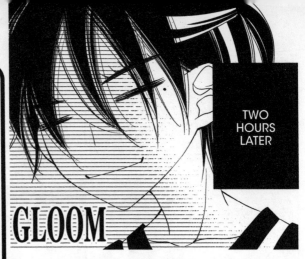

5

So once again, I took a research trip to Rock in Japan 2017! This was the fourth year in a row? I think? And once again, I had a total blast! The weather was perfect—the cloud cover kept the temperature down, and the sea breeze felt amazing as I ran around taking my reference photos.
I won't soon forget dining on Ibaraki craft sake and abalone with my new editor... It was sooo good. And this year, for the first time, we just set up on the grass and stayed there. (Because it felt too good to leave.) It was so much fun. I can't wait to go back!
I really have no interest in anything related to the outdoors, but festivals are the one exception. Probably because of the music—as long as music is the focus, I can enjoy myself anywhere. My sincerest thanks to the organizers. I hope they'll have me back next year!

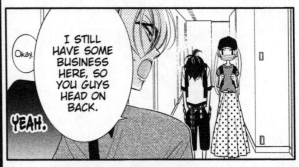

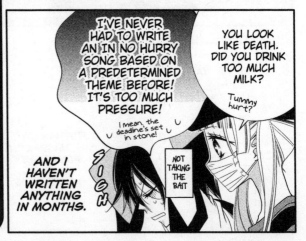

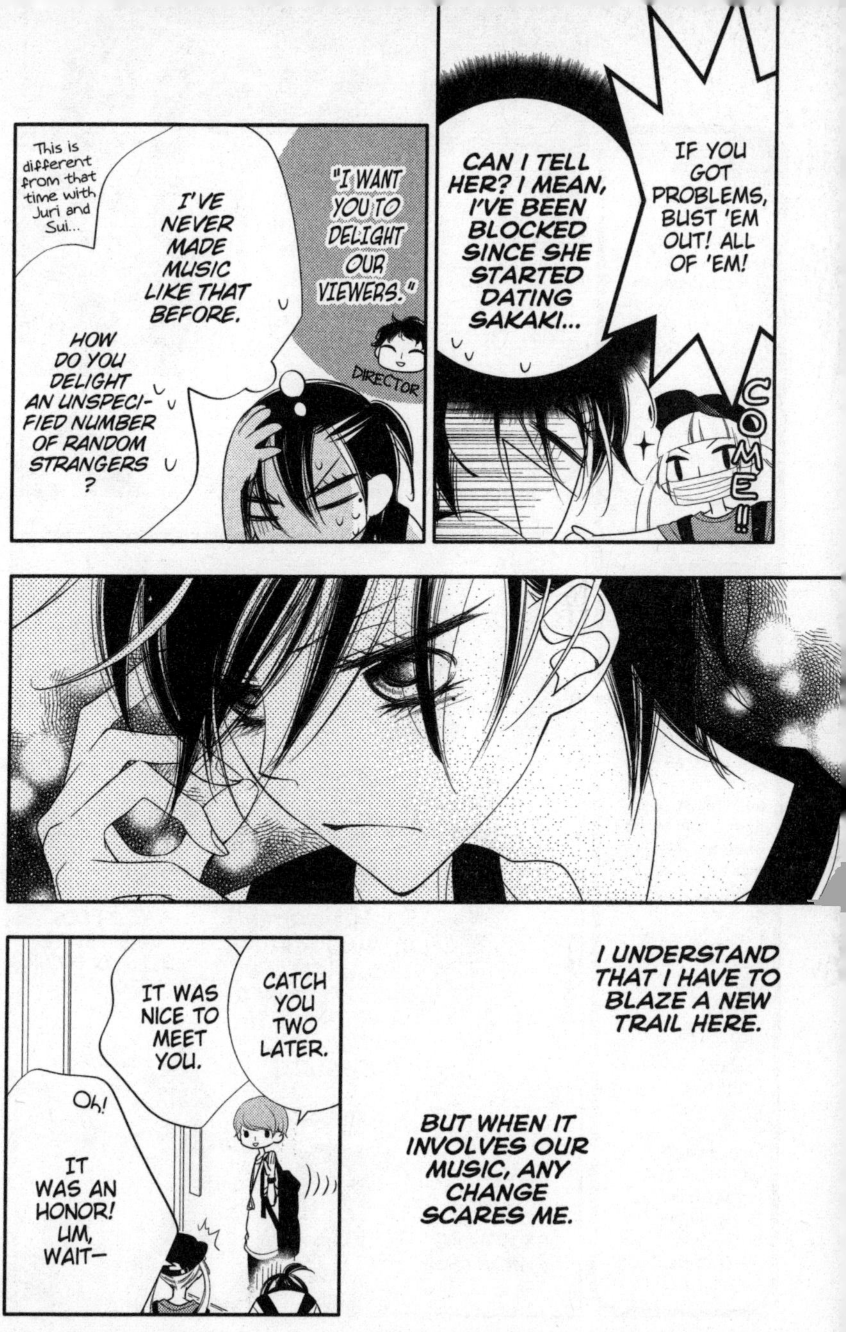
IF YOU GOT PROBLEMS, BUST 'EM OUT! ALL OF 'EM!
CAN I TELL HER? I MEAN, I'VE BEEN BLOCKED SINCE SHE STARTED DATING SAKAKI...
COME!!
"I WANT YOU TO DELIGHT OUR VIEWERS."
DIRECTOR
I'VE NEVER MADE MUSIC LIKE THAT BEFORE.
This is different from that time with Juri and Sui...
HOW DO YOU DELIGHT AN UNSPECIFIED NUMBER OF RANDOM STRANGERS?
I UNDERSTAND THAT I HAVE TO BLAZE A NEW TRAIL HERE.
BUT WHEN IT INVOLVES OUR MUSIC, ANY CHANGE SCARES ME.
CATCH YOU TWO LATER.
IT WAS NICE TO MEET YOU.
Oh!
IT WAS AN HONOR! UM, WAIT—

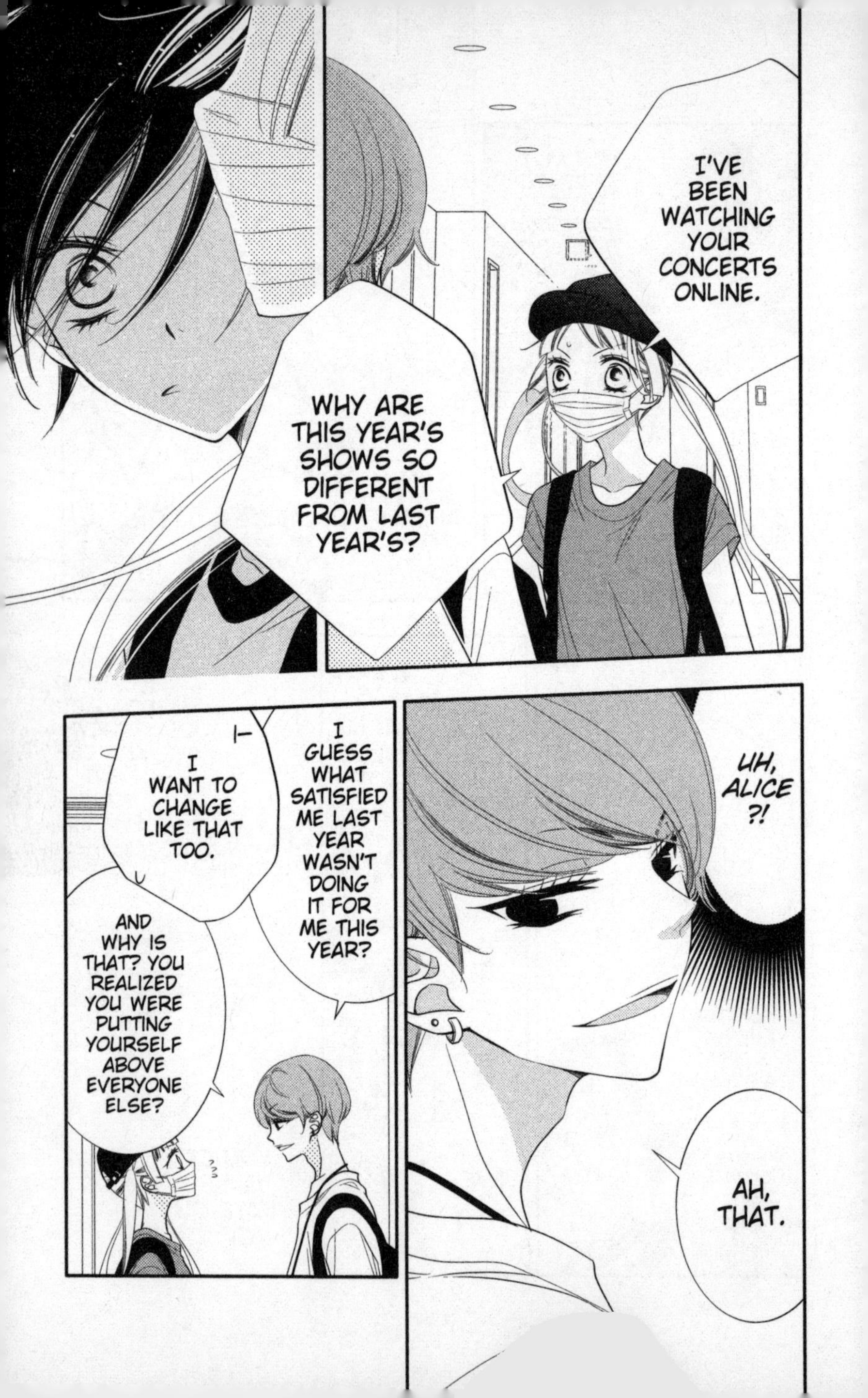
I'VE BEEN WATCHING YOUR CONCERTS ONLINE.
WHY ARE THIS YEAR'S SHOWS SO DIFFERENT FROM LAST YEAR'S?
UH, ALICE?!
AH, THAT.
I GUESS WHAT SATISFIED ME LAST YEAR WASN'T DOING IT FOR ME THIS YEAR?
I— I WANT TO CHANGE LIKE THAT TOO.
AND WHY IS THAT? YOU REALIZED YOU WERE PUTTING YOURSELF ABOVE EVERYONE ELSE?

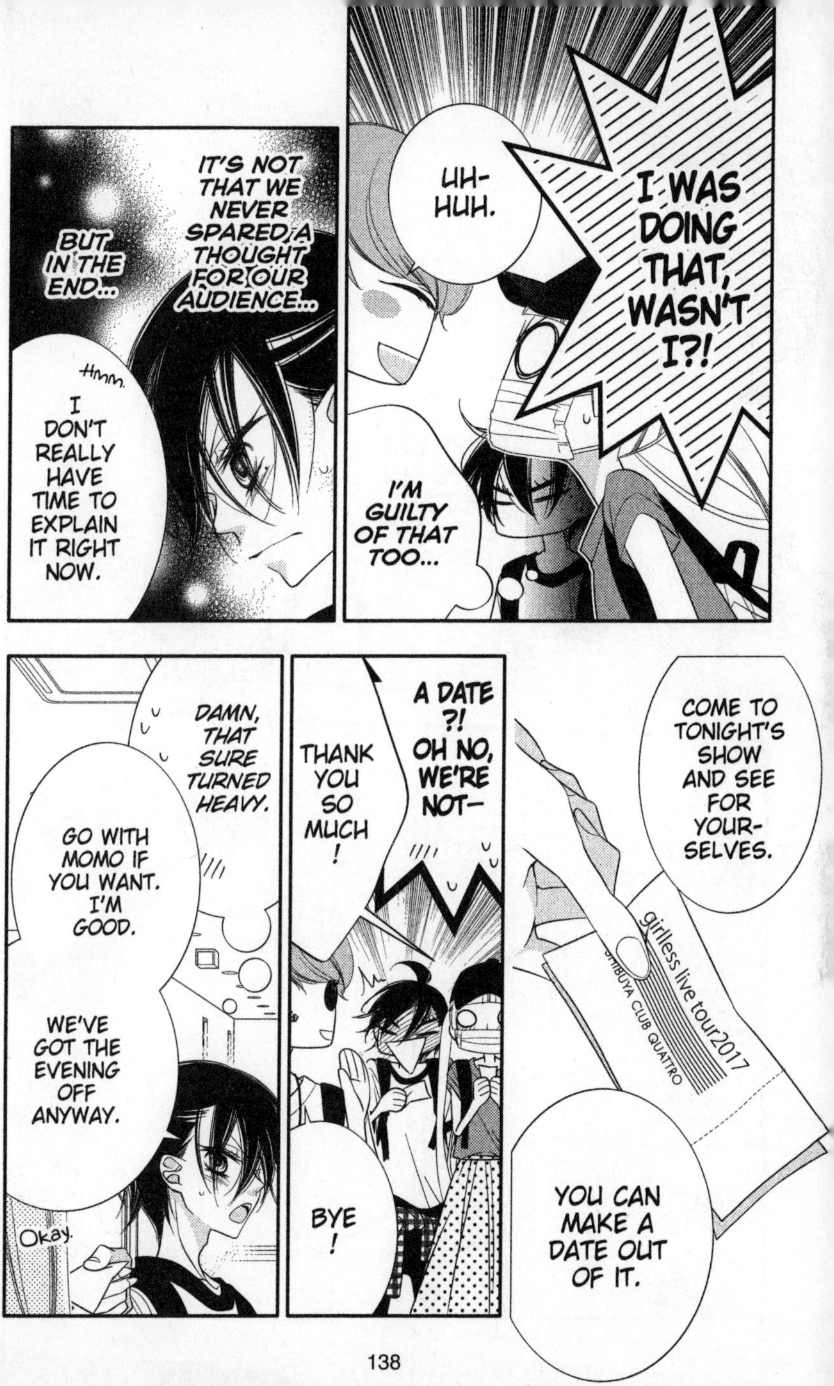

I WAS DOING THAT, WASN'T I?!
UH-HUH.
I'M GUILTY OF THAT TOO...
IT'S NOT THAT WE NEVER SPARED A THOUGHT FOR OUR AUDIENCE...
BUT IN THE END...
Hmm.
I DON'T REALLY HAVE TIME TO EXPLAIN IT RIGHT NOW.
COME TO TONIGHT'S SHOW AND SEE FOR YOURSELVES.
girlless live tour2017
SHIBUYA CLUB QUATTRO
YOU CAN MAKE A DATE OUT OF IT.
A DATE?! OH NO, WE'RE NOT—
THANK YOU SO MUCH!
BYE!
DAMN, THAT SURE TURNED HEAVY.
GO WITH MOMO IF YOU WANT. I'M GOOD.
WE'VE GOT THE EVENING OFF ANYWAY.
Okay.

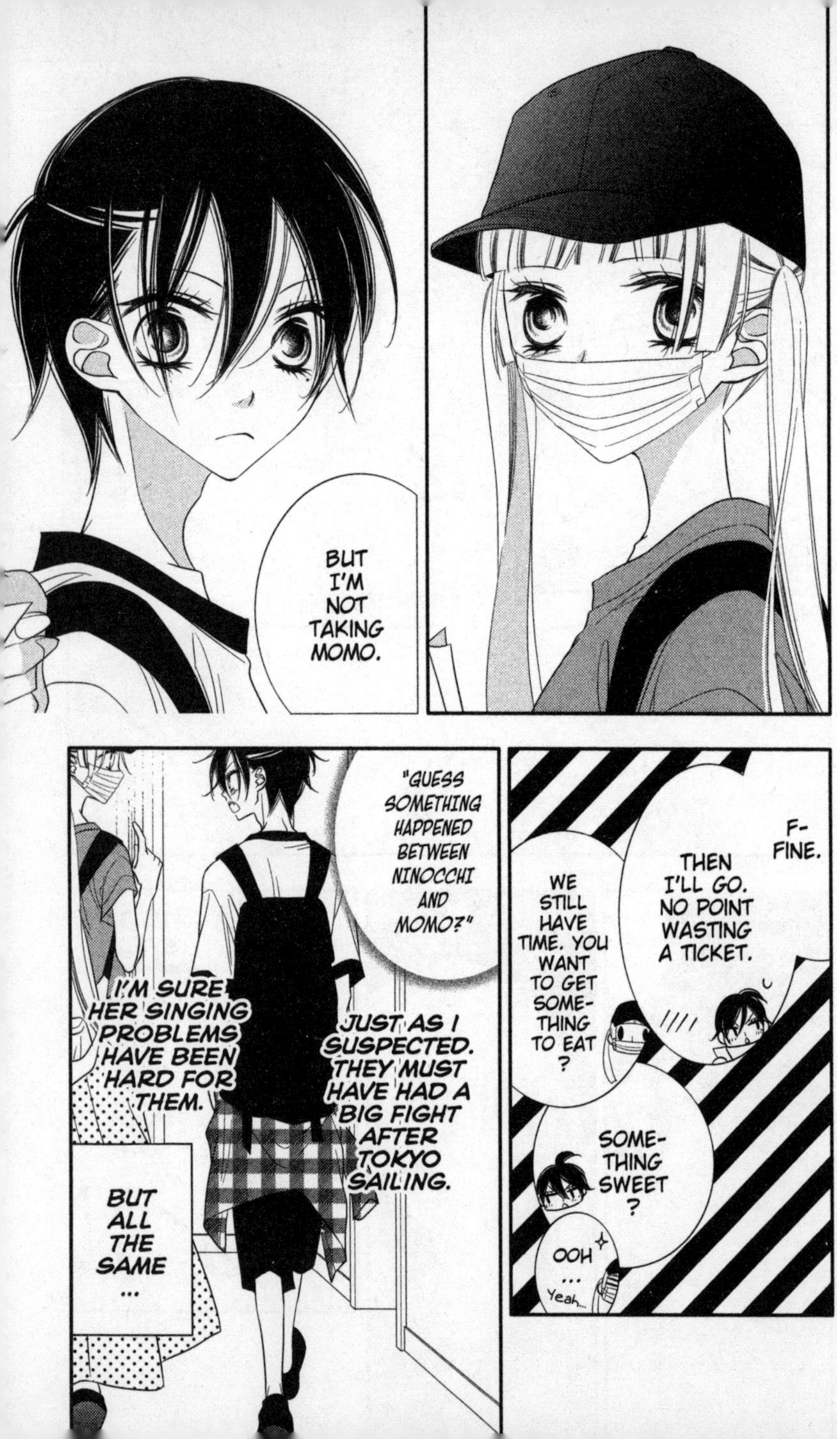
BUT I'M NOT TAKING MOMO.
F- FINE.
THEN I'LL GO. NO POINT WASTING A TICKET.
WE STILL HAVE TIME. YOU WANT TO GET SOME-THING TO EAT?
SOME-THING SWEET?
OOH...
Yeah...
"GUESS SOMETHING HAPPENED BETWEEN NINOCCHI AND MOMO?"
JUST AS I SUSPECTED. THEY MUST HAVE HAD A BIG FIGHT AFTER TOKYO SAILING.
I'M SURE HER SINGING PROBLEMS HAVE BEEN HARD FOR THEM.
BUT ALL THE SAME...

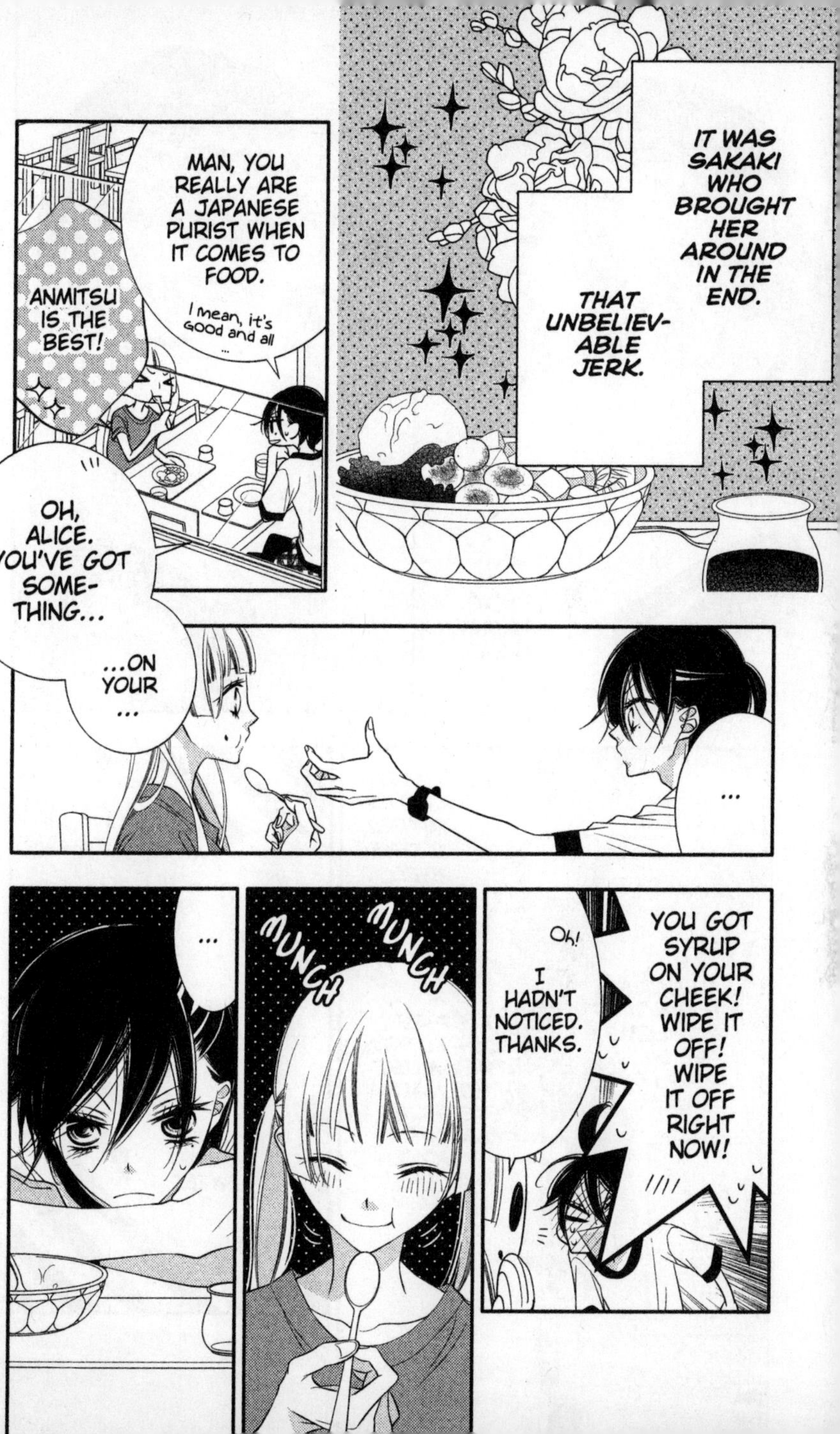
IT WAS SAKAKI WHO BROUGHT HER AROUND IN THE END.
THAT UNBELIEVABLE JERK.
MAN, YOU REALLY ARE A JAPANESE PURIST WHEN IT COMES TO FOOD.
I mean, it's good and all ...
ANMITSU IS THE BEST!
OH, ALICE. YOU'VE GOT SOMETHING...
...ON YOUR ...
...
YOU GOT SYRUP ON YOUR CHEEK! WIPE IT OFF! WIPE IT OFF RIGHT NOW!
Oh!
I HADN'T NOTICED. THANKS.
MUNCH
MUNCH
...

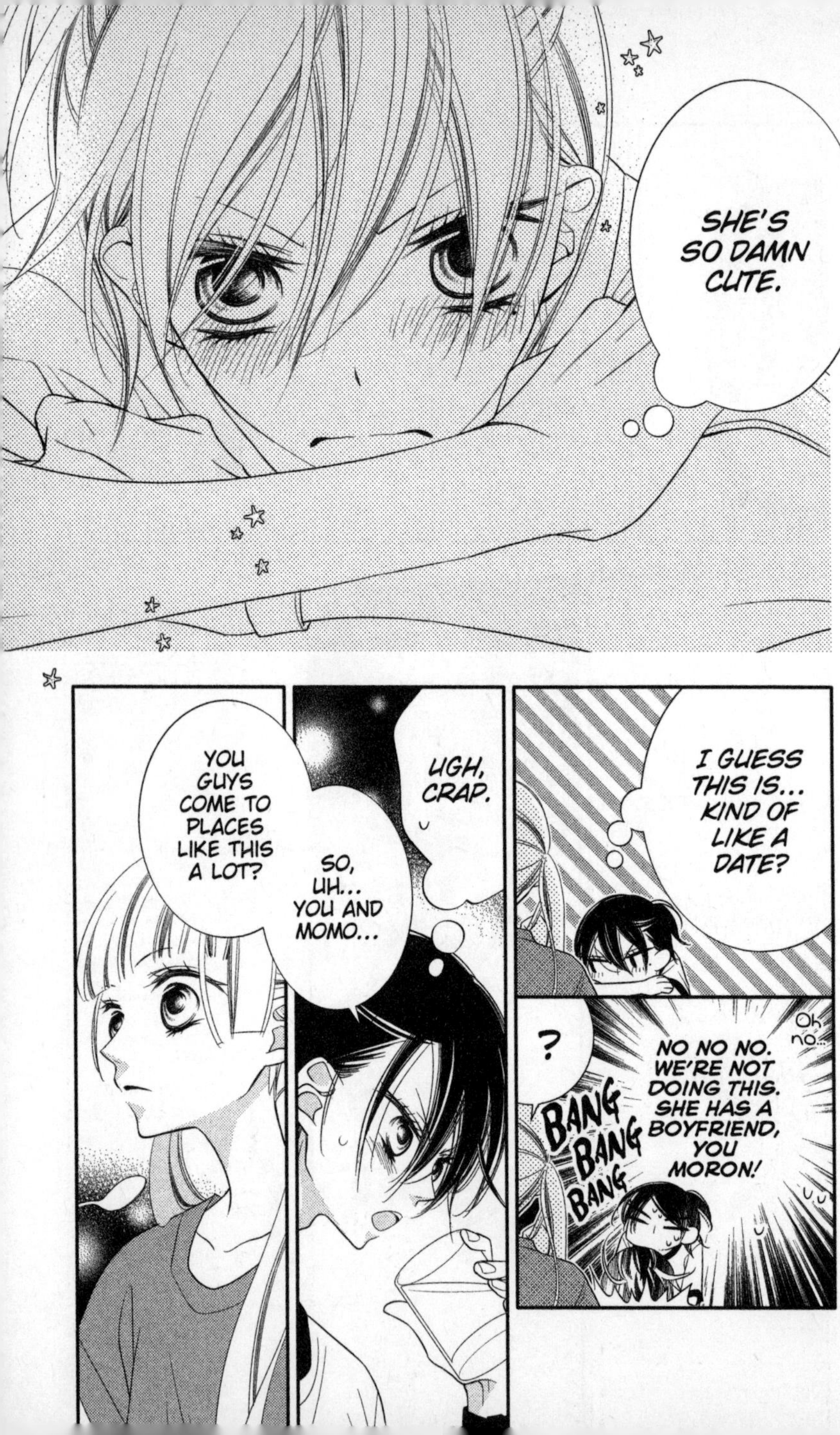
SHE'S SO DAMN CUTE.
I GUESS THIS IS... KIND OF LIKE A DATE?
Oh no...
NO NO NO. WE'RE NOT DOING THIS. SHE HAS A BOYFRIEND, YOU MORON!
?
BANG BANG BANG
UGH, CRAP.
SO, UH... YOU AND MOMO...
YOU GUYS COME TO PLACES LIKE THIS A LOT?

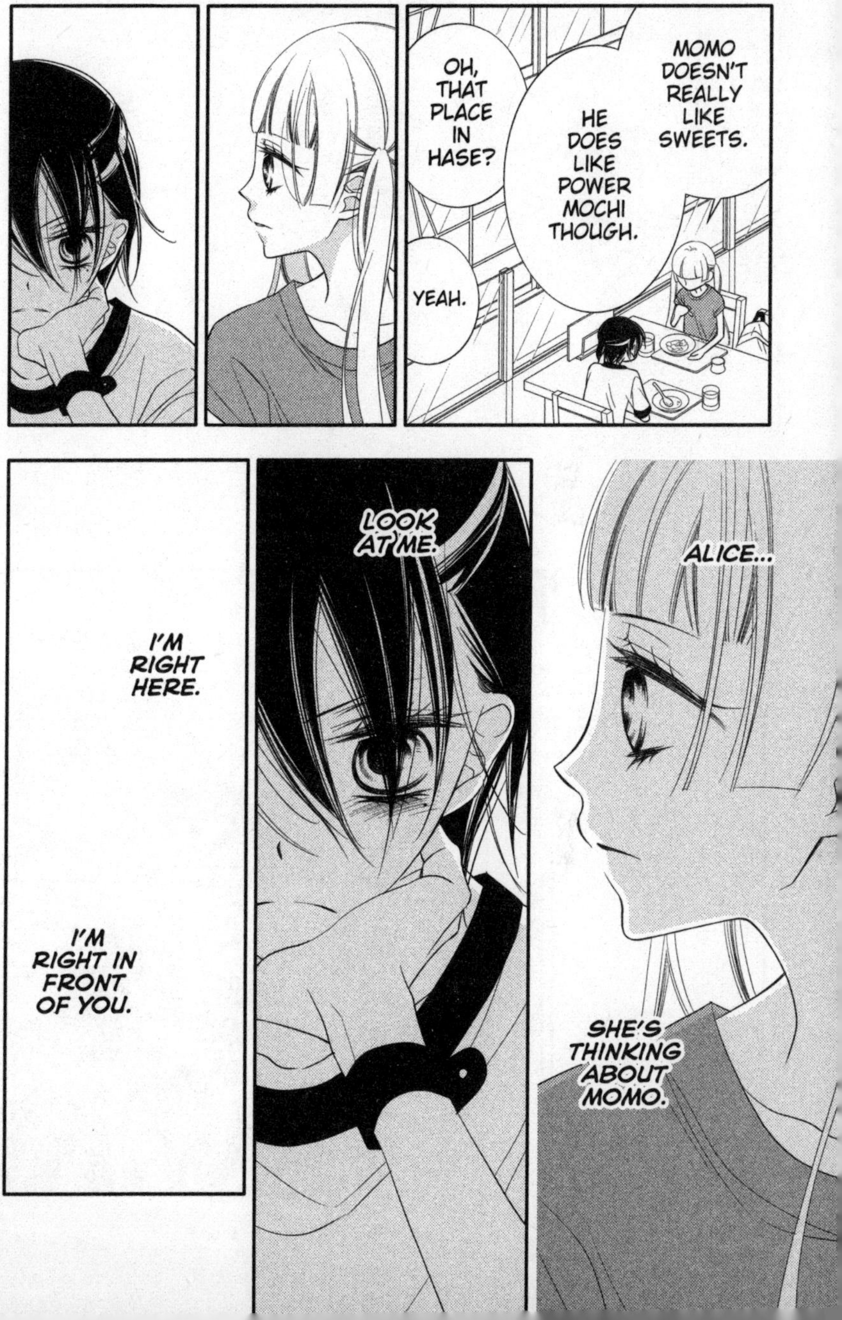
MOMO DOESN'T REALLY LIKE SWEETS.
HE DOES LIKE POWER MOCHI THOUGH.
OH, THAT PLACE IN HASE?
YEAH.
ALICE...
SHE'S THINKING ABOUT MOMO.
LOOK AT ME.
I'M RIGHT HERE.
I'M RIGHT IN FRONT OF YOU.

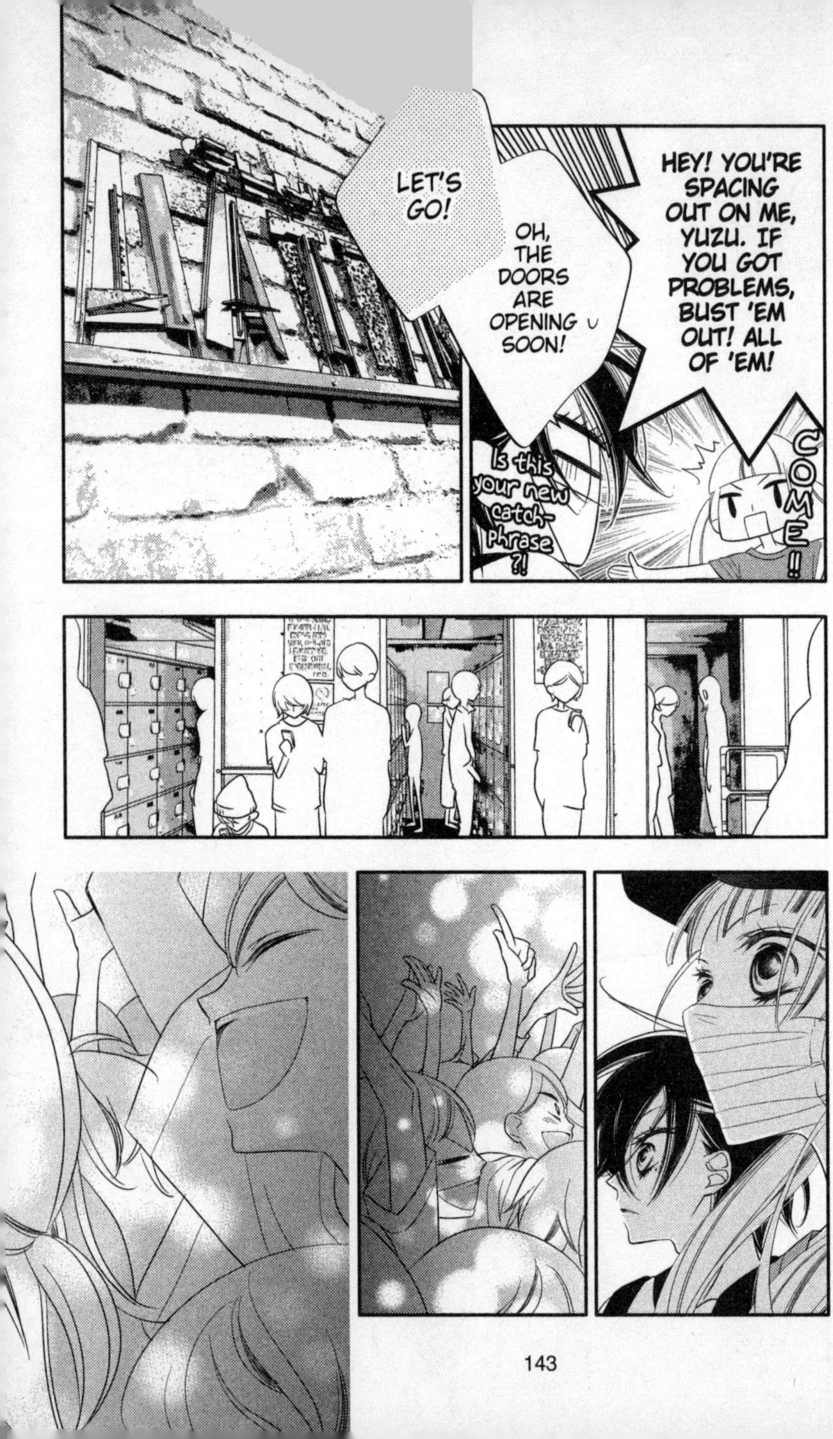
HEY! YOU'RE SPACING OUT ON ME, YUZU. IF YOU GOT PROBLEMS, BUST 'EM OUT! ALL OF 'EM!
COME!!
OH, THE DOORS ARE OPENING SOON!
Is this your new catch-phrase?!
LET'S GO!

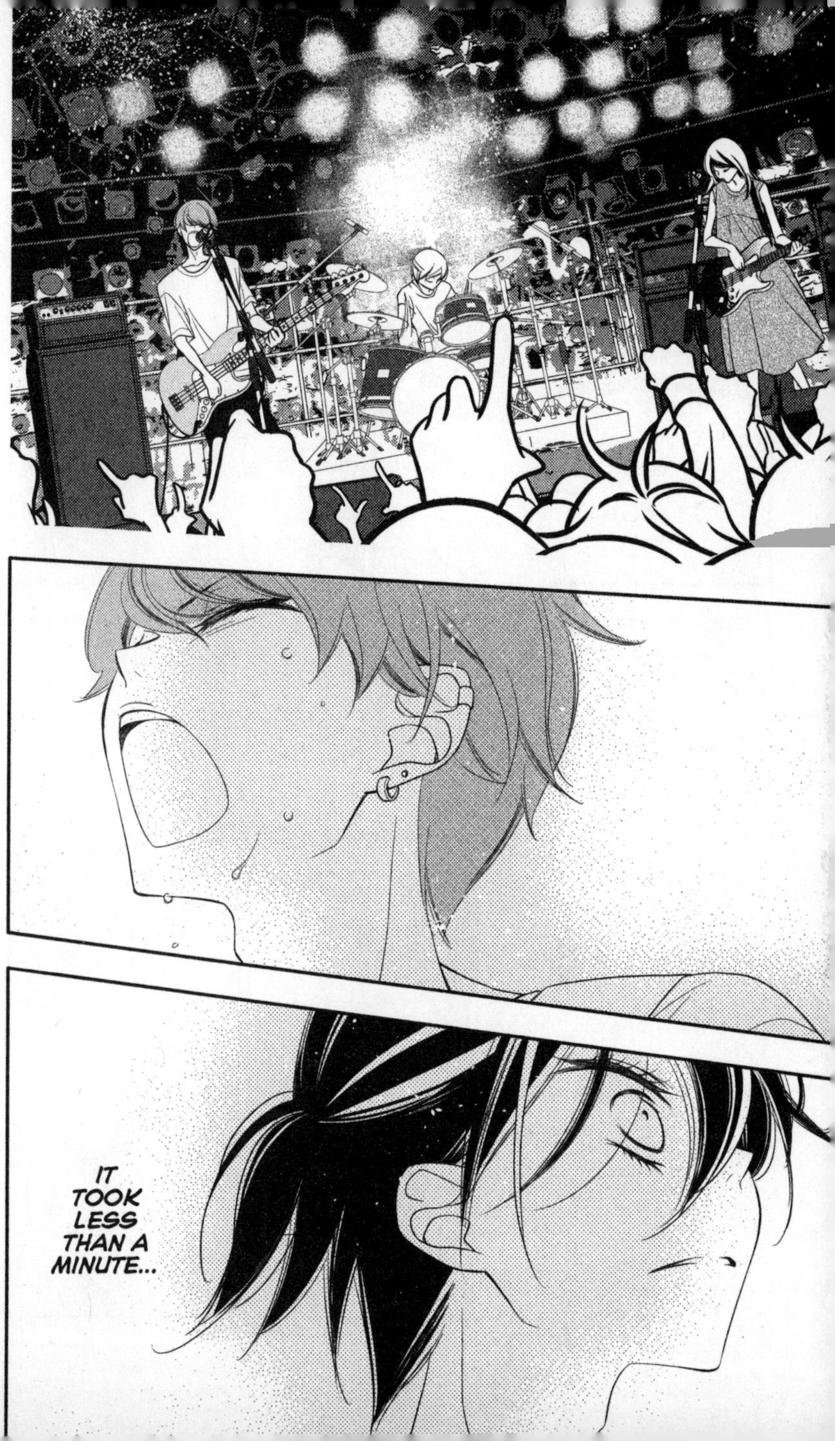
IT TOOK LESS THAN A MINUTE...

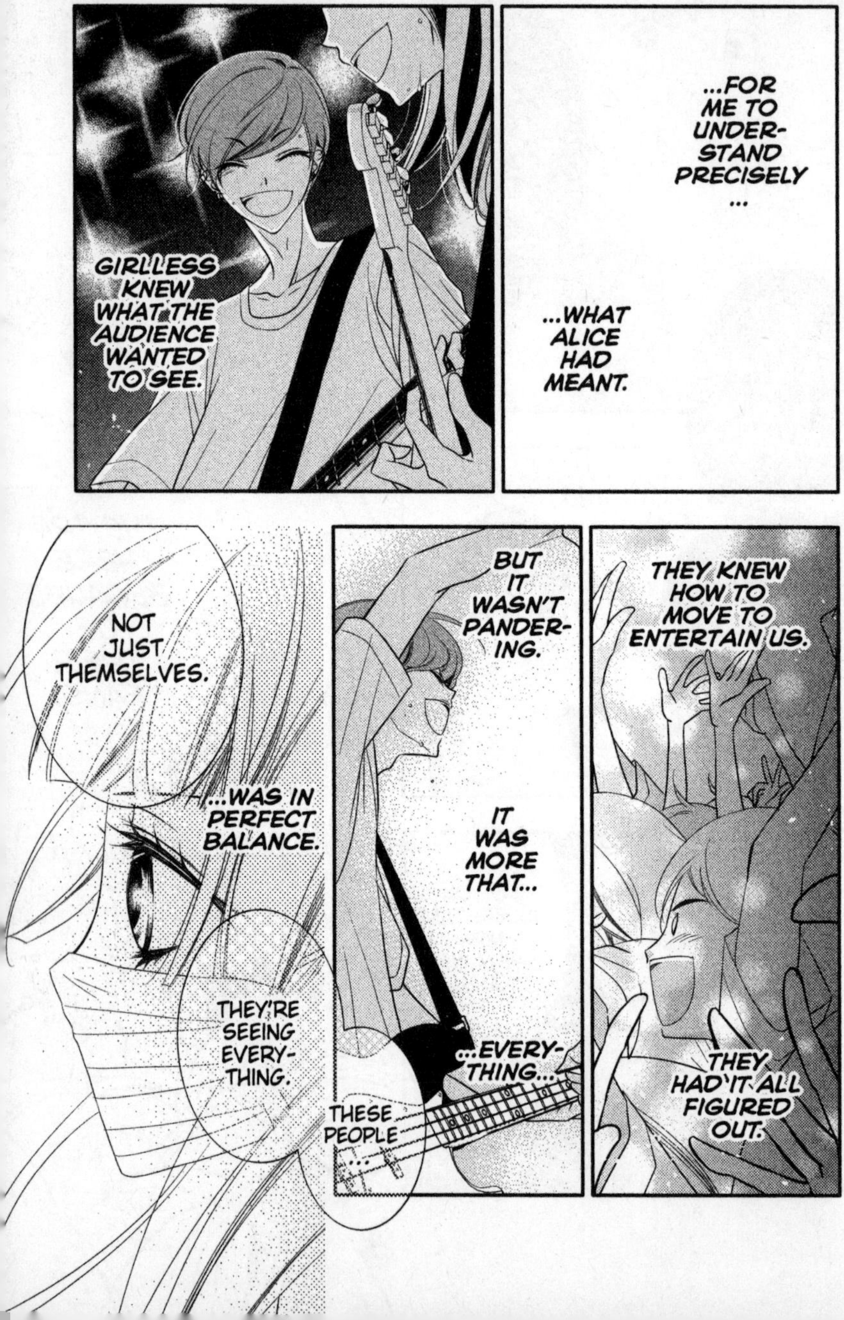
...FOR ME TO UNDERSTAND PRECISELY ...
...WHAT ALICE HAD MEANT.
GIRLLESS KNEW WHAT THE AUDIENCE WANTED TO SEE.
THEY KNEW HOW TO MOVE TO ENTERTAIN US.
THEY HAD IT ALL FIGURED OUT.
BUT IT WASN'T PANDERING.
IT WAS MORE THAT...
...EVERYTHING...
THESE PEOPLE ...
NOT JUST THEMSELVES.
...WAS IN PERFECT BALANCE.
THEY'RE SEEING EVERYTHING.

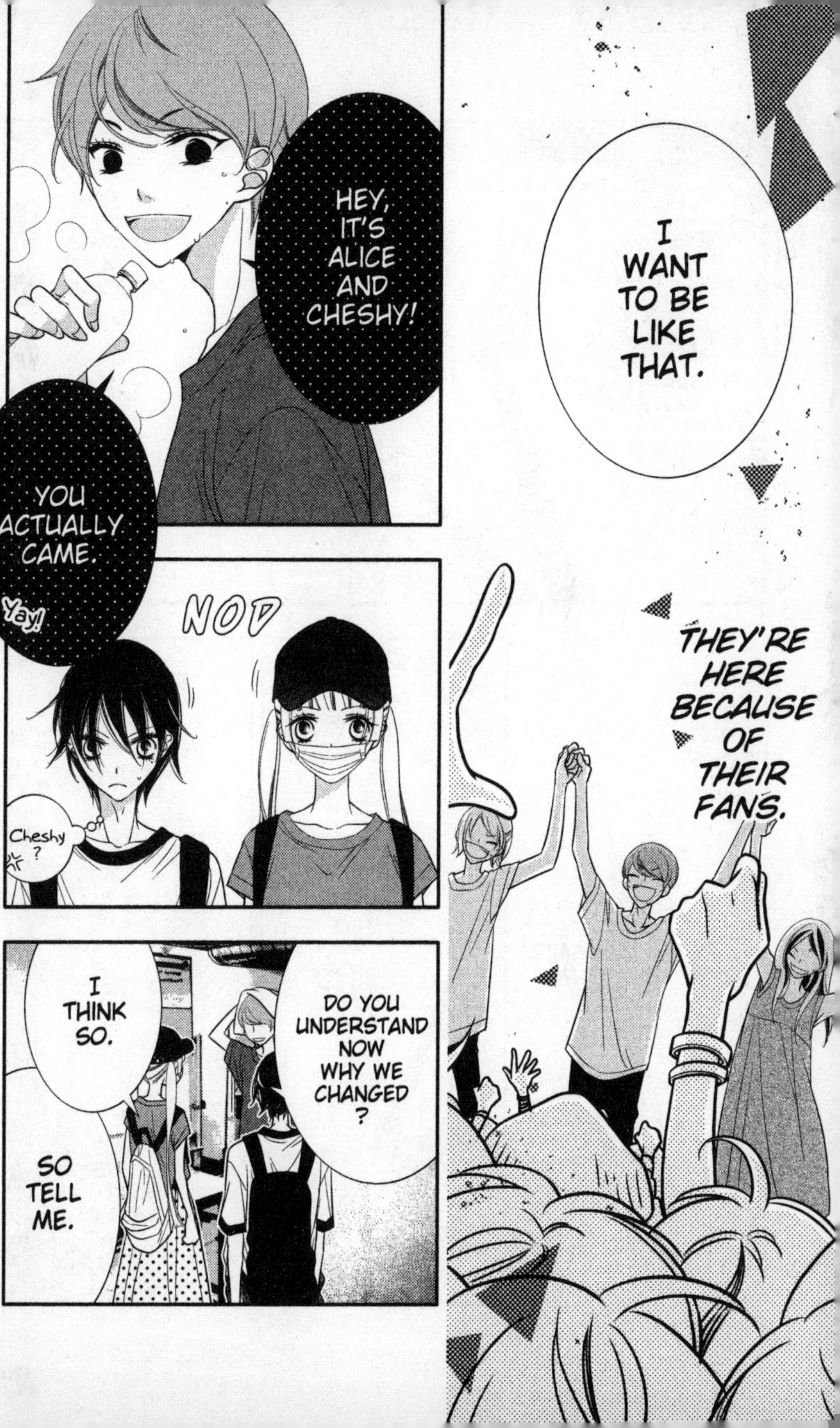
I WANT TO BE LIKE THAT.
THEY'RE HERE BECAUSE OF THEIR FANS.
HEY, IT'S ALICE AND CHESHY!
YOU ACTUALLY CAME.
Yay!
NOD
Cheshy ?
DO YOU UNDERSTAND NOW WHY WE CHANGED ?
I THINK SO.
SO TELL ME.

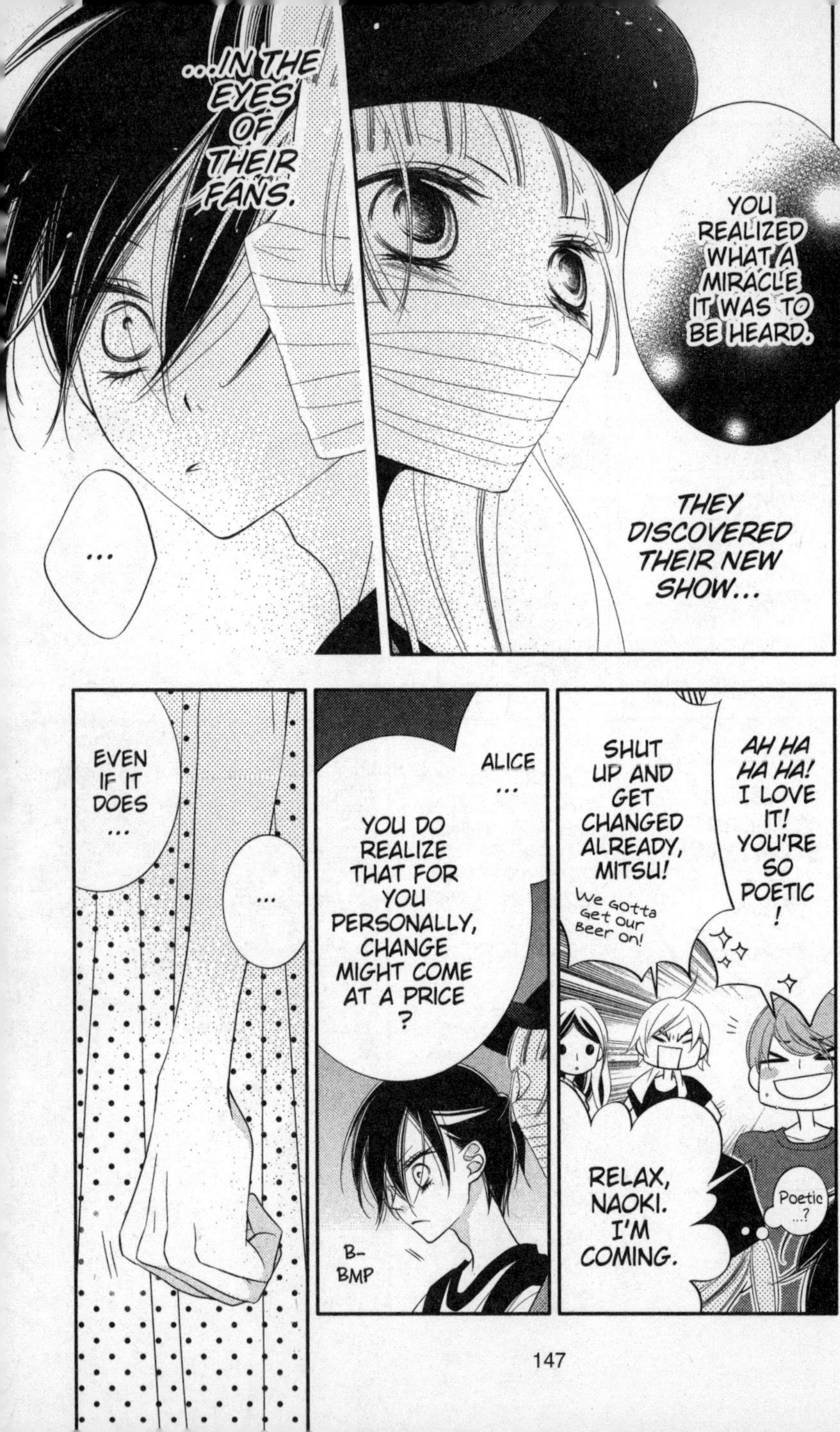

YOU REALIZED WHAT A MIRACLE IT WAS TO BE HEARD.
THEY DISCOVERED THEIR NEW SHOW...
...IN THE EYES OF THEIR FANS.
...
AH HA HA HA! I LOVE IT! YOU'RE SO POETIC!
SHUT UP AND GET CHANGED ALREADY, MITSU!
We gotta get our beer on!
Poetic...?
RELAX, NAOKI. I'M COMING.
ALICE...
YOU DO REALIZE THAT FOR YOU PERSONALLY, CHANGE MIGHT COME AT A PRICE?
B-BMP
EVEN IF IT DOES...
...

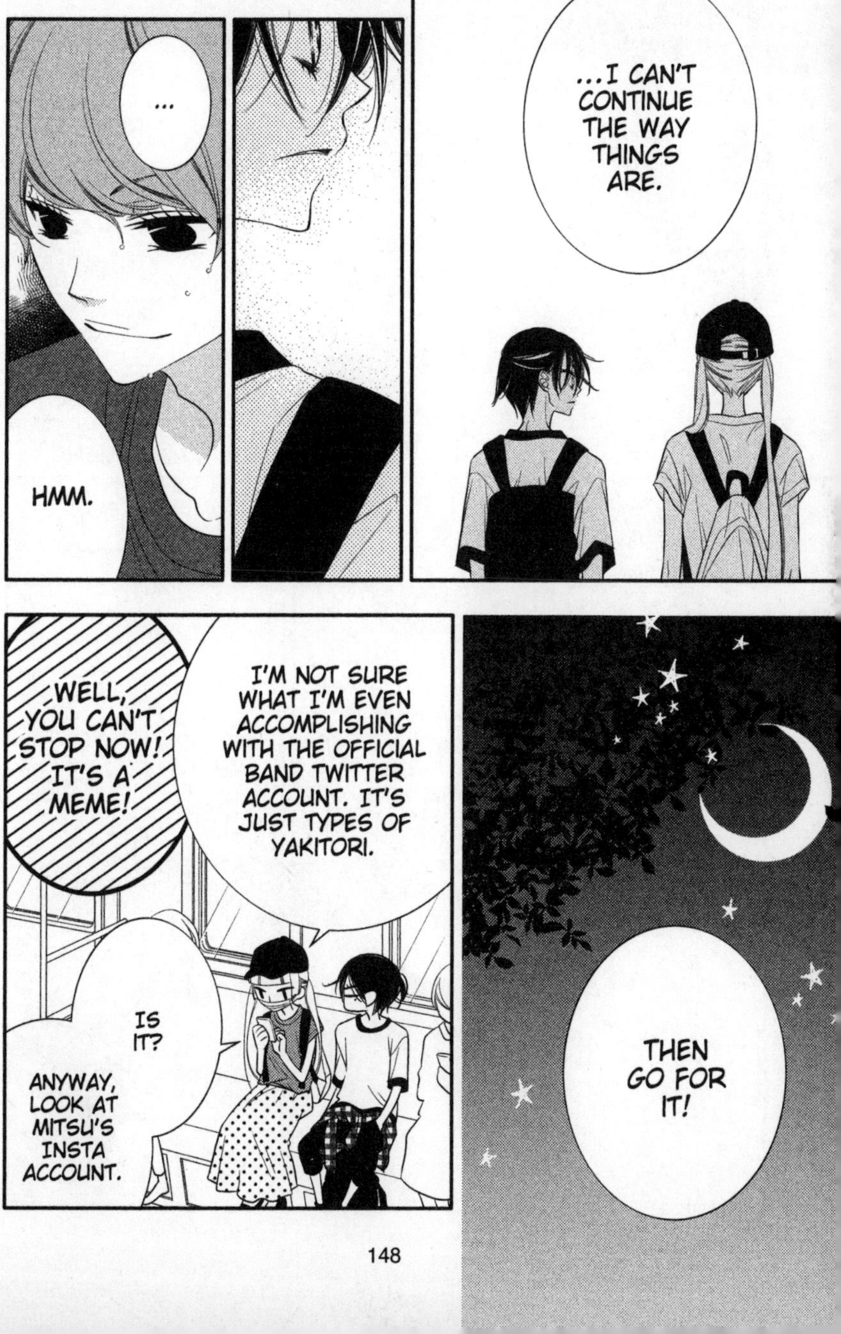
...I CAN'T CONTINUE THE WAY THINGS ARE.
...
HMM.
THEN GO FOR IT!
I'M NOT SURE WHAT I'M EVEN ACCOMPLISHING WITH THE OFFICIAL BAND TWITTER ACCOUNT. IT'S JUST TYPES OF YAKITORI.
WELL, YOU CAN'T STOP NOW! IT'S A MEME!
IS IT?
ANYWAY, LOOK AT MITSU'S INSTA ACCOUNT.

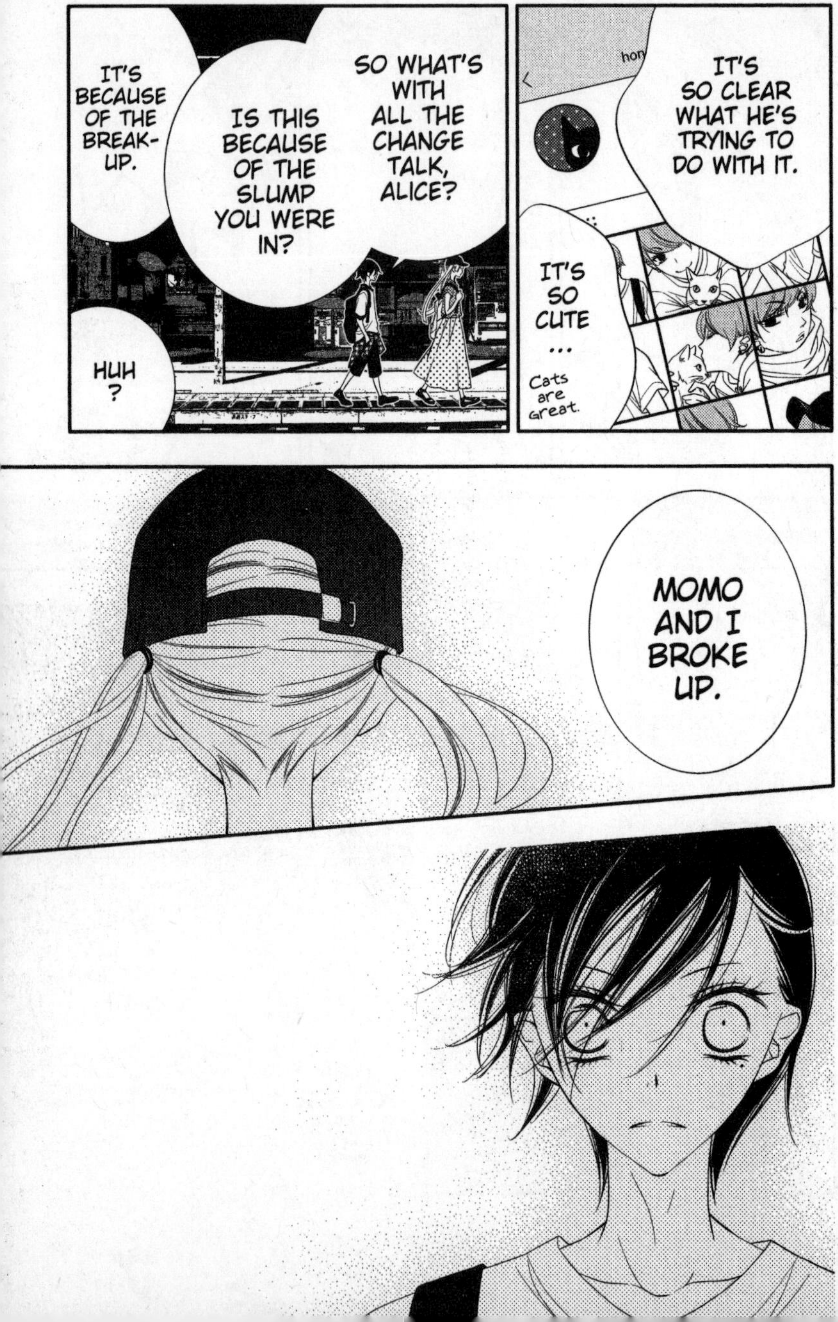
IT'S SO CLEAR WHAT HE'S TRYING TO DO WITH IT.
IT'S SO CUTE ...
Cats are Great.
SO WHAT'S WITH ALL THE CHANGE TALK, ALICE?
IS THIS BECAUSE OF THE SLUMP YOU WERE IN?
IT'S BECAUSE OF THE BREAK-UP.
HUH?
MOMO AND I BROKE UP.

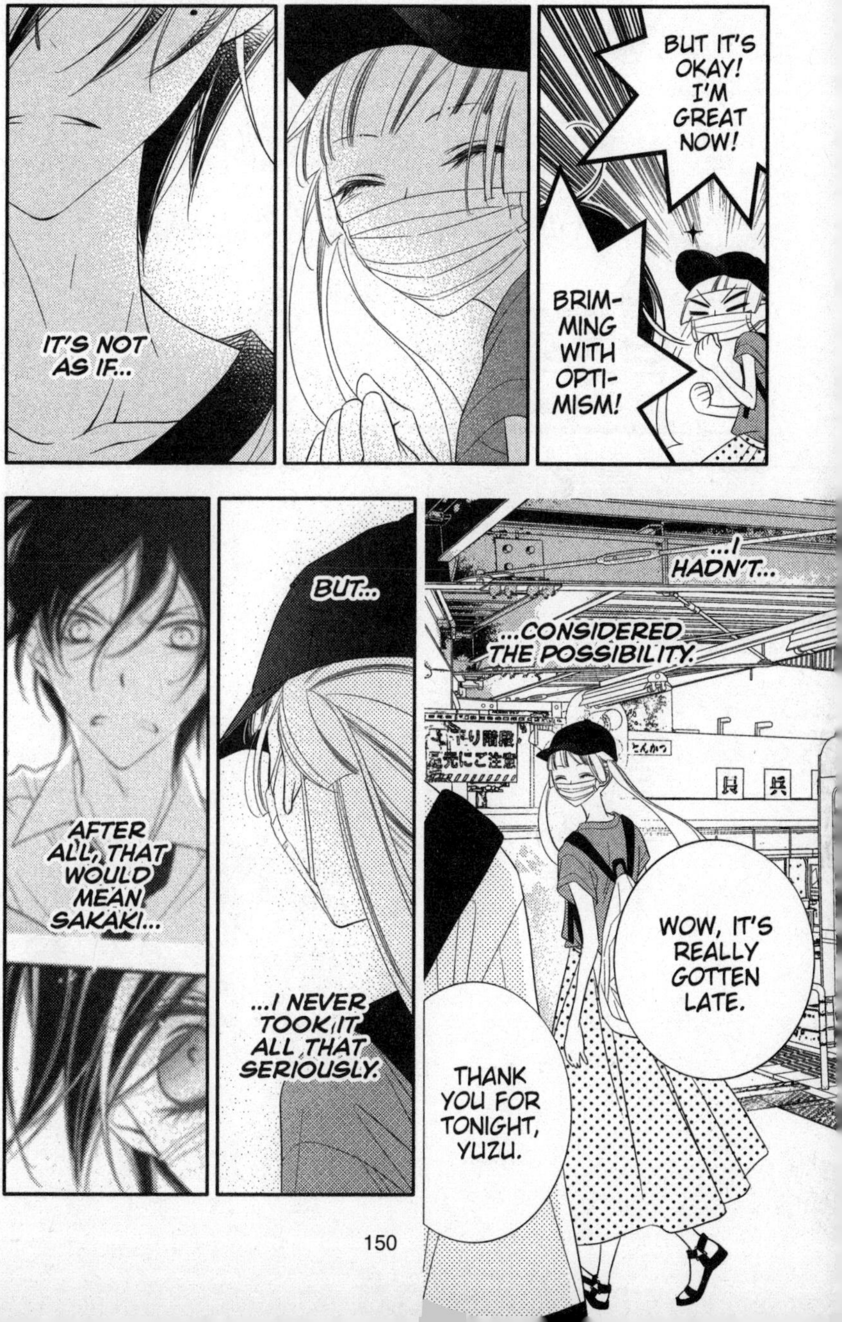
BUT IT'S OKAY! I'M GREAT NOW!
BRIMMING WITH OPTIMISM!
IT'S NOT AS IF...
...I HADN'T...
...CONSIDERED THE POSSIBILITY.
WOW, IT'S REALLY GOTTEN LATE.
THANK YOU FOR TONIGHT, YUZU.
BUT...
...I NEVER TOOK IT ALL THAT SERIOUSLY.
AFTER ALL, THAT WOULD MEAN SAKAKI...

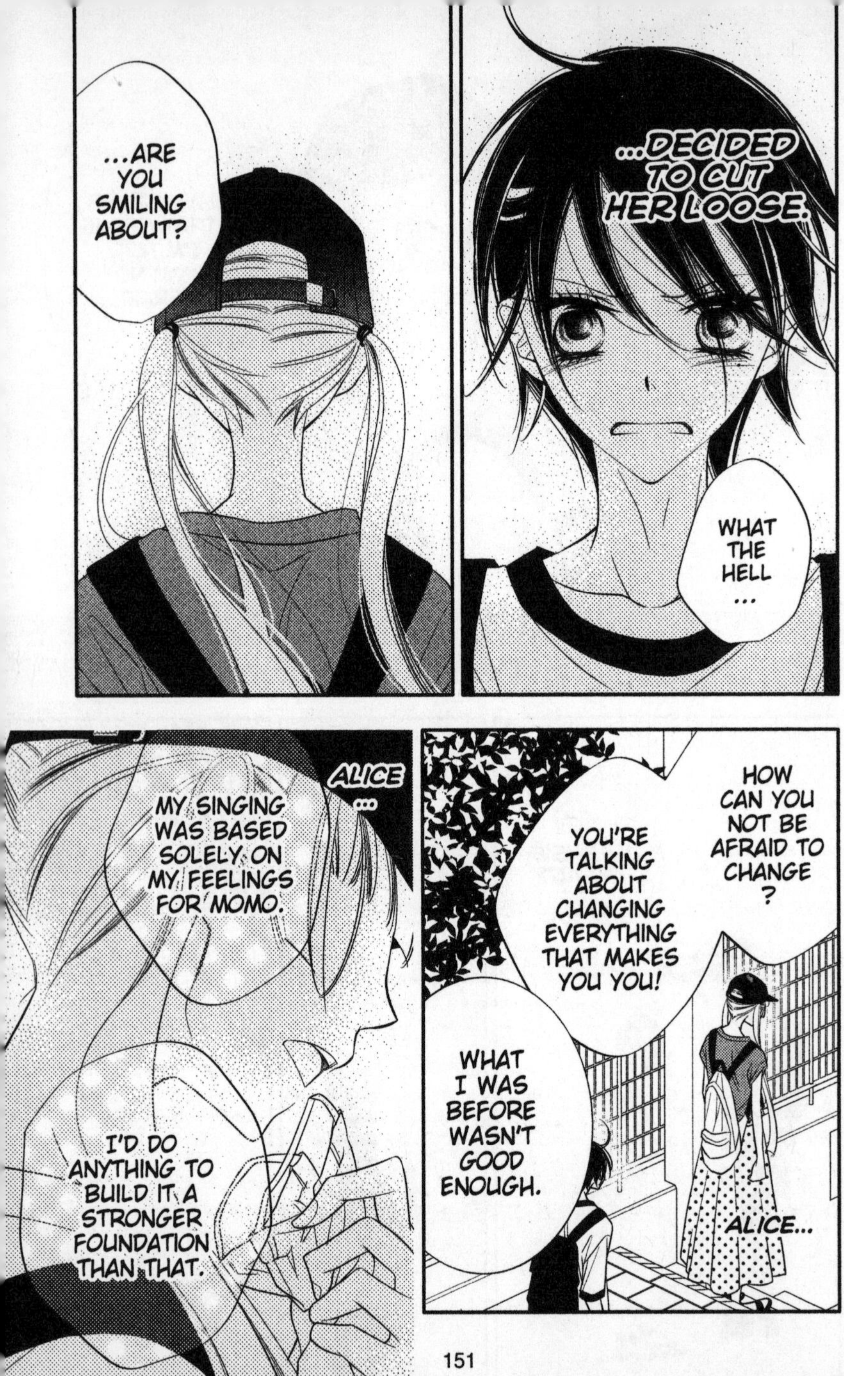
...DECIDED TO CUT HER LOOSE.
WHAT THE HELL ...
...ARE YOU SMILING ABOUT?
HOW CAN YOU NOT BE AFRAID TO CHANGE ?
YOU'RE TALKING ABOUT CHANGING EVERYTHING THAT MAKES YOU YOU!
WHAT I WAS BEFORE WASN'T GOOD ENOUGH.
ALICE...
ALICE ...
MY SINGING WAS BASED SOLELY ON MY FEELINGS FOR MOMO.
I'D DO ANYTHING TO BUILD IT A STRONGER FOUNDATION THAN THAT.

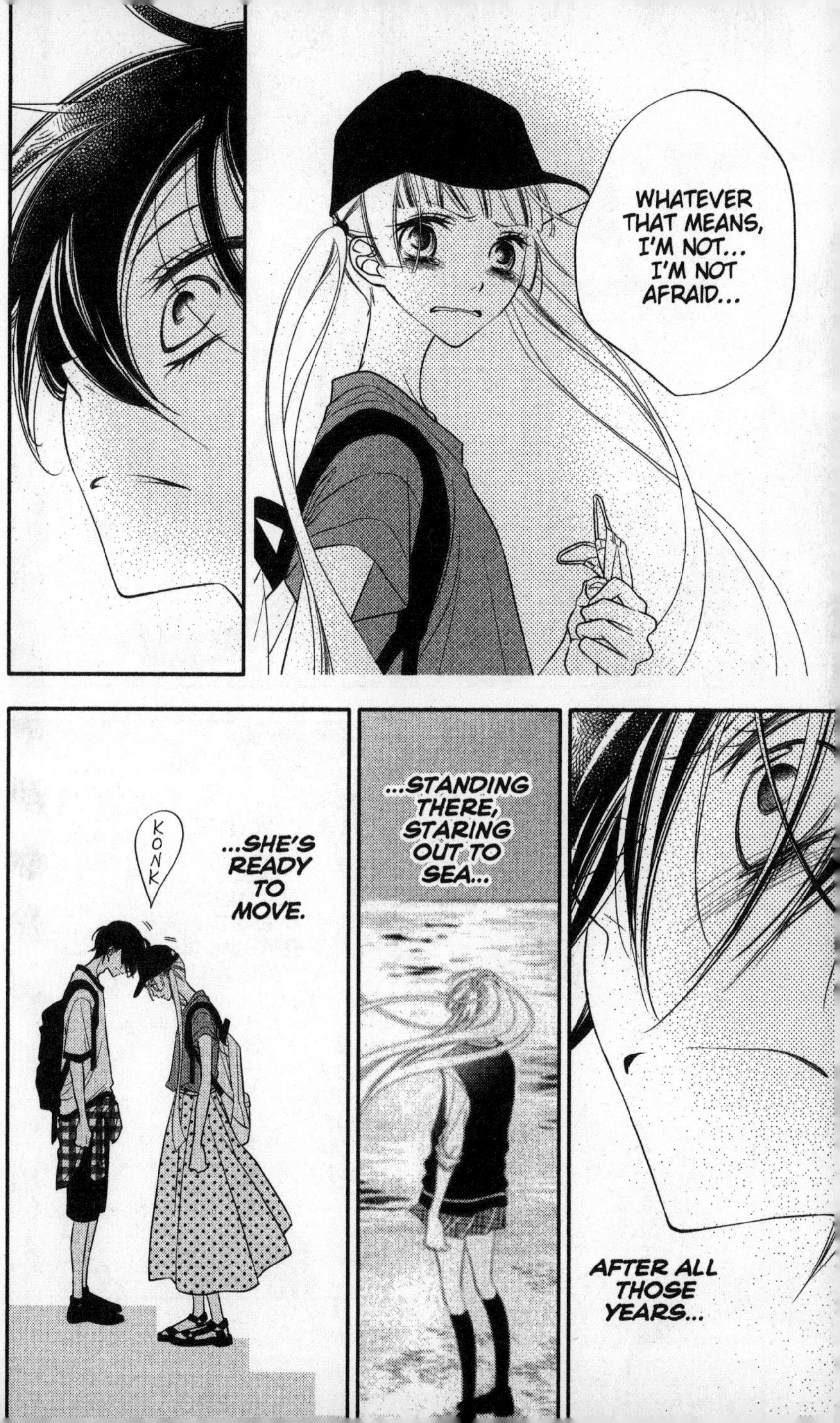
WHATEVER THAT MEANS, I'M NOT... I'M NOT AFRAID...
AFTER ALL THOSE YEARS...
...STANDING THERE, STARING OUT TO SEA...
...SHE'S READY TO MOVE.
KONK

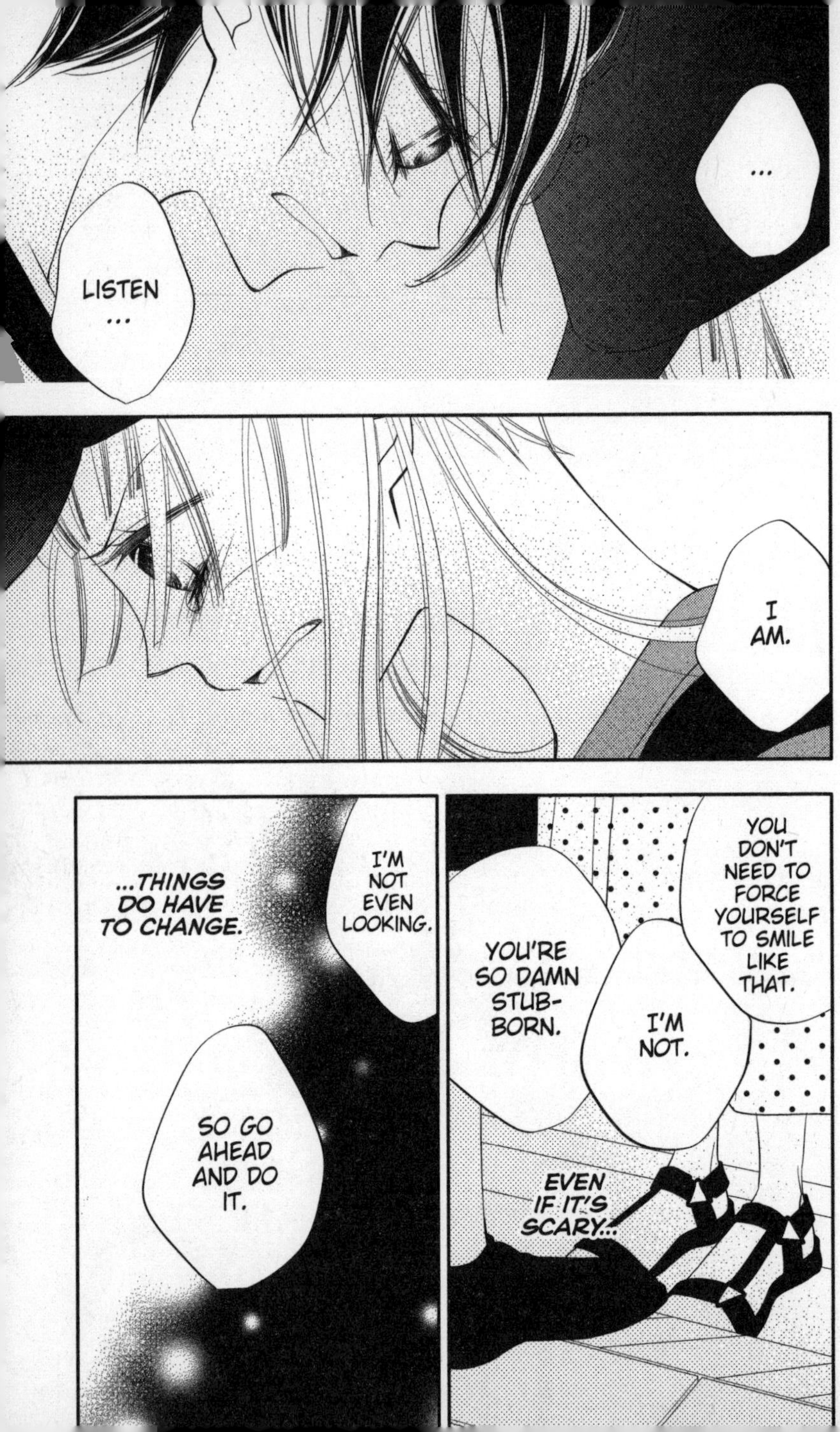
...
LISTEN ...
I AM.
YOU DON'T NEED TO FORCE YOURSELF TO SMILE LIKE THAT.
I'M NOT.
YOU'RE SO DAMN STUB-BORN.
EVEN IF IT'S SCARY...
I'M NOT EVEN LOOKING.
...THINGS DO HAVE TO CHANGE.
SO GO AHEAD AND DO IT.

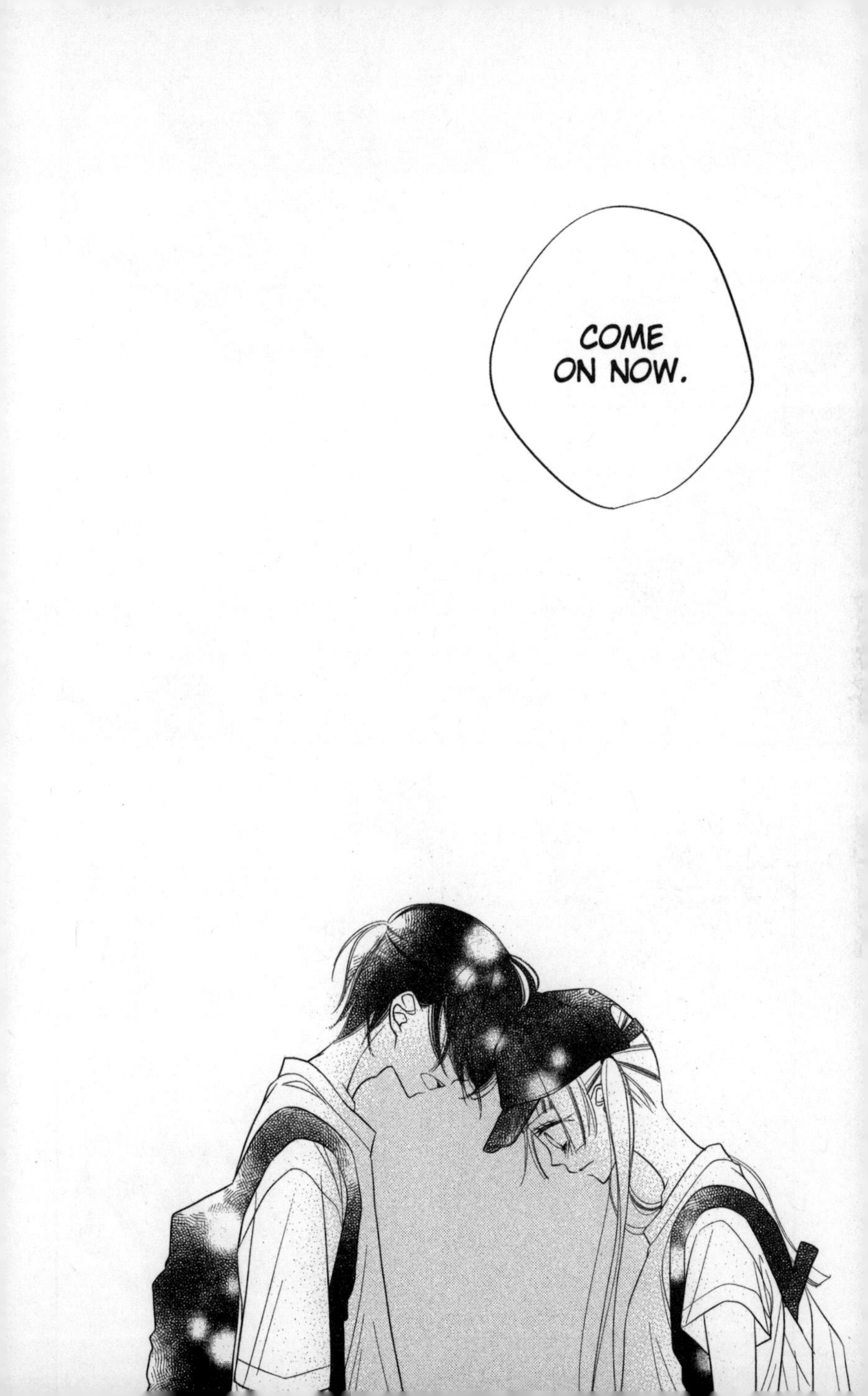
COME ON NOW.

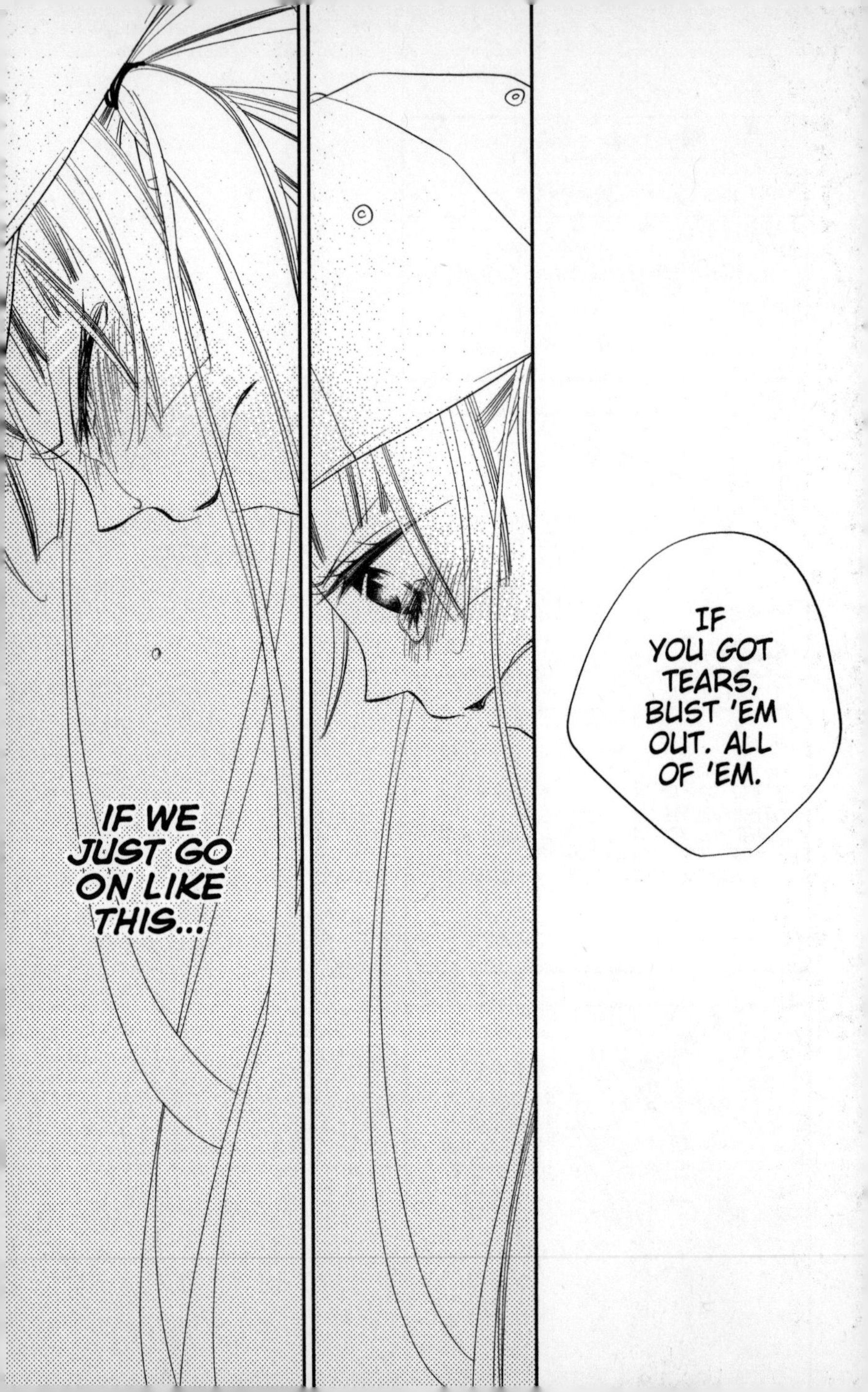
IF YOU GOT TEARS, BUST 'EM OUT. ALL OF 'EM.
IF WE JUST GO ON LIKE THIS...

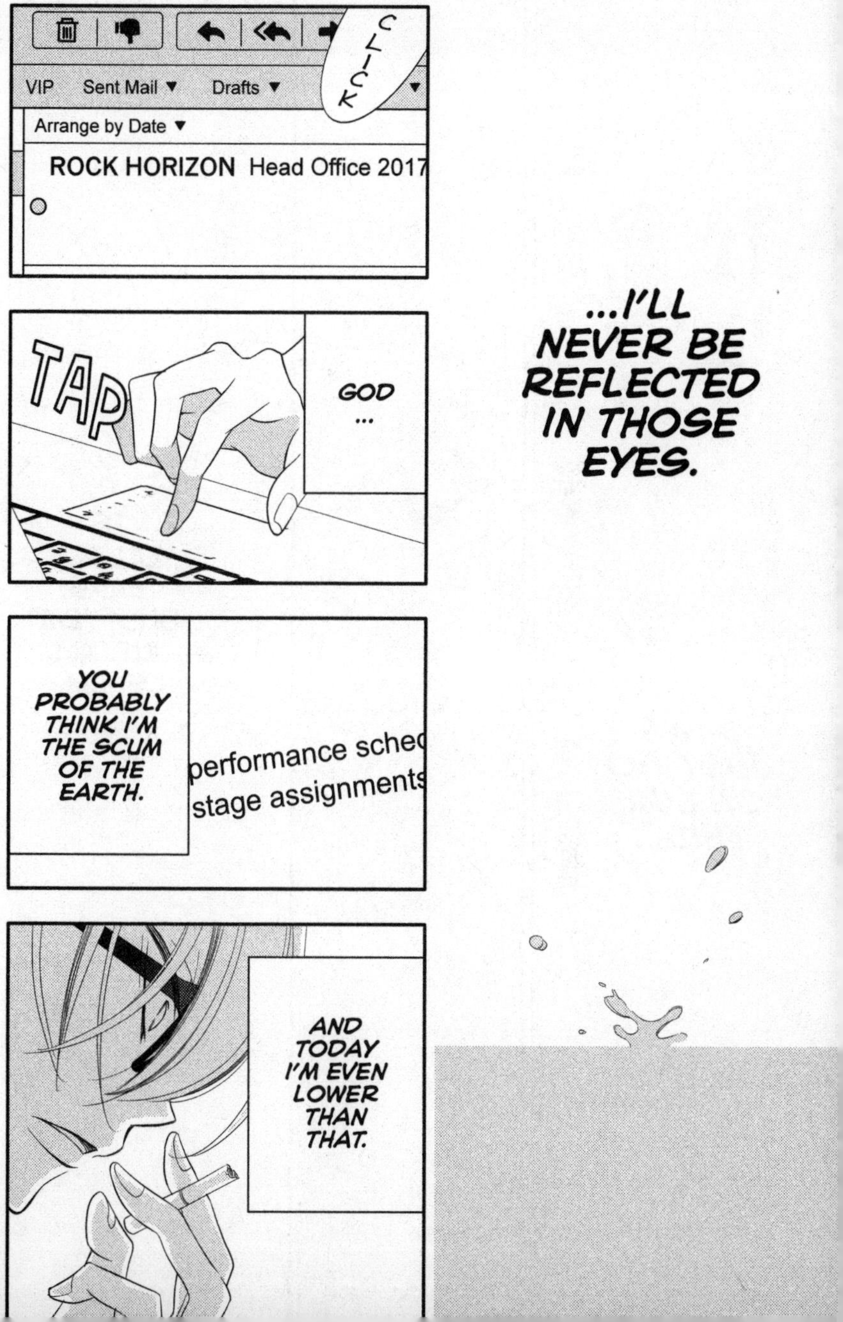

...I'LL NEVER BE REFLECTED IN THOSE EYES.
CLICK
VIP Sent Mail ▼ Drafts ▼
Arrange by Date ▼
ROCK HORIZON Head Office 2017
GOD ...
TAP
YOU PROBABLY THINK I'M THE SCUM OF THE EARTH.
performance schec
stage assignments
AND TODAY I'M EVEN LOWER THAN THAT.

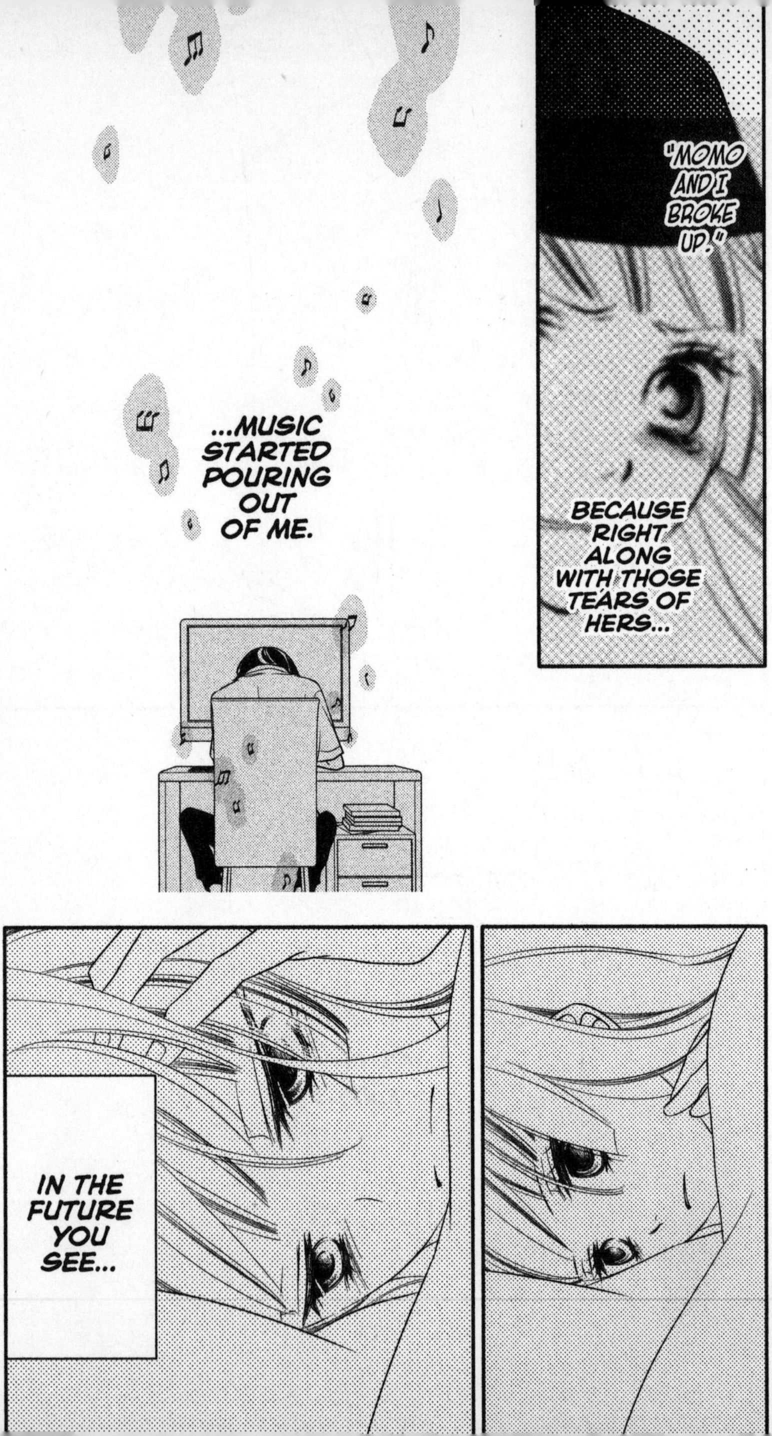
"MOMO AND I BROKE UP."
BECAUSE RIGHT ALONG WITH THOSE TEARS OF HERS...
...MUSIC STARTED POURING OUT OF ME.
IN THE FUTURE YOU SEE...

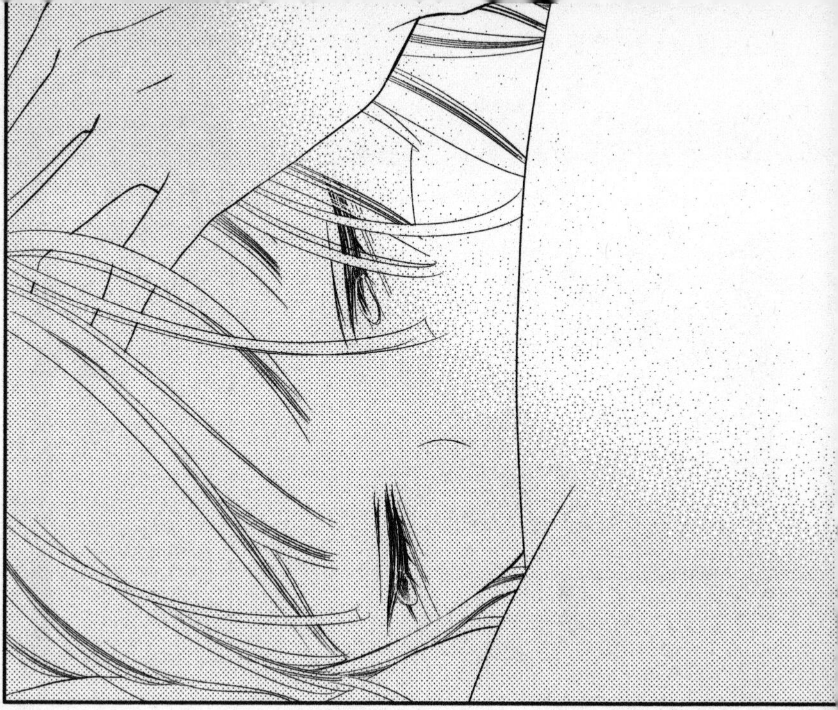

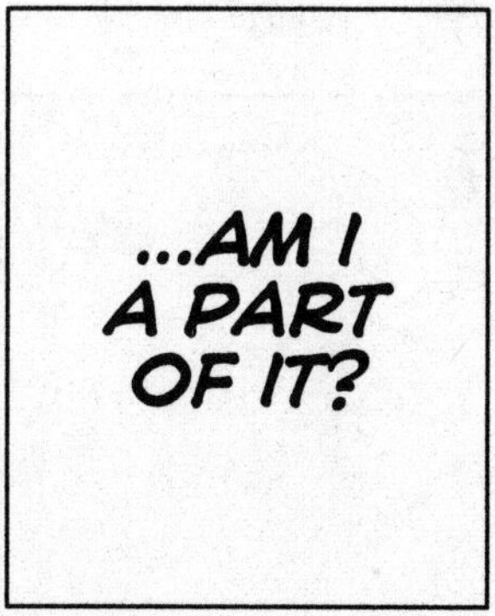
...AM I
A PART
OF IT?

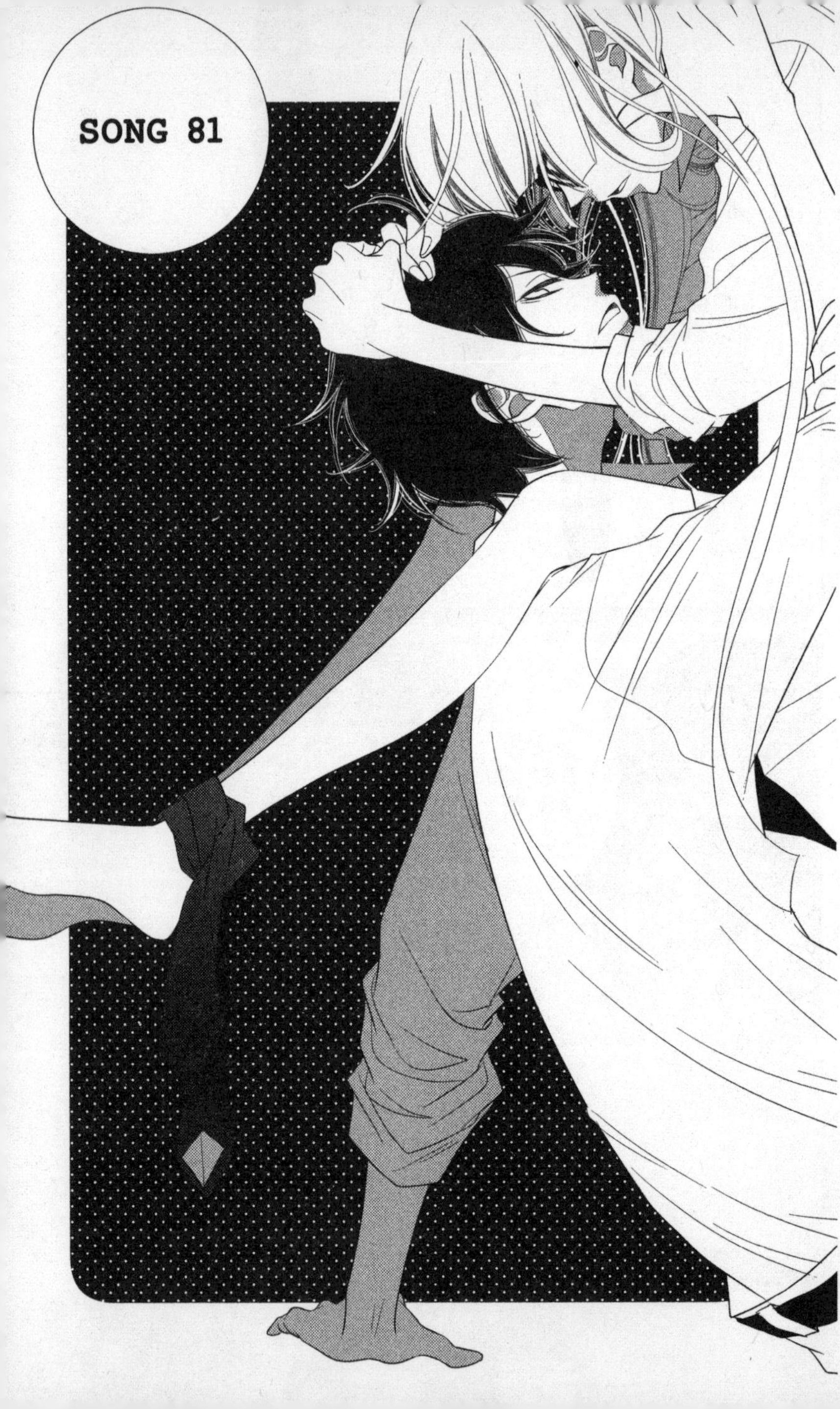
SONG 81

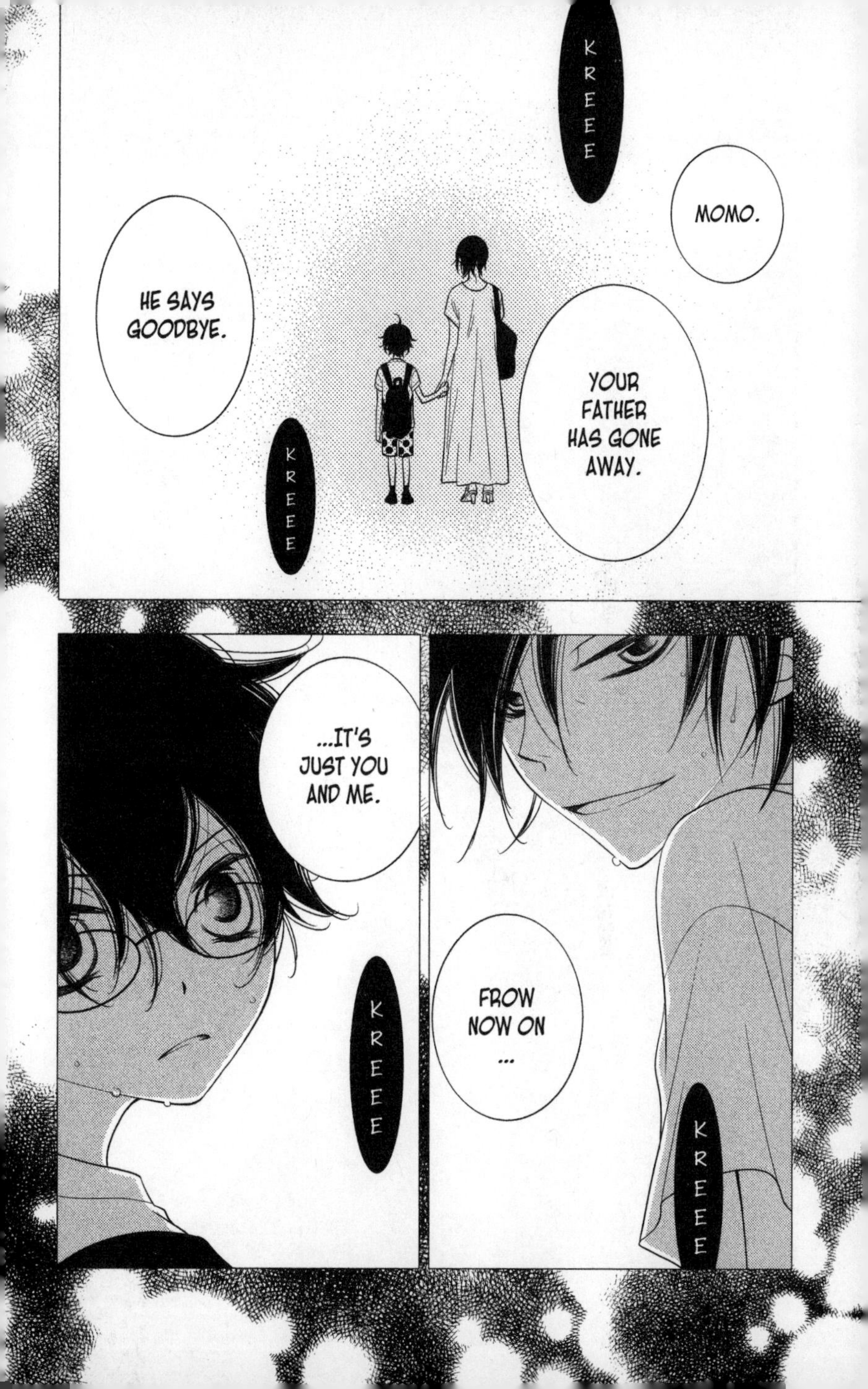
KREEE
MOMO.
YOUR FATHER HAS GONE AWAY.
HE SAYS GOODBYE.
KREEE
FROW NOW ON ...
KREEE
...IT'S JUST YOU AND ME.
KREEE

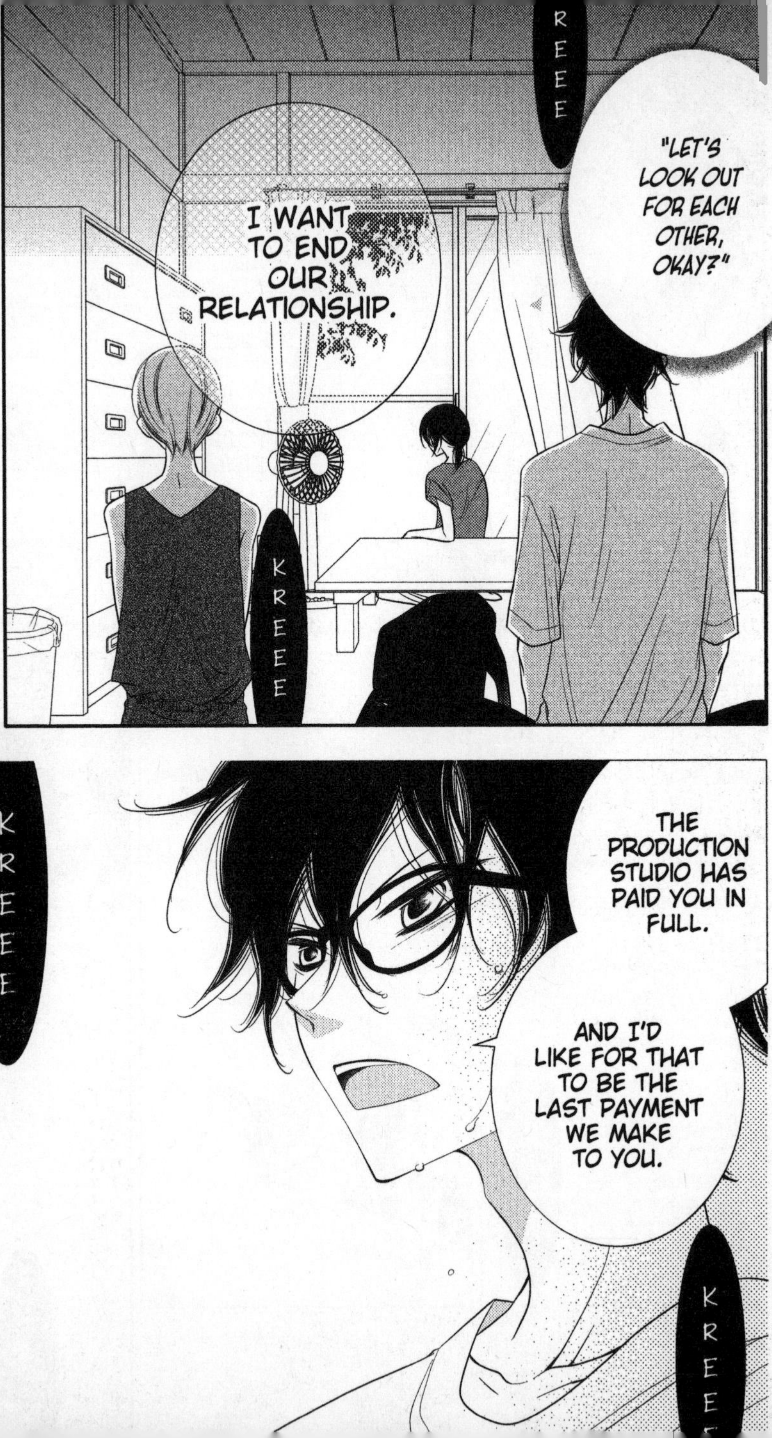

KREEE
"LET'S LOOK OUT FOR EACH OTHER, OKAY?"
I WANT TO END OUR RELATIONSHIP.
KREEE
THE PRODUCTION STUDIO HAS PAID YOU IN FULL.
AND I'D LIKE FOR THAT TO BE THE LAST PAYMENT WE MAKE TO YOU.
KREEE
KREE

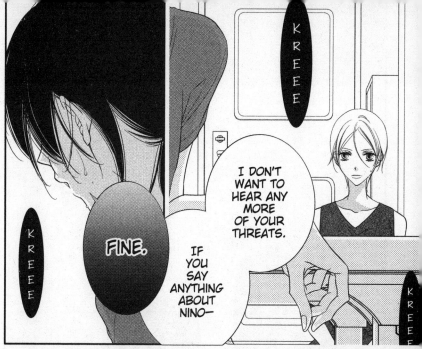

KREEE

I DON'T WANT TO HEAR ANY MORE OF YOUR THREATS.

FINE.

IF YOU SAY ANYTHING ABOUT NINO—

KREEE

KREE

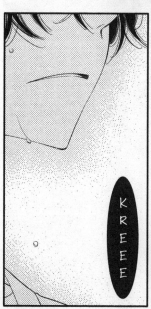

KREEE

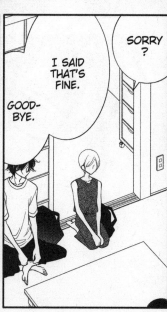

SORRY ?

I SAID THAT'S FINE.

GOOD-BYE.

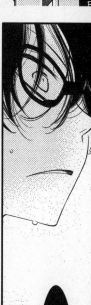

KREE

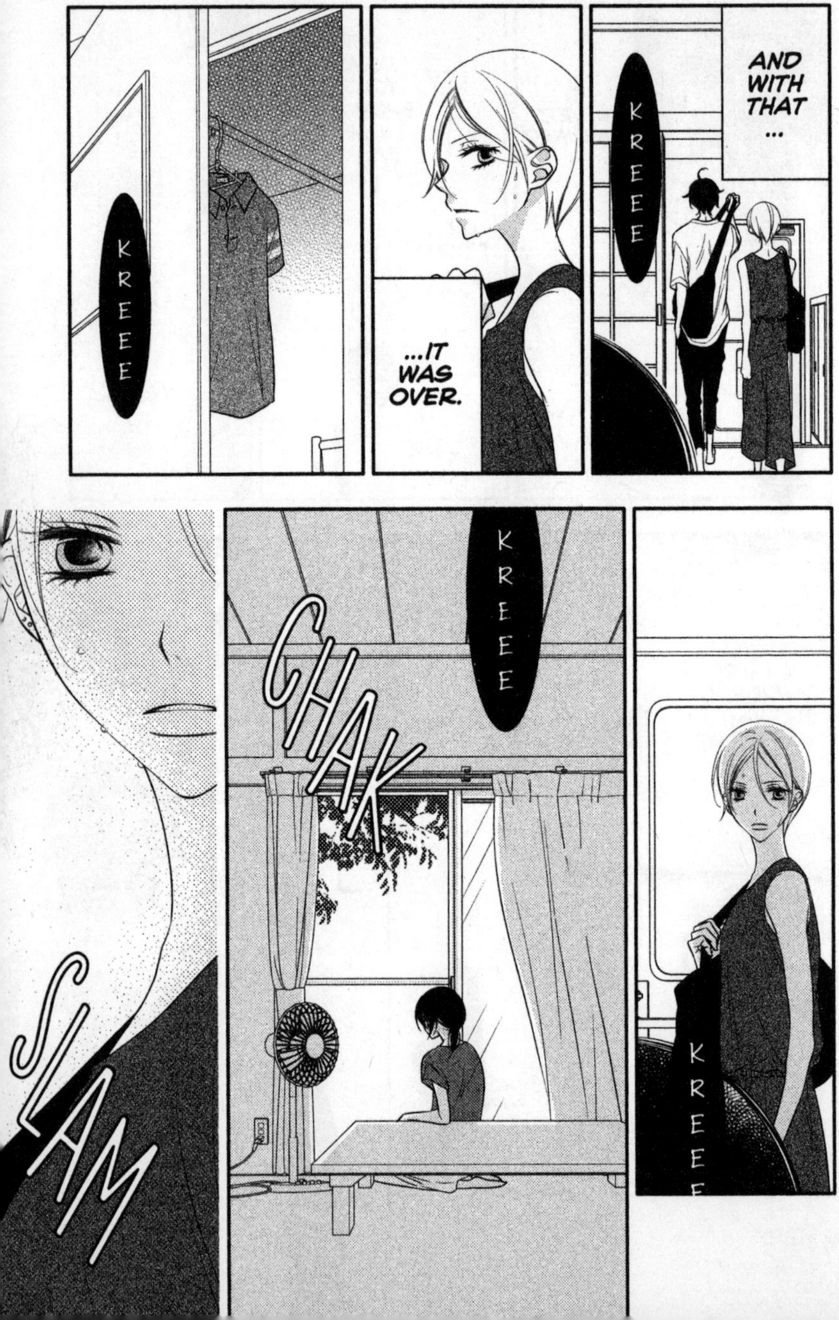
AND WITH THAT ...
KREEE
...IT WAS OVER.
KREEE
KREEE
KREEE
CHAK
SLAM

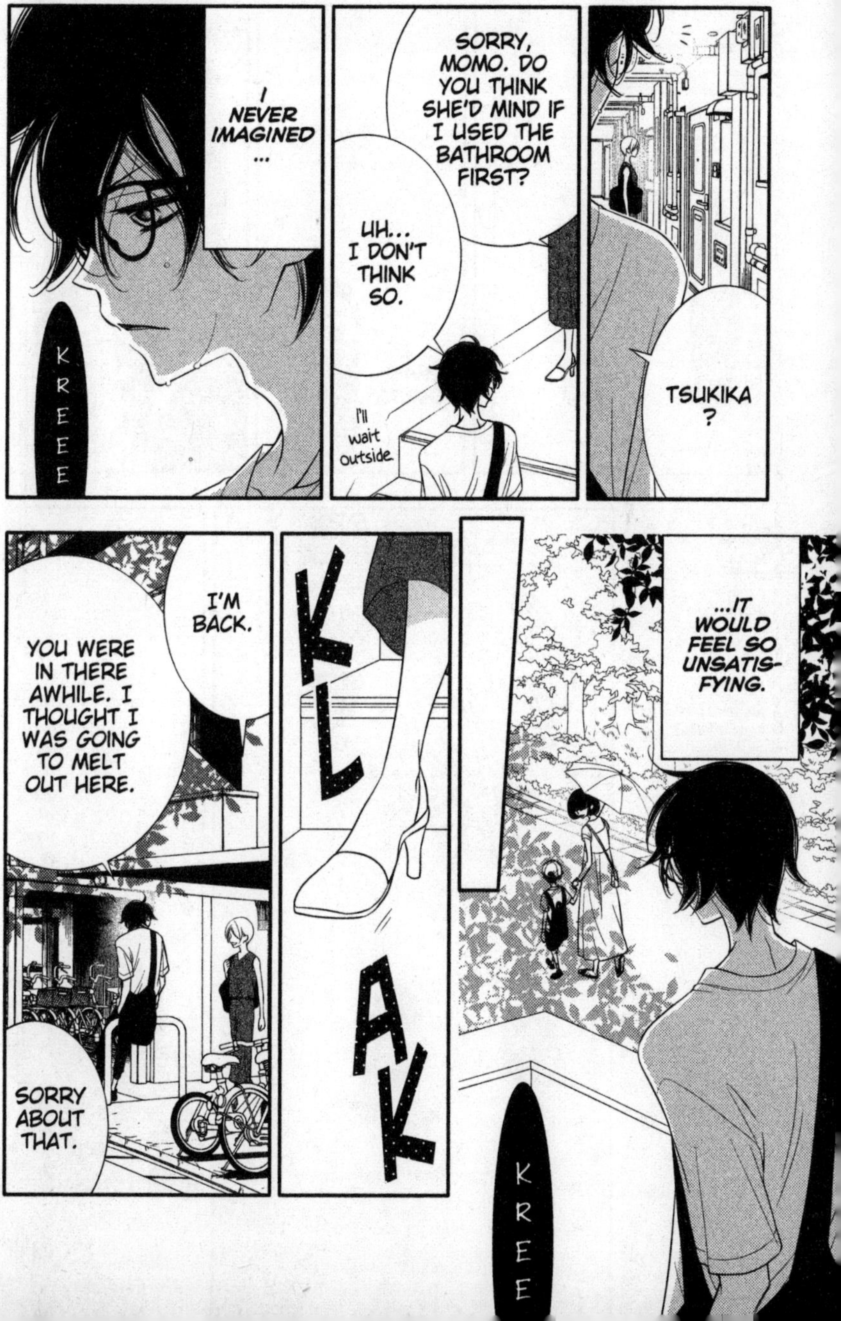
TSUKIKA?
SORRY, MOMO. DO YOU THINK SHE'D MIND IF I USED THE BATHROOM FIRST?
UH... I DON'T THINK SO.
I'll wait outside.
I NEVER IMAGINED...
KREEE
...IT WOULD FEEL SO UNSATIS-FYING.
KREE
KLAK
I'M BACK.
YOU WERE IN THERE AWHILE. I THOUGHT I WAS GOING TO MELT OUT HERE.
SORRY ABOUT THAT.

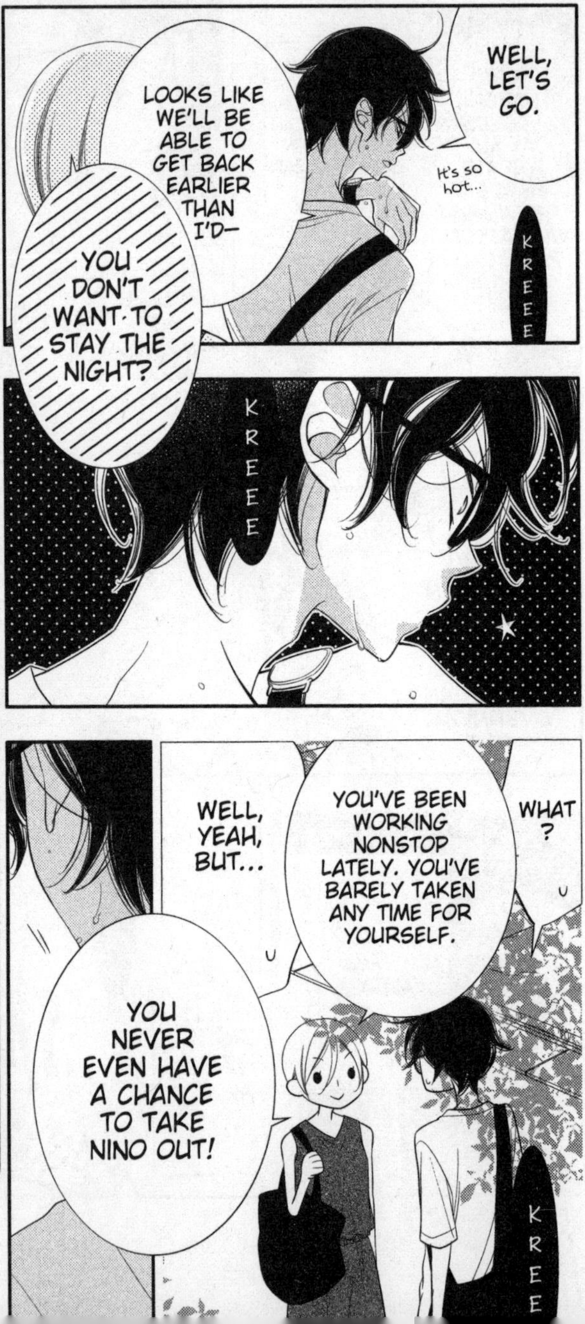
WELL, LET'S GO.
It's so hot...
KREEE
LOOKS LIKE WE'LL BE ABLE TO GET BACK EARLIER THAN I'D—
YOU DON'T WANT TO STAY THE NIGHT?
KREEE
WHAT?
YOU'VE BEEN WORKING NONSTOP LATELY. YOU'VE BARELY TAKEN ANY TIME FOR YOURSELF.
WELL, YEAH, BUT...
YOU NEVER EVEN HAVE A CHANCE TO TAKE NINO OUT!
KREE

6

I know I've discussed it on Twitter, but let's talk about the limited-edition drama CD I forgot to write about in volume 13!
The idea was to do a parallel story that was closer to the comics than the anime in terms of chronology and subject matter. I did the same thing with the drama CD for this volume! I do hope you'll give them both a listen.
Oh! This is my last column! So, how did you like volume 14? I wanted to keep this one free of any concert stuff, but the next volume begins the second Rock Horizon arc. I'm writing it now for the magazine, and I'm having a lot of fun with it. I really hope you'll like it! See you again in volume 15! Till then!

Ryoko Fukuyama
11/20/2017

[SPECIAL THANKS]
MOSAGE
TAKAYUKI NAGASHIMA
IKUMI ISHIGAKI
KENJU NORO
MY FAMILY
MY FRIENDS
AND YOU!!

Ryoko Fukuyama
c/o Anonymous Noise Editor
VIZ Media
P.O. Box 77010
San Francisco, CA 94107

HP http://ryoconet/
@ryocoryocoryoco
https://www.instagram.com/ryocofukuyama/

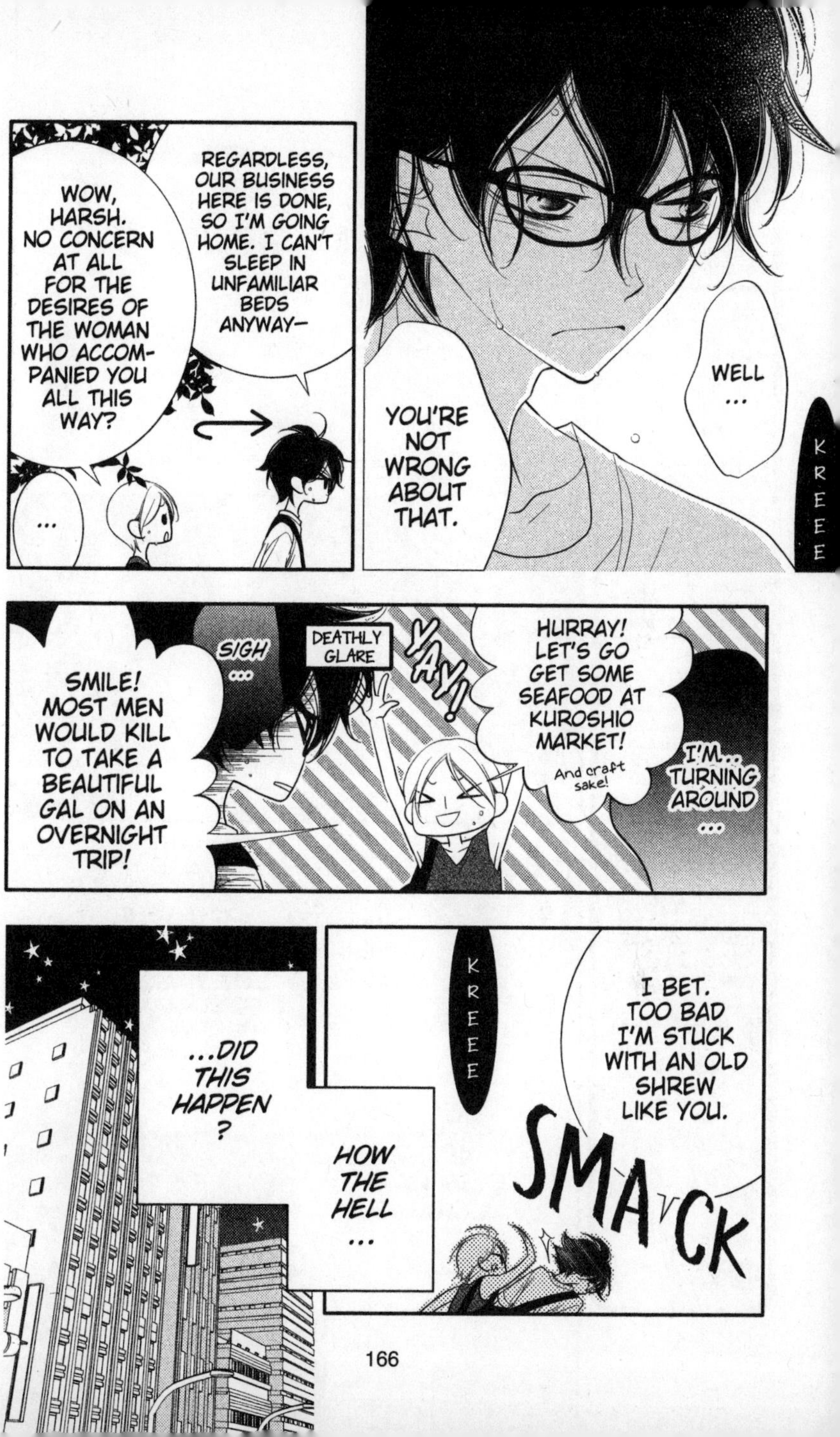
WELL...
YOU'RE NOT WRONG ABOUT THAT.
KREEE
REGARDLESS, OUR BUSINESS HERE IS DONE, SO I'M GOING HOME. I CAN'T SLEEP IN UNFAMILIAR BEDS ANYWAY—
WOW, HARSH. NO CONCERN AT ALL FOR THE DESIRES OF THE WOMAN WHO ACCOMPANIED YOU ALL THIS WAY?
...
HURRAY! LET'S GO GET SOME SEAFOOD AT KUROSHIO MARKET!
And craft sake!
I'M... TURNING AROUND...
YAY!
DEATHLY GLARE
SIGH...
SMILE! MOST MEN WOULD KILL TO TAKE A BEAUTIFUL GAL ON AN OVERNIGHT TRIP!
I BET. TOO BAD I'M STUCK WITH AN OLD SHREW LIKE YOU.
KREEE
SMACK
HOW THE HELL...
...DID THIS HAPPEN?

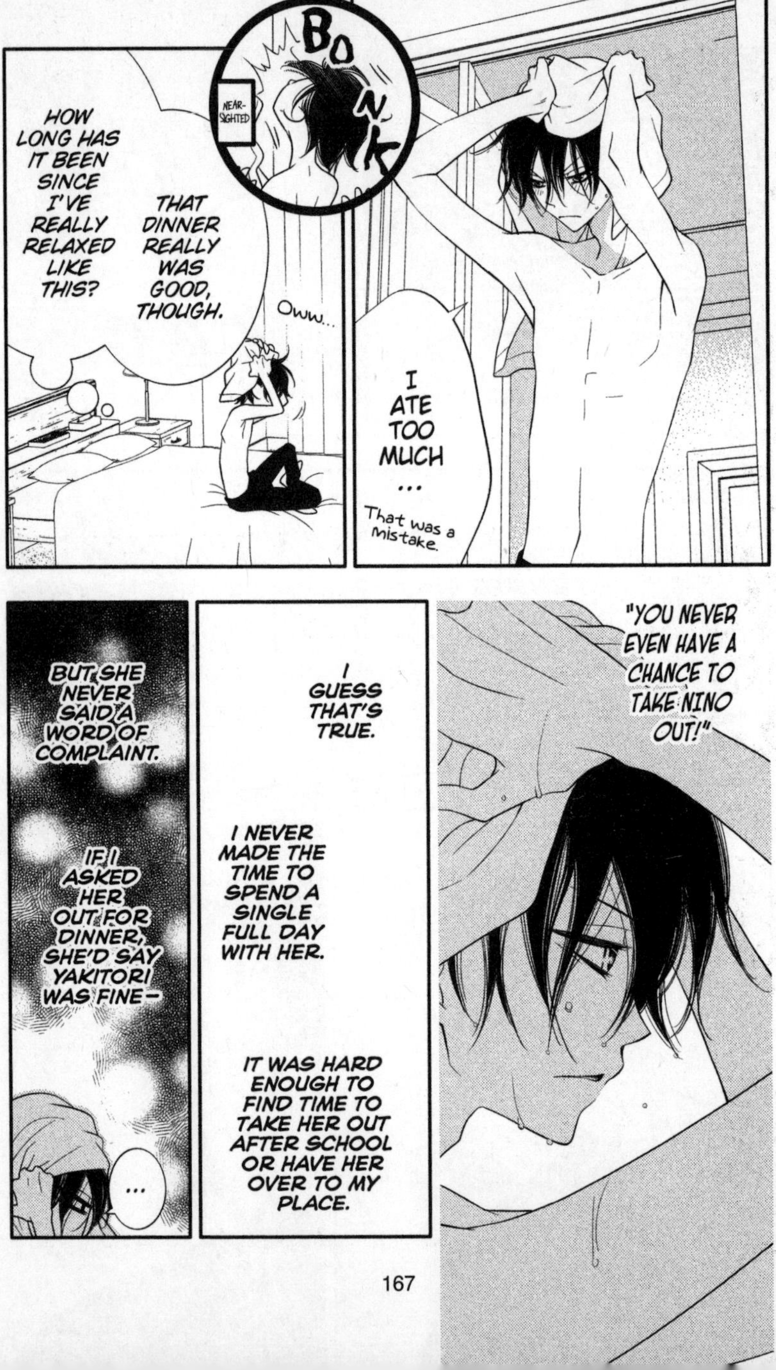
I ATE TOO MUCH...
That was a Mistake.
BONK
NEAR-SIGHTED
THAT DINNER REALLY WAS GOOD, THOUGH.
HOW LONG HAS IT BEEN SINCE I'VE REALLY RELAXED LIKE THIS?
Oww...
"YOU NEVER EVEN HAVE A CHANCE TO TAKE NINO OUT!"
I GUESS THAT'S TRUE.
I NEVER MADE THE TIME TO SPEND A SINGLE FULL DAY WITH HER.
IT WAS HARD ENOUGH TO FIND TIME TO TAKE HER OUT AFTER SCHOOL OR HAVE HER OVER TO MY PLACE.
BUT SHE NEVER SAID A WORD OF COMPLAINT.
IF I ASKED HER OUT FOR DINNER, SHE'D SAY YAKITORI WAS FINE—
...

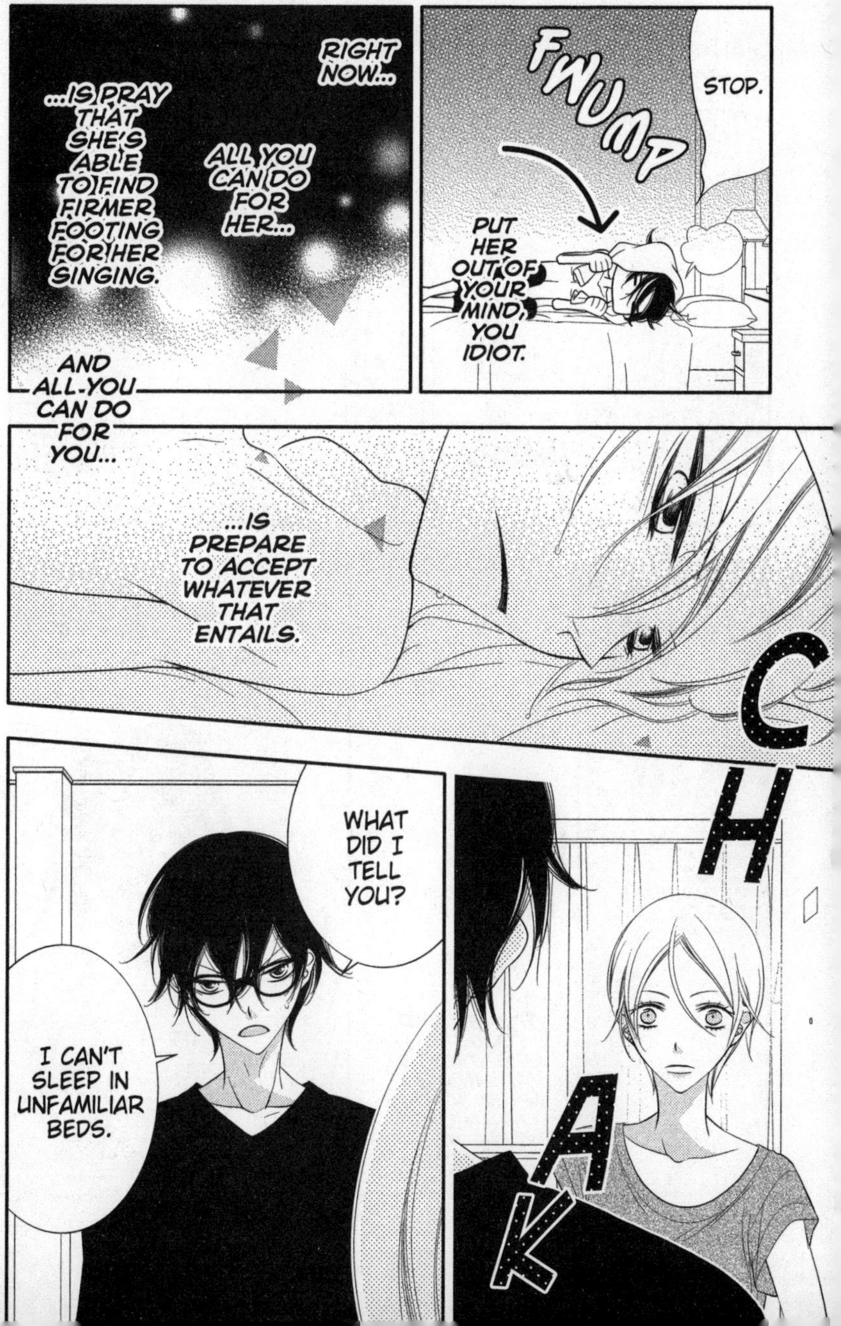
STOP.
FWUMP
PUT HER OUT OF YOUR MIND, YOU IDIOT.
RIGHT NOW...
ALL YOU CAN DO FOR HER...
...IS PRAY THAT SHE'S ABLE TO FIND FIRMER FOOTING FOR HER SINGING.
AND ALL YOU CAN DO FOR YOU...
...IS PREPARE TO ACCEPT WHATEVER THAT ENTAILS.
CHAK
WHAT DID I TELL YOU?
I CAN'T SLEEP IN UNFAMILIAR BEDS.

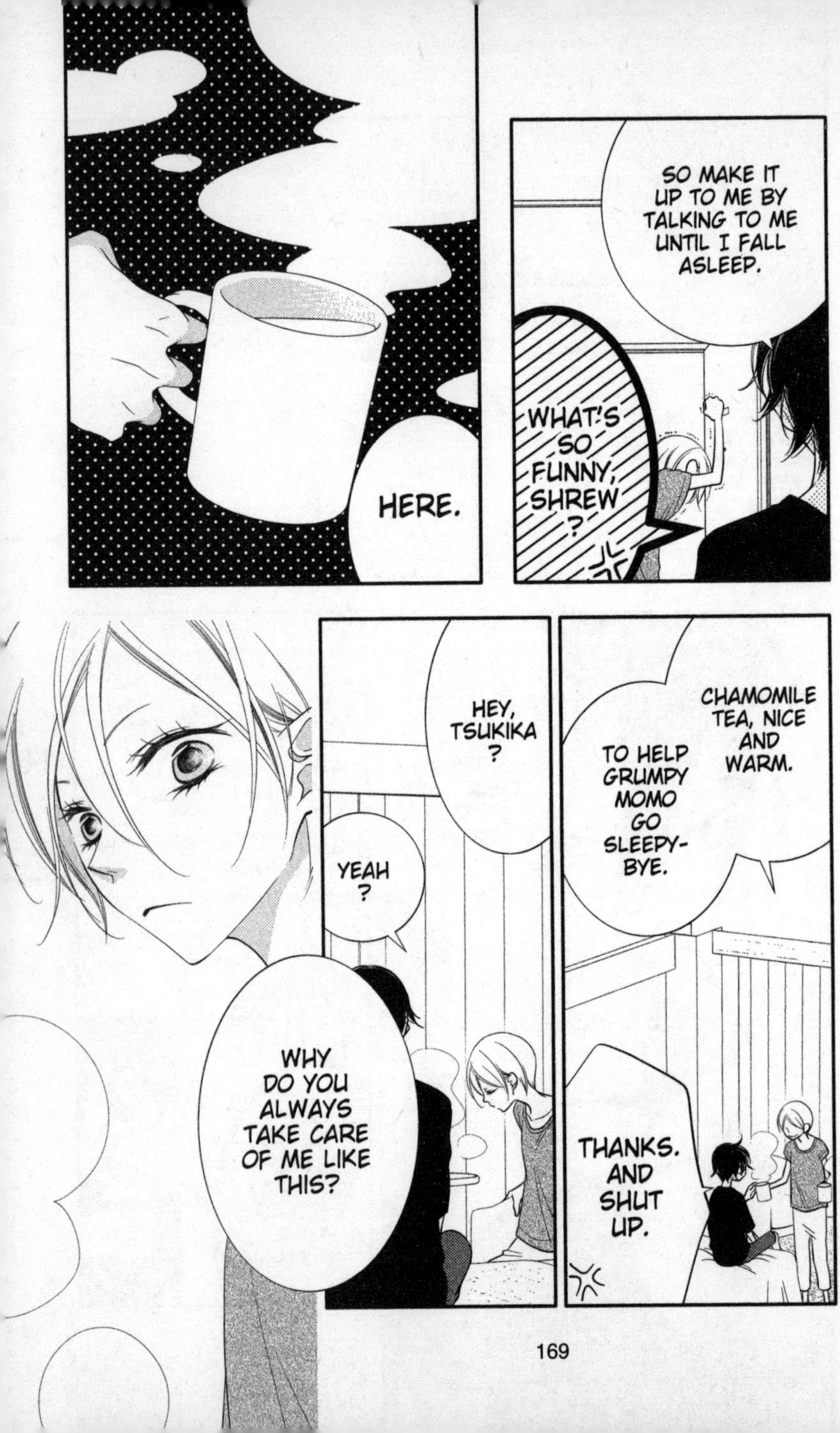
SO MAKE IT UP TO ME BY TALKING TO ME UNTIL I FALL ASLEEP.
WHAT'S SO FUNNY, SHREW?
HERE.
CHAMOMILE TEA, NICE AND WARM.
TO HELP GRUMPY MOMO GO SLEEPY-BYE.
THANKS. AND SHUT UP.
HEY, TSUKIKA?
YEAH?
WHY DO YOU ALWAYS TAKE CARE OF ME LIKE THIS?

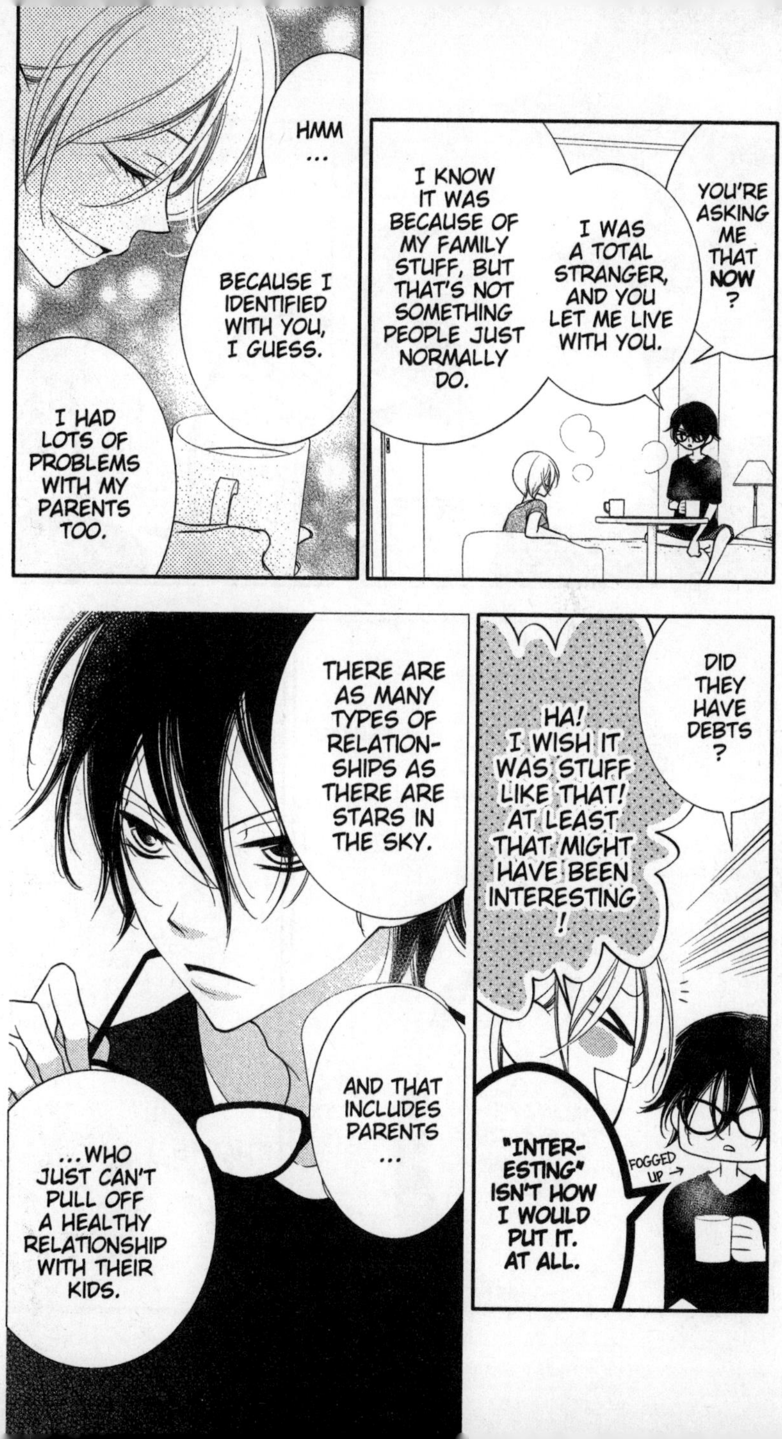
YOU'RE ASKING ME THAT NOW?
I WAS A TOTAL STRANGER, AND YOU LET ME LIVE WITH YOU.
I KNOW IT WAS BECAUSE OF MY FAMILY STUFF, BUT THAT'S NOT SOMETHING PEOPLE JUST NORMALLY DO.
HMM...
BECAUSE I IDENTIFIED WITH YOU, I GUESS.
I HAD LOTS OF PROBLEMS WITH MY PARENTS TOO.
DID THEY HAVE DEBTS?
HA! I WISH IT WAS STUFF LIKE THAT! AT LEAST THAT MIGHT HAVE BEEN INTERESTING!
"INTER-ESTING" ISN'T HOW I WOULD PUT IT. AT ALL.
FOGGED UP →
THERE ARE AS MANY TYPES OF RELATION-SHIPS AS THERE ARE STARS IN THE SKY.
AND THAT INCLUDES PARENTS...
...WHO JUST CAN'T PULL OFF A HEALTHY RELATIONSHIP WITH THEIR KIDS.

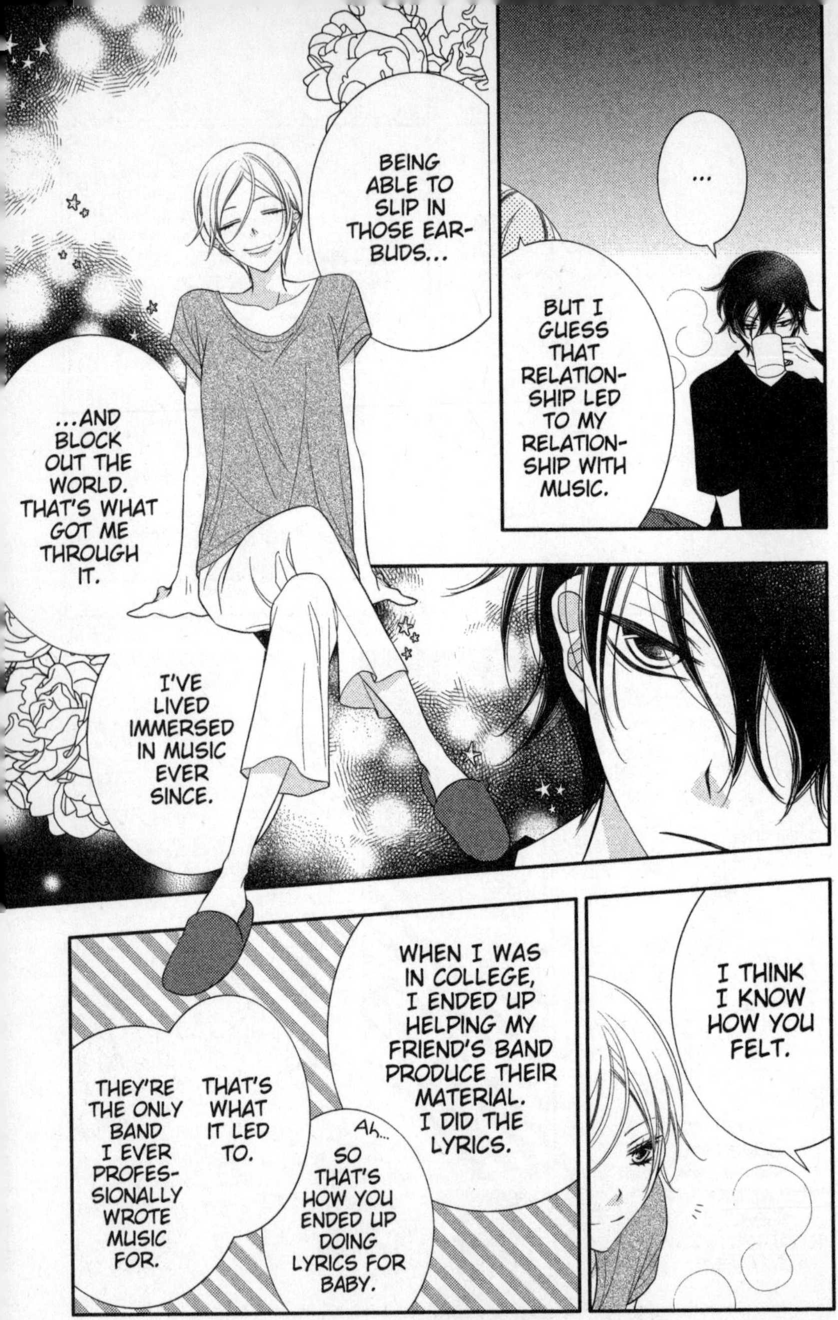
...
BUT I GUESS THAT RELATIONSHIP LED TO MY RELATIONSHIP WITH MUSIC.
BEING ABLE TO SLIP IN THOSE EAR-BUDS...
...AND BLOCK OUT THE WORLD. THAT'S WHAT GOT ME THROUGH IT.
I'VE LIVED IMMERSED IN MUSIC EVER SINCE.
I THINK I KNOW HOW YOU FELT.
WHEN I WAS IN COLLEGE, I ENDED UP HELPING MY FRIEND'S BAND PRODUCE THEIR MATERIAL. I DID THE LYRICS.
Ah... SO THAT'S HOW YOU ENDED UP DOING LYRICS FOR BABY.
THAT'S WHAT IT LED TO.
THEY'RE THE ONLY BAND I EVER PROFES-SIONALLY WROTE MUSIC FOR.

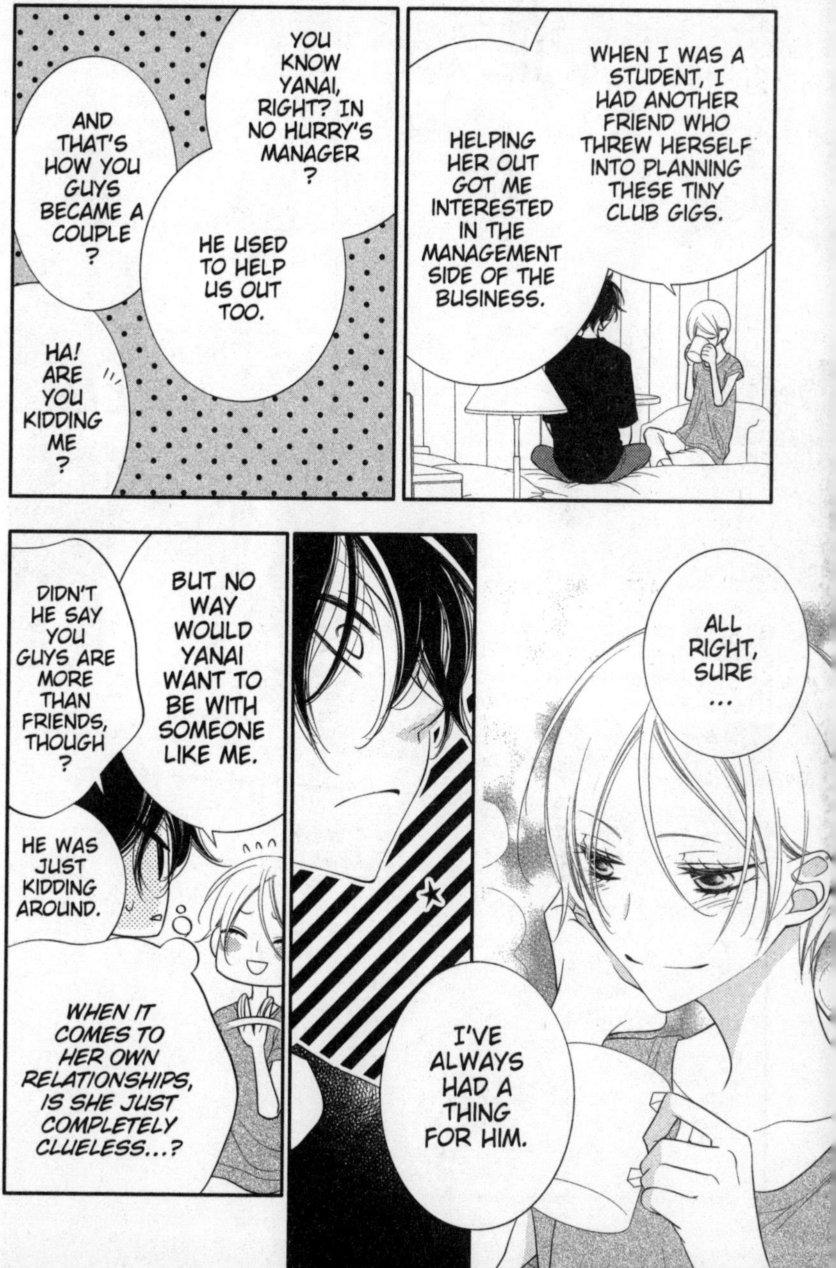

WHEN I WAS A STUDENT, I HAD ANOTHER FRIEND WHO THREW HERSELF INTO PLANNING THESE TINY CLUB GIGS.
HELPING HER OUT GOT ME INTERESTED IN THE MANAGEMENT SIDE OF THE BUSINESS.
YOU KNOW YANAI, RIGHT? IN NO HURRY'S MANAGER?
HE USED TO HELP US OUT TOO.
AND THAT'S HOW YOU GUYS BECAME A COUPLE?
HA! ARE YOU KIDDING ME?
ALL RIGHT, SURE...
I'VE ALWAYS HAD A THING FOR HIM.
BUT NO WAY WOULD YANAI WANT TO BE WITH SOMEONE LIKE ME.
DIDN'T HE SAY YOU GUYS ARE MORE THAN FRIENDS, THOUGH?
HE WAS JUST KIDDING AROUND.
WHEN IT COMES TO HER OWN RELATIONSHIPS, IS SHE JUST COMPLETELY CLUELESS...?

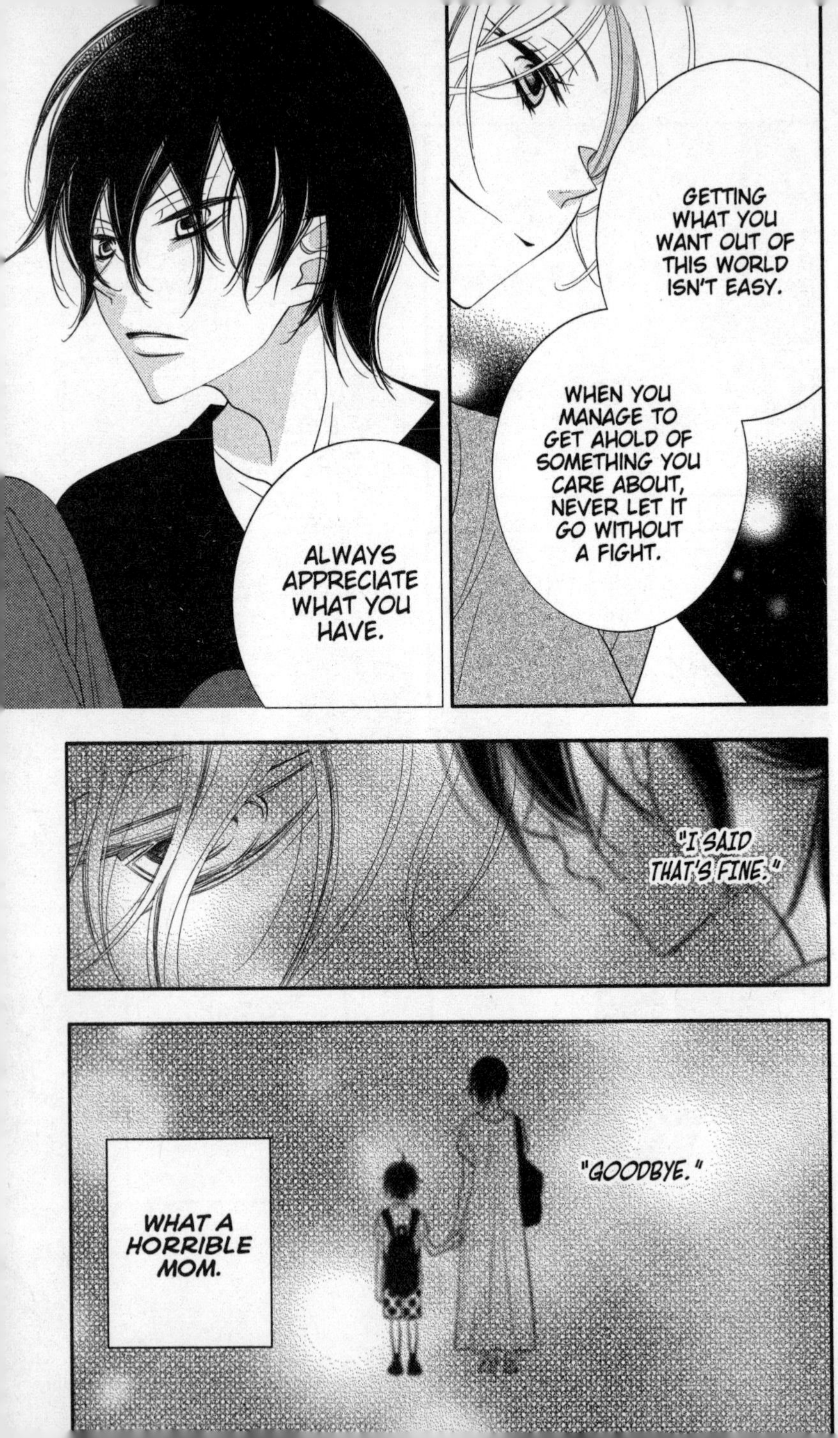
GETTING WHAT YOU WANT OUT OF THIS WORLD ISN'T EASY.
WHEN YOU MANAGE TO GET AHOLD OF SOMETHING YOU CARE ABOUT, NEVER LET IT GO WITHOUT A FIGHT.
ALWAYS APPRECIATE WHAT YOU HAVE.
"I SAID THAT'S FINE."
"GOODBYE."
WHAT A HORRIBLE MOM.

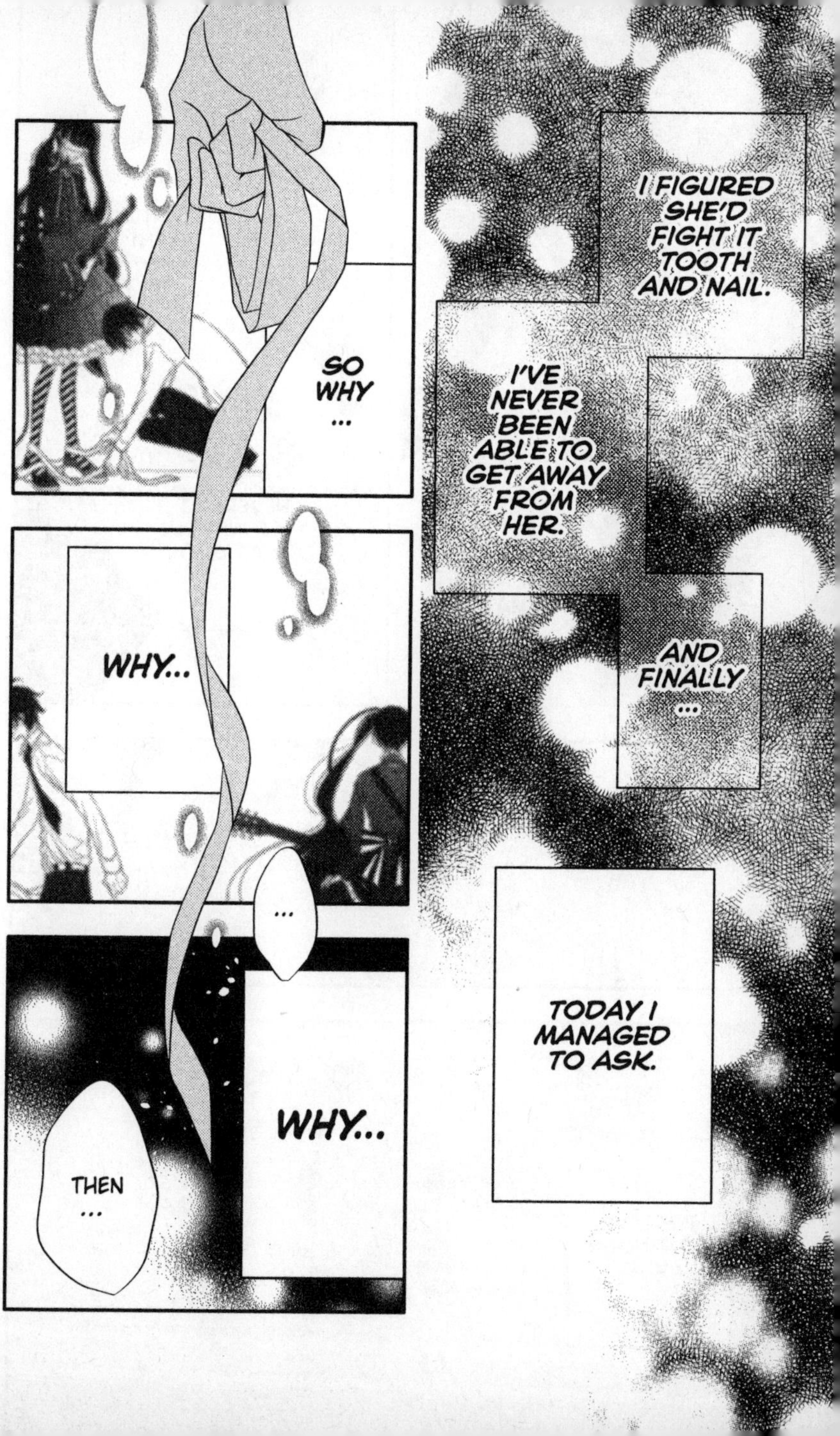
I FIGURED SHE'D FIGHT IT TOOTH AND NAIL.
I'VE NEVER BEEN ABLE TO GET AWAY FROM HER.
AND FINALLY...
TODAY I MANAGED TO ASK.
SO WHY...
WHY...
...
WHY...
THEN...

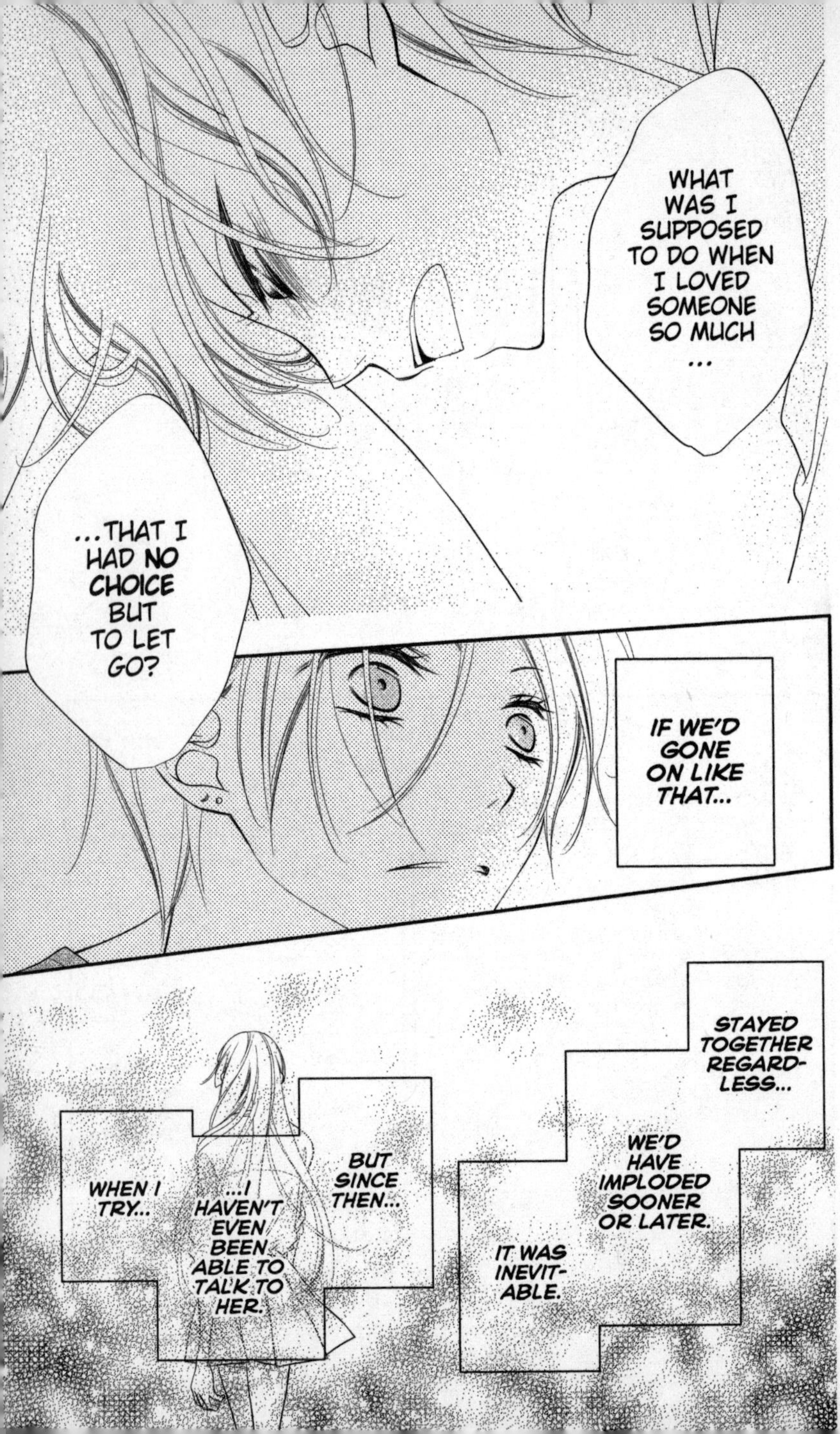
WHAT WAS I SUPPOSED TO DO WHEN I LOVED SOMEONE SO MUCH ...
...THAT I HAD NO CHOICE BUT TO LET GO?
IF WE'D GONE ON LIKE THAT...
STAYED TOGETHER REGARD-LESS...
WE'D HAVE IMPLODED SOONER OR LATER.
IT WAS INEVIT-ABLE.
BUT SINCE THEN...
...I HAVEN'T EVEN BEEN ABLE TO TALK TO HER.
WHEN I TRY...

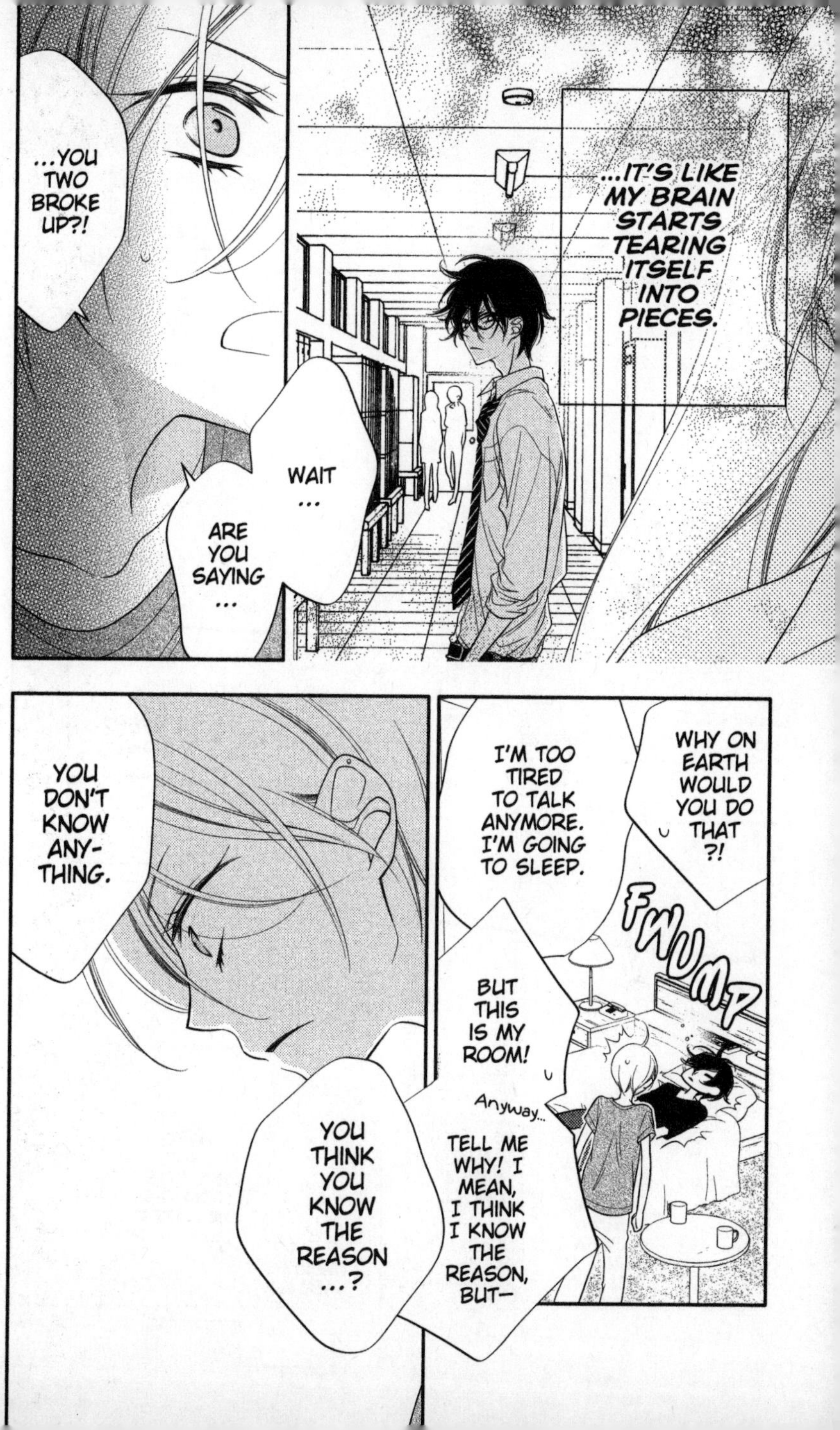
...IT'S LIKE MY BRAIN STARTS TEARING ITSELF INTO PIECES.
WAIT ... ARE YOU SAYING ...
...YOU TWO BROKE UP?!
WHY ON EARTH WOULD YOU DO THAT?!
I'M TOO TIRED TO TALK ANYMORE. I'M GOING TO SLEEP.
FWUMP
BUT THIS IS MY ROOM!
Anyway...
TELL ME WHY! I MEAN, I THINK I KNOW THE REASON, BUT—
YOU THINK YOU KNOW THE REASON ...?
YOU DON'T KNOW ANYTHING.

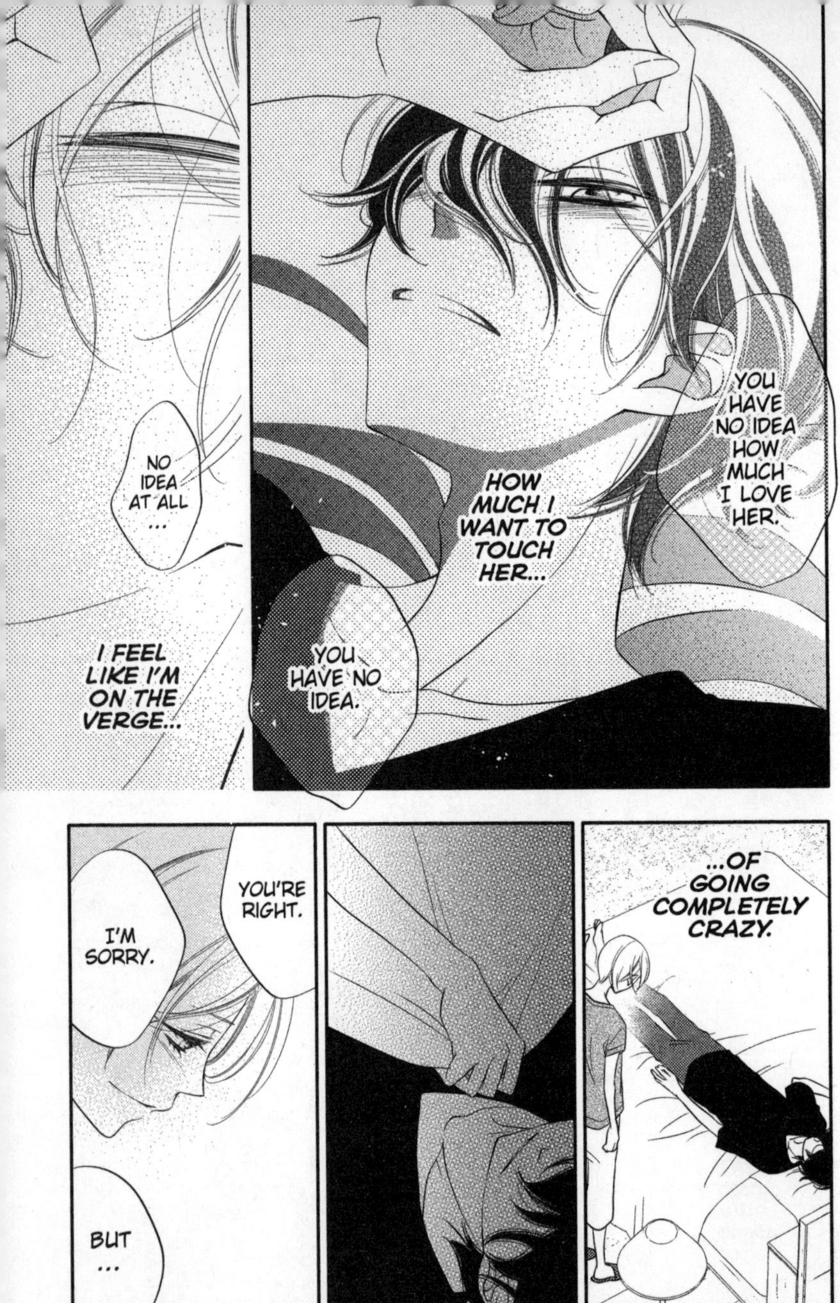
YOU HAVE NO IDEA HOW MUCH I LOVE HER.
HOW MUCH I WANT TO TOUCH HER...
YOU HAVE NO IDEA.
NO IDEA AT ALL...
I FEEL LIKE I'M ON THE VERGE...
...OF GOING COMPLETELY CRAZY.
YOU'RE RIGHT.
I'M SORRY.
BUT...

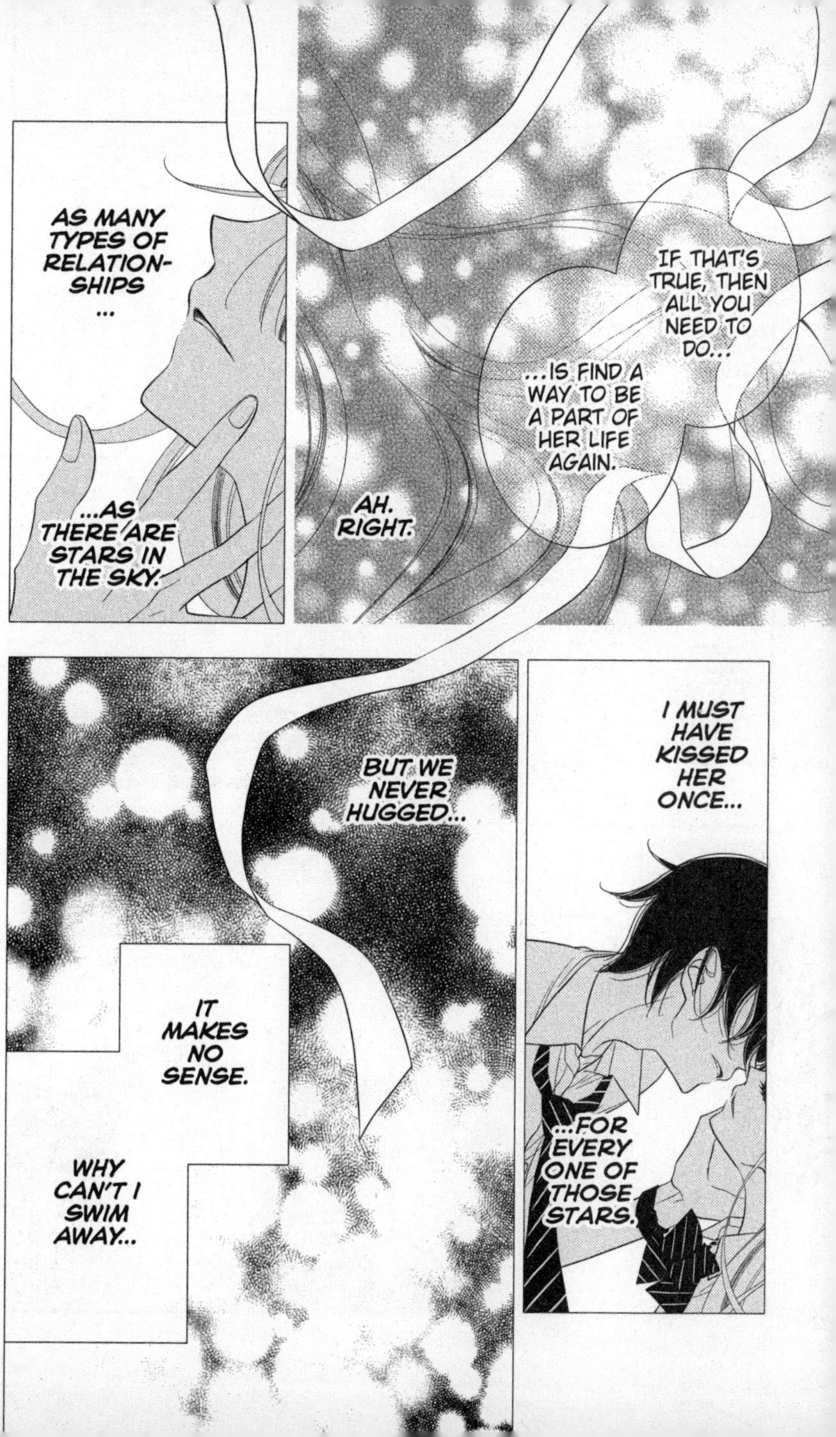
IF THAT'S TRUE, THEN ALL YOU NEED TO DO...
...IS FIND A WAY TO BE A PART OF HER LIFE AGAIN.
AH. RIGHT.
AS MANY TYPES OF RELATIONSHIPS...
...AS THERE ARE STARS IN THE SKY.
I MUST HAVE KISSED HER ONCE...
...FOR EVERY ONE OF THOSE STARS.
BUT WE NEVER HUGGED...
IT MAKES NO SENSE.
WHY CAN'T I SWIM AWAY...

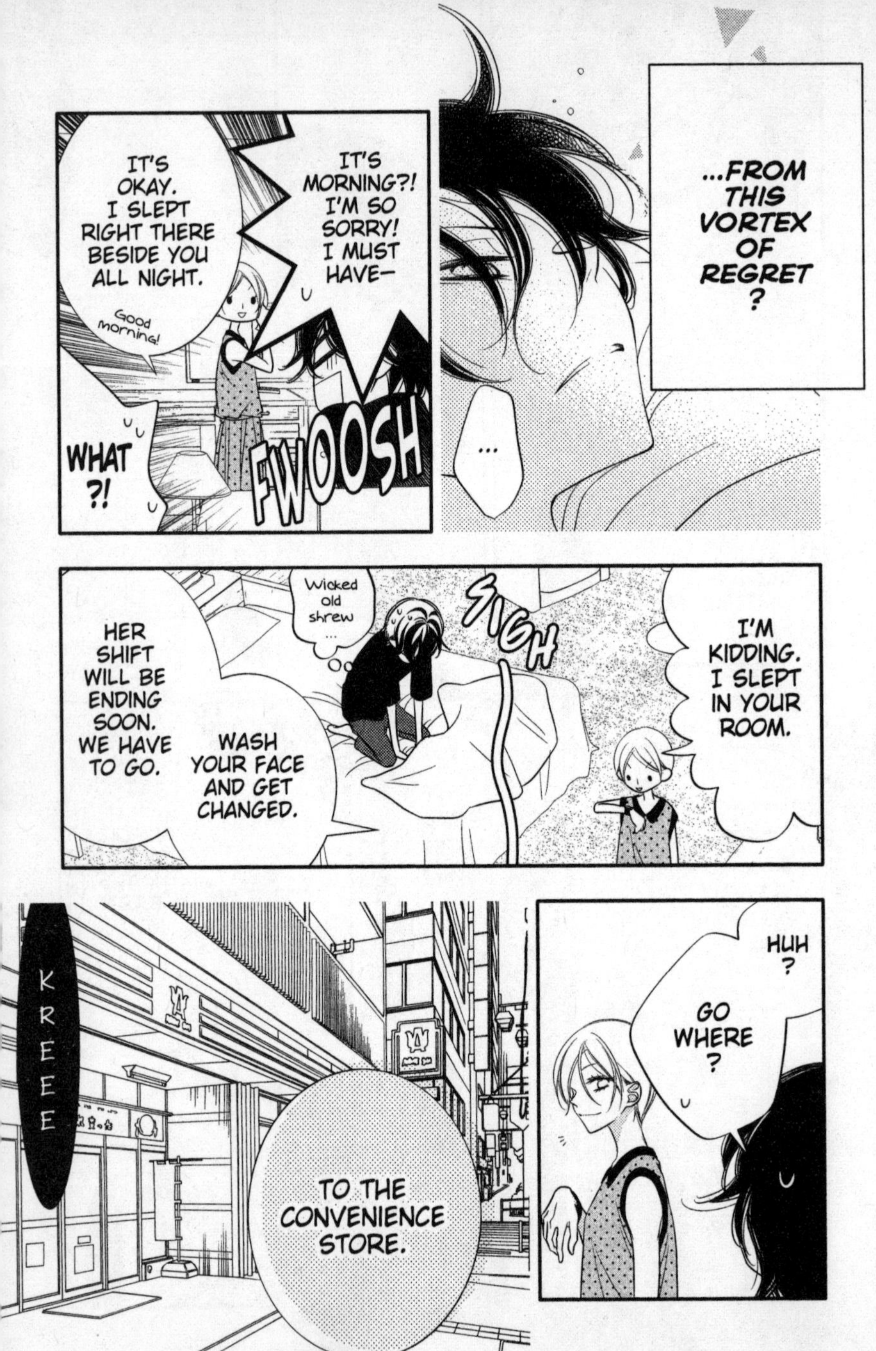
...FROM THIS VORTEX OF REGRET?
...
IT'S MORNING?! I'M SO SORRY! I MUST HAVE—
IT'S OKAY. I SLEPT RIGHT THERE BESIDE YOU ALL NIGHT.
Good morning!
FWOOSH
WHAT?!
I'M KIDDING. I SLEPT IN YOUR ROOM.
SIGH
Wicked old shrew...
WASH YOUR FACE AND GET CHANGED.
HER SHIFT WILL BE ENDING SOON. WE HAVE TO GO.
HUH?
GO WHERE?
TO THE CONVENIENCE STORE.
KREEE

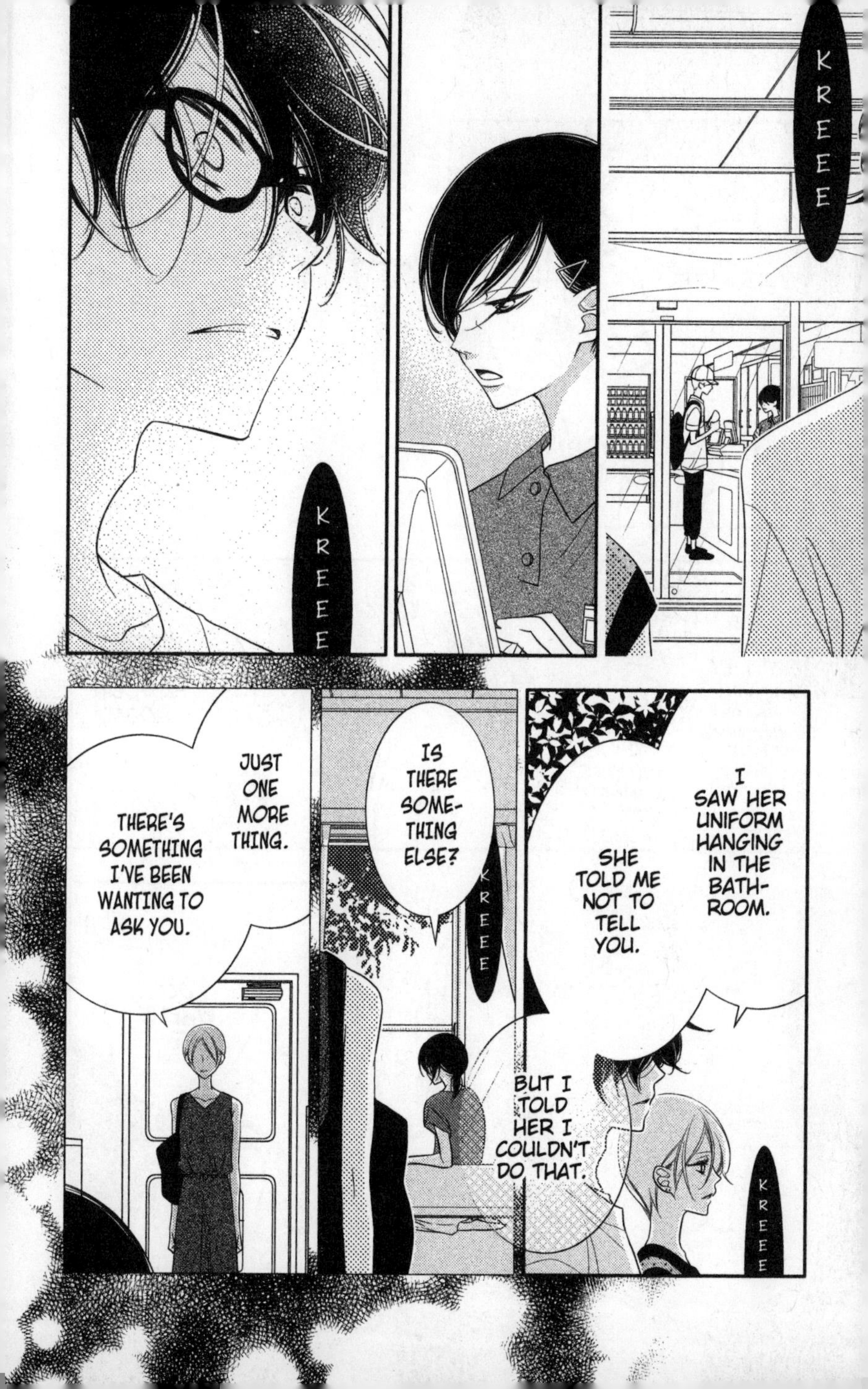
KREEE
KREEE
I SAW HER UNIFORM HANGING IN THE BATH-ROOM.
SHE TOLD ME NOT TO TELL YOU.
BUT I TOLD HER I COULDN'T DO THAT.
KREEE
IS THERE SOME-THING ELSE?
KREEE
JUST ONE MORE THING.
THERE'S SOMETHING I'VE BEEN WANTING TO ASK YOU.

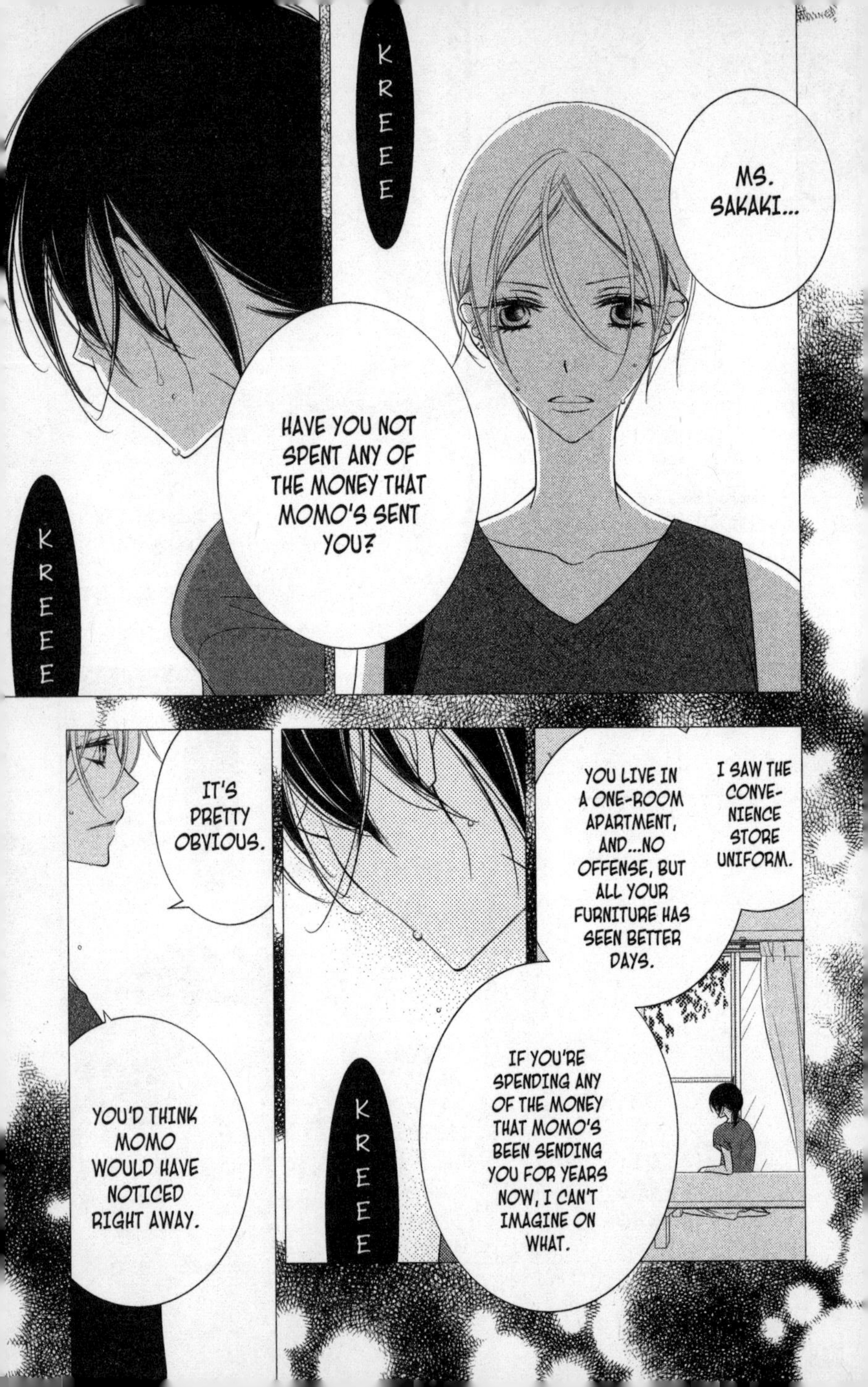
MS. SAKAKI...
KREEE
HAVE YOU NOT SPENT ANY OF THE MONEY THAT MOMO'S SENT YOU?
KREEE
I SAW THE CONVE-NIENCE STORE UNIFORM.
YOU LIVE IN A ONE-ROOM APARTMENT, AND...NO OFFENSE, BUT ALL YOUR FURNITURE HAS SEEN BETTER DAYS.
IF YOU'RE SPENDING ANY OF THE MONEY THAT MOMO'S BEEN SENDING YOU FOR YEARS NOW, I CAN'T IMAGINE ON WHAT.
KREEE
IT'S PRETTY OBVIOUS.
YOU'D THINK MOMO WOULD HAVE NOTICED RIGHT AWAY.

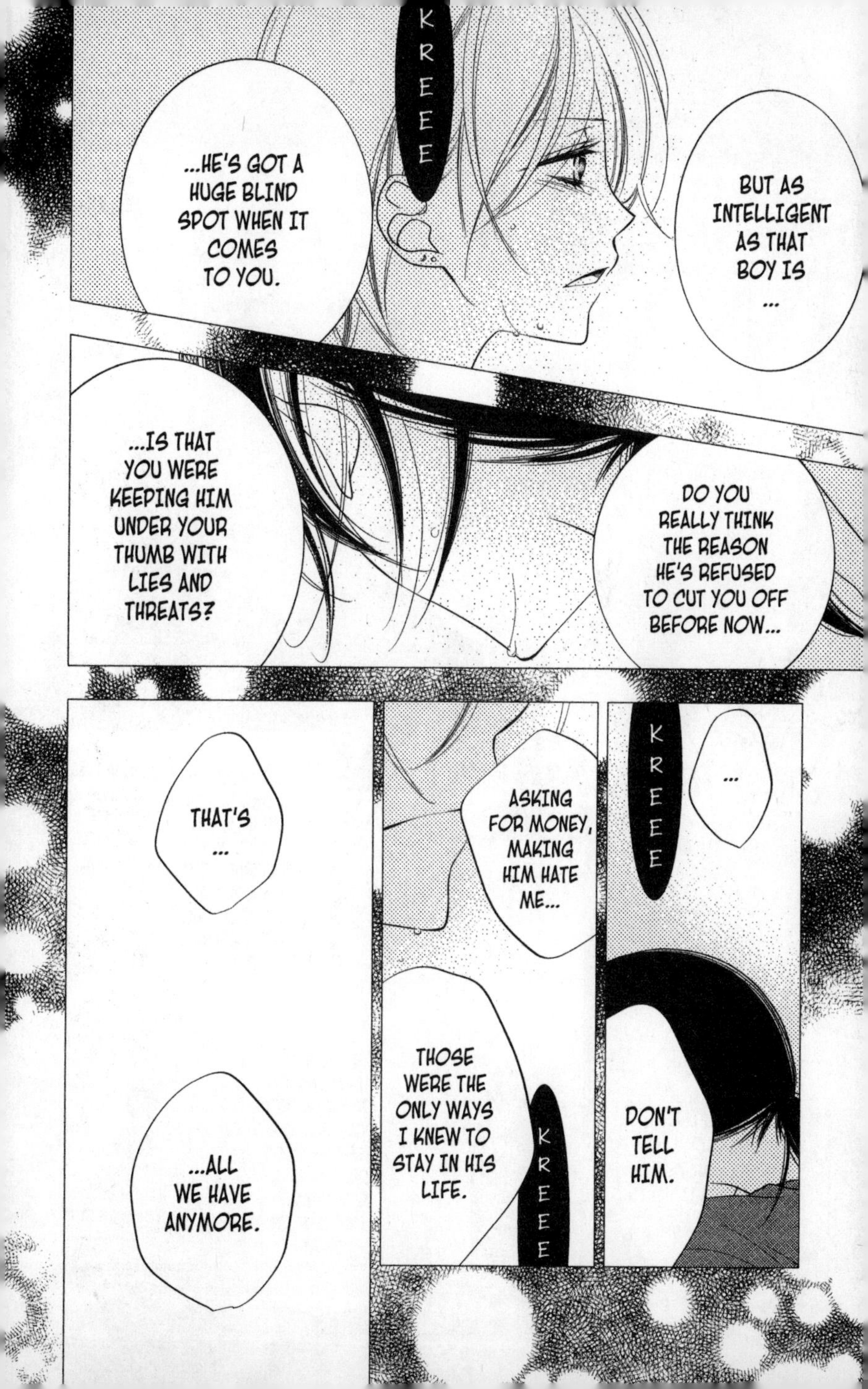
BUT AS INTELLIGENT AS THAT BOY IS ...
KREEE
...HE'S GOT A HUGE BLIND SPOT WHEN IT COMES TO YOU.
DO YOU REALLY THINK THE REASON HE'S REFUSED TO CUT YOU OFF BEFORE NOW...
...IS THAT YOU WERE KEEPING HIM UNDER YOUR THUMB WITH LIES AND THREATS?
...
KREEE
DON'T TELL HIM.
ASKING FOR MONEY, MAKING HIM HATE ME...
THOSE WERE THE ONLY WAYS I KNEW TO STAY IN HIS LIFE.
KREEE
THAT'S ...
...ALL WE HAVE ANYMORE.

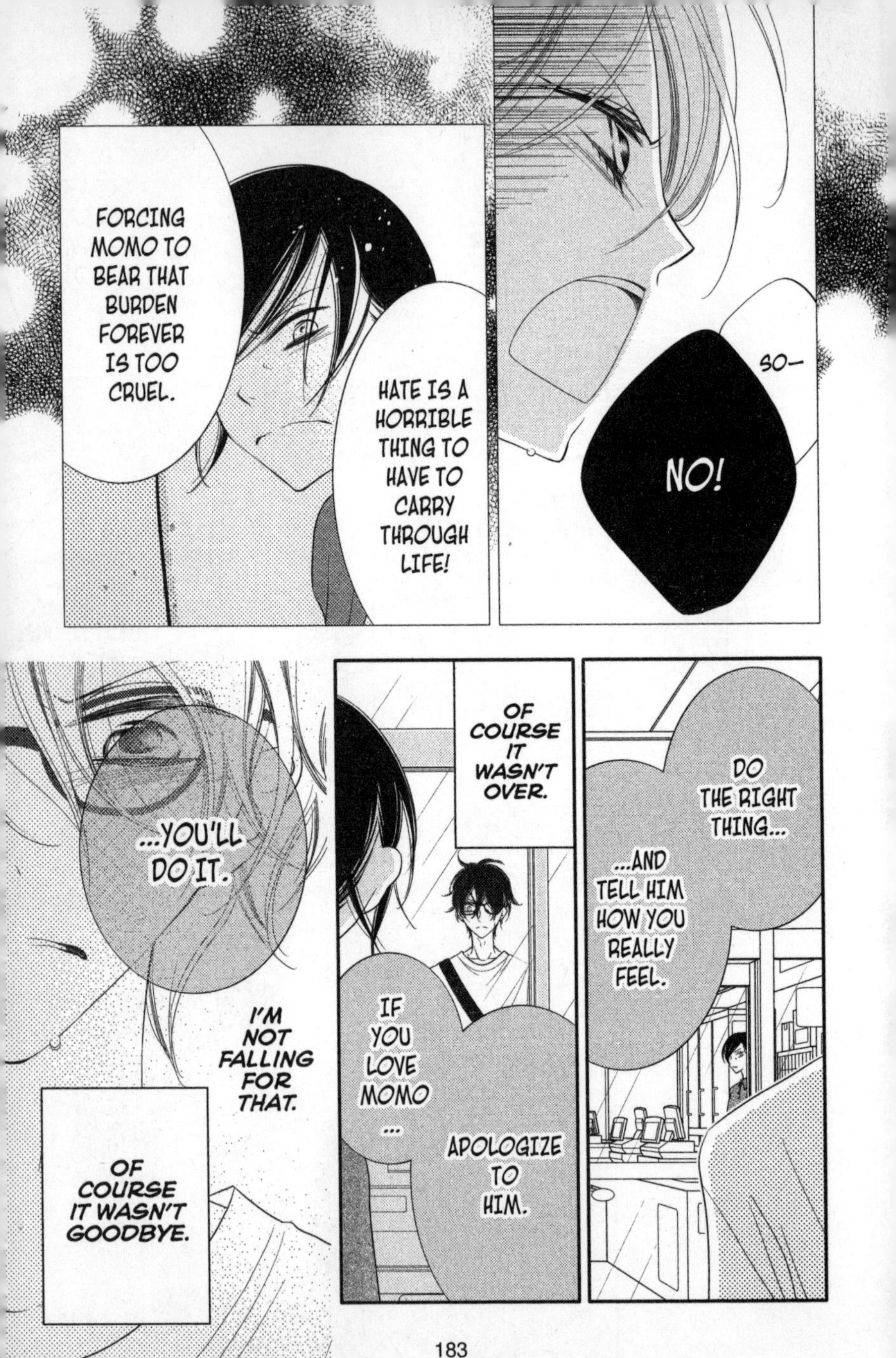
SO—
NO!
HATE IS A HORRIBLE THING TO HAVE TO CARRY THROUGH LIFE!
FORCING MOMO TO BEAR THAT BURDEN FOREVER IS TOO CRUEL.
DO THE RIGHT THING...
...AND TELL HIM HOW YOU REALLY FEEL.
OF COURSE IT WASN'T OVER.
IF YOU LOVE MOMO...
APOLOGIZE TO HIM.
...YOU'LL DO IT.
I'M NOT FALLING FOR THAT.
OF COURSE IT WASN'T GOODBYE.

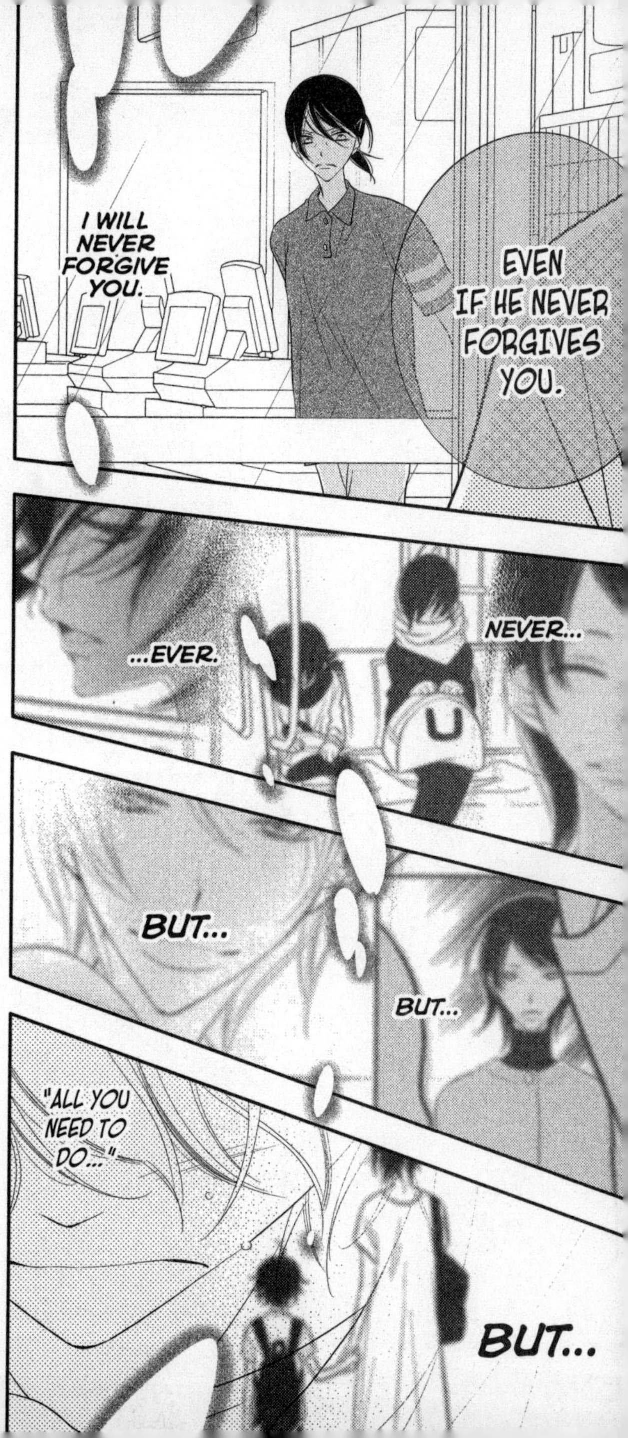
I WILL NEVER FORGIVE YOU.
EVEN IF HE NEVER FORGIVES YOU.
NEVER...
...EVER.
BUT...
BUT...
BUT...
"ALL YOU NEED TO DO..."

"...IS FIND A WAY TO BE A PART OF HER LIFE AGAIN."

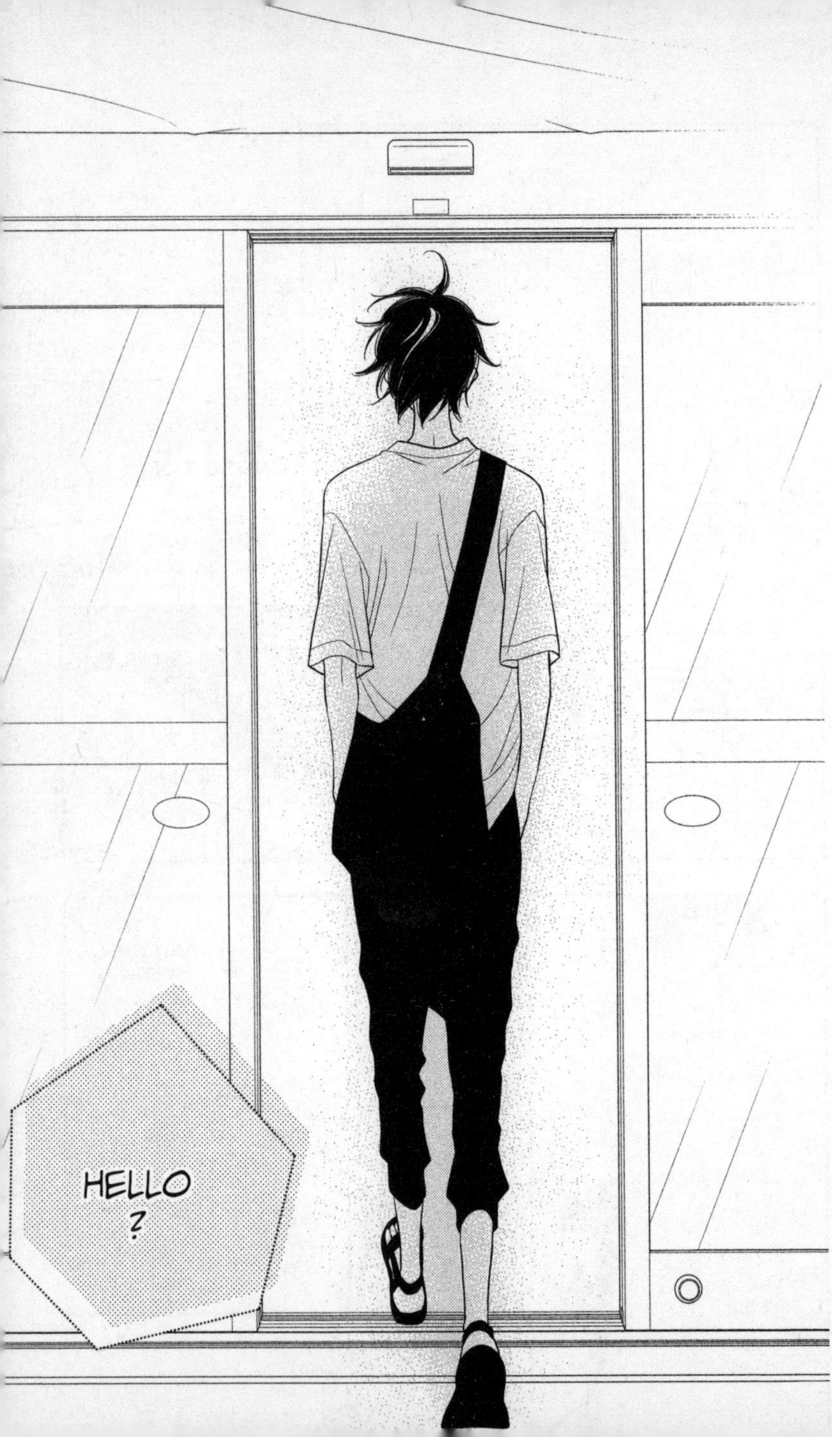
HELLO
?

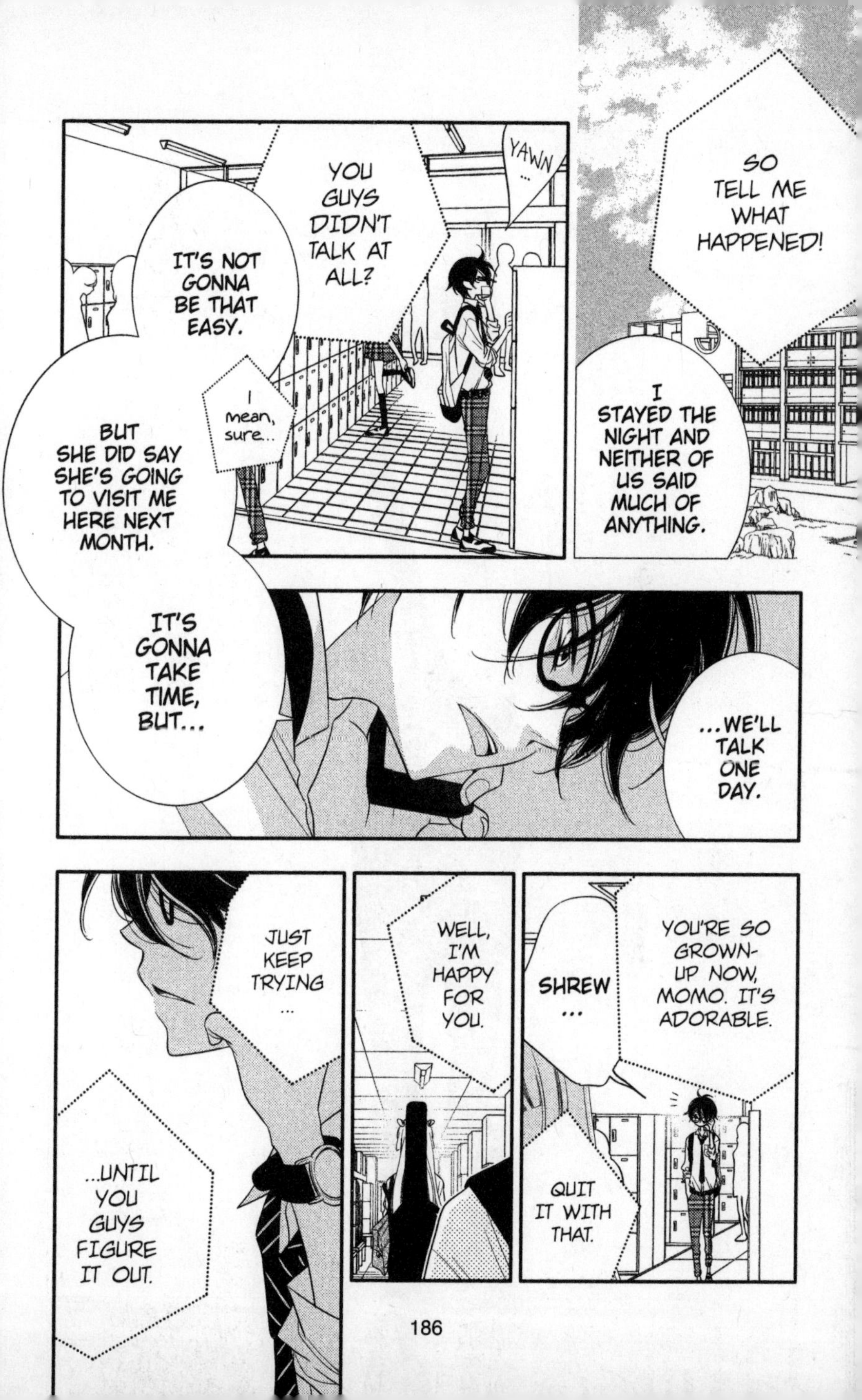
SO TELL ME WHAT HAPPENED!
I STAYED THE NIGHT AND NEITHER OF US SAID MUCH OF ANYTHING.
YAWN...
YOU GUYS DIDN'T TALK AT ALL?
IT'S NOT GONNA BE THAT EASY.
I mean, sure...
BUT SHE DID SAY SHE'S GOING TO VISIT ME HERE NEXT MONTH.
IT'S GONNA TAKE TIME, BUT...
...WE'LL TALK ONE DAY.
YOU'RE SO GROWN-UP NOW, MOMO. IT'S ADORABLE.
SHREW...
QUIT IT WITH THAT.
WELL, I'M HAPPY FOR YOU.
JUST KEEP TRYING...
...UNTIL YOU GUYS FIGURE IT OUT.

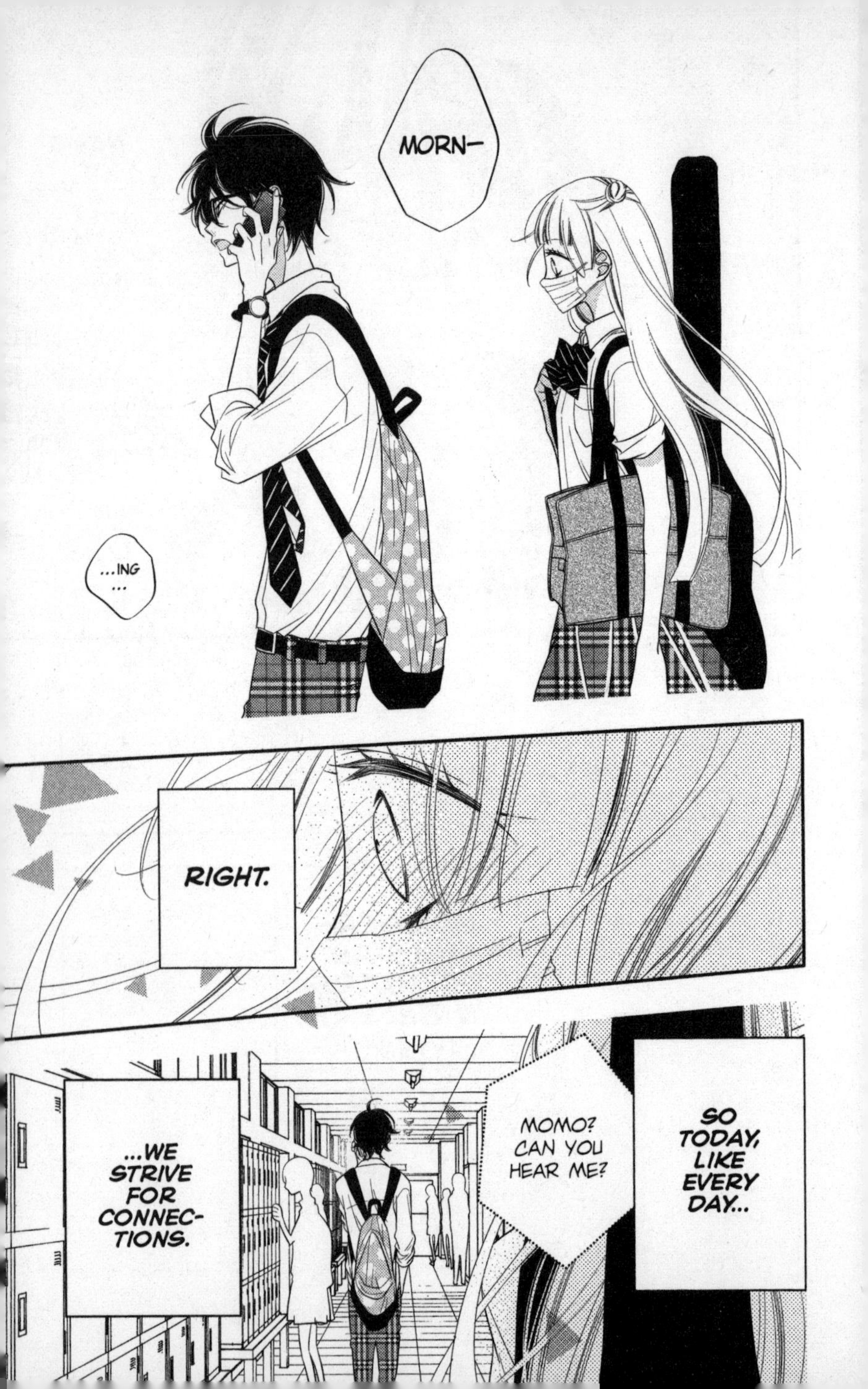
MORN—
...ING ...
RIGHT.
SO TODAY, LIKE EVERY DAY...
MOMO? CAN YOU HEAR ME?
...WE STRIVE FOR CONNEC- TIONS.

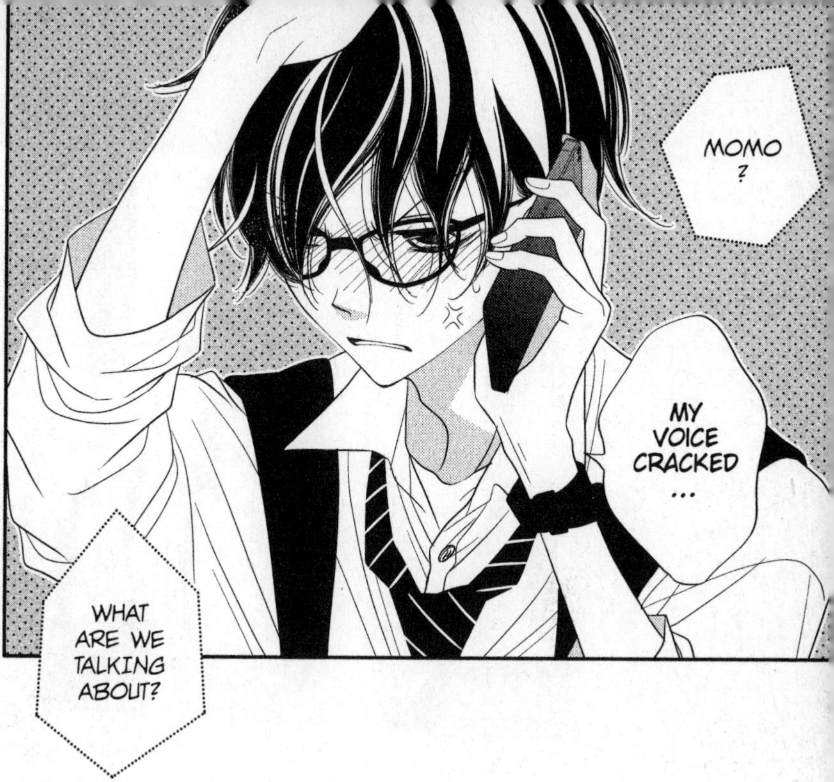
MOMO?
MY VOICE CRACKED...
WHAT ARE WE TALKING ABOUT?

INNUMERABLE AS THE STARS IN THE SKY.

ANONYMOUS NOISE ⑭ / THE END

TO BE CONTINUED IN ANONYMOUS NOISE 15

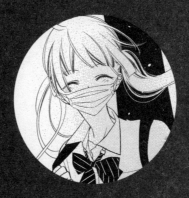

The *Anonymous Noise* movie is scheduled to debut only a few days after the release of this volume (in Japan). It would mean so very much to me if you would all head to your local cinema to see it!

- Ryoko Fukuyama

Born on January 5 in Wakayama Prefecture in Japan, Ryoko Fukuyama debuted as a manga artist after winning the Hakusensha Athena Shinjin Taisho Prize from Hakusensha's *Hana to Yume* magazine. She is also the author of *Nosatsu Junkie*. *Anonymous Noise* was adapted into an anime in 2017.

ANONYMOUS NOISE
Vol. 14
Shojo Beat Edition

STORY AND ART BY
RYOKO FUKUYAMA

English Translation & Adaptation/Casey Loe
Touch-Up Art & Lettering/Joanna Estep
Design/Yukiko Whitley
Editor/Amy Yu

Fukumenkei Noise by Ryoko Fukuyama
© Ryoko Fukuyama 2017
All rights reserved.
First published in Japan in 2017 by HAKUSENSHA, Inc., Tokyo.
English language translation rights arranged with HAKUSENSHA, Inc., Tokyo.

Printed in the U.S.A.

Published by VIZ Media, LLC
P.O. Box 77010
San Francisco, CA 94107

10 9 8 7 6 5 4 3 2 1
First printing, May 2019

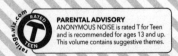

viz.com

shojobeat.com

Surpr...

You may be reading the wrong way!

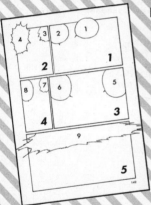

It's true: In keeping with the original Japanese comic format, this book reads from right to left—so action, sound effects and word balloons are completely reversed. This preserves the orientation of the original artwork—plus, it's fun! Check out the diagram shown here to get the hang of things, and then turn to the other side of the book to get started!

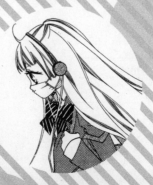

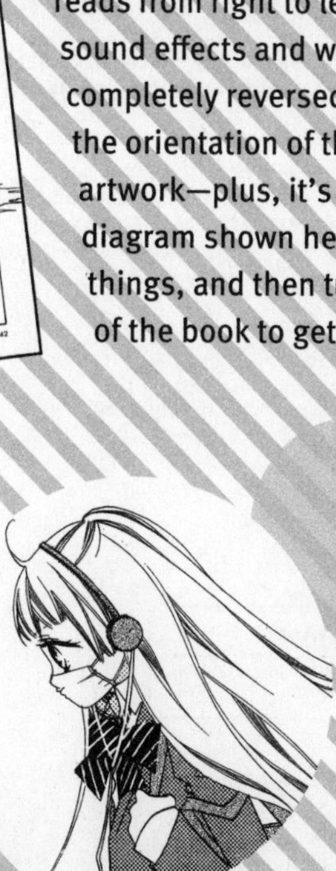